CW00547799

Ezra Pound and His Classical Sources

Historicizing Modernism

Historicizing Modernism challenges traditional literary interpretations by taking an empirical approach to modernist writing: a direct response to new documentary sources made available over the last decade.

Informed by archival research, and working beyond the usual European/American avant-garde 1900–45 parameters, this series reassesses established readings of modernist writers by developing fresh views of intellectual contexts and working methods.

Series Titles
Arun Kolatkar and Literary Modernism in India, Laetitia Zecchini
British Literature and Classical Music, David Deutsch
Broadcasting in the Modernist Era, Matthew Feldman, Henry Mead and Erik Tonning
Charles Henri Ford, Alexander Howard
Chicago and the Making of American Modernism, Michelle E. Moore
Christian Modernism in an Age of Totalitarianism, Jonas Kurlberg
Ezra Pound's Adams Cantos, David Ten Eyck
Ezra Pound and His Classical Sources, Jonathan Ullyot
Ezra Pound's Eriugena, Mark Byron

Ezra Pound's Washington Cantos and the Struggle for Light, Alec Marsh
Great War Modernisms and The New Age Magazine, Paul Jackson
Historical Modernisms, Jean-Michel Rabaté and Angeliki Spiropoulou
Historicizing Modernists, Edited by Matthew Feldman, Anna Svendsen and Erik Tonning
James Joyce and Absolute Music, Michelle Witen
James Joyce and Catholicism, Chrissie van Mierlo
James Joyce and Photography, Georgina Binnie-Wright
Jean Rhys's Modernist Bearings and Experimental Aesthetics, Sue Thomas
John Kasper and Ezra Pound, Alec Marsh
Judith Wright and Emily Carr, Anne Collett and Dorothy Jones
Katherine Mansfield and Literary Modernism, Edited by Janet Wilson, Gerri Kimber and Susan Reid
Katherine Mansfield: New Directions, Edited by Aimée Gasston, Gerri Kimber and Janet Wilson
Late Modernism and the English Intelligencer, Alex Latter
The Life and Work of Thomas MacGreevy, Susan Schreibman
Literary Impressionism, Rebecca Bowler
The Many Drafts of D. H. Lawrence, Elliott Morsia
Modern Manuscripts, Dirk Van Hulle
Modernist Authorship and Transatlantic Periodical Culture, Amanda Sigler
Modernist Lives, Claire Battershill
Modernist Wastes, Caroline Knighton
The Politics of 1930s British Literature, Natasha Periyan
Reading Mina Loy's Autobiographies, Sandeep Parmar
Reframing Yeats, Charles Ivan Armstrong
Samuel Beckett and Arnold Geulincx, David Tucker
Samuel Beckett and the Bible, Iain Bailey
Samuel Beckett and Cinema, Anthony Paraskeva
Samuel Beckett in Confinement, James Little
Samuel Beckett and Experimental Psychology, Joshua Powell
Samuel Beckett's German Diaries 1936–1937, Mark Nixon
Samuel Beckett's 'More Pricks than Kicks', John Pilling
Samuel Beckett and the Second World War, William Davies
T. E. Hulme and the Ideological Politics of Early Modernism, Henry Mead
Virginia Woolf's Late Cultural Criticism, Alice Wood

Ezra Pound and His Classical Sources

The Cantos *and the Primal Matter of Troy*

Jonathan Ullyot

BLOOMSBURY ACADEMIC
LONDON • NEW YORK • OXFORD • NEW DELHI • SYDNEY

BLOOMSBURY ACADEMIC
Bloomsbury Publishing Plc
50 Bedford Square, London, WC1B 3DP, UK
1385 Broadway, New York, NY 10018, USA
29 Earlsfort Terrace, Dublin 2, Ireland

BLOOMSBURY, BLOOMSBURY ACADEMIC and the Diana logo are trademarks of
Bloomsbury Publishing Plc

First published in Great Britain 2022

Cover design: Eleanor Rose

A catalogue record for this book is available from the British Library.

A catalog record for this book is available from the Library of Congress.

ISBN: HB: 978-1-3502-6024-5
ePDF: 978-1-3502-6023-8
eBook: 978-1-3502-6022-1

Series: Historicizing Modernism

Typeset by Integra Software Services Pvt. Ltd.

To find out more about our authors and books visit www.bloomsbury.com
and sign up for our newsletters.

Contents

List of Figures

Acknowledgments

This book grew out of an article I wrote for *Unattended Moments: The Medieval Presence in the Modernist Aesthetic* (Leiden, The Netherlands: Brill, 2018). An expanded version of this article appears as the first chapter, "*The Spirit of Romance* and the Debt to Philology." I am grateful to have received an Everett Helm Visiting Fellowship at the Lilly Library, Indiana University of Bloomington; a Research Fellowship in the Humanities to study at the Harry Ransom Center, University of Texas Austin; and an MSA Research Fellowship to study at the Beinecke Library, Yale University. The Modernist Research and Readings Group at the University of Toronto helped me clarify the argument of my early chapters. Others who offered significant feedback or helpful advice include Massimo Bacigalupo, Katarzyna Bartoszynska, Walter Baumann, Ronald Bush, Mark Byron, Marjorie Froula, Maud Ellmann, Michael Kindellan, Richard Sieburth, Leon Surrette, Demetres Tryphonopoulos, and Robert Von Hallberg.

Abbreviations

Works by Pound

ABCR *ABC of Reading* (New York: New Directions, 1960).

C *The Cantos of Ezra Pound* (New York: New Directions, 1975).

GK *Guide to Kulchur* (New York: New Directions, 1970).

LE *The Literary Essays of Ezra Pound,* ed. T. S. Eliot (London: Faber, 1960).

PT *Poems and Translations*, ed. Richard Sieburth (New York: Library of America, 2003).

L *The Letters of Ezra Pound, 1907–1941,* ed. D. D. Paige (New York: New Directions, 1951).

SP *Selected Prose, 1909–1965,* ed. William Cookson (New York: New Directions, 1973).

SR *The Spirit of Romance,* ed. Richard Sieburth (New York: New Directions, 2005).

Archives

EPC Ezra Pound Collection, Harry Ransom Humanities Research Center, University of Texas at Austin. I thank New Directions for their permission to publish excerpts of these materials. References to *EPC* are followed by box and folder number.

EPP Ezra Pound Papers, YCAL MS 43, Yale Collection of American Literature, Beinecke Rare Book and Manuscript Library, Yale University. I thank New Directions for their permission to publish excerpts of these materials. References to *EPP* are followed by a folder number.

Introduction: *The Cantos* and the Matter of Troy

Homeric scholars and comparative mythologists tell us that the stories with which the Odyssey is thick-strewn were not invented by Homer; that he took the folk-lore that lay ready to hand, and wove its diverse legends into an epic whole; that many of his myths are the common property of both Aryan and non-Aryan peoples.[1]

I have thought of the second Troy
Some little prized place in Auvergnat[2]

Late in 1934, Ezra Pound asked W. H. D. Rouse, the founding editor of the Loeb Classical Library, to undertake a plain prose translation of Homer's *Odyssey*. Rouse was a retired principal who had pioneered the Direct Method of teaching Latin and Greek to his ten- and eleven-year-old students, in which the target language is also the language of instruction. Pound wanted Rouse to resurrect Homer's clear and precise Greek from the Latinate style of George Chapman and the "King James fustian" of the Leaf-Lang translation.[3] "The modern world has LOST a kind of contact with and love for the classics which it HAD, not only in the 18th. century, and in the renaissance (part snobbism) but throughout the middle ages, when in one sense it knew much less."[4] Rouse's job was to present "Homer without a bustle. good, and without pantalettes."[5] "No poppy cock / that is the Homeric quality." Pound's letters to Rouse illuminate both the role Homer plays in *The Cantos* and the role *The Cantos* might play in our understanding of Homer.

Rouse eagerly took up the task. He sent Pound a draft of books 1–4 of the *Odyssey*. Pound bombarded him with criticism. He objected to Rouse's clunky

1 Jane Harrison, *Myths of the Odyssey* (London: Rivingtons, 1882), 1.
2 *PT*, 298.
3 *LE*, 250.
4 Ezra Pound, December 30, 1934 Letter to W. H. D. Rouse. *EPP*, 1945.
5 Ezra Pound, April 10, 1935 Letter to W. H. D. Rouse. *EPP*, 1947.

diction. "Never have I heard the word 'PLIGHT' spoken."[6] He suggested that Rouse only translate what is essential. "I just don't think you've yet got it. At any rate I'd like to see a 'rewrite' as if you didn't know the WORDS of the original, and were telling what happened."[7] He demanded that Rouse invent new phrases for the Homeric epithets. "A LIVE phrase may get one out of dead epithet."[8] He reminds Rouse of Homer's unique onomatopoeia. "What I hear in Homer with my three farden's worth of greek, is the SOUND of the old mens voices, or the poluphloisboious [loud-roaring] swish/swash on the beach."[9] In Canto 2, Pound imagines a blind Homer hearing the cicada-like voices of the old men on the Skaian gate in *Iliad* book 3 from the sound of the waves on the coast of Chios.

> And poor old Homer blind, blind, as a bat,
> Ear, ear for the sea-surge, murmur of old men's voices:
> "Let her go back to the ships."[10]

In Canto 74, Pound describes the "diminutive poluphloisboios [loud-roarings]" of Homer's sea (74/447).

But Rouse wasn't getting it. Nor did he get the whole business of modernism. "As for the modernists, Sitwells + Co, they are idiots, so far as I have managed to read, without either sound or sense, but I know little."[11] Pound sent Rouse a copy of *A Draft of XXX Cantos* (1930). Rouse was puzzled. "Your cantos are like sketches for poems, is that not so? I have not followed them yet, so forgive me if I am stupid."[12] When Rouse sent Pound his translation of book 5 of the *Odyssey*, Pound found it "just plain damn bad. Careless, frivolous, missed opportunities all over it."[13] Rouse had turned Odysseus into British gentlemen. Odysseus derives from the trickster of folklore, Pound argued: proud, lazy, impulsive:

> born un po' misero/ dont want to
> go to war / little runt who finally has to do all the
> hard work/ gets all Don Juan's chances with the ladies
> and cant really enjoy 'em/ Circe, Calypso, Nausika
> always some fly in the ointment/ last to volunteer on
> stiff jobs.[14]

[6] Ezra Pound, February [?], 1935 Letter to W. H. D. Rouse. *EPP*, 1946.
[7] Ezra Pound, March 18, 1935 Letter to W. H. D. Rouse. *EPP*, 1947.
[8] Ezra Pound, April 10, 1935 Letter to W. H. D. Rouse. *EPP*, 1947.
[9] Ezra Pound, February or March 1935 Letter to W. H. D. Rouse. *EPP*, 1947.
[10] *C*, 2/6. Hereafter quoted parenthetically in the text.
[11] W. H. D. Rouse, February 8, 1935 Letter to Ezra Pound. *EPP*, 1947.
[12] W. H. D. Rouse, March 2, 1935 Letter to Ezra Pound. *EPP*, 1947.
[13] Ezra Pound, April [?], 1935 Letter to W. H. D. Rouse. *EPP*, 1949.
[14] Ezra Pound, April 17, 1935 Letter to W. H. D. Rouse. *EPP*, 1948.

Likewise, Rouse's portrayal of Homer's gods was all wrong. They are not rational decision-makers. They derive from ancient animal spirits (with personal totem animals) and the tricky deities of folklore.

> GlAUX, owl / totem or symbolic bird / as stupid bitch HERA
> has her bull eyes / glare eyed, owl eyed Athene /
> gods connected with the divine animals
> The Apollo at Villa Giulis gives tip to
> mediterranean gods/ startling, sudden, non of that washy
> late stuff done by sculpting slave models/
> nor afternoon tea Xtian poetry. Gods tricky as nature.

Like Nietzsche, Pound champions the vitalism of archaic Greece over the decadence and rationalism of classical Greece. The "washy late stuff" of classical Athenian sculpture, such as the Apollo Lyceus, attributed to Praxiteles, epitomizes the decadent "gods in repose" style, modeled on naked slave boys.

Compare that to the Etruscan Aplu (Apollo) of Veii, a giant terracotta from the roof of a temple of Minerva (510–500 BCE), which "gives tip" to something more primordial. Apollo embodies the "startling, sudden" energy of the theriomorphic trickster god of metamorphosis and change. (See figure 0.2) Apollo strides forward to wrest the Ceryneian Hind from Heracles. Although the smile is a common feature of the archaic kouros, Apollo's smile feels exaggerated, almost demonic, like a laughing Zarathustra. The "miracle of Homer," Pound explained, "is the raw cut of concrete reality/ combined with the tremendous energy/ the contact with the natural force." Pound advised Rouse to read Ernst Fenollosa's *The Chinese Written Character as a Medium for Poetry* and study Dante's use of verbs. "The CHIEF impression in reading Homer is FRESHNESS. whether illusion or not, this is THE classic quality. 3000 years old and still FRESH. a trans/ that misses that, is bad. MUST get NEW combinations of words."[15]

Rouse could not meet Pound's demands. Pound was not really asking for a translation but a kind of poetic adaptation that would emulate the techniques and discoveries he had already made in his first thirty cantos—discoveries which Rouse didn't understand. Rouse responded on July 2, 1935:

[15] Ezra Pound, [May?] 1935 Letter to W. H. D. Rouse. *EPP*, 1950.

Figure 0.1 "Apollo Lykeios" type, Louvre Museum.

Figure 0.2 Vulca's "Apollo of Veii," National Etruscan Museum, Rome.

> Translation was in my mind all the time, i.e. such a version that a reader of Greek could find any bit of Greek in the English. That was what I asked you at the beginning. I dare say it was clear in your mind, but you did not make it clear in mine. But experience has shown me that such a translation can't be done by me.
> The question is how can it be done? And can it be true to Homer?
> I expect the whole [would] have to be done again, but never mind.[16]

Rouse's point was that if Pound wanted the *Odyssey* done right, he should translate it himself. Pound responded, "if I tried to trans the Odyssey I wd. probably make a thing of shreds and patches, all out of shape and deficient in homogeneity."[17] Pound's explanation for why he can't translate the *Odyssey* becomes a new set of demands.

> when I do sink into the greek, what I dig up
> is too concentrative,
> I dont see how to get unity of the
> WHOLE.
> I suspect neither Dante or Homer HAD the kind of
> boring "unity" of surface that we take to be characteristic
> of Pope, Racine, Corneille.
> The nekuia shouts aloud that it is OLDER than the rest/
> all that island, cretan etc/ hinter-time, that is
> NOT Praxiteles, not Athens of Pericles, but Odysseus,
> I keep nagging you, because a trans/ of the Odyssey seems to
> me so enormous an undertaking, and the requirements
> include all the possible masteries of English
> The FIRST essential is the narrative movement, forward,
> not blocking the road as Chapman does. everything that stops
> the reader must GO, be cut out.[18]

Pound first explains that his own method is too "concentrative." He can't find the unity of the whole. Then he concedes that Homer probably didn't have that unity anyway. (Meaning Pound can translate Homer.) Pound then condemns Rouse's translation of the nekyia or "questioning of the dead" in *Odyssey* 11. Rouse ought to spend more time studying Canto 1. Pound's opinion that the nekyia derives from a more primitive source than the rest of the *Odyssey* was

[16] W. H. D. Rouse, July 2, 1935 Letter to Ezra Pound. *EPP*, 1950.
[17] Ezra Pound, August 20, 1935 Letter to W. H. D. Rouse. *EPP*, 1950.
[18] Ezra Pound, August 23, 1935 Letter to W. H. D. Rouse. *EPP*, 1950.

shared by many. Jane Harrison, Johann Wilhelm Adolph Kirchoff, Andrew Lang, Albert Dieterich, Walter Leaf, and J. A. K. Thomson had argued that the nekyia reflects a more primitive religion than is found elsewhere in Homer: a cult of the dead and a goddess-based religion of fertility rituals.[19] Given that the *Odyssey* itself is made up of different layers reflecting different compositional periods, a proper translation requires all possible "masteries" of English. Pound finally suggests that Rouse not be faithful to Homer's words, but to the narrative movement forward. "Dichten = condensare."[20]

Rouse didn't reply. He was not about to translate, for example, the nekyia differently than the Circe section because it originated from an earlier source. (Pound did: Anglo Saxon English in Canto 1 and drunken Latinate English in Canto 39.) Rouse was not trying to contend with Joyce's "Oxen of the Sun." (Pound probably was.) Rouse was not going to cut whole sections out of the text, or drop or modify the epithets. (Pound did: Canto 1 condenses 140 lines of Homer into 48; his Helen has "bitch eyes" [103/750].) That would only cause confusion for those reading his translation alongside the Greek. Rouse's goal was to produce "a version that a reader of Greek could find any bit of Greek in the English."

In September of 1935, Rouse sent Pound the first few books of his completed translation. "Please say at the same time if you wish for any more. I am afraid they must bore you to criticize."[21] Pound had little to say, and their correspondence turned to the subject of Homeric color words.[22] By 1936, Pound's politics trumped what remained of their friendship: "I am so fed up with your FILTHY and disgusting government that I have to take a pull at myself to write to any Englishman who isn't out trying to prevent European war / to kill the ditch Eden and get rid of the stink of sanctions."[23] (Anthony Eden was the junior minister of the League of Nations.) Pound eventually suspended communications.

[19] Albert Dieterich, *Nekyia* (Leipzig: B. G. Teubner, 1893), 46–50, 75–7, 150–9; Jane Harrison, *Prolegomena to the Study of Greek Religion* (Cambridge: Cambridge University Press, 1908 [1903]), 333–50, 601–11; Andrew Lang, *Homer and the Epic* (London: Longmans, Green, and Company, 1893), 309–15; Walter Leaf, "Appendix L: Homeric Burial Rites," in *The Iliad*, 2nd edition, vol. 2, ed. Walter Leaf (New York: Macmillan, 1900), 618–22; J. A. K. Thomson, *Studies in the Odyssey* (Oxford: Clarendon Press, 1914), 24–30, 85–97; and Johann Kirchhoff, *Die homerische Odyssee* (Berlin: 1859), 224–34. See chapter 2.

[20] *ABCR*, 36.

[21] W. H. D. Rouse, September 16, 1935 Letter to Ezra Pound. *EPP*, 1950.

[22] See chapter 3.

[23] Ezra Pound, December [?], 1936 Letter to W. H. D. Rouse. *EPP*, 1951.

A year later, Pound came across Rouse's *The Story of Odysseus* and read the dedication: "Mr. Ezra Pound is the onlie begetter of this book. He suggested it, and he read the first part with with Odyssean patience; his trenchant comments, well deserved, gave me the courage of my convictions."[24] When Pound wrote to thank him, Rouse mentioned that he had nearly finished a translation of the *Iliad*. Pound's fury rekindled:

> If you have ALREADY finished the Iliad and sent it to press you deserve NO pity, and are a purely frivolous character. [...] It will take you FIVE years at least to rework the subtler parts of the Odyssey. NO man or god can do more than one masterpiece or two.[25]

Rouse never mentioned his intention to "rework the subtler parts of the Odyssey." Pound is only reminding him of his failure. Rouse had mentioned an interest in tackling Pindar. Pound's response: "I do NOT believe Pindar was the 67th part of Homer. All right as dilletantism for a bloke that knows Homer backwards by heart... But I wd. rather you spent the next decade REVISING yr/ Odyssey and yr Ilead."

This literary exchange is amusing for its many deadlocks. Rouse was no T. S. Eliot. Pound could not play midwife to his modernist adaptation of Homer. Rouse's intention was to produce an *Odyssey* that a young reader could enjoy. It did not require half a lifetime's rumination or a mastery of alliterative verse. Like many others, Rouse appreciated Pound's poetic insight and talent as an editor while doing his best to ignore his megalomania and crackpot politics. Pound and Rouse both agreed that Homer needed to be liberated from the high poetic English style of Chapman. Homer's stories are the stuff of folklore: rapid, fresh, and funny. But they couldn't agree beyond that. Rouse produced an *Odyssey* that anyone could read, and which greatly contributed to the popularity of the text today. His literary talent was close to null. Pound produced an *Odyssey* of shreds and patches buried within an epic that most readers find needlessly difficult and disordered.

Pound's letters to Rouse summarize, in raw form, the key features of his own translations and adaptations of the *Odyssey* buried within *The Cantos*. These include: a translation which emulates the medieval mind's love of the classics; a translation that reflects the primordial (archaic, Etruscan, "primitive") roots of Homer's gods; a translation that sacrifices literalness for freshness ("Been to

[24] Homer, *The Story of Odysseus*, trans. W. H. D. Rouse (London: Thomas Nelson and Sons, 1937), unpaginated front matter.

[25] Ezra Pound, October [22 or after], 1937 Letter to W. H. D. Rouse. *EPP*, 1954.

hell in a boat yet?" asks Circe; "my bikini is worth your raft" bargains Leucothea [39/195, 91/636]) and dead epithets for new combinations of words ("ΟΥ ΤΙΣ [*OU TIS*, 'no one'] / a man on whom the sun has gone down" [74/450]); a translation that uses different styles of English to reflect the historical stratification of Homer's text; a translation that does not impede the narrative movement forward, summarizing the action when necessary ("And he sailed, by Sirens and thence outward and away / And unto Circe" [1/5]); a translation that accentuates Homer's polyphony and his onomatopoeia, even at the cost of incomprehension or "dumping" Greek words into the text ("Thinning their oar-blades / θῖνα θαλάσσης [*thina thalassēs*, 'shore of the sea']" [98/704]); and, at least implicitly, a translation which stages its very struggle to translate Homer ("Lie quiet Divus. I mean, that is Andreas Divus," [1/5]), both celebrating and despairing of itself as "deficient in homogeneity."

The Matter of Troy

The Cantos engages with the *Odyssey* in numerous ways: it translates it; puzzles over it; interprets and misinterprets it; adapts it; critiques it; trivializes it; allegorizes it; "ritualizes" it; personalizes it; and "anthropologizes" it. There are more references to the *Odyssey* and Homer in *The Cantos* than any other text or author. *The Cantos* begins with an alliterative translation of Odysseus's visit to the underworld to visit Tiresias. Canto 2 weaves the story of Tyro from Homer's catalogue of heroines with the teichoscopy ("viewing from the walls") in *Iliad* 3. Canto 20 imagines the Lotus eaters in a chthonic paradise condemning Odysseus's selfishness. Cantos 39 and 47 recount Odysseus's sex vacation on Circe's island. Odysseus's shipwreck anchors Pound's lyrical ruminations on the destruction of Europe and his own hubris in *The Pisan Cantos*. *Rock-Drill* and *Thrones* retell Leucothea's rescue of Odysseus and his arrival in Phaeacia in sixteen fragments.

Similar to Joyce's use of a different "technic" (from τέχνη, *techne*, meaning both "craftsmanship" and "art") in each chapter of *Ulysses*, Pound uses different styles or "masteries of English" to translate Homer: an alliterative translation of the nekyia; an Ovidian *carmen petpetuum* or "endless song" of Tyro and Helen; a delirious and "doped" vision of the Lotophagoi; an erotic and ecstatic account of Odysseus and Circe's *hieros gamos* or "sacred marriage"; a lyrical and chaotic invocation of Odysseus's shipwreck; and a mystical, anagogic, and metapoetic translation of Leucothea.

Both Joyce's *Ulysses* and Eliot's interpretation of it illuminate Pound's use of the *Odyssey.* In "Ulysses" (1922), Pound describes the Homeric correspondences of *Ulysses* as "Joyce's medievalism": "a scaffold, a means of construction, justified by the result, and justifiable by it only. The result is a triumph in form, in balance, a main schema, with continuous inweaving and arabesque."[26] In "*Ulysses*, Order and Myth" (1923), Eliot identifies a "mythical method" in *Ulysses* which has replaced narrative method and represents "a step toward making the modern world possible for art."[27] The mythical method borrows developments in psychology, ethnography, and works like Frazer's *The Golden Bough* (1890–1915) in order not to adapt a canonical text but to lay bare its anthropological roots. However, the mythical method illuminates Eliot's own technique in *The Waste Land* better than Joyce's technique in *Ulysses.* Inspired by the philological technique of Jessie Weston's *From Ritual to Romance* (1920), Eliot fragments and rearranges the motifs and episodes from the Grail romance in order to reveal the primitive vegetative rituals behind them. (At least, in theory: it is difficult to make the case that *The Waste Land* fully commits to this methodology or actually achieves this.[28]) "Eliot's *Waste Land* is I think the justification of the 'movement,' of our modern experiment, since 1900," Pound explains to the Elizabethan scholar Felix Schelling in 1922.[29] "These fragments I have shored against my ruins" declares Eliot's narrator, or perhaps Fisher King.[30] Pound's version is less elegant: "These fragments you have shelved (shored). / 'Slut!' 'Bitch!' Truth and Calliope / Slanging each other sous les lauriers" (8/28). The fragmentation of the mythical method sows discord between the muses of epic poetry and eloquence.

The Cantos combines the mythical method of *The Waste Land* with the epic scope, "medievalism," and "continuous inweaving and arabesque" of *Ulysses* in order to translate or adapt the *Odyssey* not as a coherent epic but as a compendium of fragments pointing back to a primordial ritual. To put it bluntly: *The Cantos* does what Eliot (erroneously) argued Joyce had already done, and what Eliot pretended to be doing in *The Waste Land* (with Pound's help).

26 *LE,* 406.

27 T. S. Eliot, "*Ulysses*, Order, and Myth," in *Selected Prose of T. S. Eliot*, ed. Frank Kermode (London: Faber and Faber, 1975), 178.

28 See Jonathan Ullyot, "Jessie Weston and the Mythical Method of *The Waste Land*," in *The Medieval Presence in Modernism* (Cambridge: Cambridge University Press, 2016), 47–81.

29 *L*, 248.

30 T. S. Eliot, "*The Waste Land*," in *The Poems of T. S. Eliot*, vol. 1, ed. Christopher Ricks and Jim McCue (New York: Farrar, Straus and Giroux, 2018), line 430.

Certainly, this simplification would have made Pound cringe. It only tells part of the story. This book attempts to tell the rest. Pound's engagement with medieval classicism and nineteenth-century philology eclipsed that of Joyce or Eliot. Pound's readings of medieval literature in *The Spirit of Romance* (1910) are inspired by the pioneering philology of Gaston Paris, Joseph Bédier, and Walter Ker. *The Cantos* is (among so many other things) Pound's own modernist vision of the Matter of Troy, a term used by medieval authors to designate the cycle of texts based on the Trojan War and its aftereffects.[31] Specifically, *The Cantos* presents itself as a modernist *translatio studii* and *imperii* of Homer's *Odyssey.*

The medieval *translatio studii* ("transfer of knowledge and learning") is the translation and revision of classical Latin text (or Latin translation of a Greek text) to reflect contemporary tastes, morality, and truths. These include: the medieval obsession with exotic (often Eastern) affluence, early paradises, and *merveilles* ("marvels"), like the magical pavilions and automata in the *Roman d'Enéas* (*c.* 1160); the rules of courtly love as set forth in Ovid's *Amores* and the hero's refinement through "fine amor," a central theme of Benoît de Sainte-Maure's *Roman de Troie* (*c.* 1155–60); the importance of *courtoise*, or the superiority of French knighthood and learning, as evident in Chaucer's *Troilus and Cryside* (*c.* 1385); and the "truth" of Christian values and eschatology, exemplified in *L'Ovide moralisé* (*c.* 1317–28) or Dante's *Divina Commedia* (1320). The *translatio imperii*, meaning a transfer of *imperium*, or the authority to command, involves attaching a ruling family to an ancient Greek or Trojan hero. Virgil's *Aeneid* establishes the Trojan hero Aeneas as the mythic founder of Rome. Geoffrey of Monmouth's *Historia Regum Britanniae* (*c.* 1136) and Layamon's *Brut* (*c.* 1190–1215) link the founding of Albion (Britain) to the arrival of Brutus of Troy, the son of Aeneas.

In Canto 1, Pound translates a Latin translation of Odysseus's nekyia into medieval alliterative English verse: an outright declaration of his medieval classicism. Like a medieval author, Pound thanks his source, Andreas Divus. Like a medieval author, Pound presents the classical hero as a lover who epitomizes *courtoise* rather than as a brilliant tactician or doughty warrior.

[31] The Old French poet Jean Bodel classified the legendary themes and literary cycles into Three Matters: the Matter of Britain, including the legendary history of Britain and the Arthurian cycle; the Matter of France, particularly texts concerning Charlemagne and his associates; and the Matter of Rome, texts concerning Greek and Roman mythology and historical figures like Alexander the Great and Julius Cesar. The Matter of Troy was later identified as a subset of the Matter of Rome. It included any texts about the Trojan War and its aftermath, including the story of Aeneas.

Homer's Odysseus is a military hero who fends off monsters and clingy goddesses by cunning. Pound's Odysseus is a "po' misero": a passive hero who accepts the guidance of goddesses and becomes an initiate in their mysteries. He emulates what Pound calls the medieval "cult of Amor" of Ovid and the troubadour poets.[32] Like the medieval author, Pound amplifies the classical text with elaborate descriptions of earthly paradises, marvels, and exotic processions. The *Roman d'Enéas* expounds upon the dye-producing mollusks of Tyre and the magnetic fortifications of Carthage. Benoît devotes 300 lines to the alabaster Chambre de Beauté where a wounded Hector is tended: a utopia of idolatry and *courtoisie*, complete with dancing statues and an automaton that explains how a knight ought to behave.[33] Pound describes statuesque figures in marvelous floating cars passing through a Venetian jungle of crystal columns and the "Shelf of the lotophagoi, / Aerial, cut in the aether" (20/93). He turns Circe's "house of smooth stone" into a sensuous paradise of "fucked girls and fat leopards" (39/193), amplifying in over a hundred lines in Cantos 39 and 47 what Homer describes in two: "So there day after day for a full year we abode, feasting on abundant flesh and sweet wine."[34]

Pound also links Odysseus to the present day by what he calls "subject rhymes": an *imperium* of enlightened Odysseus-equivalents ("factive" personalities, or doers of the world[35]) throughout history—adventurers, entrepreneurs, lovers, scientists, patrons of the arts, and devotees of non-doctrinal religions that syncretize the best elements of paganism and Catholicism. These include Apollonius of Tyana, Sigismondo Pandolfo Malatesta, Eleanor of Acquitaine, Cunizza da Romano, Sordello da Goito, Gemistos Plethon, Niccolò III d'Este, Martin Van Buren, Thomas Jefferson, John Adams, and Benito Mussolini. The House of Este receives special attention. They traced their lineage all the way back to Troy: "And that was when Troy was down / And they came here and cut holes in rock, / Down Rome way, and put up the timbers; / And came here, condit Atesten" (20/90–91).

Traditionally, the medieval *translatio* updates the material to reflect the present, or at least to a more contemporary version of what the classical heroic age should have looked like. Benoît's Greeks and Trojans fight on horseback with axes and crossbows; they play backgammon in the off hours and worship

[32] *SR*, 97.

[33] Benoît de Saint-Maure, *Le Roman de Troie*, ed. Léopold Constans (Paris: Firmin Didot, 1904–12), lines 14631–958.

[34] Homer, *Odyssey*, trans. A. T. Murray (Cambridge, MA: Harvard University Press, 1919), 10.467–8. Hereafter quoted parenthetically in the text.

[35] *GK*, 194.

in Gothic churches; and they seem familiar with the Bible. Inspired by authors like Jane Harrison, J. A. K. Thomson, Gilbert Murray, and James Frazer, Pound updates Homer's Olympian patriarchal pantheon "backward" to its primordial, chthonic roots: female deities and dying-and-resurrecting gods associated with mystery religions and vegetative rites. He turns Odysseus from a war hero into a solar hero and fertility daimon, changing the plot of the *Odyssey* from a teleological nostos quest to a cyclical solar myth.

The Cantos is a hyperliterary translation of the *Odyssey* that demands that the reader engage with it on multiple levels: as an attempt to translate Homer; as an attempt to adapt Homer so that he is relevant today; as an attempt to emulate the way that Homer was adapted by the best medieval authors; and as an attempt to recover the *Ur-Odyssey* via the mythical method—to excavate the folklore, solar myths, and mystery rituals upon which the *Odyssey* was originally based, long before it was unified from its "confusion" by Pisistratus according to Cicero, or "anthologized" according to Pound, and long before it was expurgated and interpolated by classical and medieval scholars.[36]

Pound's ambition to excavate the primordial source of the epic was an obsession of nineteenth-century philology. Joseph Bédier had tried something similar in his hypothetical reconstruction of the putative *Ur-Tristan* in the second volume of *Le Roman de Tristan par Thomas* (1905), a work which Pound enthusiastically recommends in *The Spirit of Romance.* He also told Joyce to read it, and it became the hypotext of *Finnegans Wake.* In *The Birth of Tragedy*, Nietzsche argues that a primordial Dionysian lyric lurks behind the Apollonian tranquility of the Greek drama and epic. Vestiges remain in the "drunken" verse of Aeschylus's choruses. Nietzsche's description of the poetry of folk song, "straining to its limits *to imitate music*," can be read as a gloss on the seemingly chaotic, haphazard, and "sketchy" (as Rouse puts it) poetics of *The Cantos*:

> the melody, as it gives birth again and again, emanates sparks of imagery which in their variety, their sudden changes, their mad, head-over-heels, forward rush, reveal an energy utterly alien to the placid flow of epic semblance. Seen from the point of view of the epic, this uneven and irregular image-world of the lyric is something which must simply be condemned.[37]

[36] Before Pisistratus, writes Cicero, the books of Homer were "confusos": mixed, mingled, confounded, or "poured together" (Cicero, *De Oratore*, 3.137). "Every great culture has had such a major anthology. Pisistratus, Li Po, the Japanese Emperor who reduced the number of Noh dramas to about 450; the hackneyed Hebrew example; in less degree the Middle Ages, with the matter of Britain, of France, and of Rome le Grant" (*GK*, 394). See chapter 3.

[37] Frederic Nietzsche, *The Birth of Tragedy*, trans. Ronald Speirs (New York: Cambridge University Press, 1999), 34.

"I tried a smoother presentation and lost the metamorphosis, got to be a hurley burley," Pound explains Ford Madox Ford, who read an early draft of Canto 2.[38]

Applying the mythical method to Homer means turning the placid flow of epic semblance back into a primordial, Dionysian, melopoetic, and lyric disorder, reflecting what J. J. Bachofen identifies as matriarchal-based religions of dying-and-resurrecting gods: goddess worship, fertility rites, and mystery religions;[39] or what Jane Harrison identifies as the chthonic cults and deities that predate the "cut flowers" of Homer's Olympians:

> the Olympian gods—that is, the anthropomorphic gods of Homer and Pheidias and the mythographers—seemed to me like a bouquet of cut-flowers whose bloom is brief, because they have been severed from their roots. To find those roots we must burrow deep into a lower stratum of thought, into those chthonic cults which underlay their life and from which sprang all their brilliant blossoming.[40]

Pound's paradiso is chthonic, especially in Cantos 17, 20, and 21. In order "to write Paradise" Pound must burrow into the roots of Homer's gods (119/822). *The Cantos* is therefore a nekyia into the *Odyssey* itself. It restlessly and repeatedly summons a mythical "hinter time," long before Hades became a place of punishment like Virgil's Avernus, long before the gods were anthropomophized, allegorized, moralized, and finally exorcised by the logic of enlightenment.

> The undeniable tradition of metamorphosis teaches us that things do not remain always the same. They become other things by swift and unanalysable process. It was only when men began to mistrust the myths and to tell nasty lies about the gods for a moral purpose that these matters became hopelessly confused. When some nasty Semite or Parsee or Syrian began to use myths for social propaganda, when the myth was degraded into an allegory or a fable, that was the beginning of the end. And the Gods no longer walked in men's gardens.
>
> (*LE*, 431)

Pound's ideas are very much in line with *fin-de-siècle* intellectual school that revolted against rationalistic individualism, positivism, and democracy in favor

[38] Ezra Pound, March 21, 1922 Letter to Ford Madox Ford. *Pound/Ford: Story Of Literary Friendship* (New York: New Directions, 1981), 65.

[39] See J. J. Bachofen, *Myth, Religion, and Mother Right*, trans. Ralph Manheim (Princeton, NJ: Princeton University Press, 1967), 132–4.

[40] Jane Harrison, *Themis* (Cambridge: Cambridge University Press, 1912), xi.

of emotionalism and vitalism. The ideological roots of fascism ("some nasty Semite or Parsee or Syrian") are found here as well.

Like Proust's paradise, Pound's paradise must be written. Almost every canto reasserts a world of renewal, confusion, magical metamorphoses, and mystery. Almost every canto seeks to restore a lost mythical way of thinking which will clear the ground for a "return" of the primordial gods. Babelic melopoeia, disorder, and confusion are the prerequisites to recovering a mythical "primitive" consciousness of endless renewal: "Broken, disrupted, body eternal, / Wilderness of renewals, confusion / Basis of renewals" (20/91–92).

Pound's attempt to excavate the solar myths, fertility myths, and mystery rituals on which the *Odyssey* is based often involves the paradoxical practice of "reading" or interpreting Homer through the authors that proceeded him. Pound's innovation of the medieval *translatio* by combining it with scientific philology and comparative anthropology continues to confuse readers and critics to this day. Pound's "adapting forward" is in the service of resurrecting something much older. A few lines of Catullus or Bernart de Ventadorn restore a conception of love between Odysseus and Circe that was "expurgated" from the *Odyssey* of today. Similarly, Pound's borrowing of Neoplatonic imagery does not mean that he ascribes to the Neoplatonic philosophy of the transcendent One and the world-soul, any more than their reductive allegorical readings of Homer. Rather, Neoplatonic philosophy preserves aspects of ancient solar worship. Pound also admired their mystic reverence for Homer and their conviction that fragments of paradise were visible on earth. Likewise, Pound believed that Orphism and the Eleusinian Mysteries reflected primordial mystery religions of the dying-and-resurrecting gods that emerged from matriarchal religions.[41] Pound had no interest in the Orphic, proto-Christian, and very Unhomeric division of soul (*psyche*) and body (*soma*), nor in Orphism's rampant misogyny, asceticism, or belief in reincarnation.

The Cantos engages with the text of the *Odyssey* on at least four different levels: as a collection of ancient myths, folklore, and rituals; as an oral text composed in some mythical hinter-time, recited by bards around 850 BCE, "anthologized" by Pisistratus in 540 BCE, and edited for over a thousand years by librarians and

[41] "Whenever we encounter matriarchy, it is bound up with the mystery of the chthonian religion, whether it invokes Demeter or is embodied by an equivalent goddess" (Bachofen, *Myth, Religion, and Mother Right*, 88).

scribes; as the foundation of Western literature adapted and translated by poets like Virgil, Dante, Chapman, and Joyce; and as an artifact interpreted by the scientific philology and anthropology of Pound's day. Keeping these many layers in mind contextualizes the very deliberate disorder and polyphony of Pound's *translatio*. It also makes it a lot more pleasurable to read. For all its seeming disorder, *The Cantos* is remarkably consistent in its naive (if not romantic) attempt to resurrect a primordial poetic world of paradise and involve the reader in its mythical method.

The *Odyssey* in *The Cantos*

A brief summary of the *Odyssey* plot in *The Cantos* will illuminate the main features of Pound's *translatio*. This includes the emphasis on Odysseus as a passive hero and devotee of fertility goddesses rather than as a cunning tactician; the focus on primordial deities rather than Olympian ones; the representation of Odysseus's wanderings as cyclical rather than teleological; and the fragmentation of the Homeric text into a series of "luminous details," translation problems, and even trivia.[42] Although Pound's Homeric scaffolding is not as deliberate or as consistent as Joyce's, it is far more coherent and intricate than readers have given him credit.

The Cantos begins with a translation of the nekyia episode of *Odyssey* 11.1–112. Odysseus and his crew leave Circe's island, arrive in the land of the Kimmerians, and perform the rites to call up and question the dead. Odysseus talks to Elpenor and Tiresias, and the translation ends abruptly after Tiresias informs Odysseus that he will "Lose all companions" (1/5). Odysseus sails "outward and away / And unto Circe" in order to bury Elpenor and continue his quest. Pound briefly resumes his translation of the nekyia in Canto 2 to recount the story of Tyro's rape from *Odyssey* 11.235–59.

Canto 17 describes a Dionysian procession through a Venetian landscape at night, past "cliffs of amber" and the "Cave of Nerea," which echo Homer's description of Calypso's cave in Ogyia and Circe's cave in Aeaea (17/76). The procession continues in Canto 20 through a verdant jungle past the "shelf of the Lotophagoi" (20/93). The "Lotophagoi of the suave nails" lament the fate of the mariners Odysseus forcibly removed and "chained to the rowingbench." They

[42] "A REAL book is one whose words grow ever more luminous as one's own experience increases or as one is led or edged over into considering them with greater attention" (*GK*, 317).

"died in the whirlpool" after leaving Thrinacia, the island home of the Cattle of Helios. They didn't have "Circe to couch-mate, Circe Titania, / 'Nor had they meats of Kalüpso," nor heard they the "Ligur' aoide" ("clear, sweet song") of the Sirens, nor were buried with honors like Elpenor (20/94).

In an early typescript of Canto 20, Pound ends with a description of Odysseus and his men returning to Aeaea, with "sacks over their heads, / landed their empty casks / brought sea-gear ashore here; / here bur[]ied Elpenor / here faced again Circe."[43] Pound reworked the material and added it to Canto 23. Odysseus and his men arrive "in the morning, in the Phrygian head-sack / Barefooted, dumping sand from their boat / 'Yperionides!" (23/108). Odysseus's return to Aeaea from Hades is linked to the return of the solar deity, Helios Ὑπεριωνίδης (*Hyperiōnidēs*, "son of Hyperion") as well as the Egyptian solar deity Ra who rises over the Phyrigian (eastern) desert and gains buoyancy by dumping sand from Atet, his sun-boat.

In Canto 39, Elpenor (in Hades) muses on the long year when he lay in Circe's ingle among "fucked girls and fat leopards" (39/193). Elpenor, whom Homer describes as "not over valiant in war nor sound of understanding" (10.552), confuses the order of events of *Odyssey* book 10, repeats lines from Homer in English, Greek, and Latin like jazz refrains, and lingers on the dirty bits: "kaka pharmak edōken" ("she gave them evil drugs"); "Discuss this in bed said the lady" (39/194); "es thalamon / Ἐς θάλαμόν" ("into the bedroom"); "I think you must be Odysseus… / feel better when you have eaten…"; "Been to hell in a boat yet?" (39/195). Elpenor's satyr song climaxes with the "sacred marriage" of Odysseus and Circe: a rite of spring replete with schoolboyish innuendoes: " 'Fac Deum!' 'Est Factus'" ("Make god! It is made," but sounds like, "Fuck God; Is Fucked"); "Beaten from flesh into light / Hath swallowed the fire-ball" (39/196); "His rod hath made a god in my belly."

Canto 47 retells the story more soberly from the focalization of Circe and Odysseus. Circe (or a voice that represents her perspective) warns Odysseus of the perils to come: "Scilla's dogs snarl at the cliff's base" (47/236). She likens Odysseus's arrival to her cave to the natural compulsion of the beast to be sacrificed: "The bull runs blind on the sword, *naturans* / To the cave art thou called, Odysseus, / By Molü has though respite for a little" (47/237). She compares his nekyia to the entrance into her (literal and figural) cave: "Hast thou found a nest softer than cunnus / Or has thou found better rest / Hast'ou a deeper planting, doth thy death year / Bring swifter shoot?" (47/238). She extols

[43] Ezra Pound, "Canto XX: Typescripts." *EPP*, 3189.

the Hesiodic virtue of *aidōs* (prudence): work hard, worship the gods, and reflect on your insignificance, for "so light is thy weight on Tellus." Odysseus closes the canto with an ecstatic celebration of his sacred marriage: "By prong have I entered these hills: / That the grass grow from my body, / That I hear the roots speaking together." He links his "death" to Adonis's: "By this door have I entered the hill. / Falleth, / Adonis falleth. / Fruit cometh after." He lauds Circe as a chthonic feminine goddess of mystery religions "that hath the gift of healing, / that hath the power over wild beasts" (47/239).

The China and Adams Cantos drop the Odyssean material save one reference in 166 pages. Pound was occupied with a sustained revision of Chinese and eighteenth-century American history in light of the monetary theories of Alexander del Mar, the ethnography of Leo Frobenius, and ethnology of Thaddeus Zielinski (to name but a few). Pound "goes on a holiday" from his Odyssey *translatio* just as Odysseus does from his homeward quest in Aeaea. However, *The Pisan Cantos, Rock-Drill,* and *Thrones* reprise the Odyssey-material with renewed fervor, the material now arranged more "horizontally" than "vertically" as fragments that repeat and develop over multiple cantos.

The Pisan Cantos (Cantos 74–84) roughly recount Odysseus's journey after he leaves Calypso's island of Ogyia until he is shipwrecked and washes up on the coast of Scheria, the island of the Phaeacians from *Odyssey* 5.269–493. Pound-Odysseus clings to his raft "with the mast held by the left hand" (74/463). He reflects on his great hubris, "the folly of attacking that island [of the Cicones] / and of the force ὑπὲρ μόρον [*hyper moron,* 'beyond what is destined']" (80/532). Eventually, "the raft broke and the waters went over me" (80/533). With nothing to cling to, Odysseus-Pound swims in the "fluid ΧΘΟΝΟΣ [*CHTONOS*], strong as the undertow / of the wave receding" (82/546). He washes up on Scheria, the island of the Phacaeans, prays to "GEA TERRA," the Earth Goddess, and falls asleep as he is "drawn" into the earth (82/546).

There are over a hundred seemingly random and scattered references to the *Odyssey* in *The Pisan Cantos,* from Homer's color-words to the four winds to Odysseus's many epithets, with particular emphasis on Odysseus *outis* or "no man": the name Odysseus uses to trick Polyphemus. Odysseus (who often stands in for Pound) reflects on his past, recalling Elpenor, Tiresias, Athena, Nestor, Circe, Nausicaa, Scylla, Charybdis, the Sirens, the Cicones, and Tyro. In Canto 83, Pound re-imagines the nekyia in his Pisan tent by describing a baby wasp being born from "a squat indian bottle" that falls to the earth and descends "to them that dwell under the earth, / begotten of air, that shall sing in the bower / of Kore, Περσεφόνεια [*Persephóneia*, Persephone] / and have speech with Tiresias, Thebae" (83/552, 83/553).

Rock-Drill (Cantos 85–95) and *Thrones* (Cantos 96–109) narrate the Leucothea episode from *Odyssey* 5.333–353 in sixteen fragmentary sequences. After Odysseus's raft is wrecked by Poseidon, Leucothea emerges from the water in the form of a seagull. She instructs Odysseus to strip off Calypso's heavy garments, abandon his broken raft, swim to shore holding her magic veil (*krēdemnon*), and then return it back to the sea. "As the sea-gull Κάδμου θυγάτηρ [*Kadmou thygatēr*, 'daughter of Cadmus'] said to Odysseus / KADMOU THUGATER / 'get rid of parp[h]ernalia'" (91/635). *Rock-Drill* ends with a description of Odysseus being thrown from his raft and Leucothea taking pity on him:

And he was drawn down under wave,
The wind tossing,
Notus, Boreas,
as it were thistle-down
Then Leucothea had pity,
"mortal once
Who now is a sea-god:
νόστου [*nostou*, "to reach"]
γαίης Φαιήκων, ..." [*gaiēs Phaiēkōn*, "the land of the Phaeacians"]. (95/667)

Thrones begins with the image of Leucothea giving Odysseus her veil and disappearing into the water: "Κρήδεμνον [*Krēdemnon*, 'veil'] ... / κρήδεμνον ... / and the wave concealed her, / dark mass of great water" (96/671). Odysseus returns her veil to the sea in Canto 100: "and he dropped the scarf in the tide-rips / KREDEMNON / that it should float back to the sea, / and that quickly / DEXATO XERSI ['she gathered it in her hand'] / with a fond hand / AGERTHE ['gathered back']" (100/736–37).

Rock-Drill and *Thrones* are also full of arcane and trivial *Odyssey* allusions. For example: "'A cargo of iron' / lied Pallas" refers to Athena, disguised as Mentes, claiming to have a ship full of iron from *Odyssey* 1.184 (102/748). Pound also intentionally conflates the story of Leucothea with Leucothoe from Ovid's *Metamorphoses* 4, who "rose as an incense bush" after she resisted Apollo (98/705). Pound even imagines the Phaeacians "after 500 years / still offered that shrub to the sea-gull," as though these stories were connected (102/748).

Pound's *Odyssey*

Pound's compliant to Rouse seems to summarize the *Odyssey* within *The Cantos:* "What I dig up is too concentrative, I dont see how to get unity of the WHOLE"; "if I tried to trans the Odyssey I wd. probably make a thing of shreds and patches, all out of shape and deficient in homogeneity." However, *The Cantos* (minus the China and Adams sections) does tell a version of Homer's story. Pound's Odysseus arrives in Kimmeria, questions the ghost Tiresias, and learns that he is going to lose all his companions. He returns to Circe's island. The narrative jumps back to Odysseus's earlier visit with Circe. Odysseus's men are turned into beasts; Odysseus spends a year with Circe; and receives instructions about how to reach Tiresias. Odysseus's adventures with the Lotophagoi, the Sirens, Scylla, Charybdis, the Cicones, the Cattle of Helios, Nausicaa, and Calypso are mentioned in passing. Odysseus is eventually shipwrecked after leaving Calypso's island. Leucothea intervenes. Pound's story ends with Odysseus's arrival in Phaeacia in Canto 100, followed by a few scattered references to the Phaeacian worship of Leucothea/Leucothoe 500 years later. Although this is barely a retelling of the *Odyssey, The Cantos* does fulfill its promise to tell the story of how Odysseus will "lose all companions" and end up destitute (1/5). Pound also roughly follows the chronology of Odysseus's wanderings, unlike Homer, who begins with Odysseus's shipwreck and arrival in Phaeacia in books 5–8 and has Odysseus recount his earlier wanderings to the Phaeacian court in books 9–12.

The Cantos is populated by Homeric characters associated with ecstasy, inspiration, sex, water, and the underworld. Women outnumber men by six: Circe, Tyro, Alcmene, Proserpine, Anticlea, Helen, the Sirens, the nereids, Phatheusa, Scylla, Charybdis, Leucothea, Calypso, Nausicca, Aphrodite, Athena, and Leucothea; compared to Odysseus, Aeolus, Perimedes, Eurylochus, Elpenor, Tireseas, the Trojan elders, Proteus, Nestor, Helios (*Hyperiōnidēs*), and Zeus. Of the major divine agents in Homer's *Odyssey*—Zeus, Athena, Poseidon, Circe, and Hermes—only Circe figures significantly in *The Cantos.* Pound pairs Athena with Hermes, Dionysus, and the "*choros nympharum*" (17/77); and invokes her owl-like form, "Athenae / γλαύξ, γλαυκωπις [*glaux, glaukōpis*]" (74/458). Zeus is represented only in connection with primordial gods: as a version of Ammon, or "Zeus ram" (74/450); as paired with the god of agriculture: "Zeus lies in Ceres' bosom" (81/537); and as linked to the six-winged seraphs the fly around the throne of God in *The Book of Enoch* and the *Book of Revelation:* "Zeus with the six seraphs before him," and "Zeus, six bluejays before him" (90/627, 104/761).

The Cantos excavates Homer's pantheon back to its chthonic, primitive, shifting, and matriarchal origins. Pound's Homeric divinities are associated with grain rites and the mystery religions: Helios, Aphrodite, Demeter, Persephone, Dionysus, Circe, Leucothea, and many nameless naiads, water-nymphs, and river goddesses. A passage from J. A. K. Thomson's *Studies in the Odyssey* (1914) summarizes Pound's pantheon:

> Helios, on the other hand, is simply the personified Sun, and he, together with Dionysos and Demeter and Persephone and certain minor divinities such as Aiolos, who has charge of the winds, Kirke, Proteus, Leukothea, and the many nymphs, river-gods, and the like, including Okeanos himself, belong to a primitive nature-religion older than Homer's Olympianism and plainly irreconcilable with it.[44]

Pound emphasizes Odysseus's role as a nomadic wanderer who performs rites, follows directions, worships goddesses, suffers under the elements, and is occasionally rewarded with a bit of terrestrial paradise. As Thomson puts it,

> Odysseus never loses the counsel and guidance of some goddess, Athena or Kalypso, Kirke or Leukothea; and when we consider that Penelope, too, was a goddess to begin with, we must conclude that the story of the Odyssey grew up among a people very observant of goddess-worship, among a people also very reverent of women, as the Odyssey uniformly is.[45]

Homer's Odysseus outsmarts Circe by eating the magical herb μῶλυ (*moly*). Pound turns *moly* into an initiation drug of their *hieros gamos*: "To the cave art thou called, Odysseus, / By Molü hast thou respite for a little" (47/237). Pound makes little to no reference to Odysseus's most memorable feats of cunning: resisting Circe's magic; outsmarting the Sirens; escaping Polyphemus's cave; navigating past Scylla; and saving himself from sucking Charybdis. Even Leopold Bloom, hardly the paragon of an active hero, successfully escapes the clutches of an anti-Semitic (monocular) Cyclops and repeatedly dodges humiliating encounters with Blazes Boylan, suitor to his wife.

Homer delights in recounting stories of Odysseus the cunning (πολύμητις, *polumetis*) tactician and teller of tales. Pound, by contrast, defines *polumetis* as a kind of well-roundedness and intelligence close to godliness:

> The things that the *polumetis* knew were the things a man then *needed* for living. The bow, the strong stroke in swimming, the how-to-provide *and* the high hat,

[44] Thomson, *Studies in the Odyssey*, 153.
[45] Thomson, *Studies in the Odyssey*, 167–8.

> the carriage of the man who knew how to rule, who had been everywhere [...] And as Zeus said: "A chap with a mind like THAT! the fellow is one of us. One of US."[46]

Pound also associates *polumetis* with quick thinking and the ability to endure suffering with "hilaritas" or cheerfulness. Pound takes the epithet *outis* ("no man") out of its original Homeric context as Odysseus's ruse to escape Polyphemus's cave ("Noman blinded me!"), and uses it instead to reflect on the destitute and shipwrecked Odysseus: "OY TIΣ / a man on whom the sun has gone down" (47/450).

Pound also rejects Homer's condemnation of Odysseus's comrades as weak, ungrateful, and ultimately deserving of their deaths. Homer introduces the idea in the proem: "Yet even so he saved not his comrades, though he desired it sore, for through their own blind folly they perished—fools, who devoured the kine of Helios Hyperion" (*Odyssey* 1.6–9). By contrast, Pound's Lotophagoi condemn Odysseus for selfishly dragging his comrades from one adventure to the next and hogging all the glimpses of earthly paradise for himself: hearing the Sirens's song, eating Calypso's meats, and sharing Circe's bed. In the *ABC of Reading*, Pound argues: "His companions have most of them something that must have been the Greek equivalent of shell-shock."[47]

Pound also suggests that Odysseus deserves his shipwreck for using a "force ὑπὲρ μόρον" ("beyond what is destined") in sacking Ismaros—an incident which did not trouble Homer or later classical and medieval authors (80/532). However, Pound's Odysseus is not sinfully arrogant like Dante's Ulysses, who sails past the Straights of Gibraltar in pursuit of "del mondo sanza gente" ("the world where no one lives"), nor is he restless like Tennyson's hackneyed Ulysses, "always roaming with a hungry heart."[48] Pound's Odysseus atones for his former arrogance and learns *aidōs* by following the directions of Circe and Leucothea.

Another striking feature of Pound's *Odyssey* is the absence of the nostos theme. The word appears only once in Canto 95 in order to call attention to this lack: "νόστου / γαίης Φαιήκων ['to reach the land of the Phacaians']" a quotation of *Odyssey* 5.344–45 (95/667). "Nostos" here does not mean "return home" but merely "arrival." Pound's Odysseus is not trying to get home to his wife or son or his native land: a motif that Homer repeats *ad nauseam*. Pound's

[46] *GK*, 146.
[47] *ABCR*, 44.
[48] Dante, *Inferno from the Divine Comedy*, trans. Allen Mandelbaum (New York: Bantam, 1982), 26.117; Alfred Tennyson, "Ulysses," in *The Major Works* (New York: Oxford University Press, 2011), 82.

Tiresias says that "'Odysseus / 'Shalt return through spiteful Neptune, over dark seas, / 'Lose all companions'" (1/4–5). He does not qualify the nature of this return. Once Divus is laid to rest, Pound summarizes: "And he sailed, by Sirens and then outward and away / And unto Circe," suggesting that the "return" is back to Circe, and emphasizing the repetitive circularity of his journey (1/5). "Ithaca" occurs only once in *The Cantos* because the translation demands it: "As set in Ithaca, sterile bulls of the best / For sacrifice" (1/3). Telemachus, Laertes, Eumaeus, Eurycleia, and the suitors receive no mention. Anticlea is twice denied a voice in Pound's underworld, nor does Pound bother to remind his readers that Anticlea is the name of Odysseus's mother: "And Anticlea came, whom I beat off"; "And then Anticlea came. / Lie quiet Divus" (1/4, 1/5). In Canto 99, Pound reduces Anticlea's pitiful death while pining for her son to: "Odysseus' old ma missed his conversation" (99/714). Penelope is referred to once in a piece of trivia relating to Odysseus's generosity: "and as to why Penelope waited / keinas … e Orgei. line 639" (102/748). Penelope explains to Medon in *Odyssey* 4.693 (not 639): "Yet he [κεῖνος, *keinos,* 'that man'] never wrought [ἐώργει, *eōrgei*] iniquity at all to any man." Pound was remarkably adept at blaming "parasites" like usurers and profiteers for all the evils of the world. Although the explicit goal of *Thrones* is to highlight the ways in which men resist such evils and establish good societies and governments, there is not one reference in *The Cantos* to Odysseus's revenge upon the suitors or his reestablishment of order in Ithaca.

Pound's Odysseus is a dying-and-resurrecting god like Adonis or Tamuz; a fertility daimon who is a consort to powerful goddesses; and a solar hero who negotiates a series of mythical "monsters" (the constellations) during his course across the sky. Odysseus's elaborate stratagems in Ithaca to slaughter of the suitors and the waiting maids might have pleased Pisistratus's audience at the Panathenaia, but to Pound, this plot is a late addition that undermines Odysseus's transformation from selfish and hubristic to an initiate of the mysteries of Circe and Leucothea.

Pound's *Odyssey* is structured as a series of cyclical repetitions which replay the metamorphosis of the hero: birth, death, rebirth; sunrise, sunset, sunrise; setting sail, arriving, setting sail; descending, ascending, descending. Pound describes the model to his father:

> Rather like, or unlike subject and response and counter subject in fugue.
>
> A. A. Live man goes down into world of Dead
>
> C. B. The "repeat in history"

B. C. The "magic moment" or moment of metamorphosis, bust thru from quotidian into
"divine or permanent world." Gods, etc.[49]

If *The Cantos* has a telos, it is the gradual stripping-away of the teleological model and the epic (Apollonian) plot. The Pound hero's goal is to attune himself to the repeat in history, to recognize moments of the permanent world and cultivate them. In the so-called Paradise Cantos (90–95), Pound invokes the blind Homer first hearing his poetry in the *polyphloisbois* of the waves and Dante's first glimpse of Beatrice:

chh   chh
          the pebbles turn with the wave
chh   ch'u
                    "fui chiamat' ["I was called"]
                                        e qui refulgo" ["and here I glow"]
Le Paradis n'est pas artificiel
                                        but is jagged,
For a flash,
                    for an hour. (92/640)

The path to paradise is as "wide as a hair" and just as fragile (93/652).

In the *Odyssey*, Odysseus's adventures represent trials to be overcome in order to successfully arrive home. The heroes of the *Odyssey* are those who maintain their loyalty despite everything: Odysseus, Laertes, Eumaeus, Penelope, and Eurycleia.[50] (Homer repeatedly suggests that Odysseus is promiscuous only by necessity, and hence not technically disloyal, although many readers have questioned this.) Homer is less kind to those who succumb to grief, like Anticlea, or who waver in their convictions, like Telemachus. He is unforgiving to those who resort to disloyalty and treachery, like Odysseus's mariners, Aegisthus, Clytemnestra, Melanthius, and the maidservants. In *The Cantos*, by contrast, the Sirens, the Lotophagoi, Circe, and Leucothea all represent opportunities for Odysseus, and ultimately the reader, to witness a primordial ritual mystery and glimpse paradise. The heroes of *The Cantos* are those who stay connected to primordial divinities and the vitalist world view: free-spirited creative intellectual explorers, pacifists, and devotees of Amor. The greatest

[49] *L*, 285.
[50] See Keri Elizabeth Ames, "The Rebirth of Heroism from Homer's Odyssey to Joyce's Ulysses," in *Twenty-First Joyce*, ed. Ellen Carol Jones and Morris Beja (Gainesville: University of Florida Press, 2004), 157–78.

tragedy, according to the Lotophagoi, is man's failure to experience, or become worthy of, divinity. Pound is especially unforgiving to those who make war ("there are no righteous wars" [82/545]), reject beauty, turn revelation into doctrine, dissect and denigrate masterpieces with philology, and profit on the loss of others.

My Approach

My reading of *The Cantos* as a *translatio* of the *Odyssey* should not be taken as overly contentious. I am not arguing that *The Cantos* is a rewriting of the *Odyssey* like Joyce's *Ulysses* or even Derek Walcott's *Omeros* (1990). However, there is far more coherence to Pound's reworking of Homer's text than critics have given credit. While a wealth of scholarship has detailed the influence of philology on Pound and the primal rites submerged beneath Pound's classical allusions,[51] no study has explored how Pound's understanding of Homer is influenced by nineteenth-century scientific philology or comparative anthropology. Likewise, although there are many excellent analyses of Pound's use of medieval sources and Pound's reworking of the *Odyssey*,[52] no study has explored how medieval classicism and the *translatio* informs the methodology of *The Cantos*, nor how Pound uses different "technics" or "masteries of English" in his adaptations of different episodes of the *Odyssey*. In fact, no study has comprehensively argued that Pound even tells a story or version of the *Odyssey*—that there is a progression or any coherence to his version.

My first chapter, "*The Spirit of Romance* and the Debt to Philology," argues that Pound teases out a definition of medieval classicism in *The Spirit of Romance* (1910) that would define (his) modernism and direct the methodology of his long poem: the "Hellenic" austerity of style; the "depersonalization" of the implied author or poet; the idea of literary composition as the compiling

[51] On philology, see, for example, Hugh Kenner, *The Pound Era* (Berkeley, CA: University of California Press, 1971); Fred Robinson, "Pound's Anglo Saxon Studies," in *Ezra Pound*, ed. Harold Bloom (New York: Chelsea House, 1987), 105–26. On Pound's Eleusis, see, for example, Leon Surette, *A Light from Eleusis* (New York: Oxford University Press, 1979); and Demetres Tryphonopoulos, *The Celestial Tradition* (Waterloo, ON: Wilfrid Laurier University Press, 1992); and chapters 2, 4, and 5.

[52] On Pound's medieval sources, see, for example, Mark Byron, *Ezra Pound's Eriugena* (London: Bloomsbury Academic, 2014); David Anderson, *Pound's Cavalcanti* (Princeton, NJ: Princeton University Press, 1983). On Pound's *Odyssey*, see, for example, Walter Baumann, "The *Odyssey* Theme in Ezra Pound's *Cantos*," in *Roses from the Steel Dust* (Orono, ME: National Poetry Foundation, 2000), 83–97; Leah Flack, *Modernism and Homer: The Odysseys of H.D., James Joyce, Osip Mandelstam, and Ezra Pound* (Cambridge: Cambridge University Press, 2015).

and arranging of fragmented sources; the proximity of literary composition to (philological) literary criticism; the use of Latin texts as necessary intermediaries to understanding Greek texts; and the practice of the medieval *translatio studii.* Pound relies on the philological scholarship of Gaston Paris, Joseph Bédier, and Walter Ker, all of whom rejected Romantic and Victorian medievalism.

The second chapter, "Odysseus among the Dead," looks at how Pound's Anglo-Saxon *translatio* of Homer in Canto 1 transforms Odysseus from a Greek warrior and family man to a fertility hero through concision and suppression of Homer's *Odyssey* 11. Pound turns Homer's description of Odysseus raising and questioning the dead into a rite of resurrecting the primordial gods. Pound also de-emphasizes and destabilizes Odysseus as independent from his men. I look at the influence of Jane Harrison's concept of the "holophrase," or a described events without a clear distinction between subject and object, on Canto 1, as well as Lucien Lévy-Bruhl's "pre-logical consciousness."

The third chapter, "Protean Homer," argues that Pound stitches fragments from Homer into an Ovidian *carmen perpetuum* ("endless song") to recreate what Nietzsche calls the Dionysian lyric lurking behind the epic form. This includes a translation of *Iliad* 3, in which the Trojan elders watch Helen approach; a "continuation" of the nekyia from Canto 1, in which Odysseus meets Tyro in the underworld and learns of her seduction by Poseidon in the guise of a river; and the tale of Dionysus's transformation of the mariners into dolphins from Hymn 7 to Dionysus and Ovid's *Metamorphoses.* Canto 2 inaugurates a poetic style which might be called, at the syntactic and metaphorical level, an aesthetics of perpetual metamorphosis, through a concatenation of imagist word-clusters. Pound expands Ovid's "magical instants" of transformation into a Dionysian rite, and presents the reader with a jagged "pre-epic" or folkloric *Ur-Odyssey.*

Chapter 4, "The Lotophagoi: Confusion and Renewal," looks at how Pound's aesthetics of confusion and delirium in Canto 20 critiques epic coherence. Pound presents a Babelic music difficult to hear and a visionary scene difficult to visualize: a "wilderness of renewals," leading to "confusion / Basis of renewals" (20/92). Lyric confusion undermines narrative coherence: from the opening search for Homer's melopoetic sound; to a philological puzzle in the text of Arnaut Daniel; to Niccolò d'Este's delirious reading of *La Chanson de Roland*; and culminating in the lament of the Lotophagoi.

Chapter 5, "Erotic Circe," looks at how Pound's *translatio* of *Odyssey* 10 and 12 performs the Eleusinian ritual of the *hieros gamos*, first through a comedic, bawdy, quasi-pornographic song in the voice of Elpenor, and then through a lyric and ecstatic hymn in the voice of Circe and Odysseus. Cantos 39 and 47 excavate Homer's Circe as a matriarchal fertility goddess and restore her as Odysseus's hierophant and spiritual guide. Circe critiques Odysseus's desire to "sail after knowledge" and argues for the necessity of adopting Hesiodic αιδώς (*aidōs*): shame, decency, and humility (47/236). Canto 47 marks Odysseus's transformation from an active epic hero—Odysseus πτολιπόρθιος (*ptolipórthios*) or "sacker of cities"—to a passive lyric hero—a dying-and-resurrecting god like Adonis.

My sixth chapter, "Pisan Wreck," argues that *The Pisan Cantos* is anchored in a specific Homeric episode: Odysseus's shipwreck after he leaves Calypso on Ogyia until he is washed up on Scheria. Pound introduces a sustained lyrical "I" while at the same time adopting an even more chaotic and polyphonic style, repeatedly invoking wind, booming waves, and fragile vessels. Homer's terrible winds become Pound's suave airs that blow from paradise; Homer's frightful waves become a percussive ritual of the Pound hero's chthonic descent; Homer's foreboding chaos of water manifests Pound's sacred disorder which leads to "the mind indestructible" and the mental state of paradise (74/450).

The last chapter, "How to Read Leucothea," argues that Leucothea represents the necessary "plunge" into difficult knowledge and arcana in order to achieve Pound's paradise. Cantos 90–95 present a paradise best described as interactive and "anagogic," a term that Pound uses to represent a type of poetry that represents the struggle of the mind to achieve the state of divine or philosophical contemplation. For Pound, paradise is less a place than a state of mind or an ability to see. It flashes in the mind "for an hour. / Then agony, / then an hour, / then agony" (92/640).

1

The Spirit of Romance and the Debt to Philology

It is impossible (as M. Gaston Paris has shown) to separate the spirit of French Romance from the spirit of Provençal lyric poetry.[1]

"I want to maintain that after a hundred years of romanticism," T. E. Hulme begins his lecture to the Quest Society in 1911, "we are in for a classical revival."[2] According to Hulme, Romanticism is the belief that man is "an infinite reservoir of possibilities," whereas classicism contends that "man is an extraordinarily fixed and limited animal whose nature is absolutely constant. It is only by tradition and organization that anything decent can be got out of him."[3] Hulme calls for a revival of "accurate, precise and definite description," "without the infinite being in some way or other dragged in," and insists that "beauty may be a small, dry thing."[4] A year earlier, in 1910, Ezra Pound wove a manifesto of classicism into his enthusiastic survey of medieval literature, *The Spirit of Romance*, based on lectures he delivered in 1909. It was later reprinted with his 1912 lecture, "Psychology and the Troubadours." Taking as his authorities the scholarly works of Gaston Paris, Joseph Bédier, and Walter Ker, Pound teases out a definition of medieval classicism that would define (his) modernism and direct the methodology of *The Cantos*: a Hellenic austerity of style; the depersonalization of the implied author or poet; a de-emphasis of originality; the idea of literary composition as the compiling and arranging of fragmented sources; the proximity of literary composition to (philological) literary criticism; the use of Latin texts as necessary intermediaries to understanding Greek texts; and the practice of the medieval *translatio* (*studii et imperii*), which means both to translate a classical text and to "transfer" (adapt, update) its material to reflect contemporary (scientific and religious) "truths."

1 Walter Ker, *Epic and Romance* (New York: Macmillan, 1897), 394.

2 T. E. Hulme, "Romanticism and Classicism," in *The Collected Writings of T. E. Hulme*, ed. Karen Csengeri (Oxford: Clarendon Press, 1984), 59–73, 59.

3 Hulme, "Romanticism and Classicism," 61.

4 Hulme, "Romanticism and Classicism," 67–8.

Part anthology and part textbook, *The Spirit of Romance* includes summaries of the "best" medieval works and Pound's working translations of Provençal and early Italian poetry. Pound's topic is devoted to literature produced in the Middle Ages derived from Latin texts. He suggests that classicism was at its finest in the Middle Ages, beginning with the *Pervigilium Veneris* or Provençal *Alba* (*c.* fourth century) and ending with Dante. Two later chapters pay homage to François Villon and Lope de Vega as the most "medieval" of the early Renaissance poets. Pound argues that the renaissance of the fifteenth century marked a decline from the golden Middle Ages, during which a pagan worship of nature and love was practiced alongside Christianity. Humanism is Romanticism disguised: a cult of the self which loses hold of living nature, the "universe of fluid force," the "universe of wood alive, of stone alive," when "man is concerned with man and forgets the whole and the flowing."[5]

Pound's understanding of medieval classicism was as much inspired by late-nineteenth-century philology as it was by the medieval texts themselves. Pound resented philologists for most of his life, and even went so far as to place them in hell with usurers and sodomites in *The Cantos*: "pets-de-loup, sitting on piles of stone books, / obscuring the texts with philology" (14/63). A *pet-de-loup* ("wolf-fart") is the name for a dusty mushroom as well as French slang for an old, doddering professor. However, Pound's university training was as a philologist. Pound studied Dante's Italian, Old English, Old French, Old Spanish, and Provençal as an undergraduate at Hamilton College in Clinton, New York, with William Pierce Shephard, an editor of Provençal poets. He received a master's degree in Romance languages at the University of Pennsylvania with Hugo Rennert, the renowned scholar and editor of medieval Spanish romances and the works of Lope de Vega. Pound registered to write a PhD on the role of the jester in Lope de Vega's plays, but never pursued the project. As James Longenbach puts it, "Pound's work often demands the source-hunting philological scholarship in which he himself was trained at the University of Pennsylvania."[6]

Throughout his life, Pound resented not the scientific technique of the philologist, but his inability to separate good work from bad. His first published essay in 1906 damns "the Germanic ideal of scholar" engaged "in endless pondering over some utterly unanswerable question of textual criticism."[7] "This

5 *SR*, 92, 93.

6 James Longenbach, *Stone Cottage: Pound, Yeats, and Modernism* (Oxford: Oxford University Press, 1991), 153.

7 Ezra Pound, "Raphaelite Latin," in *Ezra Pound: Poetry and Prose*, vol. 1, ed. Lea Baechler, A. Walton Litz, and James Longenbach (New York and London: Garland, 1991), 5.

book is not a philological work," *The Spirit of Romance* begins. "Only by courtesy can it be said to be a study in comparative literature."[8] "The history of an art is the history of masterwork, not of failures, or of mediocrity," he continues haughtily.

> I have floundered somewhat ineffectually through the slough of philology, but I look forward to the time when it will be possible for the lover of poetry to study poetry—even the poetry of recondite times and places—without burdening himself with the rage of morphology, epigraphy, *privatleben* and the kindred delights of the archaeological or "scholarly" mind.

Pound partly wants to deflect potential criticism from philologists. He knew that his book contained none of the rigors of a philological work or even a comprehensive comparative study. But Pound also admired and emulated the work of good philologists, and hoped to be accepted among them. In a 1927 letter to Richard Aldington, Pound complains that he is less interested in Routledge reprinting his "Spurt of Romance" than he is in finally getting his philological edition of Guido Cavalcanti published. He goes on: "I suggest a new vol. called Mediaeval studies, or more modestly Mediaeval notes. Studies, better I guess. [...] I have UNDERSTOOD a lot of mediaeval stuff that the profs. haven't. Any squirt of a privatdozent can go over it and put in the commas."[9]

Gaston Paris, Joseph Bédier, and Walter Ker characterize their philological method as a rejection of Romantic and Victorian medievalism. From Gaston Paris, Pound discovers the scientific method of literary analysis; the idea of the medieval text as a composite made up of disparate sources and lays; the depersonalized hero/protagonist/author who "vibrates" his subject matter; and the connection between the "cult of Amor" of the troubadours and pagan rituals. From Joseph Bédier, Pound is inspired by the idea of the medieval author as a creative scholar who translates, arranges, and refines the tradition; the importance of discovering original masterworks; and the idea that the philologist himself can channel the voice of the source texts. From Walter Ker, Pound borrows a comparativist framework through which he could identify and assess the medieval masterwork; and was inspired by the idea that the medieval *translatio* can reveal something more ancient or primitive than the classical source text itself.

Much has been written about Pound's early translations of Latin, Anglo-Saxon, and troubadour poets; his correspondence with Latin, Greek, Provençal, Anglo-Saxon, and Chinese scholars; and his three failed "philological" editions

[8] *SR*, 5.

[9] Ezra Pound, August 26, 1927 Letter to Richard Aldington. *EPC*, Box 5, Folder 4.

of Arnaut (1917–18), Cavalcanti (1929), and Confucius (1954).[10] However, little to no scholarship has been written about Pound's theory of classicism in *The Spirit of Romance*, on Pound's debt to these three philologists, or on how medieval classicism and philology inspired the methodology of *The Cantos.*

Gaston Paris

Gaston Paris was well known as a scholar and philologist to many in Pound's circle. Paris was nominated for the Nobel Prize for Literature in 1901, 1902, and 1903. The committee considered his scholarship a unique creative contribution to the world republic of letters. Pound admired his scientific technique as well as his status as a popular academic and anthologist. In 1933, Pound advises the young poet, T. C. Wilson, "anybody who can penetrate the text-book ring wd. confer a blessing. Small manifest on that subject somewhere. Gaston Paris wrote text-books, and France had some sort of culture and amenity. Also *the* most paying line, after religion."[11] *The ABC of Reading* begins:

> The author hopes to follow in the tradition of Gaston Paris and S. Reinach, that is, to produce a text-book that can also be read for "pleasure as well as profit" by those no longer in school; by those who have not been to school; or by those who in their college days suffered those things which most of my own generation suffered.[12]

Pound asked his parents in 1909 while writing *The Spirit of Romance* to mail him his Provençal anthologies by Gaston Paris and Carl Appel.[13] Pound summarizes Paris's lecture on *La Chanson de Roland* in his book and references Paris's definition of *amour courtois* (courtly love), his theory on the lyrical roots of the medieval romance, and his article connecting the May Day rituals with Provençal poetry.

The birth of medieval studies in Germany, France, and England during the late nineteenth and early twentieth centuries inaugurated not only a renaissance of interest in medieval texts but also a major shift in how the medieval text was

[10] See especially Hugh Kenner, *The Pound Era* (Berkeley, CA: University of California Press, 1971); David Anderson, *Pound's Cavalcanti* (Princeton, NJ: Princeton University Press, 1983); Richard Sieburth, "Channelling Guido: Ezra Pound's Cavalcanti Translations," in *Guido Cavalcanti tra i suoi lettori*, ed. Maria Luisa Ardizzone (Firenze: Cadmo, 2003), 249–78; and Fred Robinson, "Pound's Anglo Saxon Studies," in *Ezra Pound*, ed. Harold Bloom (New York: Chelsea House, 1987), 105–26.

[11] *L*, 331.

[12] *ABCR*, 11.

[13] See J. J. Wilhelm, *Ezra Pound in London and Paris, 1908–1925* (University Park, PA: Penn State University Press, 1990), 37.

4 MERLIN.

« solitude ! Comment a-t-il pu lui-même échap-
« per au service qu'il nous devait ? »

Un démon, élevant alors la voix : « Je sais
« l'origine de nos revers : nous avons perdu notre
« cause en croyant la rendre meilleure. Rappe-
« lez-vous les paroles dont nous ont longtemps
« fatigué les prophètes : Le Fils de Dieu, disaient-
« ils, descendra sur la terre ; il apaisera la que-
« relle commencée par Adam ; il sauvera ceux
« qu'il lui plaira de sauver. Hélas ! ils annon-
« çaient ce qui est arrivé. Leur Sauveur est
« venu, qui nous a ravi des âmes à son choix
« et les a reconquises. Nous aurions dû le de-
« viner, le prévenir peut-être. Leur Sauveur a
« fait plus : il efface le péché pris dans le
« flanc maternel, par le moyen de je ne sais
« quelle eau qu'il leur jette au nom du Père,
« du Fils et du Saint-Esprit. Nous perdons ainsi
« tous nos droits, à moins que d'eux-mêmes
« ils ne reviennent à nous. Pour comble de
« malheur, il a laissé sur la terre des ministres
« qui ont pouvoir d'effacer les iniquités succes-
« sives, si l'on vient à se repentir de les avoir
« commises. Ainsi les hommes peuvent tou-
« jours nous échapper. Est-ce là de la justice ?
« Oh ! comme il a dû subtilement ouvrer,
« et quel amour ne lui ont pas inspiré ces
« hommes, pour le décider à prendre chair au
« milieu d'eux, afin de les racheter ! Quand

Figure 1.1 Paulin Paris, from *Les Romans de la Table Ronde* (1868–77), volume 2, Walter Map's "Merlin," 4–5.

regarded. The medievalism of the Victorians, Pound writes in 1911, "was that of the romances of North Places, of magical ships, and the rest of it, of Avalons that were not; a very charming medievalism if you like it—I do more or less—but there is also the medievalism of medieval life as it was."[14] When Gaston Paris succeeded his father, Paulin Paris, as professor of medieval French literature at the Collège de France in 1872, he attacked the kind of "scholarly" editions his father was known for, such as the five-volume *Les Romans de la table ronde* (1868–77), made up of selections and abridgements of medieval texts adapted into modern French, often accompanied with illustrations.

Romance philologists were committed to discovering the unique heroic beauty of a bygone era unjustly condemned as the dark ages by Enlightenment thinkers. Their work continued the medievalism of German Romantics like Friedrich Schlegel, August Wilhelm Schlegel, Ludwig Tieck, and Johann Fichte, who regarded the Middle Ages as a golden age when church and state were unified. Paris criticizes his father for analyzing medieval texts with his heart

[14] Ezra Pound, "I Gather the Limbs of Osiris," *The New Age*, 10.9 (December 28, 1911): 201.

rather than his scientific mind, of pandering to the general public, *érudits,* and women, rather than scholars and academics.[15] Emulating the scientific rigor and the model of textual editing of the great German philologist Karl Lachmann, Paris declares that French medieval literature should be subject to the same rigorous philological scholarship given to classical literature.

Paris was responding to an increasing need to catch up with German philologists, who were publishing critical editions of Provençal poetry and robbing France of its critical heritage. This was all the more pressing after France's humiliating defeat in the Franco-Prussian War in 1871. Although François Raynouard had published *Choix de poésies originales des troubadours* (1816–21), and *Lexique roman, ou Dictionnaire de la langue des troubadours* (1838–44), his legacy was being outshone by German scholars. Friedrich Diez's *Grammar of the Romance Languages* (1836–44), and his *Etymological Dictionary of the Romance Languages* (1853) were standard editions. In 1884, Paris attacks the first critical edition of Chrétien de Troyes by Wendelin Foerster on the sole grounds that he was German.[16] In 1885, Paris published the first volume of his anthology of Provençal poetry, *La Poésie du Moyen Âge*, the same year as Carl Appel published his definitive anthology, *Provenzalische Chrestomathie.* Pound owned both books.

Over twenty journals devoted to medieval studies and philology were launched in France, beginning with the *Revue critique d'histoire et de littérature* (1866), founded by Paris and three other young philologists. Rejecting the eloquence of traditional French literary criticism, the articles were written in a simple, direct, and trenchant style. They were short, dense, rigorously scientific, and highly technical. An 1869 editorial reads: "Above all, we seek to propagate and perfect scientific methods, if possible. The inadequacy of the scientific movement in this country comes not from a lack of zeal but a lack of method."[17] The *Revue critique* was followed by *Revue des langues romanes* (1870); *Romania* (1872) (meant to rival *Germania* [1836]); *La revue de philologie française et provençale* (1887); *Le Moyen Âge* (1888); and *Annales du Midi* (1889). Paris and Paul Meyer founded

[15] See Gaston Paris, "Paulin Paris et la littérature française du moyen âge," in *La Poésie du Moyen Âge* (Paris: Librairie Hachette, 1895), 219. Pound seems to echo the sentiment regarding Victorian poetry in 1911: "As long as the poet says not what he, at the very crux of a clarified conception, means, but is content to say something ornate and approximate, just so long will serious people, intently alive, consider poetry as balderdash—a sort of embroidery for dilettantes and women" (*SP*, 41).

[16] See Isabel DiVanna, *Reconstructing the Middle Ages* (Newcastle upon Tyne: Cambridge Scholars Publishing, 2008), 139.

[17] "Ce que nous cherchons avant tout, c'est à répandre, si nous le pouvons, à perfectionner les méthodes scientifiques. La faiblesse du mouvement scientifique dans notre pays ne provient pas tant du manque de zèle que du manque de méthode." ("À nos lecteurs," *Revue critique d'histoire et de littérature*, 4.1 [January 2, 1869]. My translation.)

the Société des anciens textes français in 1875, dedicated to publishing critical editions of medieval French literature, including the French Tristan texts which Pound lauds in *The Spirit of Romance.*[18] In their program, Paris and Meyer argue that it would be in France's national interest to follow the example of Germany and teach medieval literature in schools and replace the pedagogical model of *explication du texte* with rigorous philology and phonetics. In 1880, medieval French literature was added to the prescribed syllabus for lycées, and France's national epic, *La Chanson de Roland*, became required reading.[19]

Karl Lachmann pioneered the technique of studying multiple manuscripts in order to deduce the closest form of the original. His technique marked the shift from Romantic philology to scientific philology: from a one-to-one contact between the copy and the philologist, to a comparative study of several manuscripts. Lachmann produced the first critical edition of the Greek New Testament (1831–50), restoring it to its most ancient form by relying on the Alexandrine text-type rather than the Textus Receptus. In his 1850 edition of Lucretius's *De Rerum Natura*, Lachmann demonstrates that the three main manuscripts derived from one lost archetype, which itself derives from a manuscript written in a miniscule hand, which itself derives from a fourth- or fifth-century manuscript written in rustic capitals. Lachmann also applied his philological technique to medieval literature, publishing the *Nibelungenlied* (1826), the poetry of Walter von der Vogelweide (1827), Hartmann von Aue's *Iwein* (1827), and the works of Wolfram von Eschenbach (1833). However, Lachmann found his own technique too difficult given the multiplicity of medieval manuscripts and the amount of textual divergence. He often contents himself with a few good manuscripts, providing his readers with an "image" of the original.[20]

When Gaston Paris imported the "German method" to the study of the medieval French texts, he was quick to point out Lachmann's own shortcomings when it came to editing medieval texts. Paris's 1872 edition of *La Vie de Saint Alexis* revolutionized the way French philologists would edit texts. The text is placed out scientifically, with the stanzas numerated, and often a half page or more of footnotes discussing variants from twelfth-, thirteenth-, and fourteenth-century manuscripts.

[18] *SR*, 82.

[19] See Janine Dakyns, *The Middle Ages in French Literature: 1851–1900* (London: Oxford University Press, 1973), 199–209.

[20] See Bernard Cerquiglini, *In Praise of the Variant*, trans. Betsy Wing (Baltimore, MD: Johns Hopkins University Press, 1999), 52.

The edition was noticeable for the absence of the elaborate typefaces and pictures that characterized those of his father.[21] Dating the manuscripts as best as he could, and comparing each one, Paris produced the best "copy" of the original. He normalized the orthography and grammar of Old French, presented an entire theory of declension, and then went on to complain how countless manuscripts showed "errors of declension."[22] Paris also prefaced the text with a 138-page manifesto detailing the breakthrough of his critical and scientific method. Lachmann's name did not appear. For Paris, the new philology has "as its goal to rediscover, as much as possible, the form of the work to which it is applied had when it came from the author's hands."[23] Comparing himself to Eugène Viollet-le-Duc, Paris declares, "I have tried here to do for the French language what an architect would do who wanted to reconstruct on paper Saint-Germain-des-Prés as the eleventh century admired it."[24]

Paris was also known for arguing that the lyric origin of courtly romance was troubadour poetry and for inventing the doctrine of *amour courtois*. The famous doctrine appears as a digression in a seventy-five-page article in 1883 comparing the *Lancelot Proper* to Chrétien's *Lancelot* (1177). Courtly love, according to Paris, is an idolizing love in which the mistress is entirely independent of the lover. The lover undergoes ordeals and tests to prove his ardor and commitment. Sexual satisfaction is often not the goal or the end result, but the love is not merely Platonic.[25] Paris's doctrine was a strategy to make even (medieval) love scientific and rule-based, subsuming it under a masculine omniscience as objective, thoughtful, and active rather than subjective, naïve, and passive.[26]

Pound echoes Paris's scientific doctrine when he describes the "cult of Provence" as a "cult of emotions" defined by "its truth, by its subtlety, and by its refined exactness."[27] He links *amour courtois* to the "depersonalization" of the troubadour poet, which distinguishes him from the Renaissance poet. "Though the servants of Amor went pale and wept and suffered heat and cold, they came on nothing so apparently morbid as the 'dark night.' The electric current

[21] See Michael Camille, "Philological Iconoclasm: Edition and Image in the *Vie de Saint Alexis*," in *Medievalism and the Modernist Temper*, ed. R. Howard Bloch and Stephen G. Nichols (Baltimore: Johns Hopkins University Press, 1996), 371–401.

[22] Gaston Paris and Léopold Pannier, *La Vie de Saint Alexis* (Paris: Franck, 1872), 135. Quoted in Cerquiglini, *In Praise of the Variant*, 64.

[23] Paris and Pannier, *La Vie de Saint Alexis*, 8. Quoted in Cerquiglini, *In Praise of the Variant*, 56.

[24] Paris and Pannier, *La Vie de Saint Alexis*, 135. Quoted in Cerquiglini, *In Praise of the Variant*, 64.

[25] See Gaston Paris, "Études sur les romans de la Table Ronde: Lancelot du Lac, II: Le conte de la charrette," *Romania* 12 (1883): 459–534.

[26] See David Hult, "Gaston Paris and Courtly Love," in *Medievalism and the Modernist Temper*, ed. R. Howard Bloch and Stephen G. Nichols (Baltimore: Johns Hopkins University Press, 1996), 212.

[27] *SR*, 116.

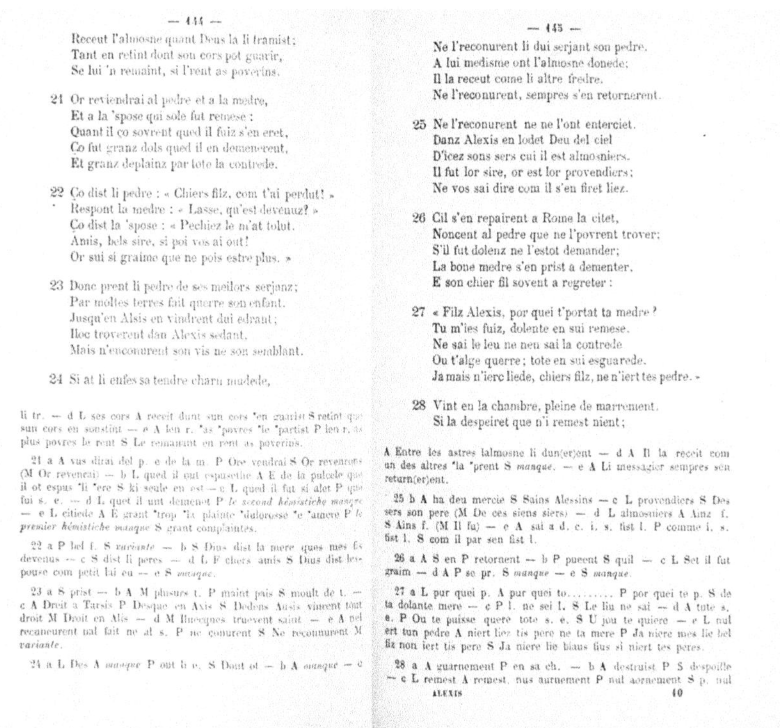

— 144 —

Receut l'almosne quant Deus la li tramist;
Tant en retint dont son cors pot guarir,
Se lui 'n remaint, si l'rent as poverins.

21 Or reviendrai al pedre et a la medre,
Et a la 'spose qui sole fut remese :
Quant il ço sovrent qued il fuiz s'en eret,
Ço fut granz dols qued il en demenerent,
Et granz deplainz par tote la contrede.

22 Ço dist li pedre : « Chiers filz, com t'ai perdut! »
Respont la medre : « Lasse, qu'est devenuz? »
Ço dist la 'spose : « Pechiez le m'at tolut.
Amis, bels sire, si poi vos ai out!
Or sui si graime que ne pois estre plus. »

23 Donc prent li pedre de ses meilors serjanz;
Par moltes terres fait querre son enfant.
Jusqu'en Alsis en vindrent dui edrant;
Iloc troverent dan Alexis sedant,
Mais n'enconurent son vis ne son semblant.

24 Si at li enfes sa tendre charn mudede,

li tr. — d L ses cors A receit dunt sun cors 'en guarist S retint que sun cors en soustint — e A len r. 'as 'povres 'le 'partist P len r. as plus povres le rent S Le remanant en rent as poverins.

21 a A vus dirai del p. e de la m. P Ore vendrai S Or revenrons (M Or revenrai) — b L qued il out espusethe A E de la pulcele que il ot espus 'li 'ere S ki seule en est — c L qued il fut si alet P que fui s. e. — d L quet il unt demenet P *le second hémistiche manque* — e L citiede A E grant 'trop 'la plainte 'dulorose 'e 'amere P *le premier hémistiche manque* S grant complaintes.

22 a P bel f. S *variante* — b S Dius dist la mere ques mes fis devenus — c S dist li peres — d L F chers amis S Dius dist lespouse com petit lai eu — e S *manque*.

23 a S prist — b A M plusurs t. P maint pais S moult de t. — c A Dreit a Tarsis P Desque en Axis S Dedens Aussis vinrent tout droit M Droit en Alis — d M Iluecques truevent saint — e A nel recanurent nal fait ne al s. P ne conurent S Ne reconnurent M *variante*.

24 a L Des A *manque* P out li e. S Dout ot — b A *manque* — c

— 145 —

Ne l'reconurent li dui serjant son pedre.
A lui medisme ont l'almosne donede;
Il la receut come li altre fredre.
Ne l'reconurent, sempres s'en retornerent.

25 Ne l'reconurent ne ne l'ont enterciet.
Danz Alexis en lodet Deu del ciel
D'icez sons sers cui il est almosniers.
Il fut lor sire, or est lor provendiers;
Ne vos sai dire com il s'en firet liez.

26 Cil s'en repairent a Rome la citet,
Noncent al pedre que ne l'povrent trover;
S'il fut dolenz ne l'estot demander;
La bone medre s'en prist a dementer,
E son chier fil sovent a regreter :

27 « Filz Alexis, por quei t'portat ta medre?
Tu m'ies fuiz, dolente en sui remese.
Ne sai le leu ne nen sai la contrede
Ou t'alge querre; tote en sui esguarede.
Ja mais n'ierc liede, chiers filz, ne n'iert tes pedre. »

28 Vint en la chambre, pleine de marrement,
Si la despeiret que n'i remest nient;

A Entre les astres lalmosne li dun(er)ent — d A Il la receit com un des altres 'la 'prent S *manque*. — e A Li messagier sempres sen return(er)ent.

25 b A ha deu mercie S Sains Alessins — c L provendiers S Des sers son pere (M De ces siens siers) — d L almosniers A Ainz f. S Ains f. (M Il fu) — e A sai a d. c. i. s. fist l. P comme i. s. fist l. S com il par sen fist l.

26 a A S en P retornent — b P pueent S quil — c L Set il fut graim — d A P se pr. S *manque* — e S *manque*.

27 a L pur quei p. A pur quei to......... P por quei te p. S de ta dolante mere — c P l. ne sei l. S Le liu ne sai — d A tute s. e. P Ou te puisse quere tote s. e. S U jou te quiere — e L nul ert tun pedre A niert liez tis pere ne ta mere P Ja niere mes lie bel fiz non iert tis pere S Ja niere lie biaus fius si niert tes peres.

28 a A guarnement P en sa ch. — b A destruist P S despoille — c L remest A remest, nus aurnement P nul aornement S p. nul

ALEXIS 10

Figure 1.2 Gaston Paris, *La Vie de Saint Alexis* (1872), 144–5.

gives light where it meets resistance."[28] Given a subject, the medieval poet vibrates "different intensities."[29] The lover is nothing without his lady-love; the troubadour poet is nothing without his subject. "Man is a mechanism," Pound explains. "Chemically he is a few buckets of water tied up in a complicated sort of fig-leaf."[30] This may be an echo of Hulme's distinction between romanticism and classicism: "To the one party man's nature is like a well, to the other like a bucket."[31]

In a famous article published in 1891–92, "Les origines de la poèsie lyrique en France," Paris connects the tradition of troubadour poetry with May Day festivals.[32] In *The Spirit of Romance*, Pound connects the tradition of troubadour

[28] *SR*, 97.
[29] *SR*, 94.
[30] *SR*, 92.
[31] Hulme, "Romanticism and Classicism."
[32] See Gaston Paris, *Mélanges de littérature française du Moyen Âge* (Paris: H. Champion, 1912), 539–615.

poetry with May Day festivals, the "cult of Amor," and the Eleusinian mysteries.[33] Pound explains that the late Latin poem *Pervigilium Veneris*, depicts "a Greek feast, which had been transplanted into Italy, and recently revived by Hadrian; the feast of the Venus Genetrix, which survived as May Day."[34] "If paganism survived anywhere it would have been, unofficially, in the Langue d'Oc."[35] In his "Credo" of 1930, Pound declares, "I believe that a light from Eleusis persisted throughout the middle ages and set beauty in the song of Provence and of Italy."[36]

Joseph Bédier

Gaston Paris's student and successor at the Collège de France, Joseph Bédier, continued his battle to "reclaim" medieval texts for France. Bédier was even more of an antiromantic and Germanophobe than Paris. Like Paris, Bédier systematically discredited the theories of his predecessor. *Les fabliaux* (1893) attacks Paris's idea that the medieval French *fabliaux* originated from Arabic sources. Bédier argues that they are quintessentially French. "France did not need inferior colonies for inspiration."[37] *Les Légendes épiques: Recherches sur la formation des chansons de geste* (1908–13) was a systematic rejection of Paris's idea that *La Chanson de Roland* and other *chansons de geste* are products of a gradual process of collective creation. Bédier stresses instead the importance of a single genius, arguing that the belief in an anonymous "folk" is romantic.[38] He published two different critical editions of *La Chanson de Roland* in 1920 and 1922, as well as a critical commentary in 1927.

Pound links *La Chanson de Roland* to what Gaston Paris called "the national style" in order to highlight the idea of the "depersonalized" medieval author: "the personality of the author is said to be 'suppressed,' although it might be more exact to say that it has been worn away by continuous oral transmission."[39] Pound was probably unfamiliar with *Les Lègends épiques*, but he generally sides

33 Pound was partly inspired by Joesph Péladan's *Le Secret des troubadours* (1906), itself influenced by Paris's scholarship. See Peter Makin, *Provence and Pound* (Berkeley: University of California Press, 1978), 244.

34 *SR*, 18.

35 *SR*, 90.

36 *SP*, 53.

37 Michelle Warren, *Creole Medievalism* (Minneapolis: University of Minnesota Press, 2011), 126.

38 Peter Nykrog, "A Warrior Scholar at the Collège de France: Joseph Bédier," in *Medievalism and the Modernist Temper*, ed. R. Howard Bloch and Stephen G. Nichols (Baltimore: Johns Hopkins University Press, 1996), 288.

39 *SR*, 74.

with Bédier concerning the importance of individual genius over a medieval "folk." In "The Tradition" (1914), he credits Walter Ker for deflating such a myth about Anglo Saxon poetry: "Dr. Ker has put an end to much babble about folk song by showing us *Summer is ycummen in* written beneath the Latin words of a very old canon."[40]

Bédier developed a revolutionary philological technique of his own which contradicted Paris's Lachmannian method. Bédier noticed that 95 percent of Lachmann's stemns begin with a perfect binary: first the original, followed by two copies, followed by three or more copies of those copies. "The flora of philology knows only trees of a single kind," he explains. "A trunk always divides into two dominant branches, and only into two [...] A bifid tree is not all strange, but a clump of bifid trees, a grove, a forest? *Silva potentosa* ['a wondrous forest']."[41] Bédier argues that the Lachmannian technique follows an "unconscious" Freudian desire for symmetry. His new method was less distrustful of scribes. He considered each (early) version of the text its own unique version. As John Graham puts it: "the lapses, parapraxes, and judgments committed by the scribe are more interesting than those of the editor because they are closer in time to the original work. In such a perspective, the original itself becomes a function of the unconscious of its scribes."[42] Bédier's 1913 edition of Jean Renart's *Le Lai de l'Ombre,* presents the three "good" manuscripts of the text (versions A, E, and F) in their entirety, as well as a list of other variants. Each version is considered different but equally coherent forms of the text.

Bédier was best known in his day for his editions of the Tristan legend: his composite *Roman de Tristan* (1900) written for a popular audience; his reconstruction of *Le Roman de Tristan par Thomas* (1902); and his hypothetical reconstruction of the putative *Ur-Tristan* in the second volume of *Le Roman de Tristan par Thomas* (1905). Pound recommends his readers consult all three, as well as Ernest Muret's *Le roman de Tristan, par Béroul et un anonyme* (1903). Bédier's editions of Tristan influenced the work of

40 *LE*, 92.

41 Joseph Bédier, "La tradition manuscrite du *Lai de l'Ombre*," quoted in Sebastiano Timpanaro, *The Genesis of Lachmann's Method*, ed. and trans. Glen Most (Chicago: University of Chicago Press, 2005), 158. Bédier first expressed his objection to Paris's Lachmannian technique in *Le Lai de l'Ombre* (1913).

42 John Graham, "National Identity and the Politics of Publishing the Troubadours," in *Medievalism and the Modernist Temper*, ed. R. Howard Bloch and Stephen G. Nichols (Baltimore: Johns Hopkins University Press, 1996), 82.

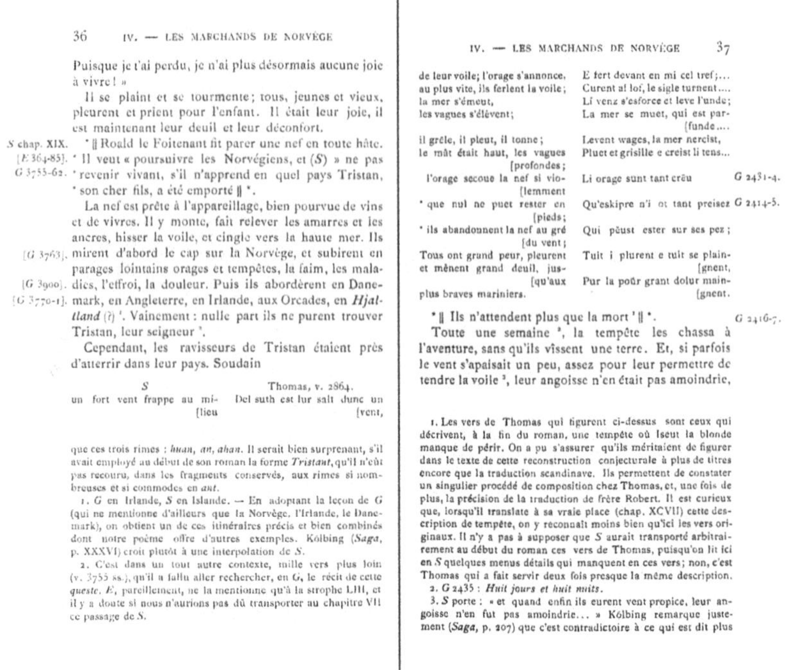

36 IV. — LES MARCHANDS DE NORVÉGE

Puisque je t'ai perdu, je n'ai plus désormais aucune joie à vivre! »

Il se plaint et se tourmente; tous, jeunes et vieux, pleurent et prient pour l'enfant. Il était leur joie, il est maintenant leur deuil et leur déconfort.

S chap. XIX. * ‖ Roald le Foitenant fit parer une nef en toute hâte.
[E 364-85]. * Il veut « poursuivre les Norvégiens, et (S) » ne pas
G 3755-62. * revenir vivant, s'il n'apprend en quel pays Tristan,
* son cher fils, a été emporté ‖ *.

La nef est prête à l'appareillage, bien pourvue de vins et de vivres. Il y monte, fait relever les amarres et les ancres, hisser la voile, et cingle vers la haute mer. Ils
[G 3763]. mirent d'abord le cap sur la Norvége, et subirent en parages lointains orages et tempêtes, la faim, les mala-
[G 3900]. dies, l'effroi, la douleur. Puis ils abordèrent en Dane-
[G 3770-1]. mark, en Angleterre, en Irlande, aux Orcades, en *Hjaltland* (?) [1]. Vainement : nulle part ils ne purent trouver Tristan, leur seigneur [2].

Cependant, les ravisseurs de Tristan étaient près d'atterrir dans leur pays. Soudain

S	Thomas, v. 2864.	
un fort vent frappe au mi- [lieu	Del suth est lur salt dunc un [vent,	
de leur voile; l'orage s'annonce,	E fert devant en mi cel tref;...	
au plus vite, ils ferlent la voile;	Curent al lof, le sigle turnent....	
la mer s'émeut,	Li venz s'esforce et leve l'unde;	
les vagues s'élèvent;	La mer se muet, qui est par- [funde....	
il grêle, il pleut, il tonne;	Levent wages, la mer nercist,	
le mât était haut, les vagues [profondes;	Pluet et grisille e creist li tens...	
l'orage secoue la nef si vio- [lemment	Li orage sunt tant crêu	G 2431-4.
* que nul ne puet rester en [pieds;	Qu'eskipre n'i ot tant preisez	G 2414-5.
* ils abandonnent la nef au gré [du vent;	Qui pëust ester sur ses pez;	
Tous ont grand peur, pleurent et mènent grand deuil, jus- [qu'aux plus braves mariniers.	Tuit i plurent e tuit se plain- [gnent, Pur la poür grant dolur main- [gnent.	

* ‖ Ils n'attendent plus que la mort [1] ‖ *. G 2416-7.

Toute une semaine [2], la tempête les chassa à l'aventure, sans qu'ils vîssent une terre. Et, si parfois le vent s'apaisait un peu, assez pour leur permettre de tendre la voile [3], leur angoisse n'en était pas amoindrie,

que ces trois rimes : *huan, an, ahan*. Il serait bien surprenant, s'il avait employé au début de son roman la forme *Tristant*, qu'il n'eût pas recouru, dans les fragments conservés, aux rimes si nombreuses et si commodes en *ant*.

1. *G* en Irlande, *S* en Islande. — En adoptant la leçon de *G* (qui ne mentionne d'ailleurs que la Norvége, l'Irlande, le Danemark), on obtient un de ces itinéraires précis et bien combinés dont notre poème offre d'autres exemples. Kölbing (*Saga*, p. XXXVI) croit plutôt à une interpolation de *S*.

2. C'est dans un tout autre contexte, mille vers plus loin (v. 3755 ss.), qu'il a fallu aller rechercher, en *G*, le récit de cette *queste*. *E*, pareillement, ne la mentionne qu'à la strophe LIII, et il y a doute si nous n'aurions pas dû transporter au chapitre VII ce passage de *S*.

37

1. Les vers de Thomas qui figurent ci-dessus sont ceux qui décrivent, à la fin du roman, une tempête où Iseut la blonde manque de périr. On a pu s'assurer qu'ils méritaient de figurer dans le texte de cette reconstruction conjecturale à plus de titres encore que la traduction scandinave. Ils permettent de constater un singulier procédé de composition chez Thomas, et, une fois de plus, la précision de la traduction de frère Robert. Il est curieux que, lorsqu'il translate à sa vraie place (chap. XCVII) cette description de tempête, on y reconnaît moins bien qu'ici les vers originaux. Il n'y a pas à supposer que *S* aurait transporté arbitrairement au début du roman ces vers de Thomas, puisqu'on lit ici en *S* quelques menus détails qui manquent en ces vers; non, c'est Thomas qui a fait servir deux fois presque la même description.

2. *G* 2435 : *Huit jours et huit nuits*.

3. *S* porte : « et quand enfin ils eurent vent propice, leur angoisse n'en fut pas amoindrie... » Kölbing remarque justement (*Saga*, p. 207) que c'est contradictoire à ce qui est dit plus

Figure 1.3 Joseph Bédier, *Roman de Tristan* (1900), volume 1, 36–7.

Charles Péguy, Arthur Rimbaud, Guillaume Apollinaire, Jean Cocteau, and James Joyce.[43] Pound describes Bédier's *Roman de Tristan* as a "reconstruction of the tale from compared texts" of the Tristan legend.[44] Hilaire Belloc translated it in 1903, and Florence Simonds retranslated it in 1910. In his prefatory note, which came after Gaston Paris's laudatory preface, Bédier explains, "my text is a very composite one, and were I to attempt to list my sources in detail, I'd have to put at the bottom of this little book's pages as many footnotes as Becq de Fouquières used in his edition of the poetry of André Chénier."[45]

[43] See Alain Corbellari, "Joseph Bédier, Philologist and Writer," in *Medievalism and the Modernist Temper*, ed. R. Howard Bloch and Stephen G. Nichols (Baltimore: Johns Hopkins University Press, 1996), 269–85; and Timothy Martin, *Joyce and Wagner* (Cambridge: Cambridge University Press, 1991), 97–101.

[44] *SR*, 82.

[45] Joseph Bédier, "Prefatory Note," in *The Romance of Tristan and Iseut*, trans. Edward J. Gallagher (Indianapolis: Hackett, 2013), xlviii.

Bédier's sources were mainly Old French manuscripts, especially those of Thomas of Britain and Béroul, which he pointed out are the earlier and more authentic sources of the myth than the German versions by Gottfried von Strassburg and Eilhard von Oberge. Bédier's *Roman de Tristan* dealt a blow to the Wagner mania that swept nineteenth-century French letters. Wagner's medieval sources, Gottfried for the Tristan legend and Wolfram von Eschenbach for the Parsifal legend, were both derivative of French medieval authors. The myth underlying *Tristan und Isolde* (1865) was no more German than that of *Parsifal* (1882).

Gaston Paris argued voluminously that the Tristan romance was an amalgamation of earlier lais derived from Celtic sources.[46] Bédier systematically dismantles his theories, claiming instead that the author was a very French Celtophile. Similar to his argument about the origin of *La Chanson de Roland*, Bédier argues in 1904,

> We must imagine one great workman instead of this anonymous and almost unconscious activity of several generations of jongleurs, acting by fragmentary inventions and unwittingly collaborating; instead of this indefinite development of the poem from generation to generation, we must picture one sovereign hour, one moment when the man, the individual appears, the conscious poet, the Homer who, taking possession of the vague, amorphous formation of earlier times, destined, but for him, to oblivion, laid his law upon them, breathed into them the life of his genius, and alone, the true creator, formed them for the coming ages.[47]

Bédier posits a single Old French romance prior to the earliest surviving French texts, and then sets about reconstructing it.

Pound singles out the French Tristan legend as one that "stands apart from the other romances. The original energy and beauty of its *motif* have survived even the ignoble later versions, and have drawn to them beautiful words and beautiful minor incidents."[48] Pound was fascinated by its composite nature as a patchwork of disparate fragments, translations, and bits of older myth. He plays the role of philologist-guide in his summary, explaining that the tale "has been elaborated by various hands."[49] He describes the second Ysolt as an

[46] See DiVanna, *Reconstructing the Middle Ages*, 152–5.

[47] Joseph Bédier, "The Legend of Tristan and Isolt," in *The Romance of Tristan and Iseut*, trans. Susan Taber (Indianapolis: Hackett, 2013) 123.

[48] *SR*, 82.

[49] *SR*, 83.

interpolation. He speculates about lost manuscripts. "Presumably, in some lost version, their tragic death occurs about this time; but later interest demands that their adventures be prolonged."

> The incandescent fairy dog Pticru creeps into the tale from some Celtic source. The shining house of crystal and rose is discovered by someone; and a great artist designs the death scene[,] remembering Ovid, when he tells of the ship's sails and the fatal confusion of their colors. The Celtic origin of the tale is almost beyond dispute. But one never knows what strange lore came into Ireland during that earlier period of her culture, the fifth century, when Ireland made manuscripts for Europe.

Bédier obviously would not have fully agreed with Pound's summary. Pound gestures to the possibility that this great romance derives from an ancient source.

The thirteen pages of Pound's notes on Bédier's editions of the Tristan myth in the Beinecke Library at Yale University evidence a deep fascination and familiarity with the sources. Pound's notes are replete with line citations from *Le Roman de Tristan par Thomas* of 1902. Bédier's composite edition of Thomas stitches together eight fragments, moving from prose to poetry, filling the margins with citations and usually half the page with footnotes, and splitting the text into two columns for comparison if the variance is significant. At one point, Pound notes, "Text here [mixed?] and obscure / as Bed. admits / as text of one meaning / rehashed to other might well be."[50] Pound suspects the line from the Turin fragment, "Des quant avez este Richolt," which he translates, "Is not Trists story older than 'Richolt'" (i.e., *Richeut* [1159], the earliest known fabliau) "looks like a later graft."[51] He complains of the "endless talk between Isolt and Brangvain [Iseult's servant] / Entire loss of vigor of first part of story / drag drag drag." He notes at one point how Arthur's court is "dragged in." He compares Thomas's style with Chrétien at numerous instances ("vers freer. + better") but also notes cryptically: "Master works of C. du Troyes / to be recognized." Concerning the "Hall of Images" episode, in which Tristan carves a statue of Iseut beneath the vault of a cave, implants a container of aromatics in her heart cavity so that pleasant smells issue from her lips and the nape of her neck, and worships it like a sacred relic, Pound notes, "sensuous inauguration of medieval decadence."

Bédier's virtuosic philological technique of reconstructing the original Tristan myth through a series of fragments was of greater interest to Pound

[50] Ezra Pound, "Tristan of Bedier." *EPP*, 3742.
[51] Joseph Bédier, *Le Roman de Tristan par Thomas* (Paris: Didot, 1902), 346.

than his gallophilic theories. In his preface to the *Le Roman de Tristan*, Gaston Paris calls Bédier a "worthy heir to the poets of old," who has revived the legend "faced with a pile of ruins."[52] He describes Bédier's process of refashioning a head and limbs to this trunk "not by a mechanical juxtapositioning, but by a kind of organic regeneration, like that achieved by animals who, once mutilated, are made whole again using their own internal force following the model of their original form."[53] He characterizes him as a "modern day Béroul" who rescued the tale "even more complete no doubt, more brilliant, and more supple than when Béroul had launched it of old."[54] Bédier later describes his process by citing a work by Jean-Marie Guyau, *l'Art au point de vue sociologique* (1889), which describes an example of "sympathetic pain in experimental hypnosis," in order to explain how the philologist must sympathize with his text. "I believe that the old texts have a soul and that it's useless to waste one's time deciphering them if one does not feel one's soul in sympathy with them," he explains in a 1921 interview.[55] "There should not be any difference between the work of the scholar and that of the novelist."

Bédier's reconstructions are regarded less highly today than they were in his day. Many of his choices were conventional. In *Le Roman de Tristan,* he suppresses the savagery and sexuality of the source texts, enhances courtly manners, reduces ambiguity, unifies the tone, and even incorporates explanatory notes into the text.[56] In his reconstruction of Thomas's text, Bédier justifies his smoothing over of certain things by suggesting that Thomas's text falls short of the original *Ur-Tristan,* which Bédier had in fact posited.[57] However, Bédier showcases the philologist's ability to read between the lines of the medieval manuscript, to decipher the original "authentic" copy, and then to actually reconstruct it. Bédier's editions of *Tristan* represent a *tour de force* of the new scientific philology, recalling Lachmann's virtuosic reading of Lucretius. Bédier also demonstrates how close philology was to literary creation. He channels or "vibrates" with the sources, as Pound would put it, until he is able to "continue" Béroul, restore Thomas, and recreate the original masterwork, *Ur-Tristan.* Bédier argued that the medieval author was not a jongleur, but an academic,

52 Gaston Paris, "Original Preface by Gaston Paris," in *The Romance of Tristan and Iseut*, trans. Edward J. Gallagher (Indianapolis: Hackett, 2013), 115, 116.

53 Paris, "Original Preface," 116–17.

54 Paris, "Original Preface," 117.

55 Joseph Bédier, Interview with Marcel Pays, October 4, 1921. Quoted in Warren, *Creole Medievalism*, 135.

56 For a detailed analysis, see Edward J. Gallagher, "Introduction" to *The Romance of Tristan and Iseut* (Indianapolis: Hackett, 2013), xxi–xl.

57 See Warren, *Creole Medievalism*, 133.

compiler, and translator, who, in one "sovereign hour," arranges the disparate elements of a tradition together—"to have gathered in the air a live tradition," in Pound's words (81/542). Bédier's medieval author is, in some ways, an inspired philologist. His philological technique of considering all the "good" versions of the medieval text as equally valid further blurs the lines between the original source or manuscript and that scribe or academic who could "channel," translate, and arrange the best—and therefore the most "original"—version of the story.

Walter Ker

The most influential book written in reaction to the cottage industry of publishing "new" (French) medieval classics was Walter Ker's *Epic and Romance* (1897), which set the agenda for many generations of English medievalists. Pound recommends his readers consult Ker's work directly. He quibbles with one of Ker's readings of Dante. Generally, however, Pound echoes Ker's opinions and aesthetic assessments. Ker's comment about Gaston Paris may even have inspired Pound's title: "It is impossible (as M. Gaston Paris has shown) to separate the spirit of French Romance from the spirit of Provençal lyric poetry."[58]

Ker champions the medieval epic as original, heroic, realist, and lofty, while the medieval romance is secondary, refined, chivalric, unrealistic, and decadent. "The composite far-fetched romance of the age of chivalry," Ker argues, is merely an outgrowth of the epic.[59] "The history of the early heroic literature of the Teutonic tongues, and of the epics of old France, comes to an end in the victory of various romantic schools, and of various restricted and one-sided forms of narrative."[60] Pound agrees with Ker that the medieval romance is a decadent, "feminine," and less serious outgrowth of the epic:

> The literary artist objects to being bound by actual events, and the folk cry out for marvels. Moreover, there are ladies to be entertained; ladies, bored somewhat by constant and lengthy descriptions of combats, not greatly differing one from another. The songs of more or less historical happenings go out of vogue; the romances—weaker sisters of the songs of deed—gradually usurp the first place in the interest of the general.[61]

58 Ker, *Epic and Romance*, 394.
59 Ker, *Epic and Romance*, 57.
60 Ker, *Epic and Romance*, 39.
61 *SR*, 79.

Chrétien, according to Ker, "generally substituted a more shallow, formal, limited set of characters for the larger and freer portraits of the heroic age, making up for this defect in the personages by extravagance in other respects—in the incidents, the phrasing, the sentimental pathos, the rhetorical conceits."[62] Ker considers chivalry and courtly behavior a very French, cosmopolitan, and effeminate form of dandyism: "Odysseus would never have complained about having to ride in a cart."[63] Pound concedes that Chrétien is the "recognized master" of the medieval romance in order to make the point that his stories "move more swiftly" than those of Malory and so undermine the Pre-Raphaelite Bible.[64] However, Pound concedes, "as art, they are certainly no advance on Apuleius's *Cupid and Psyche.*"[65]

Ker argues that the best medieval romances are the oldest and simplest ones: the lays of Marie de France, the anonymous *Guingamor*, and the prose of Thomas. "The poetical genius of Thomas is shown in his abstinence of effort. Hardly anything could be simpler. He does very little to fill out or to elaborate the story; he does nothing to vitiate his style; there is little ornament or emphasis."[66] Pound explains that the poetry of Marie "is perhaps the most readable"; he offers a full summary of *Guingamor*; and he praises the austerity of Thomas's style in a similar manner.[67] Ker describes the medieval *chantfable* ("sung story"), *Aucassin et Nicolette*, as "one of the few perfectly beautiful stories in the world," and the "quintessence of the romantic imagination."[68] Pound describes it as "the most exquisite Picard comedy [...] which owes its immortal youth purely to the grace of its telling."[69]

Ker favors Old English and Old Norse epics over Old French ones. He compares the style of *La Chanson de Roland* to *Beowulf*, the fragmentary *Battle of Maldon*, the *Short Lay of Sigurd*, and the Icelandic sagas, concluding that French epics are not as "sincere" as Icelandic and Teutonic ones, which are closer to Homer's style.[70] "There are no such masterpieces in the French epic as in the Icelandic prose."[71] Pound offers a summary of *La Chanson de Roland*, singling out the passage of Roland's death: "He is the perfect hero of pre-realist

[62] Ker, *Epic and Romance*, 354.
[63] Ker, *Epic and Romance*, 8.
[64] *SR*, 79, 82.
[65] *SR*, 82.
[66] Ker, *Epic and Romance*, 393.
[67] *SR*, 79.
[68] Ker, *Epic and Romance*, 374.
[69] *SR*, 83–4.
[70] Ker, *Epic and Romance*, 24.
[71] Ker, *Epic and Romance*, 330.

literature."[72] Because his study is limited to Romance languages, Pound attempts to illustrate how the Castilian *El Cantar de Mio Cid* is a better text: "In its swiftness of narration, its vigor, the humanness of its characters, for its inability to grow old, the Spanish 'geste' seems to me to surpass its French predecessor."[73]

At times, Ker shifts between a comparison of the genre of romance versus epic to the style and subject matter of romance versus epic. This allows him the claim that there are often more beautiful "romantic" elements in epic poetry.

> Romance in many varieties is to be found inherent in epic and tragedy; for some readers, possibly, the great and magnificent forms of poetry are the most attractive when from time to time they forget their severity, and when the tragic strength is allowed to rest, as in the fairy interludes of the *Odyssey,* or the similes of the clouds, winds, and mountain-waters in the *Iliad.*[74]

"There is more of the pure romantic element in the poems of Brynhild, the story of Njal, in the *Song of Roland,* than in the famous romances of Chrestien of Troyes, or any of his imitators."[75] Pound utilizes a similar technique by quoting a long passage from Sophocles's *Oedipus at Colonus* in order to demonstrate that it contains "all the paraphernalia of the 'Romantic' school, and something besides."[76]

Pound's description of the "Hellenic" austerity of style in the early Middle Ages is indebted to Ker, who repeatedly stresses that the classical epic is simple and precise, free of ornament, written with "allusive brevity" and "simplicity and grandeur."[77] "Speaking generally," Pound explains, "the spells or equations of 'classic' art invoke the beauty of the normal, and spells of 'romantic' art are said to invoke the beauty of the unusual."[78] Pound characterizes the best poetry of the early Middle Ages as having the "charm of neatness" and being "vivid and accurate"[79] "It is in the spirit of this period to be precise."[80] The exactness and precision of the troubadour poets hearken back to Greek models. Arnaut Daniel's canzoni satisfy "the ear trained in Roman and Hellenic music."[81] Dante "displays a certain quality of calm power, allegedly denied all authors save the Greek."[82]

[72] *SR*, 78.
[73] *SR*, 66.
[74] Ker, *Epic and Romance*, 367.
[75] Ker, *Epic and Romance*, 373.
[76] *SR*, 13.
[77] Ker, *Epic and Romance*, 333, 338.
[78] *SR*, 14.
[79] *SR*, 18, 28.
[80] *SR*, 106.
[81] *SR*, 22.
[82] *SR*, 129.

Unsurprisingly, Ker describes the technique of medieval *translatio* as a degradation of the source text. "The Celtic spirit is not in the French *Tristran*, just as Virgil's genius is not in *Roman d'Enéas*," because they are "translated by minds imperfectly responsive."[83] To make his point, Ker offers an analysis of the *Roman de Troie* (*c.* 1155–60), Benoît de Saint-Maure's immensely popular medieval *translatio* of the "first hand" accounts of the Trojan War written by Dares Cretensis and Dictus Phrygius. Ker describes the injection of lavish description and contemporary medieval fashion as "overdone."[84] "Hector is brought home wounded to a room which is described in 300 lines."[85] "There is, for example, a long description of the precious clothes of Briseide (Cressida) at her departure, especially of her mantle, which had been given to Calchas by an Indian poet in Upper India." Pound epitomizes this risible aspect of the medieval *translatio*:

> Whatever we can learn from the medieval redaction of the events of Greek and Roman antiquity can be more easily learned from the beautiful illumination of an early fifteenth century book, which has recently been displayed in the National Gallery. It represents Caesar crossing the Rubicon, he and his hosts being arrayed in the smartest fashions of the late Middle Ages.[86]

However, Ker does contend that a medieval *translatio* can give "new value" to a classical text, even uncover its pagan or "primitive" source. "It may be held that the Welsh stories gave a new value to the classical authorities, and suggested new imaginative readings."[87] "Jason got a new reading by Benoît when it was read in the light of the Celtic romance," he explains.

> The quest of the golden Fleece and the labors of Jason are all reduced from the rhetoric of Ovid, from their classical dignity, to something like what their original shape may have been when the story that now is told in Argyll and Connaught of the *King's Son of Ireland* was told or chanted, ages before Homer, of a king's son of the Greeks and an enchantress beyond sea.

Similarly, Pound hints that the "strange lore" of ancient pagan stories was injected into manuscripts copied by Celtic scribes in the fifth century, and argues that Provençal poetry revives the pagan "cult of Amor" more successfully than Roman poetry. "I suggest that the living conditions of Provence gave the necessary restraint, produced the tension sufficient for the results, a tension

[83] Ker, *Epic and Romance*, 385.
[84] Ker, *Epic and Romance*, 379.
[85] Ker, *Epic and Romance*, 377.
[86] *SR*, 79.
[87] Ker, *Epic and Romance*, 382.

unattainable under, let us say, the living conditions of imperial Rome."[88] For Pound, the Christian Provençal poets were more pagan and "classical" than the pagan Romans. Pound goes so far as to define medieval Christianity as closest to its "ecstatic" roots. It is neither dogmatic nor concerned with ethics. Its "general object appears to be to stimulate a sort of confidence in the life-force."[89]

Ker's general formula runs as follows: Medieval French romances (Chrétien and everything later which "comes from the mills of a thousand active literary men"[90]) are derivative of simpler, earlier French romances (Thomas, *Aucassin et Nicolette*, Marie de France); which are derivative of the troubadour lyrics (although Ker only mentions this in passing); and, more importantly, the *chansons de geste*; which are derivative of Old English and Old Norse epics; which are derivative of Homer. Pound's general formula spans a greater time period and limits itself to (medieval) romance languages: Victorian Romanticism (Tennyson, Swinburne) is derivative of the early Renaissance; which is derivative of late medieval writing (Malory, Villon, Lope de Vega); which is derivative of French medieval romance (Chrétien and his imitators); which is derivative of simpler, earlier French romances (Thomas, Béroul, *Aucassin et Nicolette,* Marie de France); which is derivative of Provençal poetry. At this point, Pound's formula becomes less linear. The Provençal poets are derivative, but in some ways more "Hellenic" than Latin writers of antiquity (Virgil, Ovid, Apuleius); who are derivative of the Greeks (Sappho, Homer, Sophocles).

Pound's Troy in *Three Cantos*

"When it does come we may not even recognize it as classical," Hulme predicts in "Romanticism and Classicism."[91] "Although it will be classical it will be different because it has passed through a romantic period." Hulme's prophesy "that a period of dry, hard, classical verse is coming" may have anticipated the contours of imagism, but not the medieval classicism of Pound, inaugurated by his *translatio* of Homer, "Canto III," published in *Poetry* in 1917, before Pound witnessed Joyce's own *translatio* of Homer (serialized from 1918 to 1920), and helped shape Eliot's own unique *translatio* of the Grail myth, *The Waste Land*, inspired by the philology of Jessie Weston, a student of Gaston Paris.

88 *SR*, 97.
89 *SR*, 95.
90 Ker, *Epic and Romance*, 371.
91 Hulme, "Romanticism and Classicism," 65.

Pound's version of Homer's nekyia episode in book 11 of *the Odyssey* is an instance of Bédier's inspired philology in action. Pound uses an alliterative Anglo-Saxon style not only because he is trying to make English "medieval" again and so situate his own translation of Homer as a medieval *translatio*, but also because Anglo-Saxon poetry (according to Ker) displays the "Hellenic" concision of language that is closer to Homer's style. Pound's *translatio* is an anthropological attempt to reveal the *Ur-Odyssey* in line with Ker's description of Benoît's tales of Jason, "reduced from their classical dignity, to something like what their original shape may have been [...] ages before Homer." As Pound explains to William Rouse in 1935: "The nekuia shouts aloud that it is OLDER than the rest/ all that island, cretan etc/ hinter-time, that is NOT Praxiteles, not Athens of Pericles, but Odysseus."[92] Note Pound's language here: the nekyia episode does not reach back to the age of Homer, but to the age of Odysseus: the age of heroes, a mythical time hundreds of years before Homer lived. In the first of *Three Cantos of a Poem of Some Length* (1917), Pound announces its ambition to resurrect those spirits:

Not *lemures,* not dark and shadowy ghosts,
But the ancient living, wood-white,
Smooth as the inner bark, and firm of aspect
And all agleam with colors—no, not agleam
But colored like the lake and like the olive trees,
Glaukopos, clothes like the poppies, wearing golden greaves,
Light on the air.
Are they Etruscan gods?[93]

Pound's *Ur-nekyia* is an act of philological hubris more ambitious than Bédier's attempt to reconstruct the *Ur-Tristan*. Like the medieval *translatio*, Pound takes liberties with the text, not by expansion, as Benoît or Guido Cavalcanti do, but condensation. 112 lines of Homer's dactylic hexameter become 67 lines of alliterative "dry, hard, classical verse," as Hulme puts it.

Certainly, one can imagine Gaston Paris, Joseph Bédier, and Walter Ker's bafflement in reading *The Cantos,* just as one can imagine Jessie Weston scratching her head after reading *The Waste Land.* Understanding Pound's debt to philology reveals just how creatively he paid it back.

[92] Ezra Pound, August 23, 1935 Letter to W. H. D. Rouse. *EPP*, 1950.
[93] *PT*, 319–20.

2

Odysseus among the Dead: Primitive Homer

> *"If my contention be right that the cult of the collective daimon, the king and the fertility-spirit is primary, Homer's conception of the hero as the gallant individual, the soldier of fortune or the gentleman of property is secondary and late."*[1]

Seven years after *The Spirit of Romance*, Pound's translation of Homer's nekyia in "Canto III" appeared in *Poetry* in 1917. Five years later, this translation inaugurated his long poem in *A Draft of XVI Cantos* (1922). During this period, Pound cultivated an interest in primitivism, comparative anthropology, and the Cambridge Ritualists. Pound's nekyia in Canto 1 is an excavation of the folkloric and primordial rituals in the *Odyssey*. His Odysseus is not a war hero trying to return home and restore order but a fertility daimon and solar hero whose adventures, sufferings, and sexual exploits reflect the seasonal processes of nature.

In 1934, a puzzled W. B. Yeats describes how Pound

> is mid-way in an immense poem in *vers libre* called for the moment *The Cantos,* where the metamorphosis of Dionysus, the descent of Odysseus into Hades, repeat themselves in various disguises, always in association with some third that is not repeated. [...] He hopes to give the impression that all is living, that there are no edges, no convexities, nothing to check the flow; but can such a poem have a mathematical structure? Can impressions that are in part visual, in part metrical, be related like the notes of a symphony; has the author been carried beyond reason by a theoretical conception? His belief in his own conception is so great that since the appearance of the first Canto I have tried to suspend judgment.[2]

[1] Jane Harrison, *Themis* (Cambridge: Cambridge University Press, 1912), 335.

[2] W. B. Yeats, "Introduction" to ed. W. B. Yeats *The Oxford Book of Modern Verse* (Oxford: Oxford University Press, 1936), xxiv–xxv.

Yeats acknowledges Pound's repetitive fugal structure as well as his ideal of primitive vitalism, but otherwise finds only paradoxes. Why must his system have a mathematical structure at all? Why doesn't Pound just allow his poetry to give way to an unchecked flow of "all that is living"? Yeats does not seem to grasp Pound's classicism. The goal is not to "give the impression" of a vitalistic universe but to invoke it through fugal repetition and rhythm. The sun rises and sets in almost every one of Pound's early cantos; the earth is fructified; the hero washes away the hell-ticks. The reader of *The Cantos* must become an amateur philologist and comparative anthropologist in order to recognize patterns and interpret its mathematical or symphonic operations. *The Cantos* is about as impressionistic as *The Divine Comedy.*

While Yeats's aesthetic ideal is a momentary recall of the primordial past, Pound cultivates its return to the present. In what follows, I look at how the primordial gods in Pound's early poetry inaugurate this return. Pound's poetry does not describe but invokes the primordial world in order to reunite poetry and ritual. I then outline Pound's ideal of an anti-humanist primitivist classicism that he presents in "The New Sculpture" (1914). For Pound, the best classical art has no moral or cathartic use; it asserts a primordial unstable "order" of inchoate gods that demand reverence and admiration. I next investigate how Pound's Anglo-Saxon nekyia transforms Odysseus from a warrior and family man to a fertility hero via concision and suppression of Homer's text. Pound undermines the importance of a narrative telos while emphasizing Odysseus's cyclical return. Odysseus's interrogation of the dead becomes a rite of resurrecting the primordial gods. Inspired by Jane Harrison's reading of the nekyia, Pound de-emphasizes and destabilizes Odysseus as independent from his men. Odysseus is a collective daimon whose soul is "congregationalized," as Jane Harrison puts it.[3] He epitomizes Lucien Lévy-Bruhl's "pre-logical consciousness" or what Harrison calls a "holopsychosis": an understanding of the world without a clear distinction between subject and object.

A lot of criticism about Canto 1 emphasizes the Odysseus-Pound parallel: here Pound "questions the ghosts" of his literary past (Homer, Virgil, Dante) in order to clear the ground for his own modernist epic.[4] Little attention has been paid to Pound's attempt to present a Homer "that it is OLDER than the rest." Pound's nekyia is one into the *Odyssey* itself: to excavate pre-Olympian mystery religions and (matriarchal) hero worship. Pound's debt to cultural anthropology and the

3 Harrison, *Themis,* 474.

4 See, for example, Hugh Kenner; *The Pound Era;* and Ronald Bush, *The Genesis of Ezra Pound's Cantos* (Princeton, NJ: Princeton University Press, 1976).

Cambridge Ritualists has been mostly ignored. This is partly because Pound was reluctant to credit any influences that he shared with his contemporaries, especially Eliot, for whom there could be no mythical method without authors like Edward Tylor, Jane Harrison, Lucien Lévy-Bruhl, or Émile Durkheim.

Time Burns Back: Pound's Early Poetry

"We have about us the universe of fluid force, and below us the germinal universe of wood alive, of stone alive," Pound declares in "Psychology and the Troubadours" (1914).[5] This is partly an echo of Yeats, who argues in "Magic" (1901) that the forerunners of modern poets imagined "themselves to be stocks and stones and beasts of the wood, till the images were so vivid that the passers-by became but a part of the imagination of the dreamer."[6] However, Pound's poetic ideal is not to withdraw into the primordial past but to cultivate moments of its return when the ancient gods become unsettlingly present. Pound also avoids words like "dream" and "imagination" because they invoke Romanticism or humanism. Pound emulates historical moments when the "germinal universe" was most present to poetic consciousness: archaic Greece, the High Middle Ages, or fifteenth-century Venice. The primordial gods of Pound's early poetry are pre-Olympian deities: matriarchal figures like Dione or Cybele; chthonic deities like Demeter and Persephone; dying-and-resurrecting gods like Adonis and Dionysus Zagreus; and the many minor gods, nymphs, demigods, heroes, and daimons or guiding spirits that are often left unnamed in ancient texts. "Sub Mare" (1912), for example, invokes the primordial region beneath the "slow green surgings of the underwave, / 'Mid these things older than the names they have."[7]

In "Cino" (1908), Pound imagines the obscure troubadour Cino da Pistoia (1270–1337) renouncing his love poetry for nature poetry. "I have sung women in three cities, / But it is all the same; / And I will sing of the sun."[8] "Cino" dramatizes the moment when the young troubadour discovers his true subject: not the actual women he praises, but the "strange spells of old deity" that are invoked through his song. Cino devotes his future songs to the animate, vital world: "the white birds / In the blue waters of heaven, / The clouds that are spray

5 *SR*, 92.

6 W. B. Yeats, "Magic," in *Essays and Introductions* (New York: Macmillan, 1961), 43. On the similarity of Pound's early thinking with Yeats, see Terrence Diggory, *Yeats and American Poetry* (Princeton, NJ: Princeton University Press, 1983), 31–58.

7 *PT*, 242.

8 *PT*, 24.

to its sea."[9] His realization is marked by pagan invocations to "'Pollo Phoibee," and "Zeus' aegis-day."

"The Flame" (1911) develops the themes of "Cino" into an aesthetic. The poet claims that the traditional subjects of troubadour poetry are not what they seem: "'Tis not a game that plays at mates and mating, / Provençe knew / 'Tis not a game of barter, lands and houses, / Provençe knew."[10]

> 'Tis not "of days and nights" and troubling years,
> Of cheeks grown sunken and glad hair gone gray;
> There *is* the subtler music,
> We are not shut from all the thousand heavens:
> Lo, there are many gods whom we have seen.[11]

Provençal poets knew that their poetry transcended its subject: be it courtly love (the "game that plays at mates and mating"); the exploits of winning and losing castles; the chronicles of sorrow and difficult years; or the threnody to time passing. The poet's quest is to find that "subtler music": the "clear light" of the primordial past burning near the "eternal embers." That past is represented by "all the thousand heavens" and all the "many gods" of long-forgotten religions.

The second half of "The Flame" invokes the "clear light" that rushes forward to the poet from a primordial past, albeit in language dripping with Swinburnian archaisms that Pound would later abandon: "Thou hooded opal, thou eternal pearl, / Oh thou dark secret with a shimmering floor." "Oh thou anxious thou, / Who call'st about my gates for some lost me; / I say my soul flowed back, became translucent." The protean and quasi-Neoplatonic images of the hooded opal and eternal pearl reflect the inchoate quality of this realm. Because an opal is often found encased, "hooded," or "enveloped" in another rock, it also suggests the auric egg of the theosophical tradition: the envelope that contains all the principal parts of a human being which endure through the cycles of regeneration, or "the preserver of every Karmic record" as Helena Blavatsky puts it.[12] This became the butt of a joke in *Ulysses* that is oddly apposite here: "People do not know how dangerous lovesongs can be, the auric egg of Russell warned occultly."[13] Pound

9 *PT*, 25.
10 *PT*, 168.
11 *PT*, 169.
12 Helena Blavatsky, *Collected Writings*, vol. 12, ed. Boris De Zirkoff (Wheaton, IL: The Theosophical Publishing House, 1980), 608.
13 Joyce, *Ulysses*, ed. Walter Gabler (New York: Vintage, 1986), 9.103–104. Earlier, J. J. O'Molloy asks Stephen what he thinks of "that hermetic crowd, the opal hush poets: A. E. the mastermystic? That Blavatsky woman started it" (7.782–3). Opal hush was a drink of claret and lemonade purportedly invented by W. B. Yeats.

might also have been thinking of Rilke's "Archaic Torso of Apollo" (1907), which is "suffused with brilliance from inside, / like a lamp" and which glistens "like a wild beast's fur," forcing the imperative on the viewer: "Du musst dein Leben andern": "you must change your life."[14] However, in "The Flame," the "I" and the "Thou" are blurred and intertwined. Pound's primordial Thou is both anxious and a creator of anxiety. It demands that the poet retrieve his primordial self ("some lost me") in order to respond to it. This primordial self is not a state of mind, but an emptying out of subjectivity: the soul becomes "translucent" (as many opals are), and rushes backwards to greet the (forward rushing) Thou. Pound's concept of the primordial always implies a dissolution of the self, which is why his classicism is essentially anti-humanist.

"In Durance" (1909) begins as a traditional poem of exile but develops into a yearning for a primordial time. "Durance" means forced confinement; the speaker is homesick "after mine own kind."[15] These are the inchoate daimons of the past.

> Aye, I am wistful for my kin of the spirit
> And have none about me save in the shadows
> When come *they*, surging of power, "DAEMON,"
> "Quasi KALOUN." S.T. says, Beauty is most that, a
>   "calling to the soul."
> When then, so call they, the swirlers out of the mist
>   of my soul,
> They that come mewards, bearing old magic.[16]

The poet's "kin of the spirit" are not the exalted company of Dante or Villon but a primordial *they* that swirls out of the mist of his soul. In "On the Principles of Genial Criticism" (1814), Samuel Taylor Coleridge ("S. T.") writes:

> As light to the eye, even such is beauty to the mind, which cannot but have complacently in whatever is perceived as pre-configured to its living faculties. Hence the Greeks called a beautiful object καλόν quasi καλοῦν, i.e., *calling on* the soul, which receives it instantly, and welcomes it as something connatural."[17]

Coleridge goes on to quote Plotinus's *Ennead* 1:6 which asserts that the soul "speaks of the beautiful as if it were familiar with it, recognizes and welcomes

14 Rainer Maria Rilke, *Selected Poetry*, trans. Stephen Mitchell (New York: Vintage, 1989), 60–1.

15 *PT*, 89.

16 *PT*, 90.

17 Samuel Taylor Coleridge, "Essays on the Principles of Genial Criticism," [1814] in *The Collected Works of Samuel Taylor Coleridge: Shorter Works and Fragments*, ed. H. J. Jackson and J. R. de J. Jackson, vol. 2 (London: Princeton University Press, 1995), 378–9.

and, so to speak, adapts itself to it." But Pound resists the Neoplatonic connection, opting instead to invoke the "daimon," from the Greek δαίμων (*daimon*), which means "god," "godlike," "power," or "fate," but refers specifically to a primordial nature spirit, ghost, chthonic hero, or spirit guide. Jane Harrison's *Prolegomena to the Study of Greek Religion* (1903) includes a ninety-page investigation of Greek daimons and Keres (the more malevolent version of a daimons) because, she argues, they are essential to understanding primordial pre-Olympian religions.[18] For Pound, these daimons bear "old magic," and swirl "out of the mist of my soul." Frazer's *The Golden Bough* was considered the authoritative text on primitive magic. Although the word "magic" would soon drop from Pound's vocabulary, in a 1927 letter to his father, Pound explains that the fugal structure of *The Cantos* culminates in the "the magic moment or moment of metamorphosis" that is a temporary illumination of the "divine or permanent world."[19] "Old magic," therefore, marks the sudden return of primordial gods and the vital universe which Pound equates with paradise.

"The Return" (1912) is Pound's most accomplished and unsettling invocation of the primordial "Muse" and, ultimately, a statement of Pound's mythical method—long before Eliot coined the term. Here the nameless "they" return "with fear, as half-awakened" but also threaten destruction.[20] These nameless gods bear only their epithets:

> See, they return; ah, see the tentative
> Movements, and the slow feet,
> The trouble in the pace and the uncertain
> Wavering!
>
> See, they return, one, and by one,
> With fear, as half-awakened;
> As if the snow should hesitate
> And murmur in the wind,
> and half turn back;
> These were the "Wing'd-with-Awe,"
> Inviolable.

[18] Harrison, *Prolegomena to the Study of Greek Religion,* 163–256. For W. B. Yeats, the daimon refers to a summoned spirit of the dead which is antithetical to the self but compliments it. His idea is informed by the Hermetic Order of the Golden Dawn and probably not what Pound refers to here, since Pound's daimon is part of a plurality. See W. B. Yeats, *Per Amica Silentia Lunae* (New York: Macmillan, 1918), 37–40, 84–7.

[19] *L*, 285.

[20] *PT*, 244.

Gods of the wingèd shoe!
With them the silver hounds,
                    sniffing the trace of air!

Haie! Haie!
          These were the swift to harry;
          These the keen-scented;
          These were the souls of blood.

Slow on the leash,
                    pallid the leash-men![21]

When Pound explained to Rouse in 1935 that "A LIVE phrase may get one out of dead epithet," he might have referred Rouse to this poem.[22] Because these gods are "older than the names they have," as the narrator of "Sub Mare" puts it, they exist only as fragmented, vivid epithets. "Wing'd-with-Awe" suggests winged Athena or Nike, as well as ἐπαινὴ (*epaine*), meaning fearful or awesome, usually attributed to Demeter or Persephone. "Inviolable" suggests Artemis Ἁγνη (*Hagne*), meaning "chaste," or "holy" in the sense of an in inviolate and inviolable virgin; or perhaps Mercury *Terminorum* (cognate of τέρμα ["a goal"] and τέρμων ["border"]), meaning "of boundaries unviolated." "Gods of the wingèd shoe" invokes the messenger god Hermes, who traditionally wears the *talaria* or winged sandals (πτηνοπέδῖλος [*ptēnopédilos*] or πτερόεντα πέδιλα [*pteróenta pédila*]). "Silver dogs" might refer to Homer's description of the animate gold and silver dogs at the palace of Alcinous in Phaecia: "On either side of the door there stood gold and silver dogs, which Hephaestus had fashioned with cunning skill to guard the palace of great-hearted Alcinous; immortal were they and ageless all their days" (7.91–94). However, these dogs are "sniffing the trace of air," recalling Artemis's hunting dogs who tear Acteon apart. A later poem, "The Coming of War: Actaeon" (1915), likens the onset of war with the return of old gods, "Hosts of an ancient people, / The silent cortège."[23] Just as war is imminent in Europe, the ancient deities in "The Return" hasten to our doorstep, and will soon be unleashed and tear us to pieces. The epithet "swift to harry" suggests the winged Keres or the Erinyes (Furies), who drive Orestes mad after he kills his mother and nearly drive the seer Melampus to destruction.[24] Aeschylus's Erinyes track

[21] *PT*, 244–45.

[22] Ezra Pound, April 10, 1935 Letter to W. H. D. Rouse. *EPP*, 1947.

[23] *PT*, 285.

[24] *Odyssey* 15.223–42.

Orestes by following the scent of Clytemnestra's blood. "Keen-scented" recalls the chorus of old men in the *Agamemnon* who compare Cassandra to a Fury: "ἔοικεν εὔρις ἡ ξένη κυνὸς δίκην / εἶναι, ματεύει δ' ὧν ἀνευρήσει φόνον" (*eoiken euris hē xenē kynos dikēn / einai, mateuei d' hōn aneurēsei phonon*); "The stranger seems keen-scented as a hound; she is on the trail where she will discover blood."[25] The epithet "pallid" might also have originated from the *Agamemnon*. When the chorus likens Cassandra to an "Ἐρινὺ" (*Erinyn*), their blood turns *krokobaphēs*: "ἐπὶ δὲ καρδίαν ἔδραμε κροκοβαφὴς / σταγών" (*epi de kardian edrame krokobaphēs / stagōn*); "back to my heart runs pallid drops [of blood]."[26] Liddell and Scott define *krokobaphēs*, which literally means "crocus-dyed" or "saffron-dyed," as the "sallow, sickly blood-drop such as might be supposed to run to the heart of dying men."[27] Robes worn by priests of Dionysus were also *krokobaphēs*. Pound's"pallid" leash-men also suggest a daimon thirsty for vengeance or blood, like the "impetuous, impotent dead" that crowd upon Odysseus when he offers them the blood drink, and the subsequent "pallor" that overtakes Odysseus (1/4).

The power of "The Return" is that it does not describe but invokes, wakens, and hastens these inviolable and inchoate gods from the primordial past. Their return unsettles and harries the narrator ("See, they return"), similar to, but more vividly than the "hooded opal" and the "anxious thou" of "The Flame." Pound gives the impression of speed—of these strange unnamed gods hastening toward the reader—while repeatedly insisting that they are slow. They are tentative, uncertain, wavering, troubled in pace, half-awakened, hesitant—and yet they seem menacing and blood-hungry. We are told that these gods were once "the swift to harry" and "the keen-scented," which suggests that they will soon be again. The poem itself gathers their momentum. They will not be slow on the leash for long.

W. B. Yeats thought "The Return" one of Pound's finest poems, but his reading betrays his inability to grasp it. "Even where the style is sustained throughout one gets an impression, especially when he is writing in *vers libre*, that he has not got all the wine into the bowl, that he is a brilliant improvisator translating at sight from an unknown Greek masterpiece."[28] Yeats's Victorian classicist metaphor of the (not) brimming wine bowl is ill-suited to the vitalism of "The Return." Pound's speaker is inextricably involved in the action: summoning,

[25] Aeschylus, *Agamemnon*, trans. Herbert Weir Smyth, in *Aeschylus*, vol. 2 (Cambridge, MA: Harvard University Press, 1926), lines 1093–4.

[26] Aeschylus, *Agamemnon*, lines 1119, 1120–1.

[27] Liddell and Scott, "κροκοβαφής," in *A Greek-English Lexicon*, 8th edition (Oxford: Clarendon Press, 1901), 847.

[28] W. B. Yeats, "Introduction" to the *Oxford Book of Modern Verse*, xxv–xxvi.

hastening, being visited and even threatened by the primordial past. "The Return" asserts Pound's anti-humanist classicism and announces the death of the "cult of humanism." It is also a version of "the mythical method" long before Eliot "discovered" it. Pound's task is to "translate" an ancient text back into its most primordial (if invented) ritual.

Pound's early poetry evolves out of Victorian imagery, description, "romanticism" and personal statements of poetic philosophy to translation, invocation, and the fragmented, hurried, "notational" style of *The Cantos*. However, it is consistent in its main contention that primordial religions represent a vitalism which has been lost with the cult of humanism. Poetry must enact the return of the primordial past. In "Salutation the Second" (1913), Pound commands his songs to "Go! rejuvenate things!"[29] "Dance and make people blush, / Dance the dance of the phallus / and tell anecdotes of Cybele!" Cybele is as primordial as it gets: an ancient Anatolian mother goddess adopted by the Greeks as Gaia and the harvest goddess Demeter. In her earliest manifestation she is a *Potnia Theron*, or "Mistress of Animals," to whom Frazer devotes a chapter in *The Golden Bough*: "The Myth and Ritual of Attis." Cybele was worshiped in subterranean chambers; her lover (or son) Attis was slain by a boar's tusk like Adonis and rejuvenated in the spring.[30] Pound's ideal poet does not just "tell anecdotes" of Cybele, he dances the dance of the phallus and reawakens the spring.

Primitivism and "The New Sculpture"

In "The New Sculpture" (1914) Pound offers something of a manifesto of his anti-humanist primitivism by contrasting Classical Greece, which he allies with Victorian aestheticism, fashion, and popular art, with Archaic Greece, which he allies with futurism and primitivism. Pound suggests that the Attic sculptor Praxiteles made the equivalent of "super-fashion plates" and that Classical Greek sculpture "reminds all rightly constituted young futurists of cake-icing and plaster of Paris."[31]

> Their sculpture has at certain recurring periods been an idea for super-aesthetes and matinee girls. The placid have excused the Greek drama by the Aristotelian fable that it was made for purgation, that you beheld Clytemnestra and then

[29] *PT*, 266.

[30] See James Frazer, *The Golden Bough*, vol. 6 (London: Macmillan, 1914), 263–76.

[31] Ezra Pound, "The New Sculpture," in *Ezra Pound and Visual Arts*, ed. Harriet Zinnes (New York: New Directions, 1980), 179.

> retreated home to do differently. You exhausted your unseemly emotions by the use of vicarious horror and returned to an orderly life.
>
> Of course the Greeks never did return to an orderly life. They were addicted to more disreputable vices than can be mentioned in modern society or even in "Modern Society." With the exception of a few plausible writers they were probably the most unpleasant set of people who ever existed.

Pound's goal is to offend devotees of the Victorian aesthetics of Walter Pater and Johann Winckelmann, who hailed Greek art as the ideal fusion of individual being and Platonic form. Pound echoes Nietzsche in *The Birth of Tragedy*, which argues that Aristotle's reading of tragedy as cathartic therapy is a castrated and philosophical (moralistic) interpretation of primordial Dionysian ritual.[32] While Aristotle's reading might explain the late dramatist Euripides, it fails to grasp the terrifying worldview of Aeschylus. In Pound's words, the Greeks "had tragedy to remind them of chaos and death and the then inexplicable forces of destiny and nothingness and beyond."[33] This paraphrases Nietzsche's Bacchic daimon Silenus to King Midas: "The very best thing is utterly beyond your reach: not to have been born, not to *be*, to be *nothing*."[34]

Pound declares that he cannot explain Jacob Epstein's "Female Figure" (1913) because he is too busy being moved by it:

> Art is to be admired rather than explained. The jargon of these sculptors is beyond me. I do not precisely know why I admire a green granite, female, apparently pregnant monster with one eye going around a square corner.[35]

Pound claims that Epstein's grotesques undermine the cult of humanism which has "taken refuge in the arts."[36] "The introduction of djinn, tribal gods, fetishes, etc. into the arts is therefore a happy presage."

> The artist recognizes his life in terms of the Tahitian savage. His chance for existence is equal to that of the bushman. His dangers are as subtle and sudden.
>
> He must live by craft and violence. His gods are violent gods. A religion of fashion plates has little to say to him, and that little is nauseous. An art of fashion plates does not express him.[37]

Pound refers here to the Tahitian savages of Gauguin, one of the pioneers of primitivist art. The djinns are described in Charles Doughty's *Travels in Arabia*

32 See Nietzsche, *The Birth of Tragedy*, 54–75.
33 Pound, "The New Sculpture," 179.
34 Nietzsche, *The Birth of Tragedy*, 23.
35 Pound, "The New Sculpture," 181.
36 Pound, "The New Sculpture," 180.
37 Pound, "The New Sculpture," 181.

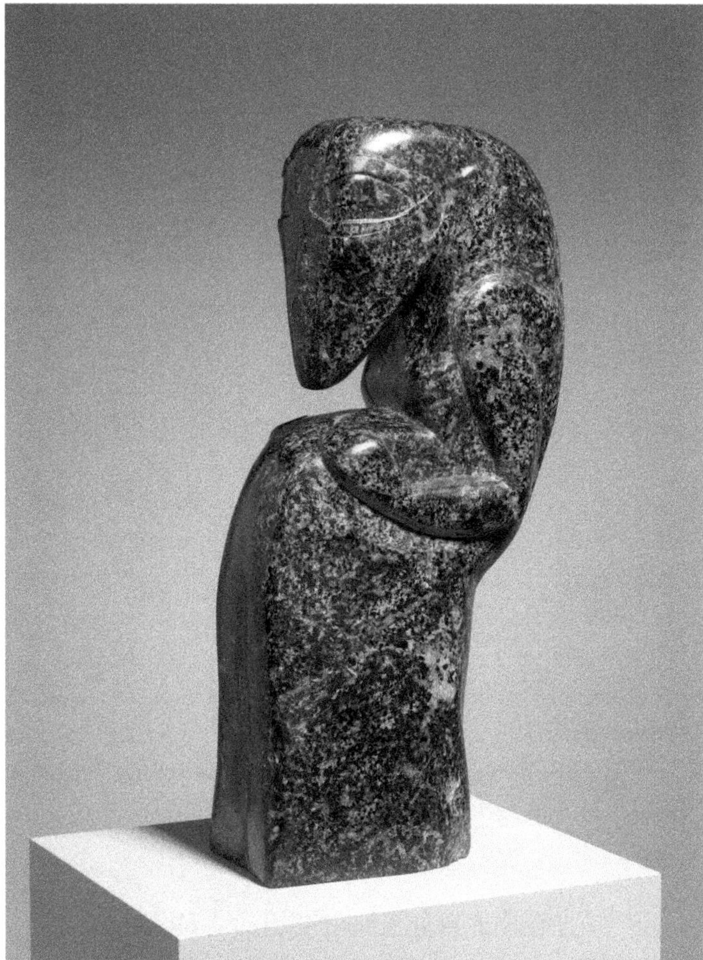

Figure 2.1 Epstein, "Female Figure" (1913), Minneapolis Institute of Art.

Deserta (1888) which Pound read with Yeats during their winters at the stone cottage between 1913 and 1916. "Did we ever get to the end of Doughty: / The Dawn in Britain? / perhaps not" (83/554). Doughty's description of the djinn is an apt comparison with Epstein's female figures:

> some [are] tall, and some be of little stature, their looks are very horrible; certain of them have but one eye in the midst of their faces; other jins' visages be drawn awry in fearful manner, or their face is short and round, and the lips of many jins hang down to their middles.[38]

[38] Charles Doughty, *Travels in Arabia Deserta*, vol. 2 (London: Jonathan Cape, 1921 [1888]), 3.

"The New Sculpture" concludes with a bold declaration of a new aristocracy of the artist:

> We turn back, we artists, to the powers of the air, to the djinns who were our allies aforetime, to the spirits of our ancestors. It is by them that we have ruled and shall rule, and by their connivance that we shall mount again into our hierarchy. The aristocracy of entail and of title has decayed, the aristocracy of commerce is decaying, the aristocracy of the arts is ready again for its service.

Pound's anti-humanist futurism demands that the artist turn back to the most primitive gods and ancestors. Primitivism marks the collapse of humanism and the pragmatic or "use-based" theory of art as moral or cathartic or verisimilar. Art must strive to resurrect the primordial and unstable "order." It must confront us with the inchoate early gods and monsters. Art should have a magical role, and not in the Frazerian pragmatic sense of "making the crops grow." Art must address other worlds. Its language must radiate with mystery and power that even the speaker cannot fully comprehend.

The poet's task is therefore to "translate" the ancient text back to its most primordial version as an invocation of ancient deities, like Pound does in "The Return." Pound would apply this strategy to create the modernist epic: mine the "authoritative" epic of Homer for its oldest material, then shred that down so that it might have the same invocative power as "The Return." The task was to make Homer even more primitive.

Primitive Homer = Medieval Homer

"Early Translations of Homer" is a composite of three short essays written in 1918 and 1919 in which Pound offers a preliminary defense for his Anglo-Saxon translation of Homer's nekyia in "Canto III." Pound lauds Hugh Salel's Middle French translation of Homer by claiming that Homer's style is closest to medieval poetry.

> Homer *is* a little *rustre,* a little, or perhaps a good deal, medieval, he has not the dovetailing of Ovid. He has onomatopoeia, as of poetry sung out; he has authenticity of conversation as would be demanded by an intelligent audience not yet laminated with aesthetics; capable of recognizing reality. He has the repetitions of the *chanson de geste.*[39]

[39] *LE*, 254.

Homer is *rustre:* rustic, uncouth, boorish. He is closer to the orality of Middle Ages (Anglo-Saxon poetry, *La Chanson de Roland,* the Crusade cycle) than to Classical Athens (the "laminated" aesthetics of Praxilites) or to Ancient Rome (Ovid's dovetailing).

Pound also relates Anglo-Saxon consciousness and the oral poetry of Homer with primitive mentality. In *Guide to Kulchur* (1938), Pound suggests that comparative studies of primitive consciousness are the only way to illuminate the Anglo-Saxon mind:

> The study of savages has in our time come to be regarded as almost the sole guide to anglo-saxon psychology. If we reflect on African and oriental vagueness as to time, if we reflect on what is often called "feminine" lack of punctuality among our more irritating acquaintance, it shd. not unduly astonish us that the idea of a MEASURE of value has taken shape slowly in human consciousness. Savages or small boys swapping jack-knives... Mischung von Totemismus... Papua-Sprachen... die Idee eines Wertmessers noch nicht scharf ausgepragt ["mixture of totemism... Papuan speaking... the idea of a measure of value not yet sharply defined"] (Helmut Petri, *Die Geldenform der Sudsee*). The idea of a measure of value not yet sharply defined. (Ausgepragt also monetize or coin.[40])

Rather than cite a more familiar name like Jane Harrison or Gilbert Murray, Pound refers to an untranslated book by Helmut Petri about currencies in the South Pacific that even a learned reader like Eliot had probably never heard of. Pound suggests that the Anglo-Saxon mind had no defined and measured values, including clock- or chronological time (punctuality), as well as the worth of an object to enable "fair" trade. He cites fragments from Petri's book that refer to this "blending" of concepts and indistinct idea of values among the totemic clans of the Papuan speaking people.

"Early Translations of Homer" can be read as Pound's own declaration of his method in Canto 1: to make Homer *rustre* again with an Anglo-Saxon alliterative style. Canto 1 emphasizes many of the qualities he associates with primitive thought: the importance of the collective, rather than the individual, hero; the deliberate elision (*Mischung*) of subjects and objects, agents and patients; invocation rather than description; and a general emphasis on magic, ritual, states of fear, confusion, and disorder.

40 *GK*, 162.

Canto 1: The Ocean Flowing Backward

Pound's *translatio* of the nekyia undermines Homer's epic plot. Pound's Odysseus is a collective everyman rather than an individual hero trying to get home. Pound emphasizes the summoning of the ghosts and ignores the practical advice Odysseus receives.

Canto 1 uses an alliterative style similar to Pound's 1912 translation of "The Seafarer," especially in the use of archaic Anglo-Saxon diction. These include "swartest night" (Old English: *sweart*, "black"); "the ell-square pitkin" (a word invented by Pound to mean "little pit," but suggested by the Dutch prefix *-ken* which denotes a diminutive, such as *katteken*, "kitten," or *menneken*, "a very small person"); "dreory arms" (Old English: *dreor*, "gore"; Pound footnotes it later as "bloody"[41]); "ingle" ("fireplace," from Lowland Scottish: *aingeal*, "light," "fire"); "bever" (Lowland Scottish: *bever*, "drink," hence "beverage"); "fosse" (Middle English, from Latin: *fossa*, "ditch"); and "soothsay" (Old English: *sōth*, "truth"). "Poured ointment, cried to the gods," might confuse a reader until she considers the Latin root of "ointment," *unguentum*, or "salve," or the Old French *oindre*, "to anoint," and realizes that it refers to the libations of mead and sweet wine mentioned earlier.

Like alliterative poetry, the majority of Pound's lines are broken by mid-line breaks or caesurae. (Although the caesura is associated with Latin metrics rather than Anglo-Saxon poetry, the word will serve because Pound was translating Andreas Divus's Latin.) Pound generally follows the traditional formula of alliterative verse in which the first and sometimes second lift in the a-verse alliterates with the first lift of the b-verse. For example: "Bore sheep aboard her, and our bodies also"; "Bore us out onward with bellying canvas"; "Thus with stretched sail, we went over sea till day's end"; "Battle spoil, bearing yet dreory arms"; "Slaughtered the herds, sheep slain of bronze"; "To Pluto the strong, and praised Proserpine"; "But first Elpenor came, our friend Elpenor"; and "For soothsay. / And I stepped back." Half-lines and short sentences create unexpected syntactic and rhythmic breaks, such as "Aforesaid by Circe" and "Pitiful spirit." Inversions like "men many" and other difficult grammatical constructions trip the reader up. "Since toils urged other," for example, has the meaning of, "this other labor pressed us."

Unlike the heavy-handed alliterative style of "The Seafarer," however, with its regular stress pattern, Canto 1 utilizes complex stress and rhythmic patterns.[42]

[41] *ABCR*, 115.
[42] See Chris Jones, *Strange Likeness* (Oxford: Oxford University Press, 2006), 44–7.

Pound's Anglo-Saxon Homer has an incantatory quality. The opening lines string clauses and coordinating conjunctions together in order to create a feeling of breathless parataxis, of a sentence caught in *medias res* trying to find its way:

> And then went down to the ship,
> Set keel to breakers, forth on the godly sea, and
> We set up mast and sail on that swart ship,
> Bore sheep aboard her, and our bodies also
> Heavy with weeping, and winds from sternward
> Bore us out onward with bellying canvas,
> Circe's this craft, the trim-coifed goddess. (1/3)

The actions are concatenated with coordinating conjunctions rather than subordinating ones. Each has equal importance. Elision of articles and pronouns, a feature of Saxon verse, suggests hurriedness. "And then went down to the ship" alters Homer's "'αὐτὰρ ἐπεί ῥ' ἐπὶ νῆα κατήλθομεν" (*autar epei rh' epi nēa katēlthomen*, literally: "but when we went down to the ship") and Divus's "At postquam ad navem descendimus" ("but after we went down to the ship"). The conjunction ἀτάρ marks a strong contrast. It is best translated as "but." "Postquam" is best rendered as "after that," or "as soon as."[43] Pound changes Homer's ἀτάρ into καί (*kai*, "and")—perhaps καί ῥα (*kai rha*, "and so") or καί νύ (*kai ny*, "and now")—as though we were catching the bard in mid-sentence.

The actions of hauling the ship into the breakers, setting the mast, unfurling the sails, loading the sheep, loading the men, and launching out to sea takes priority over any designation of grammatical agents. The men are referred to only three times: "we," "our bodies," and "us," meaning the men and the ship. By contrast, the ship and parts of the ship are named repeatedly: "ship," "ship," "her," "bellying canvas," and "craft." Pound repeats the verb "bore" in parallel structures, shuffling the subjects and objects, grammatical agents and patients: "[we] bore sheep aboard her, and [bore] our bodies also / Heavy with weeping, and winds from sternward / Bore us out." The tense shifts to the present: "Circe's this craft, the trim-coiffed goddess," condensing two lines of Homer: "And for our aid in the wake of our dark-prowed ship a fair wind that filled the sail, a goodly comrade, was sent by fair-tressed Circe" (11.7–8). Pound's version is a simple assertion: Circe owns, or is the true pilot of, this craft. It feels like an afterthought, or the

[43] Hugh Kenner is incorrect when he writes: "That canto's resonant 'And then went down to the ship' follows Divus's 'At postquam ad navem descendimus,' which in turn follows Homer's 'Autar epeí hr' epì nea katelthomen.' *Autar*, and; *epei*, then; *epi nea*, to the ship; *katelthomen*, we went down" (Hugh Kenner, "Pound and Homer," in *Ezra Pound among the Poets*, ed. George Bornstein [Chicago: University of Chicago Press, 1985], 4–5).

men's realization, in indirect free speech, that Circe must be propelling them. The switch to the present tense blurs the line between the narrative and narrated time. (Technically, Odysseus is telling this story to the court of Alcinous in Scheria.) Pound will use the same technique more dramatically in Canto 2 with Acoetes's account of the transformation of the mariners. The narration of a past event transforms into the invocation of a present one.

Pound's concise translation of the journey to Cimmeria invokes a journey backward in time:

> Came we then to the bounds of deepest water,
> To the Kimmerian lands, and peopled cities
> Covered with close-webbed mist, unpierced ever
> With glitter of sun-rays
> Nor with stars stretched, nor looking back from heaven
> Swartest night stretched over wretched men there.
> The ocean flowing backward, came we then to the place
> Aforesaid by Circe.

This is mostly a faithful translation save the interpolation of the river Oceanus as backward-flowing. Homer calls it "βαθυρρόου Ὠκεανοῖο" (*bathyrroou Ōkeanoio*), which means "deep-flowing ocean," and Divus has "profundi Oceani" which means "deep ocean" or "profound ocean" (11.13). A. T. Murray, Samuel Butler, and Samuel Butcher/Andrew Lang all translate it as such. However, Homer does refer to Oceanus as "ἀψόρροος" (*apsórroos*) or "backward-flowing" in *Iliad* 18.399 and *Odyssey* 20.65, when Penelope prays to Artemis "that a storm-wind might catch me up and bear me hence over the murky ways, and cast me forth at the mouth of backward-flowing Oceanus" (20.63–65). However, Homer's ἀψόρροος means "flowing back to itself, circular," not flowing the wrong way. This is why Hephaestus rings Achilles's shield with it: "Εν δ' ἐτίθει ποταμοῖο μέγα σθένος Ὠκεανοῖο / ἄντυγα πὰρ πυμάτην σάκεος πύκα ποιητοῖο"; "Therein he set also the great might of the river Oceanus, / around the uttermost rim of the strongly-wrought shield."[44] Pound's translation is more ambiguous. While Homer's Cimmerian land is on the Pontic Steppe, or the northern shores of the Black Sea, Pound's transplanted "backward flowing" river suggests a journey backward in time; and the "swart night stretched over wretched men there" invokes the "dark continent" of Africa. In *Heart of Darkness,* Marlow likens his journey up the Congo River to a return to a prehistoric time: "Going up

[44] Homer, *Iliad*, trans. A.T. Murray (Cambridge, MA: Harvard University Press, 1924), 18.607–608.

that river was like traveling back to the earliest beginnings of the world, when vegetation rioted on the earth and the big trees were kings. An empty stream, a great silence, an impenetrable forest."[45] Like Odysseus, Marlow reaches "the tenebrous land invaded by these mean and greedy phantoms."[46]

Pound's translation and condensation of Odysseus's sacrifice to the dead obscures narrated and narrative time in order to suggest a rite being performed while spoken. Homer's account is straightforward:

> Here Perimedes and Eurylochus held the victims, while I drew my sharp sword from beside my thigh, and dug a pit of a cubit's length this way and that, and around it poured a libation to all the dead, first with milk and honey, thereafter with sweet wine, and in the third place with water, and I sprinkled thereon white barley meal. And I earnestly entreated the powerless heads of the dead, vowing that when I came to Ithaca I would sacrifice in my halls a barren heifer, the best I had, and pile the altar with goodly gifts, and to Tiresias alone would sacrifice separately a ram, wholly black, the goodliest of my flocks.
>
> (11.23–34)

Pound muddles the past present with the past future and the present narrative with the past narrative time. Odysseus's vow is conflated with the present sacrifice.

> Here did they rites, Perimedes and Eurylochus,
> And drawing sword from my hip
> I dug the ell-square pitkin;
> Poured we libations unto each the dead,
> First mead and then sweet wine, water mixed with white flour.
> Then prayed I many a prayer to the sickly death's-heads;
> As set in Ithaca, sterile bulls of the best
> For sacrifice, heaping the pyre with goods,
> A sheep to Tiresias only, black and a bell-sheep.
> Dark blood flowed in the fosse. (1/3)

"As set in Ithaca" is Pound's shorthand for, "as it was set (instructed, decided on) by Circe, in Ithaca I would sacrifice." However, it also nonsensically suggests, "as it was decided in Ithaca." The lack of agent confuses the nature of the promise. Instead of "promising that I would sacrifice the best sterile bull," Pound has, "sterile bulls of the best / For sacrifice." Moreover, the three actions are not

[45] Joseph Conrad, *Heart of Darkness* (New York: Penguin, 2017), 38.
[46] Conrad, *Heart of Darkness*, 78.

clearly separated: Odysseus promises to sacrifice a barren heifer (even Divus has *sterilem bovem,* but for some reason Pound makes it plural); to heap the pyre with treasure; and to set aside and sacrifice the black sheep for Tiresias. Pound uses "heaping" instead of "to heap" suggesting that this is isn't a promise of a future event but is (somehow) happening in the present. Homer also specifies that "Perimedes and Eurylochus held the victims" while Odysseus digs the pit, and "when with vows and prayers I had made supplication to the tribes of the dead, I took the sheep and cut their throats over the pit, and the dark blood ran forth" (11.34–36). Pound translates only the final line, "Dark blood flowed in the fosse," suggesting that it is the black bell sheep that is being sacrificed. Pound's condensation emphasizes the disorder of the scene, but also makes it seem "present," muddling and negating Ithaca as Odysseus's ultimate goal. (This is the only time the word "Ithaca" appears in *The Cantos.*)

Pound's version might represent Odysseus's own shorthand. Odysseus's description of the sacrifice in book 11 repeats almost verbatim what Circe tells Odysseus to do in 10.521–25. But readers of Canto 1 wouldn't necessarily remember that; and Pound was well aware that repetition is a feature of oral poetry. The *Odyssey* and *The Cantos* are full of it. More plausibly, the condensation reflects the harried emotional state of Odysseus quickly trying to remember the promises Circe told him to make in this frightful place: as it was decided, in Ithaca, sterile bulls, the best, for sacrifice; heap the pyre with goods; a sheep for Tiresias, black, a bell-sheep. Pound's condensation turns narration into an act and struggle to recollect, giving the impression not of something that happened long ago but of something that is happening again as it is being recollected.

The shift from narration and description to invocation is more striking when the dead emerge. Pound withholds the verb and the grammatical patient and marches the ghostly figures toward the reader in a frenzied parataxis:

Dark blood flowed in the fosse,
Souls out of Erebus, cadaverous dead, of brides
Of youths and of the old who had borne much;
Souls stained with recent tears, girls tender,
Men many, mauled with bronze lance heads,
Battle spoil, bearing yet dreory arms,
These many crowded about me; with shouting,
Pallor upon me, cried to my men for more beasts;
Slaughtered the herds, sheep slain of bronze;
Poured ointment, cried to the gods,
To Pluto the strong, and praised Proserpine;

Unsheathed the narrow sword,
I sat to keep off the impetuous impotent dead,
Till I should hear Tiresias. (1/3–4)

The spirits of the dead crowd upon Odysseus so quickly he hasn't time to explain that souls *came* suddenly out of the earth the moment the blood flowed into the fosse. Divus uses the passive verb, "congregataeque sunt" ("they were gathered together"), which is a translation of Homer's "ἀγέροντο" (*ageronto*) in the aorist middle voice, which is reflexive: the dead gathered themselves together: "αἱ δ' ἀγέροντο / ψυχαὶ ὑπὲξ Ἐρέβευς νεκύων κατατεθνηώτων" (*hai d' ageronto psychai hypex Erebeus nekyōn katatethnēōtōn*, "then there gathered from out of Erebus the spirits of those that are dead"). Pound withholds the verb because it is obvious, and because the presence of the dead is more important than their coming and gathering. Once they arrive, however, the action hurtles forward in a string of clauses introduced by active verbs: "cried," "slaughtered," "slain," "poured," "cried," and "unsheathed." Homer's Odysseus urges (ἐκέλευσα, *ekeleusa*) and Divus's Odysseus commands (*iussi*) his men to flay and burn the *already*-killed sheep, and make prayer (ἐπεύχομαι, *epeúchomai, supplicare*) to Pluto and Proserpine. There is no pouring of libations a second time. Pound's Odysseus cries to his men, seems to have them sacrifice another herd of animals, pours more libations, and cries to the gods below. The dead are being invoked, but it is not clear who is doing what. Only once Odysseus distances himself from the dead and arms himself does the syntax settle into a standard word order of subject, verb, object, and subjunctive conjunction: "I sat to keep off the impetuous impotent dead / Till I should hear Tiresias." The "collective" individual who partakes of the rite gives way to the heroic "I" who commands, interrogates, and arranges the action.

Pound's *translatio* of Homer's nekyia deemphasizes and destabilizes Odysseus as a narrator, similar to the way Pound blurs the "I" and the "Thou" in "The Flame." Pound makes objects of collective attention, such as the ship, more important than who is paying attention to them. He emphasizes actions rather than actors. He creates confusion about what happened in the past and what was happening in the present. The men are bearing animals, they are bearing their sufferings, and they are borne by the ship. The rites are sometimes performed by Perimedes, Eurylochus, and Odysseus, but more often by a collective. The dead are shouting, but so are, presumably, Odysseus and his men. Some animals are being sacrificed now, some need to be sacrificed in the future, some have already been sacrificed. In Pound's version it is as though the sacrifice is happening (again) each time it is described. According to Jane Harrison, the origin of epic poetry and drama was not a description of events, but a *dromenon*, a thing done.[47] A rite spoken is a rite performed.

Odysseus Shalt Return

Pound's condensed translation of the conversations Odysseus has in the underworld with Elpenor, his mother, and Tiresias further serves to depersonalize Odysseus, transforming him from the Homeric epic hero to the collective fertility hero. Pound suppresses all information that connects Odysseus to Ithaca or defines his quest as teleological. Homer's Odysseus goes to the underworld in order to learn information about how to return home and appease the wrath of Poseidon. Pound's Odysseus is also looking for Tiresias, but Tiresias is initially surprised to see Odysseus "a second time," offers him no useful information, and ends by prophesying that Odysseus "shalt return." Return where? For Pound, Odysseus's descent into the underworld reflects the cyclical pattern of the fertility or solar hero, who dies and is resurrected yearly, if not daily.

In the initial encounter with Elpenor, Pound suppresses all of Homer's references to Odysseus's personal life, including his individual compassion:

> But first Elpenor came, our friend Elpenor,
> Unburied, cast on the wide earth,
> Limbs that we left in the house of Circe,
> Unwept, unwrapped in sepulchre, since toils urged other.
> Pitiful spirit. And I cried in hurried speech:
> "Elpenor, how art thou come to this dark coast?
> "Cam'st thou afoot, outstripping seamen?" (1/4)

Elpenor is "*our* friend Elpenor"; his are "limbs that *we* left in the house of Circe"; he was left unburied "since [their collective] toils urged other." This is faithful to Homer's text, but Pound cuts the next lines which draw attention to Odysseus: "When I saw him I wept, and my heart had compassion on him; and I spoke and addressed him with winged words" (11.55–56). Pound's Odysseus only cries in "hurried speech."

[47] "Ritual then involves imitation but does not arise out of it. It desires to recreate an emotion, not to reproduce an object. A rite is [...] a sort of stereotyped action, not really practical, but yet not wholly cut loose from practice, a reminiscence or an anticipation of actual practical doing; it is fitly, though not quite correctly, called by the Greeks a *dromenon*, 'a thing done.'" (Jane Harrison, *Ancient Art and Ritual* [London: Williams and Norgate, 1914], 25–6).

Elpenor's response in Homer takes up nineteen lines. Pound condenses it to eight, removing all references to Odysseus's family:

> And he in heavy speech:
> "Ill fate and abundant wine. I slept in Circe's ingle.
> "Going down the long ladder unguarded,
> "I fell against the buttress,
> "Shattered the nape-nerve, the soul sought Avernus.
> "But thou, O King, I bid remember me, unwept, unburied,
> "Heap up mine arms, be tomb by sea-bord, and inscribed:
> "*A man of no fortune, and with a name to come.*
> "And set my oar up, that I swung mid fellows."

All that remains of Odysseus's status is the abstract "O King." The *Hamlet*-like imperative "remember me" is Pound's radical condensation of Elpenor's much more thorough plea:

> Now I beseech thee by those whom we left behind, who are not present with us, by thy wife and thy father who reared thee when a babe, and by Telemachus whom thou didst leave an only son in thy halls; for I know that as thou goest hence from the house of Hades thou wilt touch at the Aeaean isle with thy well-built ship.
>
> (11.66–70)

Pound omits Odysseus's familiar obligations, his goal of returning home, and the caveat that Odysseus men will be passing Aeaea on their way back from Cimmeria *anyway*. Loyalty to a fallen comrade needs no such incentives.

While Pound's careful truncation of Elpenor's speech might pass unnoticed by a reader, his silencing of Anticlea does not, further de-emphasizing Odysseus as the compassionate individual hero and family-man.

> And Anticlea came, whom I beat off, and then Tiresias Theban,
> Holding his golden wand, knew me

Compare this to Homer:

> Then there came up the spirit of my dead mother, Anticleia, the daughter of great-hearted Autolycus, whom I had left alive when I departed for sacred Ilios. At sight of her I wept, and my heart had compassion on her, but even so I would not suffer [εἴων, *eiōn*] her to come near the blood, for all my great sorrow, until I had enquired of Teiresias.
>
> (11.84–89)

Pound does not even bother to remind the reader that Anticlea is the name of Odysseus's mother. In "Canto III," Pound refers to her as just "another ghost," almost encouraging the reader to forget their relationship: "Came then another ghost, whom I beat off, Anticlea."[48] In Canto 1, Odysseus beats her off like a venomous harpy. Homer uses the same verb that he uses earlier to indicate Odysseus's resistance to the thirsty ghosts, εἴων (*eiōn*), the first person indicative active of ἐάω (*eaō*), "suffer" or "permit." Divus uses *permisi* ("allow," "grant," "permit") and *licet* ("allow," "permit"). "Beating off" recalls Dante Pilgrim in the *Inferno*, who learns to abandon his sympathy for the condemned for righteous anger. His harsh treatment of the wrathful Filippo of Argenti earns Virgil's praise.[49] But even Dante Pilgrim's heart is "choked with pity" when he encounters the suicide Pier Delle Vigne.[50] One might expect that Anticlea, who dies of grief for Odysseus, would elicit some compassion, but Pound's curt formulation evinces none.

Leah Flack calls this "a cold and detached compression that omits the pathos of the Homeric scene and that therefore fundamentally transforms Homer's hero into an impersonal high modernist persona."[51] But Pound's Odysseus is hardly impersonal in other moments. He is "heavy with weeping" when he leaves Circe; he turns white when the dead crowd upon him; he cries for more sacrifices than Homer's Odysseus does; and his compassion for Elpenor is moving. So why doesn't he care about his mother? Is Pound suggesting that Anticlea is not really his mother—or at least that this fact is unimportant? Odysseus embodies the abstract King like Frazer's King of the Wood or *Rex Nemorensis*. He is a collective fertility spirit and solar hero like Eliot's nameless quester, not a hero on a mission with a complex relationship to his home and his mother like Oedipus, Perceval, or Hamlet. Pound's *translatio* comically beats off the old Homeric baggage of Odysseus the family man, who is here burdened with guilt for causing the death of his mother.

After Odysseus speaks to Tiresias, Pound mentions Anticlea a second time, only to abruptly end his translation: "And then Anticlea came. / Lie quiet Divus" (1/5). Her name never appears again in *The Cantos*. If she is so unimportant, why mention her a second time, unless to call our attention to her deliberate suppression? Anticlea is unworthy of Pound's modernist *Odyssey* just as Elepenor's vow is. Dante's Ulysses sinfully forsakes the obligations of his family

48 *PT*, 320.
49 *Inferno* 8.43–44.
50 *Inferno* 13.84.
51 Flack, *Modernism and Homer*, 154.

on his quest for ultimate knowledge. Pound's Odysseus, by contrast, does not learn any of the crucial information that would make him obliged to that family. Anticlea's grief is silenced: "It was longing for thee, and for thy counsels, glorious Odysseus, and for thy tender-heartedness, that robbed me of honey-sweet life" (11.202–203). Ninety-eight cantos later, Pound renders these lines in another comic abridgment: "Odysseus's old ma missed his conversation" (99/714).

Pound's original version of the encounter in "Canto III" includes some of the conversation between Odysseus and Anticlea, but Pound evidently felt he was giving away too much:

> Came then Anticlea, to whom I answered:
> "Fate drives me on through these deeps; I sought Tiresias."
> I told her news of Troy, and thrice her shadow
> Faded in my embrace.
> Then had I news of many faded women—
> Tyro, Alcmena, Chloris—
> Heard out their tales by that dark fosse.[52]

Anticlea's question is presumably unworthy of being written, which creates the awkward first line, "Came then Anticlea, to whom I answered." Homer's Odysseus does not tell his mother "news of Troy." The war has been over for three years; most of the heroes have returned; and the bards in Ithaca are already singing the stories. Homer's Anticlea asks Odysseus where he has been and whether he has already been to Ithaca. Odysseus explains that he has been trying to get home for the past three years. Anticlea tells him that the suitors have taken over his palace; Penelope is having trouble holding them off; Telemachus is in danger; Laertes has not long to live; and that she died of grief for him. Pound omits all of this. He includes only Odysseus's failure to embrace her, which is confusing given their dry conversation. Anticlea is then subsumed among many other "faded" women, all of whom share their sad tales by the dark fosse. Like Canto 1, "Canto III" calls attention to the suppression of Anticlea, but at the cost of a redundancy, some confusing syntax, and a hint of Odysseus's emotion towards his mother. "And Anticlea came. Lie Quiet Divus" is much more concise.

Pound also shortens Tiresias's speech so that Tiresias seems to have no real information to share with Odysseus and no significant soothsaying abilities:

> and then Tiresias Theban,
> Holding his golden wand, knew me, and spoke first:

[52] *PT*, 320.

"A second time? why? man of ill star,
"Facing the sunless dead and this joyless region?
"Stand from the fosse, leave me my bloody bever
"For soothsay."
        And I stepped back,
And he strong with the blood, said then: "Odysseus
"Shalt return through spiteful Neptune, over dark seas,
"Lose all companions." (1/4–5)

Pound's strange translation of Tiresias's first words is partly explained by a mistake in Divus, "Cur iterum o infelix liquens lumen Solis / venisti"; "Why do you come again (*iterum*), unhappy man, to the place of no light?" (11.92–93). *Iterum* is Divus's translation of "δίγονος" (*digonos*), meaning "twice-born" or "double." The corrected text is διογενὲς (*diogenes*), meaning "noble" or "sprung from Zeus."[53] But Pound was well aware that Odysseus has never been to the underworld or visited Tiresias before. No translator, including Chapman, Butcher/Lang, Butler, or A. T. Murray, makes this mistake; and every Greek text that Pound might have consulted would read διογενὲς. In "Canto III," Pound translates, "man of ill hour, why come a second time?" He chose to emphasize the error seven years later, changing it to, "A second time? why?" One reason for this might have been to preserve the spirit of medieval *translatio.* The epithet "δίγονος" is also commonly used for Dionysus because he was born from Semele and then from Zeus's thigh. It appears in Canto 48 as "twice-born" (48/241) and in Canto 74, where Pound fuses Dionysus with Christ and refers to him as "the twice crucified" (74/445). The uncorrected text therefore aids Pound in restoring Odysseus back to his original nature as a dying-and-resurrecting god like Dionysus Zagreus, who was the original subject of Greek epic and drama, as Nietzsche and Harrison tirelessly point out.[54] This is an ideal example of how a medieval "error" in translation excavates the primordial origins of the source text.

Pound's Tiresias is redundant. In Homer, Tiresias explains to Odysseus that Poseidon is angry with him for blinding his son Polyphemus, and warns him that he must "curb his spirit [θυμὸν, *thymon*]" if he ever wants to get home (11.105). Tiresias warns Odysseus not to eat Helios's sacred cattle when he reaches Thrinacia. Tiresias then gives Odysseus detailed instructions about the journey he must make to appease Poseidon after he kills the

[53] See Terrell, *A Companion*, 2.

[54] See especially Nietzsche, *The Birth of Tragedy*, 29–34, 51–3; Harrison, *Ancient Art and Ritual*, 13–15, 112–15, 153–9; *Prolegomena to the Study of Greek Religion*, 364–444.

suitors, the subject of the lost *Telegony* (576/7 BCE). Pound's Tiresias says only that "'Odysseus / 'Shalt return through spiteful Neptune, over dark seas, / 'Lose all companions'" (1/4–5). He offers him no advice, directions, or specific details. This is especially surprising given that Pound is careful to include earlier the detail that Odysseus fends off other spirits and beats his mother off "Till I should hear Tiresias." In "Canto III," he even feels the need to explain to his mother, "I sought Tiresias."

Tiresias's words suggest that Odysseus will return *home*, but Pound keeps his translation deliberately vague. Odysseus shalt return, perhaps, like the inchoate gods of "The Return" do. Once Pound puts Divus to rest, he offers his own summary of what happened next: "And he sailed, by Sirens and thence outward and away / And unto Circe" (1/5). Homer's Odysseus doesn't sail by the Sirens until after he returns to Circe and gets a new set of directions. "And unto Circe" makes an incidental stopover sound like a completion of the journey. Canto 1 begins with Odysseus leaving Circe and ends with him returning to her. Tiresias emphasizes the circularity of Odysseus's quest which mirrors Pound's own "epic structure" of descent (death), metamorphosis, and ascent (rebirth). Even the emphasized mistranslation of a "second time, why?" comically suggests that Odysseus was just in Hades yesterday, and Tiresias has nothing new to tell him except that he'll probably "return" tomorrow.

The Golden Bough of Argicida

The final lines of Canto 1 present Pound's anthropological-philological-poetic method of *translatio* in a nutshell. The authoritative text of the *Odyssey* is translated, updated, interpreted, and excavated through a series of later texts: Virgil's *Aeneid*, Divus's *Odyssey*, Georgius Dartona's Latin translation of the Homeric Hymn to Aphrodite, Frazer's *Golden Bough*, and perhaps Eliot's *The Waste Land*. Rather than update the Homeric hero like Joyce's advertising agent Leopold Bloom, Pound excavates him as a fertility daimon and King of the Wood.

> Lie quiet Divus. I mean, that is Andreas Divus,
> In officina Wecheli, 1538, out of Homer.
> And he sailed, by Sirens and thence outward and away
> And unto Circe.
> Venerandam,
> In the Cretan's phrase, with the golden crown, Aphrodite,
> Cypri munimenta sortita est, mirthful, orichalchi, with golden

> Girdles and breast bands, thou with dark eyelids
> Bearing the golden bough of Argicida. (1/5)

Pound leaves one *translatio* only to take up another: Georgius Dartona Cretensis's Medieval Latin translation of the Homeric Hymn to Aphrodite. Those inclined to retrieve Pound's actual edition of Divus (publication details provided) might be gratified to discover that Dartona's translations of the Homeric Hymns are appended. Pound's Anglo-Saxon English transforms into a decadent polysyllabic Greek and Latin vocabulary: "Venerandam," meaning "worthy of veneration," and "orichalchi," Medieval Latin for "coppery," from the Greek *chalkós*. Dartona's verbose Latin translation of the Homeric Hymn marks a deterioration of the stylistic precision of Divus. Pound's own poetic style becomes difficult and cryptic, marking the shift from the "medieval" narrative poetry of Homer to the erudite condensed lyric of *The Cantos.*

Pound juxtaposes two unrelated quotations in these last five lines. Aphrodite is described as "worthy of veneration" (*venerandum*) and one who "holds sway over the Cyprian heights" (*Cypri munimenta sortita est*).[55] Over a hundred lines later, Aphrodite narrates to Anchises how when she was just a girl "ἀνήρπαξε χρυσόρραπις Ἀργειφόντης" (*anērpaxe chrysorrapis Argeiphontēs*) "the one with the golden wand, the Argos-killer [Hermes], abducted me."[56] Dartona translates *Argeiphontes* (Slayer of Argos) as *Argicida,* which means "slayer of the Greeks" but also literally "Slayer of Argos." Apollo gave Hermes the golden caduceus or healing staff; it was later transferred to Asclepius. But Pound probably doesn't expect his readers to know that. His juxtaposition suggests that Aphrodite is the "thou" bearing the golden wand. However, by calling it a golden *bough* Pound suggests that Aeneas bears it. Virgil recounts how Aeneas must retrieve the golden bough that grows in the woods near Avernus and deliver it to Proserpina, the queen of the underworld, in order to speak to his father. According to Frazer, Virgil based this story on an ancient fertility cult, in which a hero must slay the king or priest who guards the sacred tree of Diana Nemorensis (Queen of the Wood) near the shores of Lake Nemi in order to become the new King of the Wood (Rex Nemorensis).[57] This represents a sacred marriage of the hero with the earth. Breaking a branch of her sacred tree was presumably part of this ritual.

[55] "Hymn 5 to Aphrodite," trans. Georgius Dartona, lines 1–3. Quoted in *LE,* 266.

[56] "Hymn 5 to Aphrodite," From Hesiod, Homeric Hymns, Epic Cycle, and Homerica, trans. H. G. Evelyn-White (Harvard: Harvard University Press, 1914), 406–28, line 117.

[57] See Frazer, *The Golden Bough*, vol. 1, 11.

In *The ABC of Reading*, Pound makes a contrast between the "epic" and the "folkloric" aspects of the *Aeneid.*

> Virgil came to life again in 1514 partly or possibly because Gavin Douglas knew the sea better than Virgil had.
>
> The lover of Virgil who wishes to bring a libel action against me would be well advised to begin his attack by separating the part of the Aeneid in which Virgil was directly interested (one might almost say, the folk-lore element) from the parts he wrote chiefly because he was trying to write an epic poem.[58]

For Pound, the *Aeneid* can be separated into what Virgil was "directly interested" in, the folk-lore element, and the requirements of the epic narrative, such as the quest plot or vivid descriptions of Aeneas's sea journey. If Gavin Douglas's Middle Scots *translatio* can improve upon the latter, he improves upon the epic.

Pound's modernist *translatio*, by contrast, does away with the requirements of the epic entirely and emphasizes what authors like Virgil and (presumably) Homer were really interested in: the folklore element. One of the oldest vestiges of folkloric myth in the *Aeneid*, according to Frazer, is the story of the golden bough. Because it reflects material older than Homer's epic, Pound finds no contradiction in grafting Aeneas's visit to the underworld on Odysseus's nekyia. This explains why Pound translates Elpenor's line, "ψυχὴ δ' Ἄϊδόσδε κατῆλθε" (*psychē d' Aidosde katēlthe*, "my spirit went down to the house of Hades"), which in Divus is, "anima autem infernum descendit" ("the soul descended to the lower regions") as "the soul sought Avernus" (11.65). Avernus is the ancient name for the volcanic crater near Cumae, and the entrance to the underworld in Virgil's *Aeneid.*

Pound's truncation of Dartona's Latin translation of the Homeric Hymn to Aphrodite reinterprets and "continues" Odysseus's nekyia. Odysseus (as Aeneas, as the King of the Wood) bears the golden bough. This suggests that Pound's Odysseus sought Tiresias not for his advice on how to return home, but simply in order to partake of a ritual to revive the earth. Homer's Tiresias holds the "χρύσεον σκῆπτρον" (*chryseon skēptron*, "golden staff") (11.91) which Divus translates as the "aureum sceptrum" ("golden scepter"). Pound specifies that "Tiresias Theban, / Holding his golden wand, knew me." Apollodorus describes this as the blue staff made of cornel wood given to Tiresias by Athena after she blinds him.[59] She also gives Tiresias the power to understand the language of

[58] *ABCR*, 45.

[59] Apollodorus, *The Library* 3.6.7.

birds. Later, Zeus grants him the power to prophecy. Homer describes the staff as golden, and Pound can't resist the association. In a passage from book 10 that Pound will quote in Greek in Canto 39 and translate in Canto 47, Circe explains to Odysseus that Persephone granted reason only to Tiresias:

> but you must first complete another journey, and come to the house of Hades and dread Persephone, to seek soothsaying of the spirit of Theban Teiresias, the blind seer, whose mind abides steadfast. To him even in death Persephone has granted reason, that he alone should have understanding; but the others flit about as shadows.
>
> (10.490–95)

Persephone grants Tiresias reason among the dead, just as Athena granted him knowledge of the green language, and Zeus the power of prophecy. Tiresias's golden staff represents his wisdom, his soothsaying abilities, and his powers of intellect. Pound's Odysseus ventures to Hades/Avernus not for advice, but to replace the aged King of the Wood, to take his golden bough, and (perhaps) to deliver it (back) to Persephone/Proserpine, as Aeneas does. Given that many of Pound's readers associate Tiresias with the author of *The Waste Land*,[60] Pound also suggests that *The Cantos* will replace Eliot's flaccid attempt to revitalize the dead tradition. There's a new King of the Wood. Perhaps that is why Tiresias complains of being resurrected "a second time." This one better count.

Jane Harrison and Ritual Theory

Pound's insight that "the nekuia shouts aloud that it is OLDER than the rest" was far from original. Many scholars, including, Jane Harrison, Johann Kirchhoff, Andrew Lang, Albert Dieterich, Walter Leaf, and J. A. K. Thomson, argued that the nekyia reflects a more primitive religion than is found elsewhere in Homer: a cult of the dead and a goddess-based religion of fertility rituals.[61] "I cannot avoid believing that the whole of Book XI, with the exception of a few

[60] Eliot explains in a note that Tiresias is "the most important personage in the poem, uniting all the rest" (*The Waste Land*, note for line 218). "What Tiresias *sees*, in fact, is the substance of the poem."

[61] See Albert Dieterich, *Nekyia* (Leipzig: B. G. Teubner, 1893), 46–50, 75–7, 150–9; Jane Harrison, *Prolegomena to the Study of Greek Religion* (Cambridge: Cambridge University Press, 1908 [1903]), 333–50, 601–11, and below; Andrew Lang, *Homer and the Epic* (London: Longmans, Green, and Company, 1893), 309–15; Walter Leaf, "Appendix L: Homeric Burial Rites," in ed. Walter Leaf, 2nd edition, *The Iliad*, vol. 2 (New York: Macmillan, 1900), 618–22; J. A. K. Thomson, *Studies in the Odyssey* (Oxford: Clarendon Press, 1914), 24–30, 85–97; and Johann Kirchhoff, *Die homerische Odyssee* (Berlin: W. Hertz, 1859), 224–34.

passages [...] is a fragment of the old *nostos* and therefore of the oldest part of the poem," writes Kirchhoff in 1859.[62] As J. A. K. Thomson puts it in 1914:

> Is the Visit to the Dead an original part of the Odysseus-saga? The answer is, yes; there is no part older than that. For Odysseus is one of those divine or supernatural beings, made familiar to us by the *Golden Bough*, who are thought to die and come to life again, or to be obscured for a season only to reappear in renewed splendor. Unable to invent a better term, I have followed Miss Harrison in calling such a being an Einautos-Daimon.[63]

By far the most formidable, outspoken, and influential author on this subject was Jane Harrison. Harrison devotes most of her scholarship to excavating vestiges of pre-Olympian, chthonic, matriarchal goddess- and hero-worship in Homer and other Greek texts. Although Pound never mentions her by name, her influence would have been unavoidable in his extensive research into mystery religions and the worship of Dionysus Zagreus and other dying-and-resurrecting gods. Harrison was the leading and eldest figure among the Cambridge Ritualists, who included Gilbert Murray, Francis Cornford, and A. B. Cook. W. B. Yeats, H.D., James Joyce, T. S. Eliot, D. H. Lawrence, E. M. Forester, and Virginia Woolf all read Harrison avidly.[64]

Harrison's monumental *Prolegomena to the Study of Greek Religion* (1903, revised in 1908 and 1922) investigates the matriarchal and chthonic roots of Homer's Olympian gods, and was the authority on harvest festivals, mystery religions, and the worship of Dionysus and Orpheus. As Gilbert Murray puts it, this study "transformed the whole approach of the study of Greek

[62] Kirchhoff, *Die homerische Odyssee*, 226–7. Translation by Edmund Jephcott in Max Horkheimer and Theodor Adorno, *Dialectic of Enlightenment*, trans. Edmund Jephcott (Stanford: Stanford University Press, 2002), 59n55. By "old nostos" Kirchhoff refers to his theory, long defunct by Pound's day, that Odysseus's *Apologia*, or account of his wanderings, originally comprised only the episode of the Cicones, the Lotus-eaters, the Cyclops, and a shortened version of the descent into Hades. A later bard added the "new nostos": the episode of Aeolus, the Laestrygonians, and Circe. See Joan Bollack, "Odysseus among the Philologists," in *The Art of Reading: From Homer to Paul Celan*, trans. Catherine Porter, Susan Tarrow, and Bruce King (Washington, DC: Center for Hellenic Studies, 2016), 16–45.

[63] Thomson, *Studies in the Odyssey*, vii.

[64] For Yeats, see Martha Carpentier, "Jane Ellen Harrison and the Ritual Theory," *Journal of Ritual Studies* 8.1 (1994): 11–26. For H.D., see Eileen Gregory, *H. D. and Hellenism* (Cambridge: Cambridge University Press, 2009), 109–11. For Woolf, see Martha Carpentier, *Ritual, Myth, and the Modernist Text* (Abingdon: Routledge, 1998), 150–80; and Jean Mills, *Virginia Woolf, Jane Ellen Harrison, and the Spirit of Modernist Classicism* (Columbus, OH: Ohio State University Press, 2014). For Eliot, see Robert Crawford, *The Savage and the City in the Work of T. S. Eliot* (New York: Clarendon Press, 1987). For Joyce, see Daniel M. Shea, *James Joyce and the Mythology of Modernism* (Stuttgart: Ibidem-Verlag, 2006); and Doreen Gillam, "Stephen Kouros," *James Joyce Quarterly* 8 (1971): 221–32. For Lawrence, see William York Tindall, "D. H. Lawrence and the Primitive," *The Sewanee Review* 45.2 (1937): 198–211; and Deborah Spillman, "Miming Made Modern: D. H. Lawrence, Jane Harrison, and the Novel," *The D.H. Lawrence Review* 42.1–2 (2017): 123–45.

religion."[65] James Frazer's chapter on Dionysus in *The Spirit of The Corn* cites Harrison seven times.[66] Harrison's *Themis: A Study of the Social Origins of Greek Religion* (1912, revised in 1927) was even more influential, pioneering the "ritual theory" for which she became famous. Harrison links the "Kouretes," or the leaping, dancing worshippers of (pre-Homeric) Zeus, to the modern-day artist, incorporating Freud's *Totem and Taboo* (1912), William James's studies of mysticism, Émile Durkheim's collectivism, Henri Bergson's duration, and Lucien Lévy-Bruhl's pre-logical mentality. Harrison next wrote *Ancient Art and Ritual* (1913) for the Oxford Home University Library, a series designed to make classical scholarship more accessible to the public. *Ancient Art and Ritual* describes how Greek drama evolved from rhythmic dances and dithyrambs celebrating the springtime rebirth of Dionysus Zagreus: "a leaping, inspired dance."[67] These dances or *dromena* ("things done") are the origin of epic and drama. In the spirit of *The Birth of Tragedy*, Harrison argues that the organization of rituals into dramatic festivals by Greek city states marked the "decay of religious faith."[68] "The new wine that was poured into the old bottles of the *dromena* at the Spring Festival [of Athens] was the heroic saga."[69] The "life story of the life-spirit" gave way to plots about "human individual heroes."[70] Epic and drama were born, and man became isolated from god. "Man has come out from action, he is separate from the dancers, and has become a spectator."[71] As Pound would say, "man is concerned with man and forgets the whole and the flowing."[72]

Harrison rebelled against the rationalism that dominated her contemporaries like James Frazer. She argues that one cannot use intellectual concepts to understand primitive man. For Harrison, primitivism represents a higher form of life because it is experiential and emotional rather than rational. Frazer, by contrast, was steeped in nineteenth-century rationalism. *The Golden Bough* relies on rational concepts to explain primitive consciousness in the spirit of Edward Burnett Tylor's *Primitive Culture* (1871), itself a much more theoretically accomplished work. (D. H. Lawrence admitted he got a lot more from reading

[65] Gilbert Murray, *Jane Ellen Harrison, an Address Delivered at Newnham College* (Cambridge: W. Heffer, 1928), 11.

[66] James Frazer, *The Golden Bough*, vol. 7 (London: Macmillan, 1912), 1–34.

[67] Harrison, *Ancient Art and Ritual*, 77.

[68] Harrison, *Ancient Art and Ritual*, 137.

[69] Harrison, *Ancient Art and Ritual*, 146.

[70] Harrison, *Ancient Art and Ritual*, 145.

[71] Harrison, *Ancient Art and Ritual*, 136.

[72] *SR*, 93.

Tylor than Frazer.[73]) Frazer regards magic as false science and a rational misconception of nature's laws. The savage jumps while planting to make the corn grow; he lights a candle to make the sun rise; he drowns an old king (or a puppet of one) to usher in the spring. For Frazer, the evolution from magic to religion (deity-worship) represents a triumph of abstract thought and human reason. Religious man elevates himself above the savage by virtue of his superior intellect.

> This deepening sense of religion, this more perfect submission to the divine will in all things, affects only those higher intelligences who have breadth of view enough to comprehend the vastness of the universe and the littleness of man. Small minds cannot grasp great ideas; to their narrow comprehension, their purblind vision, nothing seems really great and important but themselves. Small minds hardly rise to religion at all.[74]

Frazer's *oeuvre* vacillates between empathy and a general contempt for primitive peoples. He describes "the muzzy mind of the Sicilian bumpkin who looked with blind devotion" to his goddess.[75] Frazer's primitive is trapped in an egotistical barbarity as he tries to control the world. Harrison's primitive expresses a pre-intellectual vitalism: the lost spiritual force inherent in nature and man.

Martha Carpentier and Jean Mills document how the misogyny of the academy and a series of poorly written biographies deflated the importance of Jane Harrison to the Cambridge Anthropologists.[76] Studies like John Vickery's *The Literary Impact of the Golden Bough* (1973) overemphasize Frazer's importance to literary modernity and all but ignore Jane Harrison. *The Golden Bough* was admired by academics and artists as an anthology of ancient religions, but it was generally looked down upon as a work of comparative anthropology. In his 1913 review of Allen Upward's anthropological study of Christian mythology, *The Divine Mystery*, Pound praises Upward because he

> has been "resident" in Nigeria; he has had much at first hand, and in all his interpretation of documents he has never for an instant forgotten that documents are but the shadow of the fact. He has never forgotten the very real

[73] D. H. Lawrence, *Letters of D. H. Lawrence*, vol. 2, ed. James Boulton (Cambridge: Cambridge University Press, 1981), 259 and 630.

[74] Frazer, *The Golden Bough*, vol. 1, 240.

[75] Frazer, *The Golden Bough*, vol. 7, 59.

[76] See Carpentier, *Ritual, Myth, and the Modernist Text*, 39–67; Carpentier, "Jane Ellen Harrison and the Ritual Theory," 12; and Mills, *Virginia Woolf, Jane Ellen Harrison, and the Spirit of Modernist Classicism*.

> man inside the event or the history. It is this which distinguishes him from all the encyclopaedists who have written endlessly upon corn gods, etc.[77]

Frazer was the quintessential armchair anthropologist, who culled from other studies in order to create an anthology of primitive practices. When he offered commentary, it was often more rationalist than his source texts. Jane Harrison, by contrast, traveled to museums and archaeological excavations across Europe to advance her unique theories. As Martha Carpentier puts it:

> In addition to the usual profuse scholastic, philological and anthropological references, Harrison's work was always filled with concrete pictorial evidence such as vase paintings, tablets, bas-reliefs and layouts of excavated temples and theaters. Her discussion of the origins of Greek drama in Dionysian ritual is supported by a detailed discussion of the excavated Dionysiac Theater at Athens.[78]

Harrison was exactly the kind of "hands-on" scholar that Pound admired in Allen Upward, and, later, the swashbuckling figure of Leo Frobenius.

To Pound's contemporaries, Jane Harrison was a household name. Harrison's writings on the ritual origins of theater had a profound influence on Yeats. In "The Theater" (1900), Yeats declares that "the theater began in ritual, and it cannot come to its greatness again without recalling words to their ancient sovereignty."[79] In "Ireland and the Arts" (1901), he describes poets as "the priesthood of an almost forgotten faith."[80] "In very early days the arts [...] were almost inseparable from religion, going side by side with it into all life."[81] Pound spent three winters with Yeats from 1913 to 1916 at the Stone Cottage at Ashdown Forest nominally acting as Yeats's secretary. They presumably discussed Harrison's ritual theory while Pound adapted Fenollosa's translations of Japanese Noh theater. In his introduction to Pound's *Certain Noble Plays of Japan* (1916), Yeats explains that the Noh drama taught its audience "to elaborate life in a ceremony, the playing of football, the drinking of tea, and all great events of State, becoming a ritual."[82] He imagines that the performer of his Cuchulain "wearing this noble, half-Greek, half-Asiatic face, will appear perhaps like an image seen in reverie by some Orphic worshipper."[83] The narrator of "Among

[77] *SP*, 403–4.
[78] Carpentier, "Jane Ellen Harrison and the Ritual Theory," 16.
[79] W. B. Yeats, "The Theater," in *Essays and Introductions* (New York: Macmillan, 1961), 170.
[80] W. B. Yeats, "Ireland and the Arts," in *Essays and Introductions* (New York: Macmillan, 1961), 203.
[81] Yeats, "Ireland and the Arts," 204.
[82] W. B. Yeats, "Certain Noble Plays of Japan," in *Essays and Introductions* (New York: Macmillan, 1961), 235.
[83] W. B. Yeats, "Certain Noble Plays of Japan," 221.

Schoolchildren" (1928) imagines the ideal of art in terms of a ritual dance: "O body swayed to music, O brightening glance, / How can we know the dancer from the dance?"[84] These lines might have been directly inspired from Harrison's description of the dance in *Ancient Art and Ritual*:

> In the old ritual dance the individual was nothing, the choral band, the group, everything, and in this it did but reflect primitive tribal life. Now in the heroic saga the individual is everything, the mass of the people, the tribe, or the group, are but a shadowy background which throws up the brilliant, clear-cut personality into a more vivid light.[85]

The antimonies that plague Yeats's narrator between youth and old age, innocence and experience, beauty and artistic toil, are resolved in this final image of a regressive eradication of individuality through ritualistic dance.

Hope Mirrlees, a close friend of Harrison and later T. S. Eliot, was directly inspired by *Themis* in her 1919 poem *Paris,* a fragmented depiction of a night peregrination through post-war Paris, in which the narrator doubles as Dionysus descending into Hades in order to rescue Semele and revivify the spring. The narrator begins the poem in search of a "holophrase," a term Harrison defines as an utterance "of a relation in which subject and object have not yet got their heads above water but are submerged in a situation."[86] Although not as accomplished, *Paris* bears remarkable similarities to *The Waste Land* (1922), from its use of radical fragmentation, erudition, quotations in foreign languages (Mirrlees knew eleven, including Ancient Greek, Zulu, and Old Norse), explanatory footnotes, and in being inspired from a work of comparative anthropology about vegetation ceremonies. Mirrlees's nameless hero wanders through the city at night observing the detritus of capitalist culture, hearing the voices of the night wanderers: "I don't like the gurls of the night-club—they love / women."[87] She alludes to Verlaine, and repeatedly returns to the image of the river and the ghosts who cross its bridges:

> The Seine, old egotist, meanders imperturbably towards the sea,
> Ruminating on weeds and rain . . .
>   If through his sluggish watery sleep come dreams
>   They are the blue ghosts of king-fishers.[88]

[84] W. B. Yeats, *The Collected Works of W. B. Yeats*, vol. 1, ed. Richard J. Finneran (New York: Scribner, 1996), 222.

[85] Harrison, *Ancient Art and Ritual*, 159.

[86] Hope Mirrlees, *Paris: A Poem* (London: Hogarth, 1919), 3. Harrison, *Themis,* 373.

[87] Mirrlees, *Paris: A Poem,* 21.

[88] Mirrlees, *Paris: A Poem,* 14.

Mirrlees even mentions "the wicked April moon," and explains in a note: "The April moon, *la lune rousse*, is supposed to have a malign influence on vegetation."[89] Perhaps that is why Eliot's April is the cruelest month. Leonard and Virginia Woolf published *Paris* immediately after publishing Eliot's *Poems* (1919). They would publish *The Waste Land* two years later. Eliot later considered Mirrlees one of his "greatest friends," but, as Mirrlees writes in a letter, never mentioned to her that he had ever read *Paris*.[90] Perhaps he wished he had not.

Eliot was an avid reader of Harrison. "Few books are more fascinating than those of Miss Harrison, Mr. Cornford, or Mr. Cooke [*sic*], when they burrow in the origins of Greek myths and rites," he writes in "Euripides and Professor Murray" (1921), an essay that Pound admired and later quoted.[91] When Eliot defines his "mythical method" in "Ulysses, Order and Myth" (1923), he suggests that modern literature must come to terms with *The Golden Bough*. But he means Frazer's wealth of evidence, not his rationalism or his contempt for the primitive mind. (There is no evidence that Joyce had read *The Golden Bough*, but he did own Harrison's *Mythology and Monuments of Ancient Athens* [1890].[92]) Eliot enthusiastically reviewed Lévy-Bruhl's *Les fonction mentales dans les sociétées inférieures* (1910) in 1916, in which Lévy-Bruhl harshly criticizes Frazer for representing primitive logic as an inferior version of civilized Western logic. As William Harmon points out, almost all of Eliot's fascination with "primitive mentality" owes its contours and emphases to this book.[93]

Harrison's name would have been impossible for Pound to avoid. On three separate occasions between 1912 and 1931, Pound titles articles with "Prolegomena"—which to many of his contemporaries would have suggested either Harrison or Kant.[94] Akiko Miyake makes a compelling case that Harrison's *Themis* influenced the fertility rites of Canto 39, the depiction of the ox sacrifice in Canto 53, as well as Canto 71, in which John Adams is referred to as "THEMIS

[89] Mirrlees, *Paris: A Poem*, 23, note to page 14.

[90] See Michael Swanwick, *Hope-In-The-Mist: The Extraordinary Career and Mysterious Life of Hope Mirrlees* (Upper Montclair, NJ: Henry Wessells, 2009), 49; and Cyrena Pondrom, "Mirrlees, Modernism, and the Holophrase," *Time Present: The Newsletter of the T. S. Eliot Society* 74/75 (2011): 4–6.

[91] See Peter Liebregts, *Translations of Greek Tragedy in the Work of Ezra Pound* (London: Bloomsbury Academic, 2019), 6–7.

[92] Thomas Connolly, *The Personal Library of James Joyce: A Descriptive Bibliography* (Buffalo: University at Buffalo, 1955).

[93] William Harmon, "T. S. Eliot, Anthropologist and Primitive," *American Anthropologist* 78.4 (1976): 803.

[94] Ezra Pound, "Prolegomena," *Poetry Review* 1.2 (February 1912): 72–6; and Ezra Pound, "Prolegomena," *The Exile* 2 (1927): 35. "How to Read," first published in the New York Herald Tribune in 1929, was expanded into a pamphlet and re-titled *Prolegomena 1: How to Read* (Toulon: To Publishers, 1932).

CONDITOR" (71/417).[95] Although Pound never mentions Harrison, he was always reluctant to credit authors who were in vogue with his fellow modernists, just as he was quick to denounce literary movements—even ones he invented—if they became too popular. It was a commonplace by 1920 that "Christ follows Dionysus," as the narrator of *Hugh Selwyn Mauberly* puts it, who also complains of "neo-Nietzschean clatter" of his age.[96] Pound felt the need to brag that he had never read a word of Jessie Weston, the inspiration of *The Waste Land*. Just as he distanced himself from the theosophical texts that Yeats was immersed in, so he distanced himself from the comparative anthropology that Eliot and many other of his contemporaries read avidly. Pound always touted his own discoveries, however minor, probably out of fear of being regarded as derivative of Yeats, Joyce, and Eliot, such as the unremarkable Allen Upward; the mostly untranslated Leo Frobenius; and Ernest Fenollosa, whom Pound edited and published himself.

Harrison's nekyia; The Blamless Ones

Pound's ambition to excavate a primordial Pre-Homeric religion in Canto 1 derives from Harrison's research. In *Themis*, Harrison argues that the Greek hero was originally "the collective daimon, the king and fertility-spirit," and that Homer, as a late writer, had already lost this sense.[97]

> It has again and again been observed that in Homer we have no magic and no cult of the dead. Homer marks a stage when collective thinking and magical ritual are, if not dead, at least dying, when individualist thinking to which it belongs are developed to a point not far behind that of the days of Pericles.

Pound's statement that "the nekuia shouts aloud that it is OLDER than the rest/ all that island, cretan etc/ hinter-time, that is NOT Praxiteles, not Athens of Pericles, but Odysseus," might even be a paraphrase of this. In *Prolegomena to the Study of Greek Religion*, Harrison argues that Homer's nekyia is unique in that it contains vestiges of a pre-Olympian religion of magic rituals, mysteries, and a cult of the dead not fully suppressed "under the force of a hostile epic tradition" inaugurated by Pisistratus.[98] Instead of the cunning strategist and

[95] Akiko Miyake, *Ezra Pound and the Mysteries of Love* (Durham, NC: Duke University Press, 1991), 183–7.
[96] *PT*, 550, 560.
[97] Harrison, *Themis*, 335.
[98] Harrison, *Prolegomena to the Study of Greek Religion*, 335.

experienced war hero who outsmarts his adversaries, Odysseus is presented as a collective daimon and youthful fertility hero who passively follows directions, performs rites, shrinks in terror, cries for help, and weeps as he hears sad tales of wronged men and women: all of the attributes Pound emphasizes.

According to Harrison, Odysseus's blood offering to Tiresias is "a clear reminiscence of the ghost-raising that went on at many a hero's tomb, for [...] every hero was apt to be credited with mantic powers."[99] The ghosts that crowd Odysseus after the sacrifice are Keres, Harrison explains: primordial death spirits who partake of the blood feast just as the Olympian gods partake of sacrifice. "The service of the dead is here very near akin to that of the Olympians; it is no grim atonement, but at worst a bloody banquet, at best a human feast." In other words, Odysseus's sacrifice is in keeping with a regular "service of the dead" of pre-Olympian religion. It is not a specific or unusual task that Odysseus must perform in order to gain specific or unusual information (from Tiresias) or to atone for his wrongs, as Homer presents it.

Harrison describes how the underworld (d)evolved from a place of hero and goddess worship to a place of punishment. In pre-Olympian religions of Greece dominated by female goddesses and hero cults, the underworld is a holy place where goddesses and heroes happily reside. In the Olympian world, the underworld is a prison where goddesses and heroes are punished.

> It was an ingenious theological device, or rather perhaps unconscious instinct, that took these ancient hero figures, really regnant in the world below, and made the place of their rule the symbol of their punishment. According to the old faith all men, good and bad, went below the earth, great local heroes reigned below as they had reigned above; but the new faith sent its saints to a remote Elysium or to the upper air and made this underworld kingdom a place of punishment; and in that place significantly we find that the tortured criminals *are all offenders against Olympian Zeus.*[100]

Harrison similarly describes how night (d)evolved from sacred to evil. "The ritual prescription that heroes should be worshiped by night, their sacrifice consumed before dawn, no doubt helped the conviction that as they loved the night their deeds were evil."[101] Odysseus travels to a land of perpetual darkness because the cult of hero-worship is stronger there. Dante Pilgrim, by contrast, wanders through a "dark night" because his soul is in danger of corruption.

[99] Harrison, *Prolegomena to the Study of Greek Religion*, 75.
[100] Harrison, *Prolegomena to the Study of Greek Religion*, 606.
[101] Harrison, *Prolegomena to the Study of Greek Religion*, 337.

The Cantos undermines Homer's patriarchal and pro-Olympian *translatio.* Canto 17 presents a paradisal cortege of Dionysius Zagreus through Venice at night, "the trees growing in water"; "The light now, not of the sun" (17/76). The procession continues into the chthonic "general paradiso"[102] of Cantos 20 and 21, during the "night of the golden tiger," which Pound associated with the mysteries of Eleusis (21/99). In Canto 39, when Circe is giving Odysseus directions to the Cimmerians, she first jokes, "Been to hell in a boat yet?" but this is immediately qualified: "To Flora's night, with hyacinthus, / With the crocus (spring / sharp in the grass,)" (39/195). The Paradise Cantos (90–95) are full of images of goddesses rising out of Erebus into a dark paradisal landscape under the moon; lamps being pulled out to sea in the pagan rite of Adonis and Dione; and the "green deep of the sea-cave" of Queen Elizabeth's eye to the mind of Drake; or the fragile wings of "farfalla in tempesta ['butterfly in storm'] / under rain in the dark" as an image of Pound's "jagged" paradise (91/632, 92/639). As late as the "Notes for Canto 111" Pound imagines paradise as: "Amor / Cold mermaid up from black water– / Night against sea-cliffs"; "Soul melts into air, / anima into aura, / Serenitas" (111/803). For Pound, divinity is more present in darkness or the underworld.

The catalogue of heroines in *Odyssey* 11 is also a vestige of an older matriarchal religion. "And the women came, for august Persephone sent them forth" (11.225–26). As Pound summarizes in "Canto III": "Then he had news of many famous women, / Tyro, Alcmena, Chloris, / Heard out their tales by that dark fosse."[103] As Harrison explains, these tales seem out of place in Homer's text. "In general mysteries seem to occur more usually in relation to the cult of women divinities, of heroines and earth-goddesses; from the worship of the Olympians in Homer they are markedly absent."[104] Homer devotes 107 lines to fifteen tales of women, although most readers of the *Odyssey* don't remember them. Pound read them closely and adds scattered allusions to them in *The Cantos*. Homer's list includes Tyro (whose story is taken up in Canto 2), Antiope (mentioned indirectly via Dirce in Cantos 50 and 82), Alcmene (mentioned in Canto 90), Megara, Epicaste, Chloris, Pero, Leda, Iphimedeia, Phaedra, Procris, Ariadne (mentioned in Canto 116), Clymene, Maera, and Eriphyle. In Canto 90, Pound describes Tyro and Alcmene ascending on a crystal funnel of air, "out of Erebus," "ascending, / no shades more," as though to undo the damage Homer or Pisistratus did to them (90/628).

[102] *L*, 285.

[103] *PT*, 320.

[104] Harrison, *Prolegomena to the Study of Greek Religion*, 150–1. See also James Houlihan, "Incorporating the Other: The Catalogue of Women in Odyssey 11," *Electronic Antiquity* 2.1 (1994). https://scholar.lib.vt.edu/ejournals/ElAnt/V2N1/houlihan.html [Accessed March 19, 2022]

Holophrase, or Pre-logical Mentality

In *Themis,* Harrison uses the concept of the holophrase, first discussed by the historian Edward John Payne and the anthropologist Alfred Ernest Crawley, to characterize primitive mentality.[105] Holophrase, meaning "whole phrasing," expresses a complex relation in a single word before the division of subject and object.

> Language, after the purely emotional interjection, began with whole sentences, *holophrases*, utterances of a relation in which subject and object have not yet got their heads above water but are submerged in a situation. A holophrase utters a holopsychosis. Out of these *holophrases* at a later stage emerge our familiar "Parts of Speech," rightly so called, for speech was before its partition. A simple instance will make this clear.
>
> The Fuegians have a word, or rather holophrase, *mamihlapinatapari,* which means "looking-at-each-other,-hoping-that-either-will-offer-to-do-something-which-both-parties-desire-but-are-unwillling-to-do." This holophrase contains no nouns and no separate verbs, it simply expresses a tense relation—not unknown to some of us, and applicable to any and every one. Uneducated and impulsive people even today tend to show a certain holophrastic savagery. They not unfrequently plunge into a statement of relations before they tell you who they are talking about. As civilization advances, the holophrase, overcharged, disintegrates, and, bit by bit, object, subject and verb, and the other "Parts of Speech" are abstracted from the stream of warm conscious human activity in which they were once submerged.[106]

This concept resonates with Pound's definition of the image in "A Few Don'ts" (1913, a year after *Themis* appeared) as "that which presents an intellectual and emotional complex in an instant of time."[107] Similarly, Pound's concept of "paideuma" adopted from Leo Frobenius is defined as "the tangle or complex of the inrooted ideas of any period."[108] As Harrison puts it, "the

[105] Edward John Payne, *History of the New World Called America*, vol. 2 (Oxford: Clarendon Press, 1899), 114–19, 156–265; and Alfred Earnest Crawley, *The Idea of the Soul* (London: Adam and Charles Black, 1909), 31–48. Payne calls the holophrase "the collective embodiment of selected impressions," and suggests that holophrases disappear as the sense of collectivity diminishes (189). Crawley explains that the holophrase "will apply to any persons; it will apply to animals. It contains no names or nouns—they are unnecessary. In the earliest speech all holophrases are without meaning when divided. [...] At this early stage, then, articulate sounds are merely contrivances for expressing the relations between things" (34).

[106] Harrison, *Themis*, 474.

[107] *LE*, 4.

[108] *GK*, 57.

holophrase shows us man entangled as it were in his own activities, he and his environment utterly involved. He has as yet no 'soul,' but he has life, and has it more abundantly."[109] "Language tells us what we have already learnt from ritual, that the 'soul' of primitive man is 'congregationalized,' the collective daimon is before the individual ghost, and still more is he before the Olympian god." Canto 1 recreates a primitive mentality in which the hero is not clearly delineated from the group. Pound plunges the reader into statements of relations while being deliberately confusing and vague about subject and object, agent and patient. When the dead emerge from the pit, Pound piles up statements of relation with inverted syntax that seems to recreate a holopsychosis and even mimic the broken English of "savage speak" like Conrad's "Mistah Kurtz—he dead," which Eliot originally wanted as the epigraph to *The Waste Land:* "These many crowded about me; with shouting, / Pallor upon me, cried to my men for more beasts."

Harrison's analysis of the holopsychosis is itself indebted to Lucien Lévy-Bruhl's "pre-logical mentality" which inspired the representations of consciousness in *The Waste Land.* In *Les fonctions mentales dans les sociétées inférieures*, Lévy-Bruhl argues that a "pre-logical mentality" involved mystic connections between people and objects or animals and the phenomenon of multi-presence, or being in more than one place at the same time. One of Eliot's favorite examples of the pre-logical mentality is the Bororo of Brazil who can "become" parrots. As Eliot puts it in his 1918 review: "He is capable of a state of mind into which we cannot put ourselves, in which he *is* a parrot, while being at the same time a man."[110] *The Waste Land* eerily features "bats with baby faces in the violet light."[111] Eliot's characters are haunted by the unraveling of selfhood ("Are you alive or not? Is there nothing in your head?"); or a ghostly multipresence: "Who is that on the other side of you?"[112] Characters can "become" other characters: "Just as the one-eyed merchant, seller of currants, melts into the Phoenician Sailor, and the latter is not wholly distinct from Ferdinand Prince of Naples, so all the women are one woman, and the two sexes meet in Tiresias."[113]

[109] Harrison, *Themis*, 474.

[110] T. S. Eliot, "Review of *Group Theories of Religion and the Religion of the Individual*, by Clement C. J. Webb," *International Journal of Ethics* 27 (1916): 116.

[111] Eliot, *The Waste Land*, line 379.

[112] Eliot, *The Waste Land*, lines 126, 365.

[113] Eliot, *The Waste Land*, note for line 218.

Identity is similarly amorphous in Canto 1, especially in the early description of loading the ship and performing the sacrifices. Pound's interest in Lévy-Bruhl, however, was mostly linguistic. As he puts it in Canto 38 (1934),

> Bruhl found some languages full of detail
> Words that half mimic action; but
> generalization is beyond them, a white dog is
> not, let us say, a dog like a black dog. (38/189)

Pound's summary is not exactly right; Lévy-Bruhl did not argue that the savage mind does not generalize, only generalizes differently. "Words that half mimic action" speaks to Pound's own technique in Canto 1, for example, of making the description of the dead rising seem like a summoning of the dead, or even his shifting of tense to the present ("Circe's this craft"). The lines about the white and black dog recalls Pound's odd translation of Odysseus's sacrifice to Tiresias: "A sheep to Tiresias only, black and a bell-sheep." A black sheep is not, let us say, a sheep like a bell sheep. The translation suggests that Odysseus is sacrificing two separate and distinct sheep to Tiresias.

Pound's phrase, "words that half-mimic action," also recalls Harrison's description of the *dromenon* or rite as the precursor to epic and drama. "The savage is a man of action. Instead of asking a god to do what he wants done, he does it or tries to do it himself; instead of prayers he utters spells."[114]

> The word for rite, *dromenon,* "thing done," arose, of course, not from any psychological analysis, but from the simple fact that rites among primitive Greeks were *things done,* mimetic dances and the like.[115]

The song of a hero who descends into the underworld and revives the old heroes and goddesses is an act (or spell) of reawakening them: a rite of spring. Similarly, Canto 1 is an act of raising the legendary bard and changing our understanding of what function his epic originally served.

While Canto 1 is still recognizably an epic narrative, Pound is already at work in dismantling the epic's teleological plot into a cyclical and "fugal" plot of recurrence and repetition; in transforming the Homeric hero into a dying-and-resurrecting hero; in dethroning the Olympian gods and reinstating earlier deities; in truncating and disordering polished narrative poetry into an invocative lyric and "primitive" Anglo Saxon verse.

[114] Harrison, *Ancient Art and Ritual*, 30.
[115] Harrison, *Ancient Art and Ritual*, 35.

3

Protean Homer

"The time of Socratic man is past. Put on wreaths of ivy, take up the thyrsus and do not be surprised if tigers and panthers lie down, purring and curling round your legs."[1]

Canto 1 resurrects a Homer who sings of chthonic gods and fertility goddesses rather than what Jane Harrison calls the "cut flowers" of the patriarchal and anthropomorphic Olympian gods: "To find those roots we must burrow deep into a lower stratum of thought, into those chthonic cults which underlay their life and from which sprang all their brilliant blossoming."[2] Gilbert Murray, in his 1907 Harvard lecture series attended by the nineteen-year-old T. S. Eliot, argues that the *Iliad* was reworked and "updated" to reflect contemporary sensibilities as many times as *La Chanson de Roland* or *La Vie de Saint Alexis.*[3] All of the "savageness" of Homer was smoothed over, but many vestiges of it remain, like poisoned arrows, torture, or blood-hungry shades. J. A. K. Thomson argues that the *Odyssey* was a Minyan and Arcadian myth transformed into an Ionian epic and then into an Achaean epic.[4] In a 1922 letter to Ford Madox Ford, Pound describes his poetic practice in the early cantos as archaeological: reconstructing "various ichthyosauri."[5]

Canto 2 uses a new set of strategies to reconstruct an *Ur-Odyssey.* Pound transforms Homer's epic narrative into an Ovidian "carmen perpetuum" (endless song) of rhapsodic transformation. He stitches together classical fragments to invoke the Dionysian lyric behind the Apollonian epic form. Although the structure of Canto 2 might seem loose or haphazard, it reveals itself as complex and deliberate.

1 Nietzsche, *The Birth of Tragedy*, 98.
2 Harrison, *Themis*, xi.
3 See Gilbert Murray, *The Rise of the Greek Epic*, 2nd edition (Oxford: Clarendon Press, 1911), 342–9.
4 See Murray, *The Rise of the Greek Epic*, 275–97; and J. A. K. Thomson, "Preface" to *Studies in the Odyssey.*
5 Ezra Pound, January 13, 1922 Letter to Ford Madox Ford. *Pound/Ford: Story of Literary Friendship* (New York: New Directions, 1981), 63.

The canto begins with a condensed invocation of Pound's mythical method, a regression from Picasso to Robert Browning to Aeschylus to the mythical Homer who hears his poetry on the shore of Chios. Pound then translates *Iliad* 3.139–60, in which the old men of Troy on the Skaian gates remark on Helen's appearance, interpolating the story of Atalanta as told by Ovid and Hesiod's Catalogue of Women. This is followed by a "continuation" of Odysseus's nekyia from Canto 1—Homer's catalogue of heroines—in which Odysseus meets Tyro in the underworld and learns of her seduction by Poseidon in the guise of a river.[6] Tyro's story, recounted in the Old English alliterative style of *The Wanderer*, bookends the story of Dionysus's transformation of the mariners into dolphins from Hymn 7 to Dionysus and Ovid's *Metamorphosis* 3.580–733. The mariners transform back into Tyro who transforms into the natural world off Homer's Chios. The canto ends with the image of the ever-changing Proteus held down by Menelaus as described in *Odyssey* 4.454.-59: a coda to the methodology of *translatio* in Canto 2.

Injecting Ovid into the Matter of Troy (and Rome) was common to the medieval *translatio.* Benoît adds stories from Ovid's *Heroides* to the *Roman de Troie,* and the author of the *Roman d'Enéas* (*c.* 1160) embellishes the love stories of Eneas and Dido and Eneas and Lavine with echoes of Ovid's *Amores.* The story in Ovid takes place long before the action of the *Odyssey,* when Tiresias was still living and Dionysus was a young god. Pound's Protean translation of Homer grafted to Ovid unearths the rhapsodic and what Pound identifies as the "folkloric" roots of Homer before his poetry was organized and constrained by what J. A. K. Thomson calls the "epic machinery" of Pisistratus:

> In the Iliad and Odyssey we find the old way of belief asserting itself in the constant transformations of the Immortals into shapes other than their ideal or typical shapes. [...] How are we to think of these transformations? Not as part of the epic machinery, although in Homer they serve that purpose too. They are not in origin an artistic device but an article of primitive religion, as indeed we all now recognize—the dreams of men who believed that the Olympian gods in battle with the Giants assumed the forms of the mean animals, and who discovered a dreadful sanctity in an oak-grove or a blackened stone.[7]

Pound's Protean *translatio* of Homer and Ovid in Canto 2 achieves a number of things that his Anglo-Saxon *translatio* of Homer of Canto 1 does not. First, Pound grounds his technique (to say nothing of his poetic ambition) as a channeling of the green language: the mythical blind Homer who hears

[6] *Odyssey* 11.235–59.

[7] Thomson, *Studies in the Odyssey,* 4.

the voices of the old men of Troy in the sea-surge off Chios and who "sees" (or once saw) Tyro's seduction by Poseidon in the play of light on the water. Second, Pound inaugurates a poetic style which might be called, at the syntactic and metaphorical level, an aesthetics of perpetual metamorphosis through a concatenation of imagistic word-clusters, dilating Ovid's "magic instants" of transformation into a Dionysian rite. "No Greek was so interested in the magic instant as was Ovid," Pound writes.[8] Third, Canto 2 restores Dionysus as the central god and hero of the epic. Dionysus, as Gilbert Murray points out, was suppressed from the Homeric corpus because he represents an older religion of mystic communion that threatened Homer's "serene anthropomorphism."

> It is always the mystical or monstrous elements of a belief which seem to have excited the keenest religious emotions of an ancient people. The owl Athena, the cow Hera, the snake-man Cecrops; the many ghosts and shapes of terror; the mystic bull Dionysus, who *is* in some strange sense the beast which he himself tears to pieces alive, and from whose blood our souls are made: these things are cleared away from Homer's world, or else humanized and made to tone in with his general serene anthropomorphism.[9]

Harrison explains how the original spring *dromenon* or rite from which drama and epic derive reenacted the dismemberment of Dionysus (or Osiris) followed by his resurrection and rebirth. Dionysus was therefore originally not the god *of* drama, but the *subject* of the spring *dromenon* or drama. As Harrison puts it, the sole mention of Dionysus in Homer (*Iliad* 6.133–7) "glistens like an alien jewel."[10] Pound brings Dionysus back, as it were, into Homer by means of Ovid, the divine young god "loggy with vine-must" (2/7) and "lord of all that is wet and gleaming" as Harrison describes him.[11] Dionysus's presence cannot be constrained within the epic: his phantasmagoria of animals, his powers of chaos and transformation overwhelm the narrative into a ritual celebration and maenad-dance that King Pentheus tries disastrously to suppress. Acoetes, who represents the ideal (anthropological and philological) reader of both Homer and Canto 2, witnesses the miracle of nature and devoutly believes. "And I worship. / I have seen what I have seen" (2/9).

[8] Ezra Pound, "On Criticism in General," *The Criterion* 1.2 (1923), 135.

[9] Murray, *The Rise of the Greek Epic*, 279. In Harrison's words: "In the Homeric sacrifice there is communion, but not of any mystical kind; there is no question of partaking of the life and body of the god, only of dining with him. Mystical communion existed in Greece, but, as will later be seen, it was part of the worship of a god quite other than these Homeric Olympians, the god Dionysus" (Harrison, *Prolegomena*, 56).

[10] Harrison, *Prolegomena*, 397. See also Murray, *The Rise of the Greek Epic*, 199.

[11] Harrison, *Ancient Art and Ritual*, 113.

In the following, I'll first untangle Pound's comparison of the epic with the "compendium" in *The ABC of Reading;* his comparison of the figure of Homer with that of Pisistratus, whom Pound suggests "anthologized" the Homeric material; and Pound's disagreement with Eliot about Joyce's mythical method. Next I'll illustrate how Canto 2 continues Homer's nekyia by presenting a new version of Homer's catalogue of heroines: the story of Helen, of Atalanta, and of Tyro. These three figures embody three different problems of Homeric *translatio* that Canto 2 seeks to resolve: first, how to capture Homer's melopoeia of the natural world ("polyphloisboious") and the "actual swing of words spoken"; second, how to add what Pound calls "overchange" and compensate for the deficiencies in the source text as Arthur Golding did to Ovid; and third, how to translate Homeric color-words (with the help of William Gladstone). I'll then illustrate how Canto 2 climaxes with a dazzling Protean *translatio* of Homer (via Ovid) to conjure up a Dionysian lyric.

Homer, Pisistratus, Joyce

Early in Canto 2, Pound invokes Homer "blind, blind, as a bat," listening to the "sea-surge" on the coast (2/6). A few lines later, Ovid's young Dionysus is picked up in "Scios / to the left of Naxos passage" (2/7). In the classical tradition, the Homeridae or "children of Homer," who claimed to be descendants of Homer, originated in Chios.[12] The first written mention of them is Pindar in 485 BC: "the Homeridae, / singers [ἀοιδοὶ, *aoidoi*] of stitched-together verses [ῥαπτῶν ἐπέων, *rhaptōn epeōn*]."[13] At the Panathenea, instituted under Hipparkhos, son of Pisistratus, Plato tells us that it was decided that these utterances go though "in sequence [ἐφεξῆς, *ephexēs*], by relay [ἐξ ὑπολήψεως, *ex hypolēpseōs*]."[14] Cicero is the first to mention the so-called Pisistratus recension in *De Oratore* (55 BCE):

> Whose learning is reported, at the same period, to have been greater, or whose eloquence to have received more ornament from literature, than that of Pisistratus? who is said to have been the first that arranged [*disposuisse*: "disposed," "distributed," "arranged"] the books of Homer as we now have them,

[12] See Derek Collins, "Homer and Rhapsodic Competition in Performance," *Oral Tradition* 16.1 (2001): 129–67.

[13] Pindar, *Nemean* 2.1–3. Translation by Collins, "Homer and Rhapsodic Competition in Performance," 132.

[14] Plato, *Hiipparchus* 228b-c. Translation by Collins, "Homer and Rhapsodic Competition in Performance," 142–3.

> when they were previously confused [*confusos*: "mixed," "mingled," "confused," "confounded," literally: "poured together"].[15]

In *The ABC of Reading*, Pound's opinion of Homer is much in keeping with scholarship of his day—that Pisistratus shaped and trimmed the original Homeric *rhaptōn epeōn* into the two epics we have today.

> Pisistratus found the Homeric texts in disorder, we don't quite know what he did about it. The Bible is a compendium, people trimmed it to make it solid. It has gone on for ages, because it wasn't allowed to overrun all the available parchment; a Japanese emperor whose name I have forgotten and whose name you needn't remember, found that there were TOO MANY NOH PLAYS, he picked out 450 and the Noh stage LASTED from 1400 or whenever right down till the day the American navy intruded, and that didn't stop it. Umewaka Minoru started again as soon as the revolution wore off. Ovid's Metamorphoses are a compendium, not an epic like Homer's; Chaucer's Canterbury Tales are a compendium of all the good yarns Chaucer knew. The Tales have lasted through centuries while the long-winded mediaeval narratives went into museums.[16]

Pound suggests that Pisistratus "trimmed" down and collected all the "good" parts of the Homeric material into the *Iliad* and *Odyssey*, just as the Japanese emperor limited the Noh plays to 450. The long-winded medieval narratives went into museums because they had no such editor. Pound is vague about what Pisistratus actually did: shape a series of disparate songs into a coherent epic, or simply reject the duller books of the Epic Cycle (the *Cypria*, the *Aethiopis*, the *Little Iliad*, the *Iliupersis*, the *Nostoi*, and the *Telegony*). Nor does he seem to care. The epic elements of Homer are of little concern to him.

When Pound refers to secondary or literary epics, the word "epic" tends to have a negative connotation. Pound praises the form of the *Metamorphoses* as a compendium while condemning the epic elements of the *Aeneid*.

> Virgil was the official literature of the middle ages, but "everybody" went on reading Ovid. Dante makes all his acknowledgments to Virgil (having appreciated the best of him), but the direct and indirect effect of Ovid on Dante's actual writing is possibly greater than Virgil's. [...] The lover of Virgil who wishes to bring a libel action against me would be well advised to begin his attack by separating the part of the Aeneid in which Virgil was directly interested (one

[15] Cicero, *De Oratore*, 3.13. Translation by J. S. Watson, *Cicero on Oratory and Orators* (New York: Harper and Brothers, 1860), 231.

[16] *ABCR*, 92.

> might almost say, the folk-lore element) from the parts he wrote chiefly because he was trying to write an epic poem.[17]

Implicit here is the idea that medieval readers, and especially great medieval authors like Dante, were arbiters of taste. The best parts of any epic, at least of any secondary epic, are the "good yarns" and "folk-lore elements" that reflect the author's own interests. As early as 1914, Pound writes that Virgil "has no story worth telling, no sense of personality. His hero is a stick who would have contributed to *The New Statesman.*"[18]

The folklore element that Pound especially admires in Virgil is the story of the golden bough: a genuine improvement of Homer's nekyia, which is why he includes it in Canto 1. Similarly, Pound praises Chaucer as "open minded, let us say to folk-lore, to the problems Frazer broaches, in a way that Shakespeare certainly was not."[19] In other words, when an author like Shakespeare changes his source material (Ovid) to fit into his plot and bland humanistic world view, he loses its original beauty. Great minds, like Chaucer as a reader of Ovid, like Dante as a reader of Virgil, and like Pound as a reader of everyone, disregard the "epic" elements of the source text and mine it for those folkloric elements: "the subtler music, the clear light / Where time burns back about th' eternal embers."[20]

But that doesn't explain what makes Pisistratus different from Virgil, according to Pound. Wasn't Pisistratus "trying to make an epic" as well? In a piece written for *The Active Anthology* in 1933, the answer seems to be either no, or that it doesn't matter. Pound drops the distinction between epic and compendium and identifies the *Iliad* and *Odyssey* as part of a "major anthology" similar to the Bible and the 450 good Noh plays:

> Every great culture has had such a major anthology. Pisistratus, Li Po, the Japanese Emperor who reduced the number of Noh dramas to about 450; the hackneyed Hebrew example; in less degree the Middle Ages, with the matter of Britain, of France, and of Rome le Grant.[21]

Pound compares Pisistratus's efforts with the reduction of the Noh dramas, the fixing of the twenty-four books of the Masoretic Text, and "in less degree" with Jean Bodel's classification of the legendary themes and literary cycles into the Three Matters in the late twelfth century, because Bodel presumably didn't do

[17] *ABCR*, 45.
[18] *LE*, 215.
[19] *ABCR*, 102–3.
[20] *PT*, 169.
[21] *SP*, 394.

any "trimming" of them as did Pisistratus or the Church Fathers. Pisistratus, like Chaucer and Ovid, was a collector of stories. The ultimate value of the *Iliad* or the *Odyssey* is its unique arrangement of the folkloric material, not the plot.

Few scholars of Pound's day would describe the *Iliad* and *Odyssey* as "anthologies." Most readers of Homer, including Aristotle, agree that what distinguishes the *Iliad* and *Odyssey* from the rest of the Epic Cycle is the expert plotting. The *Iliad* condenses the story of a ten-year war in Troy to the representative story of Achilles's rage and the death of Hector during the ninth year, all of which take place in the space of a few weeks. The *Odyssey* recounts the *nostoi* of the Greek heroes through the story of Odysseus's ten-year journey home, which is itself condensed to the roughly two-week period from when Odysseus leaves Calypso to when he slays the suitors and establishes peace in Ithaca. The digressions in Homer are generally motivated by plot, either as essential backstory or offering thematic links to the action: very unlike the loose architecture of the *Metamorphoses* or *The Canterbury Tales*.

Pound's inability or unwillingness to praise Homer's (or Pisistratus's) plotting is a provocation, like his dismissal of the "fashion plates" of Praxiletes or Aristotle's cathartic theory of drama in "The New Sculpture." Pound alligns Pisistratus's method with his own method of adapting the *Odyssey*. Pound styles himself the new or modernist Pisistratus, who, inspired by Bédier and comparative anthropology, will arrange the *Odyssey* (and many other classical texts) back into lyric.

Pound's reading of Pisistratus as an anthologist also illuminates his opinion that the correspondences to the plot of the *Odyssey* are the least important part of Joyce's *Ulysses*. As Pound put it:

> These correspondences are part of Joyce's medievalism and are chiefly his own affair, a scaffold, a means of construction, justified by the result, and justifiable by it only. The result is a triumph in form, in balance, a main schema, with continuous inweaving and arabesque.[22]

The scaffolding of the Homeric plot is "a triumph in form" only in the sense that it allows "continuous inweaving and arabeseuqe" of Joyce's material. Pound's Joyce sounds a lot more like Pound's Ovid or Chaucer. Eliot's review of *Ulysses* a year later disputes the idea that the Homeric correspondences are "a scaffolding erected by the author for the purpose of disposing his realistic tale, of no interested in the completed structure."[23] Eliot targets Richard Aldington's 1921

[22] *LE*, 406.
[23] *Selected Prose of T. S. Eliot*, ed. Frank Kermode (London: Faber and Faber, 1975), 175.

review, but he's a straw man.[24] Aldington's review is patriarchal and vapid. While conceding that *Ulysses* "is an astonishing psychological document," he compares it to "the disgusting savagery of war," reflects on Joyce's "great undisciplined talent," and muses on how "dangerous" the book might be for a young writer.[25] "Scaffold" is Pound's word. Aldington never uses it or mentions the Homeric correspondences. Perhaps Eliot means to imply that if Homer's scaffolding is not kept constantly in mind while reading *Ulysses,* one is in danger of producing criticism as bad as Aldington's. Regardless, Pound would have agreed with Eliot that Joyce manipulates "a continuous parallel between contemporaneity and antiquity," but little else. Joyce's parallels to Homer's plot are uninteresting because Homer's epic plot itself is uninteresting. Yes, one should always be thinking of the *Odyssey* while reading *Ulysses*, but not the nostos plot. The "real" Homer didn't even write that, as Harrison and Thomson argue. One should rather think of the blind bard on the beach of Chios listening to the sound of the surf (which Stephen Dedalus channels in "Proteus") and to the Homeridae stitching ancient songs together (the compositional method of "Wandering Rocks"; the fugal and stylistic method of "Sirens"). As Eliot might recall from Gilbert Murray's Harvard lectures, the text of Homer is as philologically stratified as Joyce's "Oxen of the Sun."

"Joyce lucky in copping form of Odyssey," Pound writes to Ford Madox Ford in 1922 as he worked on a draft of Canto 8, which later became Canto 2. "But it wd.nt have done for me ANNYhow."[26] Pound wanted to turn Homer back into a "compendium" of lyrics reflecting the original folklore, just as Eliot wanted to turn the Grail romance into a Grail ritual. *The Cantos* cannot cop the form of the *Odyssey* because Pound isn't interested, like Joyce or Virgil, in "trying to make an epic" at all. Pound was always wary of calling *The Cantos* an epic. After offering his notes on Canto 8 (Canto 2), Ford remarks to Pound, "I think that, in essence, you're a mediaeval gargoyle."[27] Pound replies: "As to Gargoyles, some one has got to make the plunge, decide whether the Epic, or wottell of cosmographic volcano is extinct or not. It will take me another thirty years at least. Shall probably do vol. of first ten or fifteen cantos."[28] It didn't take him that long to decide. In 1924, Pound writes to William Bird of the Three Mountains Press, "do recall that the

[24] Richard Aldington, "The Influence of Mr. James Joyce," *English Review* 32 (1921): 333–41.

[25] Aldington, "The Influence of Mr. James Joyce," 338–9.

[26] Ezra Pound, March 21, 1922 Letter to Ford Madox Ford. *Pound/Ford,* 63.

[27] Ford Madox Ford, March 21, 1922 Letter to Ezra Pound. *Pound/Ford,* 63.

[28] Ezra Pound, March 21, 1922 Letter to Ford Madox Ford. *Pound/Ford,* 66.

title of that book is '*A DRAFT* of 16 Cantos for a poem of some length.' If you will stick to that you will produce something of gtr. val. to collectors. Also it ain't an epic. It's part of a long poem."[29] Apparently, Pound had since deemed the epic extinct.

Regardless of the terminology, Pound intended for *A Draft of XVI Cantos* to appear unfinished, even disordered, despite the enormous work of arranging, excising, and rewriting that went into its construction.[30] Pound wanted to present, as succinctly as possible, a jagged "pre-epic" long poem full of pre-Pisistratian folklore and stitched together verses (*rhaptōn epeōn*) arranged in a new fugal pattern that would reflect the mythical method. "I tried a smoother presentation and lost the metamorphosis, got to be a hurley burley," Pound explains to Ford.[31] *The Cantos* are closer, therefore, to compilations like the *Metamorphoses* than epics like the *Aeneid* or even Dante's methodically structured "cosmographic volcano."[32] "One can't follow the Dantesquan cosmos in an age of experiment,"[33] Pound explains to Donald Hall in 1962. Although he tried a "miniature" version of it in Cantos 14 and 15 (*Inferno*), 16 (*Purgatorio*), and 17, 20, and 21 (*Paradiso*).[34] After Joyce, one can't even get away with "copping form of Odyssey." Homer's Apollonian epic form is at odds with his Dionysian lyric music.

Homer Hears Helen

Isocrates recounts that "some of the Homeridae also relate that Helen appeared to Homer by night and commanded him to compose a poem on those who went on the expedition to Troy."[35] After a virtuosic invocation of the mythical method of *The Cantos*, moving from Robert Browning to Shojo to Picasso to Aeschylus,

29 *L*, 259.

30 For the composition of the early cantos see especially Ronald Bush, *The Genesis of Ezra Pound's Cantos* (Princeton, NJ: Princeton University Press, 1976); Marjorie Froula, *To Write Paradise: Style and Error in Pound's Cantos* (New Haven, CT: Yale University Press, 1985); and Lawrence Rainey, *Ezra Pound and the Monument of Culture: Text, History, and the Malatesta Cantos* (Chicago: University of Chicago Press, 1991).

31 Ezra Pound, March 21, 1922 Letter to Ford Madox Ford. *Pound/Ford*, 65.

32 On Dante's influence on *The Cantos*, see James Wilhelm, *Dante and Pound: The Epic of Judgment* (Maine: University of Maine Press, 1974).

33 Donald Hall, "Ezra Pound: An Interview," *The Paris Review* 7.28 (1962): 48–9.

34 See Ezra Pound, April 11, 1927 Letter to Homer Pound: "You have had a hell in Canti XIV, XV, purgatorio in XVI etc." (*L*, 286). See also the next chapter.

35 Isocrates, *Helen* 65. In *Isocrates*, vol. 2, trans. George Norlin (Cambridge, MA: Harvard University Press, 1980).

Canto 2 brings the reader back to that very moment when the blind bard hears the "sea-surge" off Chios and Helen "appears."

> Hang it all, Robert Browning,
> there can be but the one "Sordello."
> But Sordello, and my Sordello?
> Lo Sordels si fo di Mantovana.
> So-shu churned in the sea.
> Seal sports in the spray-whited circles of cliff-wash,
> Sleek head, daughter of Lir,
>   eyes of Picasso
> Under black fur-hood, lithe daughter of Ocean;
> And the wave runs in the beach-groove:
> Eleanor, ἑλέυαυς and ἑλέπτολις!
>   And poor old Homer blind, blind, as a bat,
> Ear, ear for the sea-surge, murmur of old men's voices:
>   "Let her go back to the ships. (2/5)

Homer is introduced through a dizzying array of allusions in the comparative anthropological style of the mythical method: Browning's resurrection of the troubadour Sordello; the brief account of Sordello "as it stands in a manuscript in the Ambrosian library in Milan. 'Lo Sordels *si fo di Mantovana*'";[36] the Japanese god of wine Shojo who is often depicted as rowing in a sake cup; the sporting seals which recall Proteus as the shepherd of seals; Finnguala the daugter of Lir who is changed into a swan; Picasso's intense eyes reflecting his shape-shifting cubist visions; the three thousand Oceanids, daughters of Titan; Eleanor of Aquitaine (1124–1204) who left Louis VII to marry Henry II and incite the Hundred Years War; and the chorus's pun on Helen's name in Aeschylus's *Agamemnon* 689–90: "ἑλένας, ἕλανδρος, ἑλέπτολις" (*helenas, helandros, heleptolis*): destroyer of men, of ships, of cities. The legendary blind Homer finally appears, and Pound modifies the story of the Homeridae that Helen appeared to Homer in a dream, perhaps to account for Homer's blindness. In the sea-surge of the waves, Pound's Homer hears the shrill sound of the old men of Troy on the Skaian gates witnessing Helen's inhuman beauty for the first time. Pound then assays a translation of the famous passage that he spent a large portion of "Early Translations of Homer" arguing was untranslatable in English.

Pound's dense allusive structure epitomizes the methodology of his mythical method. *The Cantos* aspires to resurrect Homer as Browning did Sordello;

[36] *LE*, 97.

Shojo anticipates Dionysus as the original god of epic and theater; Proteus and Finnangula anticipate the transformation of Tyro and the mariners as well as the main theme of Canto 2 which is metamorphosis; Eleanor's marriage represents the "repeat of history" of Helen's abduction; Aeschylus's chorus of Greek veterans anticipate Homer's chorus of Trojan veterans; the archaic drama of Aeschylus, and especially the chorus, is a "way in" to understanding the origin of drama and epic as ritual, as Nietzsche and Harrison argue;[37] all poetry "begins" with the legendary bard receiving a vision of Helen or hearing the language of nature off Chios. Pound's Homer is himself a subject rhyme for the young Dionysus stuck on Chios; as the origin of all tragedy and epic is folklore and the ritual recreation of Dionysus's dismemberment and rebirth.[38]

The opening lines of Canto 2 also recreate a melopoetic soundscape akin to the *poluphloisboios* Homer heard of the receding waves off Chios. Pound begins with the sibilance of the sea's hiss by repeating "Sordello" (unnecessarily) four times. "So-shu" is invoked partly because his name sounds like an oar "churned in the sea." The paddling of oars and fins and splashing of water can be heard in, "seal sports in the spray-whited circles of cliff-wash, / Sleek head" and "eyes of Picasso." The labial sound takes over with "Lir" and "lithe daughter of ocean" and ends with a modified Aeschylus: "Eleanor, *helandros, heleptolis.*" Homer is introduced by a repetition of three unique alliterations "blind, blind, as a bat," "ear, ear," and "murmur of men's." The melopoeia prepares the reader's ear for Pound's own translation of the Trojan veterans. Aeschylus's description of Helen is "given back" to Homer as though the bard himself heard it in the waves.

In "Early Translations of Homer," a composite made of three short essays written in 1918–19, Pound juxtaposes Homer's description of the sea from *Iliad* 1.34 with the "authentic cadence" of speech like the Trojan veterans on the wall in *Iliad* 3.121–244 in order to address problems of Homeric translation. Pound identifies two qualities of Homer that are seldom translated well:

> the magnificent onomatopoeia, as of the rush of the waves on the sea-beach and their recession in:
>
> παρὰ θῖνα πολυφλοίσβοιο θαλάσσης
> [*para thina polyphloisboio thalassēs*]

[37] "Beneath this splendid surface lies a stratum of religious conceptions, ideas of evil, of purification, of atonement, ignored or suppressed by Homer, but reappearing in later poets and notably in Aeschylus" (Harrison, *Prolegomena*, vii). See also Nietzsche, *The Birth of Tragedy*, 36–40; and Harrison, *Ancient Art and Ritual*, 123.

[38] "It ought to be possible to demonstrate historically that every period which was rich in the production of folk songs was agitated by Dionysiac currents, since these are always to be regarded as the precondition of folk song and as the hidden ground from which is springs." (Nietzsche, *The Birth of Tragedy*, 33)

> untranslated and untranslatable; and, secondly, the authentic cadence of speech; the absolute conviction that the words used, let us say by Achilles to the "dog-faced" chicken-hearted Agamemnon, are in the actual swing of words spoken. This quality of actual speaking is *not* untranslatable.[39]

The Greek line means literally, "along the shore of the loud-resounding sea." Pound translates it in "Mauberly" (1920) as "the imaginary / Audition of the phantasmal sea-surge."[40] He translates it in a 1935 letter to Rouse as "the turn of the wave and the scutter of receding pebbles."[41] "Years' work to get that," he adds. But in 1919, he considers the passage untranslatable, along with "the authentic cadence" of Homeric speech. Pound offers the example of the argument between Achilles and Agamemnon in *Iliad* 1, but then launches into a lengthy examination of how translators have failed to capture the cadence of the Trojan veterans in *Iliad* 3.150–60, including Samuel Clark, Nicolo Valla, and Andreas Divus in Latin; Alexander Pope and George Chapman in English; and Guillaume Dubois de Rochefort in French.

In the *Iliad,* Iris, disguised as Laodice, summons Helen to the Skaian gates to witness the duel between Paris and Menelaus. A group of old Trojan veterans sitting on the wall watch Helen approach and remark on her ominous beauty. Here is A. T. Murray's translation:

> Because of old age had they now ceased from battle, but speakers they were full good, like unto cicalas [τεττίγεσσιν, *tettigessin*] that in a forest sit upon a tree and pour forth their lily-like [λειριόεσσαν, *leirioessan*] voice; even in such wise sat the leaders of the Trojans upon the wall [ἐπὶ πύργῳ, *epi pyrgō*]. Now when they saw Helen coming upon the wall, softly they spake winged words one to another [ἦκα πρὸς ἀλλήλους, *ēka pros allēlous*: "slightly/a little towards each other"]: "Small blame that Trojans and well-greaved Achaeans should for such a woman long time suffer woes; wondrously like is she to the immortal goddesses to look upon. But even so, for all that she is such an one, let her depart [νεέσθω, *neesthō*] upon the ships, neither be left here to be a bane to us and to our children after us."[42]

Pound argues that the "quality of actual speaking" is the greatest challenge for a translator of the old men's speech. Pope's version contains an "imbecility in antithesis" in lines like, "What winning graces! What majestic mien! / She moves

[39] *LE*, 250.
[40] *PT*, 525, 561.
[41] *L*, 364.
[42] *Iliad* 3.150–60.

a goddess, and she looks a queen!"[43] "What we definitely can *not* hear is the voice of the old men speaking." "The old voices do not ring in the ear." Homer compares the old men to "cicadas," and uses the unusual adjective "λειριόεσσαν" (*leirioessan*), "lily-like," commonly translated as "delicate," to describe their voices. The word has echoes of "λιγυρήν" (*ligyrēn*), meaning "shrill, clear": an adjective commonly used to describe the cicada's song, but also the Sirens in the *Odyssey*, which is probably why Pound insists that the voices must "ring in the ear." Homer describes how the Sirens "λιγυρὴν δ' ἔντυνον ἀοιδήν" (*ligyrēn d' entynon aoidēn*) "raised their clear-toned song" (12.183). Pound shortens and elides the line to "Ligur' aoide" ("clear song") twice in Canto 20 (20/89, 20/94) and expands it to "the sharp song with sun under its radiance / λιγύρ" in Canto 74 (74/459). Homer also describes the old men's speech as "Ἦκα [*Ēka*]," which Pound glosses in a note as "low, quiet, with a secondary meaning of 'little by little.'"[44] It "might, by a slight strain, be taken to mean that the speech of the old men came little by little, a phrase from each of the elders," Pound suggests.

Pound finally settles on Hugues Salel's 1545 Middle French translation as being just "medieval" enough to capture the voice of the old men speaking:

> Là, ces Viellards assis de peur du Hasle
> Causoyent ensemble ainsi que la Cigale
> Ou deux ou trois, entre les vertes fueilles,
> En temps d'Esté gazouillant à merveilles;
> Lesquels voyans la diuine Gregeoise,
> Disoient entre eux que si la grande noise
> De ces deux camps duroit longe saison,
> Certainement ce n'estoit sans raison:
> Veu la Beaulté, et plus que humain ouvrage,
> Qui reluysoit en son diuin visaige.
> Ce neantmoins il vauldrait mieulx la rendre,
> (Ce disoyent ilz) sans guères plus attendre.
> Pour éviter le mal qui peult venir,
> Qui la voudra encores retenir.[45]

Here's a literal translation:

> There, the old men sitting in fear of siriasis [heatstroke/sunburn, from *Sirus*],
> Spoke to one another like cicadas

[43] *LE*, 251.
[44] *LE*, 252n1.
[45] *LE*, 254.

> When two, then three, among the green leaves,
> Marvelously chirped during summer.
> Those who saw the divine Greek woman
> Said that if the great noise
> Of the two camps lasted the entire season
> It was certainly not without reason
> Given such beauty, and the more-than-human features
> That illuminated her divine face.
> Nevertheless it would be better to return her
> Immediately, they told themselves, without any further delay
> In order to avoid the evil that could befall them
> Should they retain her any longer.

Pound praises Salel's "absorption" in the subject matter of Homer and aligns him with the "medieval" temperament:

> Salel is a most delightful approach to the Iliads; he is still absorbed in the subject-matter, as Douglas [translator of Virgil] and Golding [translator of Ovid] were absorbed in their subject-matter. Note how exact he is in the rendering of the old men's mental attitude.[46]

Salel's translation is devoid of dovetailing and fustian. He concatenates parataxes, which is exact "in the rendering of the old men's mental attitude." He uses alliteration ("De ces deux camps duroit longe saison"); repetition ("Causoyent ensemble," "Disoient entre eux," "Ce disoyent ilz"); and consonance or onomatopoeia, especially in the line, "Causoyent ensemble ainsi que la Cigale / Ou deux ou trois, entre les vertes fueilles, / En temps d'Esté gazouillant à merveilles," which seems to recreate the shrill sibilance of the cicada's song. He also interpolates a joke: the old men feared a sunburn.

Pound's translation in Canto 2 takes more liberties with parataxes and repetition than did Salel.

> "Let her go back to the ships,
> Back among Grecian faces, lest evil come on our own,
> Evil and further evil, and a curse cursed on our children,
> Moves, yes she moves like a goddess
> And has the face of a god
>   and the voice of Schoeney's daughters,
> And doom goes with her in walking,

[46] *LE*, 254.

Let her go back to the ships,
back among Grecian voices." (2/6)

Pound turns the line, "Let her go back to the ships" into a refrain. He repeats other words as though incanting them: "evil," "evil and further evil"; "curse cursed"; "moves, yes she moves"; "goddess," "god." The line, "and doom goes with her in walking," exemplifies how the old men's argument deteriorates before Helen's "plus que humain ouvrage," and so reflects "the old men's mental attitude." The veterans first condemn Helen as an evil curse. As she draws near, they concede that she "moves, yes, she moves like a goddess." Instead of negating the concession ("but who cares—she's trouble"), they offer two more: she "has the face of a god" and a voice like Atalanta, the ancient Boeotian king Shoeneus's daughter. Finally, the old men try to return to their argument: "And doom goes with her in walking." The line would be more coherent as, "But doom goes with her walking," but the "And" reflects the "swing of words spoken." "And" introduces another concession, but then the old men decide that they have conceded enough: she spells doom. Helen's uncanny beauty muddles their rhetoric and derails their syntax.

Homer's old men remark only that Helen looks like an immortal goddess (ἀθανάτῃσι θεῇς εἰς ὦπα ἔοικεν, *athanatēsi theēs eis ōpa eoiken*). Salel expands this to, "et plus que humain ouvrage, / Qui reluysoit en son diuin visaige." Pope adds the detail, "she moves a goddess," and Pound expands this into an emphasis of the walk of the goddess, drawing on a long tradition beginning with Virgil's description of Aeneas recognizing his mother Venus (Aphrodite) by her walk:

A roseate beam
from her bright shoulder glowed; th' ambrosial hair
breathed more than mortal sweetness, while her robes
fell rippling to her feet. Each step revealed
the veritable goddess [*et vera incessu paruit Dea*][47] (1.402–205)

Guido Cavalcanti echoes this in his seventh sonnet, "Chi è questa che vien, ch'ogni uom la mira" which Pound translates in *Sonnets and Ballate of Guido Cavalcanti* (1912) as: "Who is she coming, drawing all men's gaze."[48] Pound later creates an imagist reprise of this poem as "Gentildonna" (1913):

She passed and left no quiver in the veins, who now
Moving among the trees, and clinging

[47] Virgil, *Aeneid* 1.402–405, trans. Theodore C. Williams (Boston: Houghton Mifflin, 1910).
[48] *PT*, 199.

in the air she severed,
Fanning the grass she walked on then, endures:
Grey olive leaves beneath a rain-cold sky.[49]

Pound updates Homer's description of Helen with the Italian medieval tradition of the "walk of the lady." Pound also emphasizes the dichotomy between seeing and saying, the visual and the spoken, referring back to the idea of the blind Homer "hearing" the voices of the old men in the sea-surge. When Pound repeats his refrain, he turns "back among Grecian faces" to "back among Grecian voices." The ineffable beauty of Helen's face and gait merges with the untranslatable beauty of Homer's Greek: his onomatopoeia and the "authentic cadence of speech" of his characters.

Just as Canto 1 presents the anthropological-philological "origin" of the *Odyssey*, Canto 2 presents the biographical-mythological "origin" of the *Iliad:* the vision Homer had of Helen according to the Homeridae, or the beauty of Helen as reflected by the old men's words and as reflected by the *poluphloisboios* of the waves scuttering down the Chian coast where the bard once mused. This passage received a great deal of attention by Homeric scholars in Pound's day. Gilbert Murray offers the most apt commentary in *The Rise of the Greek Epic*.

> Think how the beauty of Helen has lived through the ages. Like the driving of Jehu, it is now an immortal thing. And the main, though not of course the sole, source of the whole conception is certainly the *Iliad*. Yet in the whole *Iliad* there is practically not a word spoken in description of Helen. As Lessing has remarked in a well-known passage of the *Laokoon,* almost the whole of our knowledge of Helen's beauty comes from a few lines in the third book, where Helen goes up to the wall of Troy to see the battle between Menelaus and Paris. [...] The elders of Troy were seated on the wall, and when they saw Helen coming, "softly they spake to one another winged words: 'Small wonder that the Trojans and mailed Greeks should endure pain through many years for such a woman. *Strangely like she is in face to some immortal spirit.*'" That is all we know. Not one of all the Homeric bards fell into the yawning trap of describing Helen, and making a catalogue of her features. She was veiled; she was weeping; and she was strangely like in face to some immortal spirit. And the old men, who strove for peace, could feel no anger at the war.[50]

Pound does not fall into the trap either; instead, he traces the origins of this famous description to the original poetic inspiration. It was not Helen's face

[49] *PT*, 272.
[50] Murray, *The Rise of Greek Epic*, 267–8.

that launched a thousand ships, but the white-veiled gait of her walk, suggested by the rhythmic ebb and flow of the sea (and spume) to a blind poet. Helen's beauty was never seen, only heard. She looks the way she sounds on the lips of the old men who first beheld her: a cicada-like murmur, a recession of water through pebbles.

Atalanta: Ovid's Overchange

Pound interpolates an unusual line in his translation of *Iliad* 3.139–60: "and the voice of Schoeney's daughters." This line, along with "back among Grecian faces," is indented, possibly to indicate that it is not in Homer. Why Atalanta? Older characters in the *Iliad* tend to compare the present unfavorably with the past. Nestor complains that Achilles and Agamemnon scarcely compare to the heroes of Jason's day. Likewise, the Trojan veterans can't help but compare Helen's beauty and voice to the ancient Boetean king Schoeneus's daughter, Atalanta. Helen is also a subject rhyme for Atalanta. As J. A. K. Thomson puts it, "Penelope and Atalante, Helen and Hippodameia, are princesses of saga, but in their original and more real nature they are divine."[51] All four grew up "wild," refused the company of men, and were eventually wooed by multiple suitors. Ovid depicts Helen as wrestling naked in Sparta as a young girl in the palestra with men.[52] Sextus Propertius describes her "on fair Eurotas' sands of yore / With the young boxer-twin and twin-born knight [Castor and Pollux] / Helen with naked breast the combat bore, / Nor blushed in her immortal brothers' sight."[53] Hesiod describes Atalanta as "swift of foot, the daughter of Schoeneus, who had the beaming eyes of the Graces, [and] though she was ripe for wedlock rejected the company of her equals and sought to avoid marriage with men who eat bread."[54]

In Canto 102, Pound associates Helen and Atalanta together by their sparkling theriomorphic eyes.

> "for my bitch eyes" in Ilion
> copper and wine like a bear cub's
> in sunlight, thus Atalant (102/750)

[51] Thomson, *Studies in the Odyssey*, 53.

[52] Ovid, *Epistles*, 16.149–52. In *The Epistles of Ovid* (London: J. Nunn, 1813).

[53] Propertius, *Elegies*, 3.14. In *The Elegies of Sextus Propertius*, trans. James Cranstoun (London: William Blackwood and Sons, 1875), 146.

[54] Hesiod, *The Homeric Hymns, Epic Cycle, and Homerica*, trans. H. G. Evelyn-White (Harvard: Harvard University Press, 1914), 163.

"For my bitch eyes" is Pound's translation of *Odyssey* 4.145, where Helen calls herself "κυνώπης," *kynōpēs*, which means "shameless me," but literally "dog-eyed." Pound connects the primitive or theriomorphic Helen to Atalanta's eyes (*Atalant* is Golding's spelling) who, according to Apollodorus, was abandoned on a mountain as a child and suckled by a she-bear, hence whose "beaming eyes" presumably resemble that of a bear cub.[55]

J. A. K. Thomson argues that the *Odyssey* was originally the story of an Einautos-Daemon or fertility god, which was then transformed into a Minyan myth from Boeotia (the "Boeotian Odyssey"), in which Odysseus was *Poseidon Hippios*. That melded with an Arcadian myth, in which Penelope was a waterfowl divinity, then was transformed into an Ionian epic (the "Arcadian Odyssey"), and finally into an Achaean Doric epic (the "Ithacan Odyssey").[56] The fact that the old men on the Skaian gates are able (via the comparative method) to recognize in Helen's beauty that of the daughter of the ancient *Boeotian* king Schoeneus might even be a nod to Thomson's theory of the "Boeotian Odyssey."

Another reason Pound interpolates Atalanta is to allude to Arthur Golding's 1567 translation of Ovid's *Metamorphoses:* "*Atlant*, a goodly Ladie, one / Of Schoeneys daughters, then a Maide."[57] This is Golding's own interpolation. Ovid does not mention Shoeneus in *Metamorphoses* 8.317, but he does call Atalanta by her patronymic Schoeneia in 10.609 and 10.660. Nor does Ovid, Apollodorus, or Hesiod (in the surviving fragments of his *Catalogue of Women*) suggest that Schoeneus had more than one daughter, or that Atalanta had a beautiful voice.

In his 1917 essay, "Notes on Elizabethan Classicists," Pound singles out Golding's translation of Ovid's story of Atalanta as an instance where the translator improves upon the original text. It is the moment Hippomenes sees Atalanta running:

> The wynd ay whisking from her feete the labells of her socks
> Uppon her back as whyght as snowe did tosse her golden locks,
> And eke thembroydred garters that were tyde beneathe her ham.
> A redness mixt with whyght uppon her tender body cam,
> As when a scarlet curtaine streynd ageinst a playstred wall
> Dooth cast like shadowe, making it seeme ruddye therewith all.[58]

[55] Apollodorus, *Library*, 3.9.2.

[56] See Thomson, *Studies in the Odyssey*, v–x.

[57] Ovid, *The Metamorphoses*, trans. Arthur Golding (London: De La More Press, 1904), 168.

[58] Ovid, *The Metamorphoses*, trans. Arthur Golding, 214.

"Is not a new beauty created, a new beauty doubled when the overchange is well done?" Pound comments.[59] The last three lines in Ovid are: "inque puellari corpus candore ruborem / traxerat, haud aliter, quam cum super atria velum / candida purpureum simulatas inficit umbras."[60] A literal translation: "and it had pulled redness on her white girlish body, as when a purple/dark-red awning/ sail above a white hall makes painted/copied shadows." Golding's line, "A redness mixt with whyght uppon her tender body cam," is slightly inaccurate: in Ovid, the redness mixes with the (preexisting) whiteness of Atalanta's body. Moreover, Ovid's "atria candida," which is a white forecourt or main hall of a house, would probably have been of marble, not plaster. Regardless, Pound admired the alliterative image of Golding's "scarlet curtaine streynd ageinst a playstred wall" enough to repeat it in Canto 7: "The scarlet curtain throws a less scarlet shadow" (7/25). "Is a fine poet ever translated until another his equal invents a new style in a later language? Can we, for our part, know our Ovid until we find him in Golding?"[61] Similar to his praise of Salel's medieval Homer, Pound praises Golding for revealing how medieval Ovid was: "One wonders, when reading [Golding's book], how much more of the Middle Ages was Ovid. We know well enough that they read him and loved him more than the more Tennysonian Virgil."[62] Golding's sixteenth-century translation allows us to see past the "dovetailing" of Ovid as the true poet of the Middle Ages.

Pound interpolates Atalanta, therefore, because it is a comparison the old men of Troy might make; it is a subject-rhyme for Helen; it draws attention to the "wild" theriomorphic goddess roots of both characters; and it prepares the reader for Pound's technique in the rest of Canto 2: to interpret Homer via Ovid (and Golding); to add "overchange" to the original (and hence make more "medieval"); and to unearth something primordial in the original. This is all the more dizzying considering that the line is Golding's own interpolation into *Metamorphoses* 8.317. When Pound returns to this speech of the old men in Canto 20, now viewed through the delirium of Niccolò III d'Este, he condenses it into Greek, American English, and *Salel's* interpolation: "Under the battlement / (Epi purgo) peur de la hasle," and "Neestho, le'er go back" (20/91) (ἐπὶ πύργῳ, "on the wall"; νεέσθω, "let her go" [*Iliad* 3.153, 159]). Salel's interpolation is an "overchange" of Homer that becomes part of Pound's *Iliad*.

[59] *LE*, 235.

[60] Ovid, *Metamorphoses*, ed. Hugo Magnus (Gotha, Germany: Friedr. Andr. Perthes,1892), 10.594–96.

[61] *LE*, 235.

[62] *LE*, 235.

Tyro: Homer on Color

In the *Iliad,* Priam asks Helen at the Skaian gates to catalogue the qualities of the most famous Achaean warriors. This teichoscopy, or "viewing from the walls" of *Iliad* 3.178–243, can be read as an epic convention: by the tenth year of the war, the Trojans would probably be able to identify Agamemnon, Ajax, and Idomeneus. Earlier in book 3, however, Menelaus and Paris decide to try to settle the dispute over Helen by single combat. Why would they wait nine years to think of that solution? In *The Rise of the Greek Epic*, Gilbert Murray argues that these episodes were interpolated from another Homeric poem about the beginning of the Trojan war.[63] It seems fitting, therefore, that Pound interpolates a much older catalogue in place of Helen's: the catalogue of heroines from *Odyssey* 11. In Harrison's words: "In Homer the hero is the strong man *alive,* mighty in battle; in cultus the hero is the strong man *after death,* dowered with a greater, because a ghostly, strength."[64] Helen's teichoscopy celebrates the new male Homeric hero ("Yon man is the son of Atreus, wide-ruling Agamemnon, that is both a noble king and a valiant spearman"[65]); the catalogue of heroines celebrates the old female heroes of the cult of the dead. "And the women came, for august Persephone sent them forth, even all those that had been the wives and the daughters of chieftains" (*Odyssey* 11.225–27). Like Atalanta, Tyro is a much older heroine than either Helen or Penelope.[66] The catalogue of heroines also reflects Homer at his most "Ovidian." It is a "compendium" of tales of women impregnated by gods, which often involves a transformation of some sort: Tyro, Antiope, Alcmene, Megara, Epicaste (Jocasta), Chloris, Leda, Iphimedeia, Phaedra, Procris, Ariadne, Clymene, Maere, and Eriplye. All of these women figure more prominently in Ovid's *oeuvre* except for Jocasta and the very obscure Maere.

According to Homer, Tyro was a Thessalian princess who was married to Cretheus but became enamored with the river god Enipeus. He refused her advances, but Poseidon, full of lust, disguised himself as Enipeus and impregnated her.

> Then verily the first that I saw was high-born Tyro, who said that she was the daughter of noble Salmoneus, and declared herself to be the wife of Cretheus,

[63] Murray, *The Rise of the Greek Epic,* 201–7.
[64] Harrison, *Prolegomena,* 333.
[65] *Iliad* 3.178–9.
[66] With empty rhetoric, the suitor Antinous claims that "even the braided girls of ancient Greece, Tyro, Alcmene, garlanded Mycene—none of them had Penelope's understanding" (*Odyssey* 2.120).

> son of Aeolus. She became enamored of the river, divine Enipeus, who is far the fairest of rivers that send forth their streams upon the earth, and she was wont to resort to the fair waters of Enipeus. But the Enfolder and Shaker of the earth took his form, and lay with her at the mouths of the eddying [δινήεντος, *dinēentos*] river. And the dark [πορφύρεον, *porphyreon*] wave stood about them like a mountain, vaulted-over [οὔρεϊ… κυρτωθέν, *ourei… kyrtōthen*, "vaulted mountain"], and hid the god and the mortal woman. And he loosed her maiden girdle, and shed sleep upon her. (11.235–45)

Pound's interest in Tyro's story is the "magic instant" when Poseidon transforms into a river and tents her body as a wave. Pound's translation reprises the alliterative style of Canto 1, combining elements of the tenth-century Old English poem, *The Wanderer*, with the landscape near Chios.

And by the beach-run, Tyro,
        Twisted arms of the sea-god,
Lithe sinews of water, gripping her, cross-hold,
And the blue-gray glass of the wave tents them,
Glare azure of water, cold-welter, close cover.
Quiet sun-tawny sand-stretch,
The gulls broad out their wings,
        nipping between the splay feathers;
Snipe come for their bath,
        bend out their wing-joints,
Spread wet wings to the sun-film,
And by Scios,
        to left of the Naxos passage,
Naviform rock overgrown,
        algæ cling to its edge,
There is a wine-red glow in the shallows,
        a tin flash in the sun-dazzle. (2/6–7)

The detail of the fallow waves and sea birds preening themselves are amplified from *The Wanderer,* Pound explains to Ford Mardox Ford.[67] The alliterative style of the translation ("Quiet sun-tawny sand-stretch"; "spread wet wings to the sun-film") as well as the numerous yoked words ("beach-run," "sea-god," "cross-hold," "blue-grey," "cold-welter," etc.) continues the

[67] "Then the friendless man awakes again and sees before him the grey waves—sees the sea-birds bathing and spreading their wings." *The Wanderer,* in *Anglo-Saxon and Norse Poems,* ed. and trans. Nora Kershaw (Cambridge: Cambridge University Press, 1922), lines 45–7. See Ezra Pound, Letter to Ford Madox Ford, March 21, 1922 in *Pound/Ford,* 65.

Anglo-Saxon translation Homer of Canto 1 and the nekyia. ("Canto III" is more explicit: "Then he had news of many famous women, / Tyro, Alcmena, Chloris, / Heard out their tales by that dark fosse."[68]) The River Enipeus is in Thessaly; but Pound's transitional line, "and by Scios," reminds the reader that all Homeric locations, be they Troy or Thessaly, originate in Chios, the mythical landscape of Homer.

Pound's translation is overabundant with images of light and color: Tyro is tented by the blue-grey glassy water which has an azure glare; the sand is tawny by the sun; the wet wings of snipe catch the sun's rays; by Scios the shallows glow red like wine; a fish flashes like tin under the sun's dazzle. By repeatedly describing the water that tents Tyro, Pound searches for a precise translation of the notoriously difficult Homeric color-word, πορφύρεον, *porphyreon*, sometimes translated as "purple," "dark," or even "surging," and which Pound renders as "blue-gray" and "glare azure." The word is connected to Homer's famous epithet for the sea, οἶνοψ, *oinops*, "wine-red" or "wine-dark," here translated as "a wine-red glow." When Pound repeats the story of Tyro near the end of Canto 2; he redoubles his efforts to translate πορφύρεον and οἶνοψ:

Lithe turning of water,
        sinews of Poseidon,
Black azure and hyaline,
        glass wave over Tyro,
Close cover, unstillness,
        bright welter of wave-cords,
Then quiet water,
        quiet in the buff sands,
Sea-fowl stretching wing-joints,
        splashing in rock-hollows and sand-hollows
In the wave-runs by the half-dune;
Glass-glint of wave in the tide-rips against sunlight,
        pallor of Hesperus,
Grey peak of the wave,
        wave, color of grape's pulp,
Olive grey in the near,
        far, smoke grey of the rock-slide,
Salmon-pink wings of the fish-hawk
        cast grey shadows in water. (2/9–10)

[68] *PT*, 320.

Pound works through different ways of representing *porphyreon* while recreating a magical metamorphosis that recurs with the ebb and flow of the waves. Pound focuses on the shifting of color; the play of light and darkness; and continuous metamorphosis; all the while pushing language to its limit: "black azure and hyaline" (azure is bright blue, not black; hyaline means translucent); "bright welter"; "quiet water" covering "buff sands"; "glass-glint"; "pallor of Hesperus" (recalling "pallor upon me" from Canto 1); "grey peak of wave"; "wave, color of grape's pulp"; "olive grey"; "smoke grey"; and the "salmon-pink wings of the fish-hawk / cast grey shadows in water" (recalling Golding's "scarlet curtaine streynd ageinst a playstred wall"). The effort to capture the magical union of Tyro with the wave is also an effort to render a difficult Greek word into English, as well as to ground Homer's puzzling color words back onto the natural world of Chios, similar to how Pound had attempted, in his abandoned *A Walking Tour in Southern France* (1912), to uncover the meaning of medieval troubadour poetry like that of Bertran de Born by "reading" Bertran's landscape. Translation is philology is metamorphosis.

Pound discussed the translation of Homeric colors in detail with Rouse in 1935. For *oinops,* Rouse suggests "wine-flush almost wine-blush" and "wide-ruddy [like] claret." "I think purple is the least offensive so far but I don't like it. The cows are also ὄινοψ / (sherry?-) brown."[69] Pound also probably knew William Gladstone's three-volume *Studies of Homer and the Homeric Age* (1858). Gladstone served as prime minister to Great Britain on four separate occasions, and represented the old Victorian ways to most modernists. As Mauberly puts it, "Gladstone was still respected, / When John Ruskin produced / 'Kings' Treasuries.'"[70] However, his book was well known for its careful analysis of Homeric colors, which are confusing to most readers. Homer uses *porphyreos* to describe blood, dark clouds, a wave of a river or sea when disturbed, a darkening sea, a rainbow, the mind brooding, and death.[71] The word κύανος (*kyanos*), or "indigo," can refer to coppery and ruddy breastplates, the beard of Odysseus, or the light-brown color of sea sand "when it has just been left by the wave."[72] The word γλαυκός, *glaukos* ("white") can refer to Minerva, the eye of a lion in wrath, and the flashing of the sea. Gladstone argues that "Homeric colors are really the modes and forms of light, and of its opposite or rather negative, darkness."[73] For

[69] W. H. D. Rouse, 1935 Letter to Ezra Pound. *EPP,* 1958.

[70] *PT*, 552.

[71] William Gladstone, *Studies on Homer and the Homeric Age*, vol. 3 (London: Oxford University Press, 1858), 461–2.

[72] Gladstone, *Studies on Homer and the Homeric Age*, 464.

[73] Gladstone, *Studies on Homer and the Homeric Age*, 489.

example, οἶνοψ, *oinops*, the word for wine, was at times accompanied by ἐρυθρὸς, *erythros* ("ruddy") and μέλας, *melas* ("black") both connoting darkness, but most often by αἴθοψ, *aithops*: "this word, which fluctuates between the ideas of flame and smoke, either means tawny, or else refers to light, and not to color, and bears the sense of sparkling."[74]

Almost all of Pound's attempts to translate Homer's color words involve light. Instead of "wine-red," he chooses "wine-red glow"; instead of "purple" or "dark," he chooses "glare azure." In Canto 102, Pound compares the "bitch-eyes" of Helen to the "copper and wine" of Atalanta's bear cub eyes "in sunlight":

> the color as *aithiops*
> the gloss probably
> *oinops*
> as lacquer in sunlight
> haliporphuros,
> russet-gold
> in the air, extant, nor carmine, not flame, oriXalko (102/750)

"*Aithops* seems to be applied to dark objects, but commonly to such dark or dull objects as are capable of brightness by reflecting light," Gladstone writes in "The Color Sense."[75] Hence Pound's "lacquer in sunlight." Pound also links "haliporphuros" ("sea-purple," "sea-dark") with "russet-gold." "Gold with Homer always belongs to light rather than to color," Gladstone explains, a succinct explication of Pound's own line, "In the gloom, the gold gathers the light against it" (11/51).[76] The difficult word, ορείχαλκος, *oreichalkos*, comes from ὄρος (*oros*), "mountain" and χαλκός (*chalkos*) meaning "copper" or "bronze." It may have referred to platinum. Pound uses the word in its medieval Latin form in Canto 1: "mirthful, orichalchi, with golden / Girdles and breast bands," referring to golden Aphrodite (1/5). Here he imagines it forming "in the air," somewhere between the color carmine and a flame.

Although the organ of color was "partially developed" among the Greeks of the heroic age, Gladstone argues, Homer's color words are more sophisticated than ours today.

> His iron-grey, his ruddy, his starry heaven, are so many modes of light. His wine-colored oxen and sea, his violet sheep, his things tawny, purple, sooty, and the rest, give us in fact a rich vocabulary of words for describing what is dark so

[74] Gladstone, *Studies on Homer and the Homeric Age*, 472.
[75] William Gladstone, "The Color-Sense," *The Nineteenth Century* 2.8 (1877): 377.
[76] Gladstone, *Studies on Homer and the Homeric Age*, 482.

> far as it has color, but what also varies between dull and bright, according to the quantity of light playing upon it. Here (for example) is the link between his αἴθοψ κάπμος [*aithops kapmos*, "dark smoke"] and αἴθοψ οἶνος [*aithops onios*, "dark wine"].[77]

While it's tempting to read the recurring visions of Tyro in Canto 2 as merely an imagistic incantation or a cubist re-assemblage, it's more accurately a series of attempts to translate *Odyssey* 11.243–44: the instant when Poseidon as a πορφύρεον wave embraces Tyro. Pound's translations or glosses of the word πορφύρεον undulate and connect with οἶνοψ and αἴθοψ: "blue-grey"; "glare azure"; "sun-tawny"; "wine-red glow"; "tin flash"; "sun-dazzle"; "black azure"; "hyaline"; "glass-glint"; "pallor of Hesperus"; "grey"; "color of grape's pulp"; "olive grey"; and "smoke-grey." Why translate it once when fifteen times will do? Homer's metamorphoses of color and light surge and recede along the beach run.

And I Worship

The Tyro scene bookends the main narrative of Canto 2, a loose translation of *Metamorphosis* 3.580–733, in which Acoetes recounts to Pentheus how a group of mariners picked up the young god Bacchus on Chios, "a young boy loggy with vine-must," tried to kidnap him, and were transformed into dolphins. Poseidon's "lithe sinews of water" that hold Tyro and the "close cover" of the stilled wave metamorphose into Bacchus's phantasmagoria of wild animals: "lifeless air become sinewed"; "beasts like shadows in glass"; and the ship stilled in the water, its "ribs stuck fast in the waves" (2/8). Pound amplifies a few lines from Ovid describing the "magic instant" of metamorphoses into a sacred disorder leading to Acoetes's revelation: "And I worship. / I have seen what I have seen" (2/9). Like Canto 1, Pound turns Acoetes's description of the miracle into a ritual reenactment of it.

Arthur Golding's translation of the section in Ovid is mostly inaccurate and distracting, and does not seem to have influenced Pound's translation. Here is Brookes More's mostly literal translation from 1922:

> The ship stood still
> as if a dry dock held it in the sea.—

[77] Gladstone, *Studies on Homer and the Homeric Age*, 490.

The wondering sailors labored at the oars,
and they unfurled the sails, in hopes to gain
some headway, with redoubled energies;
but twisting ivy tangled in the oars,
and interlacing held them by its weight.
And Bacchus in the midst of all stood crowned
with chaplets of grape-leaves, and shook a lance
covered with twisted fronds of leafy vines.
Around him crouched [*iacent*] the visionary forms [*inania simulacraque*]
of tigers, lynxes, and the mottled shapes [*fera corpora*]
of panthers.[78]

"Visionary forms" is not quite right. Ovid describes how tigers, the *inania* ("empty," "unreal") *simulacraque* ("likenesses," "images") of lynxes, and the *fera corpora* ("feral bodies") of panthers were cast [*iacent*] about him. In Pound this becomes "void air taking pelt" (2/8). He amplifies Ovid's two-line description into twenty-two lines (or thirteen, if indented lines are read as continuations of the previous line).

And, out of nothing, a breathing,
        hot breath on my ankles,
Beasts like shadows in glass,
        a furred tail upon nothingness.
Lynx-purr, and heathery smell of beasts,
        where tar smell had been,
Sniff and pad-foot of beasts,
        eye-glitter out of black air.
The sky overshot, dry, with no tempest,
Sniff and pad-foot of beasts,
        fur brushing my knee-skin,
Rustle of airy sheaths,
        dry forms in the *æther*.
And the ship like a keel in ship-yard,
        slung like an ox in smith's sling,
Ribs stuck fast in the ways,
        grape-cluster over pin-rack,
        void air taking pelt.
Lifeless air become sinewed,
        feline leisure of panthers,

[78] Ovid, the *Metamorphoses*, trans. Brookes More (Boston: Cornhill Publishing Co., 1922), 3.658–67.

Leopards sniffing the grape shoots by scupper-hole,
Crouched panthers by fore-hatch,
And the sea blue-deep about us,
        green-ruddy in shadows (2/8)

Pound's animals are not only seen but heard, smelled, and felt. They crowd Acoetes's senses like the dead who rush out of the fosse towards Odysseus. The transformation happens "out of nothing": Acoetes feels a breath on his ankle; "beasts like shadows in glass" emerge, recalling "the blue-gray glass of the wave" that tents Tyro; a furred tail appears; a lynx purrs; there is a "heathery smell"; he hears the sound of "sniff and pad-foot"; and sees an "eye glitter out of black air." The presentation is disordered, fragmentary, even chaotic, but these animals are hardly menacing. The leopards have a "feline leisure"; the panthers are "sniffing the grape shoots by scupper-hole"; recalling the bathing snipe spreading their wet wings in the sun. The "rustle of airy sheaths" recalls the cicada-like sound of the old men's voices heard in the sea-surge. "And the sea blue-deep about us, / green-ruddy in shadows" suggests that the whole scene is being conjured by a poet observing seawater change color. Pound emphasizes wonder rather than terror.

Ford Madox Ford objected to Pound's use of compound or yoked words in an earlier draft of Canto 2, particularly "slung oxen"; "pulling seas"; "spray-whited"; and "cord-welter."

> My dislike for them may be my merely personal distaste for Anglo-Saxon locutions which always affect me with nausea & yr. purpose in using them may be the purely aesthetic one of roughening up yr. surface. I mean that, if you shd. cut them out you might well get too slick an effect.[79]

Pound cut all of them but "cord-welter" and improved "slung oxen" to "slung like an ox in smith's sling." However, he reiterated Ford's insight that the poem could not have "too slick an effect." "I tried a smoother presentation and lost the metamorphosis, got to be a hurley burley, or no one believes in the change of the ship. Hence mess of tails, feet, etc."[80]

In Ovid's version, the animal simulacra are mainly a device to terrify the pirates into jumping off the ship and turning into dolphins. Ovid's source is Hymn 7 to Dionysus, in which the animals are especially vicious:

> But the god changed into a dreadful lion there on the ship, in the bows, and roared loudly: amidships also he showed his wonders and created a shaggy bear

[79] Ford Madox Ford, January 21, 1922 Letter to Ezra Pound. *Pound/Ford*, 64.
[80] Ezra Pound, March 21, 1922 Letter to Ford Madox Ford. *Pound/Ford*, 65.

> which stood up ravening, while on the forepeak was the lion glaring fiercely with scowling brows. And so the sailors fled into the stern and crowded bemused about the right-minded helmsman, until suddenly the lion sprang upon the master and seized him; and when the sailors saw it they leapt out overboard one and all into the bright sea, escaping from a miserable fate, and were changed into dolphins.[81]

Here, Dionysus's furred beasts are agents of divine justice. Pound "tames" the animals, transforming it into a kind of celebration of Dionysus's powers of transformation, an intense experience of the "hurley burley" or sacred disorder. To witness Dionysus's miracles is to become an initiate of his mysteries. The goal of the ideal reader is the same as the ideal observer, Acoetes: "And I worship. / I have seen what I have seen" (2/9).

Harrison's reading of Dionysus as a primitive god of metamorphosis in connection to Eros and Orpheus illuminates Pound's treatment of Dionysus in Canto 2, as well as Pound's obsession with the "cult of Amor" and Orphism. Homer's Olympians, Harrison argues,

> are not one with the life that is in beasts and streams and woods as well as in man. Eros, "whose feet are in the flowers," who "couches in the folds," is of all life, he is Dionysos, he is Pan. Under Athenian influence Eros secludes himself into purely human form, but the Phanes of Orpheus was polymorphic, a beast-mystery-god:
>
> Heads had he many,
> Head of a ram, a bull, a snake, and a bright-eyed lion.
>
> He is like Dionysos, to whom his Bacchants cry:
>
> Appear, appear, whatso thy shape or name,
> O Mountain Bull, Snake of the Hundred Heads,
> Lion of the Burning Flame!
> O God, Beast, Mystery, come!
>
> In theology as in ritual Orphism reverted to the more primitive forms, lending them deeper and intenser significance. These primitive forms, shifting and inchoate, were material more malleable than the articulate accomplished figures of the Olympians.[82]

81 "Hymn 7 to Dionysus," trans. Hugh G. Evelyn-White, *Hesiod, Homeric Hymns, and Homerica*, lines 45–52.

82 Harrison, *Prolegomena*, 650. The first quotation is from Proclus's *Commentary on Plato's Timaeus*, vol. 2 [130B]. The second is Euripides, *Bacchae*, line 1017–20.

The Cantos rejects the anthropomorphic Olympians for the theriomorphic, phytomorphic, and petromorphic gods of Orphism, of "wood alive and stone alive." Not only *is* Dionysus his cortege of lynxes, panthers, and leopards, but also he is the disordered, half-blind, fragmentary images and impressions of these beasts. He is a mess of "primitive" forms, "shifting and ichoate" that lead to the personal revelation of his mystery.

Accepting the incoherent, the changing, and the fragmentary as the source of divine revelation is the goal of Pound's poetics, which creates a syntax that is "shifting and inchoate." A reader of *The Cantos* might be frustrated at the way Pound refuses specificity (and coherence) in such a specific, erudite, and nuanced way. Just as Canto 1 took Homer's narrative and turned it back into a ritual of the dead, so Pound's treatment of Ovid wants to return to the source as a recreation of Dionysian worship. In Ovid, Acoetes recounts his story to king Pentheus in order to warn him not to stop the women from worshiping him. Despite a few lines reminding us of this fact, "And you, Pentheus, / Had as well listen to Tiresias, and to Cadmus, / or your luck will go out of you," Pound's Acoetes relives or recreates the Dionysian ritual before Pentheus (2/9). In the *Metamorphoses,* the recurring moral is that one should learn from stories and never defy the gods. Pentheus is a bad listener; he disastrously fails to understand Acoetes's story. In *The Cantos,* the "moral" is that those who hear (and translate) folklore properly discover that all poetry is Dionysian ritual, and thereby resurrect the gods. Poetry is a direct means to worship. In Nietzsche's words: "Yes, my friends, believe as I do in Dionysiac life and in the rebirth of tragedy. The time of Socratic man is past. Put on wreaths of ivy, take up the *thyrsus* and do not be surprised if tigers and panthers lie down, purring and curling round your legs."[83] Or as Pound puts it in "Salutation the Second" (1913): "Go! rejuvenate things!"[84] "Dance and make people blush, / Dance the dance of the phallus."

Proteus

Canto 2 sets the stage for the more involved "recreations" of Dionysian (and Orphic) ritual explored throughout *The Cantos,* from the procession of Dionysus Zagreus in Canto 17 to Canto 21 to a celebration of the rites of Circe in Cantos 39 and 47 to the many recreations of his worship in *The Pisan Cantos*. At the

[83] Nietzsche, *The Birth of Tragedy,* 98.
[84] *PT,* 266.

same time, Canto 2 grounds all of its poetry, from the vision of Helen on the battlements, to the ravishment of Tyro by Poseidon, to the transformation of the mariners, in the natural world that the mythical Homer might have seen. Meaningful ritual begins with the mysteries of nature. Pound's translation of Ovid concludes with a reminder that this happened long before Troy and Canto 1, when Tiresias was still among the living. Pound then describes mythic and natural transformations that Homer or anyone might observe by any shore:

> And you, Pentheus,
> Had as well listen to Tiresias, and to Cadmus,
> or your luck will go out of you.
> Fish-scales over groin muscles,
> lynx-purr amid sea...
> And of a later year,
> pale in the wine-red algæ,
> If you will lean over the rock,
> the coral face under wave-tinge,
> Rose-paleness under water-shift,
> Ileuthyeria, fair Dafne of sea-bords,
> The swimmer's arms turned to branches,
> Who will say in what year,
> fleeing what band of tritons,
> The smooth brows, seen, and half seen,
> now ivory stillness. (2/9)

The "you" addressed in the second half here does not seem to be Pentheus of a few lines earlier, but the general reader. Acoetes (or Pound himself) is now decisively vague about what story is being told: the sailors becoming dolphins (or porpoises, or dories); a goddess of childbirth (Eileithyria) or a marine organism of the genus of bisexual jellyfishes (Eleutheria); Daphne becoming laurel; or Medusa's head turning the reeds into coral. The emphasis is not on any particular metamorphosis but the ability of the narrator (the initiate of Dionysus's mysteries) and (hopefully) the reader to witness divinity in nature by leaning over a rock and seeing the rose-paleness of the coral. At the primordial level, as Harrison points out, Eros is Dionysus is Pan is Orpheus are the Phanes. It does not matter "in what year" or "fleeing what band of tritons."

Canto 2 concludes by reinforcing the miracle of the changing sea as the original conjurer of mythologies of transformation:

> And we have heard the fauns chiding Proteus
> in the smell of hay under the olive-trees,
> And the frogs singing against the fauns
> in the half-light. (2/10)

The line recalls the end of "The Love Song of J. Alfred Prufrock," "I have heard the mermaids singing, each to each. / I do not think that they will sing to me."[85] But Pound's fauns do sing to us. The "we" here suggests that the bard has become collective: it is no longer just the mythical Homer but the Homeridae, and Acoetes, and Ovid, and Pound. Pound asserts that the old gods and their religions still exist to poets, however synaeasthetically: we hear the fauns chiding Proteus in the smell of (or perhaps while also smelling) hay under olive trees and the sound of the frogs singing against the fauns. Pseudo-Apollodorus recounts that the Egyptian king Proteus was the first to welcome Dionysus in his wanderings in Egypt.[86] But the more specific reference is to the sea god Proteus, the epitome of the shape-shifting primitive god. Homer recounts how Menelaus holds down Proteus in Pharos, near the Nile Delta, in order to learn how to get home. "At the first he turned into a bearded lion, and then into a serpent, and a leopard, and a huge boar; then he turned into flowing water, and into a tree, high and leafy" (*Odyssey* 4.454–59). Proteus's myriad transformations reflect Pound's Homeric *translatio* in Canto 2. There is no particular reason why a group of young satyrs (fauns) chide Proteus, nor who these ("the") fauns are; but fauns are associated with maenads or followers of Dionysus. The image conjures a blending of real and mythological elements with beautiful sounds, invoking the green language of Homeric "lyric."

The "frogs singing against the fauns / in the half-light" alludes to Aristophanes's *Frogs* in which Dionysus, disguised as a lion, descends to Hades in search of a good poet, a subject rhyme with Odysseus's nekyia in Canto 1, and the structural model of Hope Mirrlees's *Paris*. The choral refrain "Βρεκεκεκὲξ κοὰξ κοάξ" (*Brekekekèx-koàx-koáx*), is as onomatopoetic or melopoetic (Homeric) as Aristophanes gets. *The Frogs* is also known for its hemichant, in which one part of the chorus (the frogs) is set against the other (the Dionysian mystics, who could be fauns). Pound described his 1908 poem, "Salve O Pontifex" [Hail, High Priest] a praise of Dionysus, as "an hemichaunt."[87] The poem praises Iacchus

85 T. S. Eliot, *The Poms of T. S. Eliot*, vol. 1, ed. Christopher Ricks and Jim McCue (New York: Farrar, Straus and Giroux, 2018), 9.

86 Apollodurus, *The Library*, vol. 1, trans. James Frazer (Cambridge, MA: Harvard University Press, 1921), 2.29.

87 *PT*, 50.

(Dionysus) as the "master of initiating / Maenads," and the creator of "entangled music that men may not / Over readily understand."[88] It ends with the image of Dionysus standing on the sea: "And becoming wave / Shalt encircle all sands, / Being transmuted thru all / The girdling of the sea."[89] Pound's primordial world is accessible to the ear attuned to the singing of chorus frogs, the nose attuned to the smell of cut hay, the eye attuned to the protean colors of the sea in the half light.

Canto 2 translates the Homeric text back to its primordial state as an Ovidian "compendium" of folklore and "lived philology" of the landscape near Chios. Pound "brings Dionysus back" into Homer by means of Ovid, the divine young god "loggy with vine-must," "lord of all that is wet and gleaming" as Harrison describes him.[90] Dionysus, who boards the ship in Chios, ultimately becomes the "original" or mythic Homer, unconstrained within Pisistratus's epic structure, whose powers of chaos and transformation overwhelm the narrative into ritual celebration. Acoetes, the ideal reader of Homer, and stand-in for Pound, witnesses the miracle of nature and devoutly believes, becoming a bard himself of the secondary epic and retelling the story in its most primordial and fragmentary form.

The structure of Canto 2 seems chaotic and haphazard, but eventually reveals itself as deliberate and complex. Canto 2 ruptures the linear "epic" plot of Odysseus's narrative which is established in Canto 1. Canto 2 "pauses" the action to tell a much older story from Homer's Catalogue of Women. Pound "stalls" the action further by translating the Tyro story twice while weaving into it the (even older) story of Dionysus, creating an endless (or endlessly deferred) catalogue of heroines: a "carmen perpetuum." Odysseus does not leave Erebus. His ship is "stuck fast in the ways." Read in the light of Canto 1, Canto 2 represents what Odysseus really "learns" in his journey to Erebus: the primordial, chthonic, "feminine" knowledge of Tyro's transformation, and the initiation into a Dionysian mystery. The distinctly Orphic and Eleusinian aspects of Odysseus's nekyia, however, will be fleshed out in the Circe cantos (Cantos 39 and 47).

[88] *PT*, 51, 52.

[89] *PT*, 53.

[90] Harrison, *Ancient Art and Ritual*, 113.

4

The Lotophagoi: Confusion and Renewal

> *"When I consider [Pound's] work as a whole I find more style than form; at moments more style, more deliberate nobility and the means to convey it than in any contemporary poet known to me, but it is constantly interrupted, broken, twisted into nothing by its direct opposite, nervous obsession, nightmare, stammering confusion."*[1]

Pound's treatment of the Lotophagoi or Lotus-eaters in Canto 20 is the most significant return to the narrative action of Homer's *Odyssey* after Cantos 1 and 2. Like Canto 2, Canto 20 begins by conjuring the melopoeia of the mythical blind Homer. It then recounts the poet's pilgrimage to Cologne to meet with Emil Levy, a German philologist, in order to decipher musical notations from a fourteenth-century manuscript of Arnaut Daniel and discover the meaning of the hapax legomenon "noigandres." It introduces a new Pound hero, Niccolò III d'Este, who suffers a delirious breakdown after beheading his son Ugo and ruminates on *Le Chanson de Roland,* the *Iliad,* and Lope de Vega's *Las almenas de Toro.* His delirium transforms into a vision of the cortege of Dionysus Zagreus through a chthonic paradisal jungle. There, Pound's Lotophagoi mourn for Odysseus's companions who died at sea and condemn Odysseus for not sharing the spiritual fruits of his journey. In earlier drafts, Canto 20 ended with a translation of *Odyssey* 12.1–15, which recounts how Odysseus and his men return to Circe's island and perform funeral rites for Elpenor as instructed by Tiresias in Canto 1.[2]

Structurally, Canto 20 is similar to but more complex than Canto 2. Canto 2 explores three different problems of translation: how to capture Homer's melopoeia and the "actual swing of words spoken"; how to include "overchange"

[1] W. B. Yeats, "Introduction," to *Oxford Book of Modern Verse,* ed. W. B. Yeats (Oxford: Oxford University Press, 1936), xxv.

[2] Pound later cut this section probably so as not to interrupt his transition into Canto 21, which deals with Niccolò's reforms to the government and his patronage of the arts.

or compensate for the deficiencies in the source text; and how to translate Homeric color-words. It culminates in an ideal "Homeric" (Ovidian) translation and Dionysus rite. Similarly, Canto 20 introduces three different problems of translation and interpretation of lyric and epic texts. In each instance, confusion or deadlock leads to insight. Pound first stitches together and confuses lyrics by classical authors into a Babelic polyglossia, recreating a version of the mythical melopoetic language of Homer. This segues into a quest to recover the (lost) music of Arnaut and the meaning of a single Provençal word which describes a flower that "wards off pain." The mock-epic deteriorates into a humorous aporia, but Pound shifts to lyric and deciphers the word by "hearing" Arnaut's music in the natural world. Third, the remorse-crazed Niccolò realizes the arrogance and pride of Roland, the folly of Sancho, the foolishness of the old men who reject Helen's beauty, and (in earlier drafts) the hubris of Odysseus. Niccolò learns that animosity, war, and revenge are evil, and that Eros should never be checked, even if it is illicit. Next, Pound presents Niccolò's (new) vision of paradiso that blends elements of Virgil's underworld and Dante's hell and purgatory; a Bacchic divine "confusion / Basis of renewals" (20/92). The vision culminates in Niccolò/ Pound's critique of the *Odyssey.* The Lotophagoi regard Odysseus's wanderings not as a series of (interesting) impediments to his nostos, but as steps or stages of initiation with primordial spirits and direct observation of the natural world: "the olives under Spartha / With the leaves green and then not green"; the "meats of Kalüpso / Or her silk shirts brushing their thighs"; and the "Ligur' aoide" or clear sweet song of the Sirens (20/94). Their critique of Odysseus's single-minded quest is a critique of epic form. A glimpse of the divine or permanent world is possible only when the teleology of the epic is interrupted or loses its way. Revelation is not for those trying to get somewhere.

While Canto 2 attempts to recreate the "hurley burley" of a Dionysian transformation, the jungle or "wilderness" of confusion in Canto 20 is the "basis of renewal, renewals" (20/91). Canto 20 emphasizes those moments of confusion and emotional collapse which augur a new perspective. Painful longing or desire, (philological) frustration, guilt, delirious madness, and intoxication derail habitual thought and offer the keys to paradise. While the technique of *translatio* in Canto 2 is Protean (interwoven and disordered), Canto 20's technique is best described as confused, aporetic, delirious, intoxicated, and "doped": a necessary stage on the way to insight.

Canto 20's complex structure has been mostly overlooked. From Homer to Tennyson to Gabriele Rossetti, the Lotophagoi are presented as antagonistic figures. In Homer, they are first in a long series of hindrances to Odysseus's homecoming. In Tennyson's "Lotus Eaters," they represent the man's desire to "cease from wanderings" and completely withdraw from life.[3] In Gabrielle Rossetti's four-volume *Il mistero dell' amor platonico del medio evo* (1840), which Pound knew well, they represent the soul's being "stuck" in matter and therefore incapable of transcendence.[4] Perhaps this is why readers of Canto 20 often insist they are "bad" hedonists, despite Pound's letter to his father linking their perspective with "general paradiso," and despite the way Pound foregrounds their insights with Niccolò's own inspired and pacifist re-readings of primary epic. As Leah Flack puts it: "Pound's hedonistic Lotus-eaters voice an anti-heroic opinion—they succumb only to pleasure and refuse pain and harm."[5] Peter Liebregts suggests that they forgo "the vision of divine light" and "unquestionably accept material reality for what it is."[6] Kevin Oderman argues that "Pound derides ascetics and fornicators, and dope fiends, in the Lotophagoi Canto."[7] However, Oderman concedes that their speech is not "an easy one to comprehend," and suggests that Pound gives them genuine insight into Pound's paradise while still condemning them for inaction.[8]

The Lotophagoi are situated in Pound's paradiso, not his inferno with the usurers, popes, and philologists of Cantos 15 and 16. They are not hedonistic. They value the ephemeral and transient miracles of paradiso terrestre that Pound obsessed over his whole life: the sound of the Sirens, or the turning of olive leaves which reveal the correct reading of the epithet *glaukopis*. Niccolò's luminous critique of Roland, King Sancho II of Castile and León, and the old men on the Skaian gates prepares the reader for the Lotophaghoi's critique of Odysseus. Like Niccolò, the "doped" delirium of the Lotophagoi affords them insight. Their condemnation of Odysseus's hubris echoes Pound's own attack of war as the tragic waste of individual potential to build and create rather than destroy and be destroyed from Canto 16, and the tragic exploitation of the common man or "tovarisch" during the failed Russian revolution in Canto 27. Their condemnation also anticipates Circe, who teaches Odysseus the virtue of Hesiodic *aidōs* (humility, reverence) in Canto 47 and Pound's own condemnation of Odysseus in his essay "Hell" (1934) and in Canto 74.

3 Alfred Lord Tennyson, *The Major Works* (New York: Oxford World's Classics, 2000), 51.

4 Gabrielle Rosetti, *Il mistero dell' amor platonico del medio evo*, vol. 1 (London: R. e G.E. Taylor, 1840), 95. See Miyake, *Ezra Pound and the Mysteries of Love*, 111–13.

5 Leah Flack, *Modernism and Homer* (Cambridge: Cambridge University Press, 2015), 54.

6 Peter Liebregts, *Ezra Pound and Neoplatonism* (Madison: Fairleigh Dickinson University Press, 2004), 181.

7 Kevin Oderman, *Ezra Pound and the Erotic Medium* (Durham, NC: Duke University Press, 1986), 38.

8 Oderman, *Ezra Pound and the Erotic Medium*, 107–8.

Quasi Tinnula

The short opening sequence of Canto 20 immerses the reader into a confusing babble of Latin, Greek, Provençal, and Italian, in order to recover the lost melopoeia of Dionysian lyric. Pound achieves this by blending sonorous verses about sound:

> Sound slender, quasi tinnula,
> Ligur' aoide: Si no'us vei, Domna don plus mi cal,
> Negus vezer mon bel pensar no val."
> Between the two almond trees flowering,
> The viel held close to his side;
> And another: s'adora".
> "Possum ego naturae
> non meminisse tuae!" Qui son Properzio ed Ovidio. (20/89)

The synesthesia of "sound slender" gives way to Latin ("quasi tinnula": "as if ringing," adapted from "voce carmina tinnula" or "a high pitched voice," from Catullus, Carmen 61); Greek ("liqur'aoide": "shrill/sharp song," used to describe the Sirens in *Odyssey* 12.183); Provençal ("If I don't see you, Lady for whom I must burn, / Even not seeing you can't match my beautiful thought of you," from Bernart de Ventadorn's "Can par la flors," "When the flower appears"); Italian ("S'adora": "She is adored," from Cavalcanti's sonnet 35); then back to Latin ("can I not remember your nature?" from Sextus Propertius 2.20.28) and Italian ("Here are Propertius and Ovid"). The play of repeating consonants *s, sl, ul, l, u,* then *mn, n, m,* and *al* create a harmony: "Sound slender, quasi tinnula, / Ligur' aoide: Si no'us vei, Domna don plus mi cal, / Negus vezer mon bel pensar no val." The liquid *l*s of Bernart echo in: "Between the two almond trees flowering, / The viel held close to his side."[9]

These verses describe a gathering of poets like the heroes in Elysium. Bernart sings with his viel, a lute-like instrument, accompanied by Cavalcanti (in a word), Propertius, and Ovid. Their flowering invokes the myth of Phyllis, the Thracian princess abandoned by Demothon on his way home from Troy. Phyllis hangs herself and is transformed into an almond tree which flowers whenever Demothon returns.[10] The verses by Bernart, Cavalcanti, and Propertius pine for

[9] Hugh Kenner glosses the percussive aural patterning of this section. See *The Pound Era*, 110–20.

[10] Maurus Servius Honoratus, *Commentary on the Eclogues of Virgil*, ed. Georgius Thilo (Leipzig: B. G. Teubner, 1881), 5.10. The flowering of the almond tree in *The Cantos* invokes, more generally, sexual potency. In Canto 47, "When the almond bough puts forth its flame," Odysseus, as fertility daimon, passes through its "gates" and enters Circe's "cave" (47/239). See chapter 5.

an absent lover. By intermingling lyric fragments about sound (which written words cannot actually recreate) and lovers (which verses cannot actually manifest), Pound draws a parallel between the absent lover and the lost music of the past. This includes the original sound of Bernart's poetry accompanied by the viel, as well as the sound of Cavalcanti, Propertius, and Ovid; the tonal sound of Greek, rather than the stressed Greek of textbooks; the sound of Homer recited at the Panathenaea accompanied by a lyre; the songs of the Homeridae of Chios, or the Dionysian music of the Greek chorus as described by Nietzsche;[11] and the mythical sound of the Sirens, a music so beautiful and intoxicating it threatens to halt the hero's quest.

Polyvocalic confusion is God's punishment for man's ambition in Genesis 11:6–7. Pound's Babelic invocation of this lost sound, by contrast, is meant to heal this confusion, by allowing different languages to "sing" together. It does not mourn the lost music; it aspires to be a new (universal) poetry, revivifying a primordial music by blending lyric fragments of later devotees of the cult of Amor.

Noigandres

Pound's concise invocation of the lost melopoeia of Dionysian lyric transitions into a prolix account of his quest as a graduate student to speak to a German philologist about the (lost) music of Arnaut. The philological quest to uncover anything interesting about Arnaut ends in a humorous aporia.

> And that year I went up to Freiburg,
> And Rennert had said: Nobody, no, nobody
> Knows anything about Provençal, or if there is anybody,
> It's old Lévy."
> And so I went up to Freiberg,
> And the vacation was just beginning,
> The students getting off for the summer,
> Freiburg im Breisgau,
> And everything clean, seeming clean, after Italy.
>
> And I went to old Lévy, and it was by then 6.30
> in the evening, and he trailed halfway across Freiburg

[11] See Nietzsche, *The Birth of Tragedy*, 19–21, 36–40.

> before dinner, to see the two strips of copy,
> Arnaut's, settant'uno R. Superiore (Ambrosiana)
> Not that I could sing him the music. (20/89)

Note the mock-epic weight here. Pound needlessly repeats the action of going up to Freiburg. The word "and" begins almost every clause, which recalls the "Si" ("And") which begins almost every other sentence in French medieval chronicles. Pound goes up to Freiberg because Hugo Rennert, the editor of Old Spanish Romances and Pound's professor at the University of Pennsylvania, suggests he should. Rennert seems to be saying that no one knows more about Provençal than Emil Levy (no accent, Pound possibly confused his surname with the French painter Émile Lévy), the author of a monograph on the obscure troubadour poet Paulet de Marselha, and the eight-volume *Provenzalisches Supplement-Wöterbuch* (1892–1924), itself a supplement of sorts to François Raynouard's *Lexique roman* (1838–44). But what Rennert is actually saying is more banal: nobody really knows anything about Provençal, but if he had to pick someone, it would be old Levy.

Pound wants to show Levy "two strips of copy" from a fourteenth-century manuscript of Arnaut Daniel on which were written staves with square notes that clarified pitch intervals in the second and eighteenth canzo.[12] Pound and Levy examine "settant'uno R. superior (Ambrosiana)": that is, seventy-one R[ecto] superior Ambrosian: that is, manuscript seventy-one in the Ambrosian library, recto (odd-numbered) side. But Pound can't sing him the music, and Levy, who is tired from his long trek across Freiburg and probably thinking about dinner, doesn't have any insights worth reporting. Pound improvises a secondary quest(ion), which also amounts to nothing, but he captures the doddering music of Levy and the casual diffidence of the graduate student with comedic effect:

> And he said: Now is there anything I can tell you?"
> And I said: I dunno, sir, or
> "Yes, Doctor, what do they mean by *noigandres?*"
> And he said: Noigandres! NOIgandres!
> "You know for seex mon's of my life
> "Effery night when I go to bett, I say to myself:
> "Noigandres, eh, *noi*gandres,
> "Now what the DEFFIL can that mean!" (20/89–90)

[12] See Kenner, *The Pound Era*, 113–14.

The question comes to Pound as an afterthought: "I dunno, sir, or / 'Yes, Doctor.'" In an earlier draft, the tone is even more casual: "and I said, I dunno, sir, / eh, oh by the wa[y] Doctor / what do they mean by noigandres."[13] If Levy cannot reveal anything about Arnaut's music, surely he can solve the problem of this hapax legomenon. But Pound would not allow him even that, reinforcing the stereotype presented in his first published essay, "Raphaelite Latin" (1906), of "the Germanic ideal of scholar" engaged "in endless pondering over some utterly unanswerable question of textual criticism, such as [...] 'is a certain word *sica* or *secat*?'"[14] The word has kept old Levy up at night for six months, during which time he could only repeat it with different stresses: "Noigandres! NOIgandres!" "Noigandres, eh *noi*gandres."

The impotence of the philologist is staged. Pound published the final version of Canto 20 in 1930. It recounts a trip he made to Freiberg in 1911. Emil Levy had solved the problem in 1904, a year before Pound began studying with Rennert. "De noigandres" was a scribal error for "d'enoi gandres." "Gandir" means to protect or ward off. "Enoi" is similar to "ennui." The error is noted in Levy's *Provenzalisches Supplement-Wöterbuch*, volume 4 (G-L) of 1904, under the seventh definition of "gandir": "sich entziehen ['escape,' 'evade'], sich weigern ['reject,' 'refuse']."[15] However, Levy never bothered to create a separate entry for "noigandres" in volume 5 (M-0) of 1907 as he did for "gander" ("gandre: sieht *gandir* Schluss ['see *gandir* conclusion']"), despite the fact that it caused him so many sleepless nights. Pound and Rennert couldn't find it. Maybe this is why Pound places philologists among usurers and sodomites in hell, "sitting on piles of stone books, / obscuring the texts with philology" (14/63). Levy solved the problem, but "sat on it," and without a separate entry for "noigandres" his *Wöterbuch* might as well have been made of stone. Levy must have told Pound the answer in 1911, but Canto 20 denies him the victory.

Prior to 1904, *noigandres* was an unanswered philological puzzle. Pound's 1883 edition of Arnaut suggests that "de noigandres" is a corruption of "de notz gandres" and translates, "e l'odore de noce reale," or, "the smell of genuine walnuts/walnut trees."[16] The Occitan "notz" can mean either "nut" or "walnut." This may be why Pound adds almond trees to his Elysium earlier in the canto (Virgil's Elysium is

13 Ezra Pound, "Canto XX: Typescripts." *EPP*, 3189.

14 Ezra Pound, "Raphaelite Latin," in *Ezra Pound's Poetry and Prose: Contributions to Periodicals*, vol. 1, ed. Lea Baechler, A. Walton Litz and James Longenbach (New York: Garland, 1991), 5.

15 Emil Levy, "gandir," in *Provenzalisches Supplement-Wöterbuch*, vol. 4, ed. Emil Levy (Leipzig: O. R. Reisland, 1904), 34.

16 Arnaut Daniel, *La vita e le opere del trovatore Arnaldo Daniello*, ed. U. A. Canello (Halle: Max Niemeyer, 1883), 112.

in an "odoratum larui nemus," or "fragrant laurel grove"[17]), and repeats the line "the smell of that place" in connection to "enoi gandres": "The ranunculæ, and almond, / Boughs set in espalier, / Duccio, Agostino; *e l'olors*— / The smell of that place—*d'enoi ganres*" (20/90). Réne Lavaud's 1910 critical reedition of Arnaut based on Canello amends the line from to "de notz gandres" to "d'enoi gandres" based on Levy's findings. In the notes, however, Lavaud argues that it must be the first meaning of "gandir"—not "banishes" as Levy argues—but "protects or preserves." Lavaud's translation: "et son parfum Préservation d'Ennui."[18]

Pound probably emended his 1883 edition of Canello based on what Levy told him in 1911, but he might also have checked Lavaud's 1910 edition. In 1920, Pound translates the stanza with the obscure word "ameises" as though pointing back to its complex textual history.

Er vei vermeills, vertz, blaus, blancs, gruocs,
Vergiers, plans, plais, tertres e vaus,
E'il votz dels auzels sona e tint
Ab doutz acort maitin e tart:
So'm met en cor q'ieu colore mon chan
D'un'aital flor don lo fruitz sia amors,
E jois lo grans, e l'olors d'enoi gandres.[19]

Pound's translation:

Vermeil, green, blue, peirs, white, cobalt.
Close orchards, hewis, holts, hows, vales.
And the bird-song that whirls and turns
Morning and late with sweet accord.
Bestir my heart to put my song in sheen,
T'equal that flower which hath such properties,
It seeds in joy, bears love, and pain ameises.

It is not clear why Pound adds the word "peires" to Arnaut's list of five colors, or what it means. "Pèira" means "stone" in Occitan. Equally curious is Pound's translation of "plans, plais, tertres" ("plains, bushes, buttes") as "hewis, holts, hows." "Hewis" might derive from Middle English, "hewen," "to hew" or "chop." A "holt" is a wood or wooded hill, neither a bush nor a butte. "Hough" or "houe" is Middle English for "heel," "hamstring," or "crook of the knee." But the most

[17] *Aeneid* 6.658.
[18] Réne Lavaud, *Les Poèsies d'Arnaut Daniel* (Toulouse: Édouard Privat, 1910), 81.
[19] *LE*, 139.

unusual word is "ameises." A reader might recognize the German word for ant, "Ameise," which could make the verb, "ameisen": to "ant" or "lessen." But there is no such verb. The German word derives from Old High German "āmeiza" ("to cut off or away"); from which is derived the Middle English "amte" ("ant"). More likely, Pound was thinking of the Greek ἀμύνω (*amynō*), meaning "to keep off," "ward off," or "protect from." Homer uses the word frequently, twice in connection with the absent Odysseus being unable to ward off ruin from his house.[20]

None of this is in Canto 20, but it helps to contextualize the lines that follow. The philologer goes silent. Through an invocation of the nature around Freiberg, Italy, and the south of France, Pound discovers the proper translation.

> "Noigandres, eh *noi*gandres,
> "Now what the DEFFIL can that mean!"
> Wind over the olive trees, ranunculae [*sic*] ordered,
> By the clear edge of the rocks
> The water runs, and the wind scented with pine
> And with hay-fields under sun-swath.
> Agostino, Jacopo, and Boccata.
> You would be happy for the smell of that place
> And never tired of being there, either alone
> Or accompanied.
> Sound: as of the nightingale too far off to be heard.
> Sandro, and Boccata, and Jacopo Sellaio;
> The ranunculæ [*sic*], and almond,
> Boughs set in espalier,
> Duccio, Agostino; *e l'olors—*
> The smell of that place — *d'enoi ganres.*
> Air moving under the boughs,
> The cedars there in the sun,
> Hay new cut on hill slope,
> And the water there in the cut
> Between the two lower meadows; sound,
> The sound, as I have said, a nightingale
> Too far off to be heard. (20/90)

The scene shifts from Frieberg to Périgord, the landscape of Arnaut. The invocation is casual, unpolished, and repetitive ("the smell of that place"; "as I have said") almost as though one were reading a poet's notebook or listening

[20] *Odyssey* 1.69–71, 17.538.

to an impromptu invocation. Pound opts for repetition and refrain rather than development of the image. An ordered landscape is invoked in a disordered way. More attention is paid to sound and smell than the visual: wind over olive trees, water running, scented wind, sound of absent nightingale, smell of the place, air moving under boughs, and smell of new cut hay. Pound almost lazily repeats a list of Italian painters, as if to say: have a look at some of their landscapes, if you need a visual reference. Perhaps the symmetrical garden in Botticelli's *Primavera,* where the trees form a broken arch to draw the eye to Venus.

This section recalls the Elysium invoked at the beginning of Canto 20: the Italy of Ovid, Propertius, and Cavalcanti, as painted by Agostino Tassi, who sculpted the bas-reliefs of Sigismundo des Malatesta's temple, Jacopo Sellaio, Sandro Botticelli, and Giovanni Boccatti; and the Périgord of Bertran and Arnaut. Suddenly, the land reveals the answer to the puzzle: the type of insight Pound searches for in his abandoned *A Walking Tour in Southern France* (1912), and in "Near Périgord" and "Provincia Deserta" (1915). In "The Normal Opportunity of the Provençal Troubadour," Pound states:

> There are three ways of "going back," of feeling as well as knowing about the troubadours, first, by way of the music, second, by way of the land, third, by way of the books themselves, for a manuscript on vellum has a sort of life and personality which no work of the press attains. The Ambrosian library

Figure 4.1 Sandro Botticelli's *La Primavera* (*c.* 1482), Uffizi Gallery, Florence.

> possesses a MS (R71 superiores), a thoroughbred, with clearly written words and music, which contains the extant tunes of Arnaut Daniel.[21]

Thanks to old Levy, neither the way of the book nor the way of the music leads back. But by smelling the new cut hay and wind scented with pine, by observing the espaliers, and by listening to the water in the cut and the nightingale too far off to be heard, "de noigandres" separates into "d'enoi gandres." The poet hears the voice of nature, as Arnaut once did.

Traditionally, the mythical language of the birds is known only by prophets like Tiresias. In medieval France, "la langue des oiseaux" referred to the secret language of the troubadours, which was often based on puns. Pound's repeated invocation of the sound of a nightingale too far off to be heard invokes the tradition of Arnaut as both prophetic and an initiate of the mysteries of Eleusis. The line also inverts Keats's famous reading of the nightingale. The sound of the nightingale wrests Keats from the "dull opiate" of everyday life, "the weariness, the fever, and the fret."[22] He longs for "a vintage," "that hath been / Cool'd a long age in the deep-delved earth" and that will taste of "dance, and Provençal song, and sunburnt mirth." But the sound quickly fades:

> Past the near meadows, over the still stream,
> Up the hill-side; and now 'tis buried deep
> In the next valley-glades:
> Was it a vision, or a waking dream?
> Fled is that music:—Do I wake or sleep?

For Pound, by contrast, it is the sound of the paradoxically absent nightingale in Périgord that resurrects dance, Provençal song, and the ancient mysteries. One also can't help but compare Keats's polished lyrical diction and meter with Pound's casual or "primitive" lyrical free verse. In the later half of Canto 20, opium and fever are not the dull features of ordinary life, but recreate the confusion and self-annihilation that leads to revelation and renewal.

Dante affords Arnaut, the better craftsman, the privilege of speaking in his native Provencal in *Purgatorio* 26. Earlier in Canto 20, Pound takes this a step further, not just by letting Homer, Catullus, Propertius, Cavalcanti, Bernart, and Dante speak in their own voices, but by subjecting one of the most beautiful

[21] Ezra Pound, *A Walking Tour in Southern France*, ed. Richard Sieburth (New York: New Directions, 1992), 84.

[22] John Keats, "Ode to a Nightingale" from *The Complete Poems*, ed. John Barnard (New York: Penguin, 1988), 346.

verses of Arnaut to philological scrutiny until Arnaut "speaks" for himself in the voice of his landscape. In an early draft of Canto 20, Pound explicitly links the revelation of Arnaut's *noigandres* to the discovery of Dante's Earthly Paradise:

E lolors de noigandres
E l olors d'enoi ganres ... l'aqua dissio, el suon
della foresta.
So that the smell of that place, and the air.[23]

In *Purgatorio* 28, once Dante Pilgrim has passed through the wall of flame, he enters a "divina foresta spessa e viva" ("divine, dense and luxuriant wood").[24] He feels an "aura dolce" ("sweet breeze") and listens to the little birds who sing in counterpoint to the rhythmic undertone of the rustling leaves.[25] He arrives at a river and sees a lady picking flowers, who promises to answer his questions. Recalling how Statius told him that there are no atmospheric changes in Purgatory, Dante Pilgrim asks her:

"L'acqua," diss'io, "e 'l suon de la foresta
impugnan dentro a me novella fede
di cosa ch'io udi' contraria a questa."[26]
[I said: "The water and the murmuring forest
contend, in me, against the recent credence
I gave to words denying their existence."]

The lady explains that the sound Dante hears is the whirling wind of paradise. The very voice of Arnaut, therefore, is linked to the "woodland sounds" of paradise, and Homer's green language. Pound places Arnaut back where he belongs in the divine forest and the Elysian groves.

In this brief section, a change in poetic form results in insight. The style begins as a (mock) epic or philological quest to understand Daniel Arnaut's poetry. The figures are not heroic and nothing is resolved. When the style becomes lyrical, the landscape of Périgord reveals what the poet sought. The Lotophagoi will have a similar insight: revelation does not happen to those trying to achieve it.

[23] Ezra Pound, "Canto XX: Autograph ms. and typescripts." *EPP*, 3192.
[24] Dante, *Purgatorio* 28.2. My translation.
[25] Dante, *Purgatorio* 28.7.
[26] Dante, *Purgatorio,* trans. Allen Mandelbaum, 28.85–87.

Niccolò's Delirium, or How to Read

The action of Canto 20 abruptly shifts to a crucial moment in the life of a historical figure connected to Sigismundo Malatesta (1417–68), whom Pound focuses on in Cantos 8 to 11. Niccolò III d'Este (1393–1441) was the Marquis of Ferrara from the age of ten until his death. He had sixteen children with at least eleven women. His second wife, Parisina Malatesta, cousin of Sigismundo, twenty years his junior, had an affair with his illegitimate son, Ugo. Niccolò had them both beheaded 1425. Canto 20 recounts the moment of Niccolò's delirium and regret after the act. He comes to realize that Eros is a force greater than any law, and that violence is always the worst response. After Canto 20, Niccolò becomes a subject rhyme for Odysseus and epitomizes the Pound hero: a virile, open-minded adventurer who always sought to "keep the peace" despite being embroiled in scandal, ushering in a golden age for Ferrara.

Pound's treatment of Niccolò's crisis is as much about destabilizing the reader of *The Cantos* as it is about representing a new take on the story of Niccolò and Parisina. The fragmentary nature of Niccolò's "candied" delirium is a metatext; or a "how to read" *The Cantos*. The (primary) texts we (and Niccolò) thought we knew well are forced into crisis. "Serious" epic and tragic material is interrupted by bawdy "pastoral action." Nietzsche's "placid flow of epic semblance" is interrupted by the repetitive "uneven and irregular image-world of the lyric."[27] The classical epic material that glorifies heroic male acts of war is supplanted by a glorification of female beauty, goddesses, male fertility, the "mysterium" of coitus, and the ideal of peace and creative flourishing.[28]

Pound's version of the story differs from earlier versions that focus on the tragedy of Parisina. Byron's 1816 long poem, *Parisina*, based on a brief summary of the story in Edward Gibbon's *Miscellaneous Works* (1796),[29] inspired Gaetano Donizetti's 1833 opera of the same name, with a libretto by Felice Romani, as well as Pietro Mascagni's 1913 opera, with a libretto by Gabriele D'Annunzio. Byron

[27] Nietzsche, *The Birth of Tragedy*, 34.

[28] "Paganism included a certain attitude toward; a certain understanding of, coitus, which is the mysterium" (*SP*, 70).

[29] "Under the reign of Nicholas III, Ferrara was polluted with a domestic tragedy. By the testimony of a maid, and his own observation, the Marquis of Este discovered the incestuous loves of his wife Parisina, and Hugo his bastard son, a beautiful and valiant youth. They were beheaded in the castle, by the sentence of a father and husband, who published his shame, and survived their execution. He was unfortunate, if they were guilty: if they were innocent, he was still more unfortunate: nor is there any possible situation in which I can sincerely approve the last act of the justice of a parent." (Edward Gibbon, *Miscellaneous Works*, vol. 3 [London: John Murray, 1814], 470.)

recounts the forbidden love between Parisina and Hugo (Ugo) in octosyllabic abab verse chock full of the Latinate syntactical inversions Pound loathed:

> And Hugo is gone to his lonely bed,
> To covet there another's bride;
> But she must lay her conscious head
> A husband's trusting heart beside.[30]

After a gruesome description of Hugo's beheading, Byron banishes his Parisina and she eventually dies of grief: a fate more fitting a romantic heroine. Azo (Niccolò) finds another bride, but he is forever haunted by regret, for there was "none so lovely and so brave / As him who withered in the grave."[31] Byron doesn't specify anything particular about the relationship between Ugo and Azo to make his readers feel Azo's grief. But it is a fitting tragic end for a romantic hero: no longer capable of feeling: a "sealed-up bosom haunted" by grief.[32]

"Leigh Hunt wrote to Byron advising him against clichés. But it did not deter Byron from clichés," in Pound's words.[33] Consulting numerous Italian sources, Pound avoids the sentimental tale of doomed love.[34] He narrates how Niccolò's shame and guilt teaches him the virtue of keeping the peace. Canto 20 introduces Niccolò in his moment of delirium after Ugo's beheading. Canto 24, however, provides some helpful backstory. Pound cites the official documents concerning Parisina's dowry, details Niccolò's voyage to the Holy Land in 1413, "in the wake of Odysseus" (24/111), and describes his crisis in 1425 with quotations from his Italian source texts:

> and after
> The Marchese asked was Ugo beheaded. And the Captain:
> "Signor ... si." and il Marchese began crying
> "Fa me hora tagliar la testa
> "dapoi cosi presto hai decapitato il mio Ugo."
> [""Now cut off my head,
> "since you've so soon decapitated my Ugo.""]
> Rodendo con denti una bachetta che havea in mani.
> ["Chewing with his teeth a stick he held in his hands."]
> And passed that night weeping, and calling Ugo, his son. (24/112)[35]

30 George Byron, *Parisina*, in *The Siege of Corinth, Parisina* (London: John Murray, 1816), lines 65–8.
31 Byron, *Parisina*, lines 531–2.
32 Byron, *Parisina*, line 556.
33 Pound, *Gaudier-Brzeska: A Memoir* (New York: New Directions, 1970), 115.
34 On Pound's Italian sources, see Terrell, *A Companion*, 80 and 95.
35 English translations by Terrell, *A Companion*, 97.

These lines contextualize Pound's mythical treatment of Niccolò in Canto 20, which plunges the reader into a delirium of detail.

> He was playing there at the palla.
> Parisina—two doves for an altar—at the window,
> "*E'l Marchese*
> *Stava per divenir pazzo*
> after it all." And that was when Troy was down
> And they came here and cut holes in rock,
> Down Rome way, and put up the timbers;
> And came here, condit Atesten . . .
>   "Peace! keep the peace, Borso."
> And he said: Some bitch has sold us
>   (that was Ganelon)
> "They wont get another such ivory."
> And he lay there on the round hill under the cedar
> A little to the left of the cut (Este speaking)
> By the side of the summit, and he said:
>   "I have broken the horn, bigod, I have"
> "Broke the best ivory, l'olofans." And he said:
> "Tan mare fustes!"
>   pulling himself over the gravel,
> "Bigod! that buggar is done for,
> "They wont get another such ivory."
> And they were there before the wall, Toro, las almenas,
> (Este, Nic Este speaking)
>   Under the battlement
> (Epi purgo) peur de la hasle,
> And the King said:
>   "God what a woman!"
> "My God what a woman" said the King telo rigido.
> "Sister!" says Ancures, "'s your sister!"
> Alf left that town to Elvira, and Sancho wanted
> It from her, Toro and Zamora.
>   "Bloody spaniard!"
> Neestho, le'er go back . . .
>   in the autumn."
> "Este, go' damn you." between the walls, arras,
> Painted to look like arras. (20/90–91)

Pound introduces a key figure of his long poem in a deliberately confusing way—not just to mirror Niccolò's own delirium, but also to make the reader interact and work for meaning. Niccolò is presumably looking down at the courtyard ("there") remembering how Ugo ("he") was once playing ball (*palla*) while Parisina was "at the window" (also looking down?). But the mention of the "altar," which is now presumably in the courtyard, and the suggestion that two doves be released, reveals that Parisina is dead. (An earlier draft reads, "take two doves for the sacrifice."[36]) Virgil's Aphrodite sends twin doves to indicate to Aeneas the location of the golden bough, suggesting Niccolò's feeling of catastrophic loss. The quoted text, from one of Pound's Italian sources, offers scant context.[37] "El Marchese" (Niccolò) has gone "pazzo" (crazy) "after it all." Pound or Niccolò then jumps back in time to establish the Este family as descendants from Troy: a feature of the *translatio imperii.* Edward Gibbon claims that the House of Este descended from the Atti family,[38] but the Estes themselves claimed to be descendants of the knights of Charlemagne, which is why Niccolò projects his own suffering onto Roland. Pound or Niccolò is vaguer: "And that was when Troy was down / And they came here and cut holes in rock / Down Rome way." Niccolò's ancestors left Troy like (or with) Aeneas and then left Rome ("down Rome way") like Brutus of Troy to Ferrara and cut holes in the rock for their houses. Pound then introduces the refrain, "Keep the peace, Borso," which is what Niccolò learns from this tragedy and passes on to the future generation: Ferrara's flourishing is dependent on its being in a subordinate position to Venice. However, it is not until well into the story of Roland (who is never actually named), that Pound clarifies who "El Marchese" is and who is speaking: "(Este speaking)" and then, "(Este, Nic Este speaking)." Precisely what he is saying is not clear; Pound's quotation marks are not consistent. Niccolò's thoughts jump from the death of Roland to King Sancho II of Castile before the walls of Toro from a play by Lope de Vega to the old men on the Skaian gates in the *Iliad.*

Polyvocality asserts itself before the figure that ventriloquizes these voices. The reader first assumes it is Ezra Pound speaking, not Nic Este, especially because Niccolò acts as a ventriloquist of Pound, presenting echoes of earlier cantos ("Neestho, le'er go back") and "luminous details" of *La Chanson de Roland* and the obscure and untranslated *Las almenas de Toro* (Lope de Vega

[36] Ezra Pound, "Canto XX: Typescript." *EPP*, 3187.

[37] Possibly Giambattista Pigna's *Historia de Principi di Este* (Vinegia: V. Valgrisi, 1572). Antonio Frizzi's text is slightly different. C.f. Antonio Frizzi, *Memorie per la Storia di Ferrara*, vol. 3 (Ferrara: A. Servadio, 1850), 452–3.

[38] Gibbon, *Miscellaneous Works,* vol. 3, 172. The Atti family included Publius Attius Atimetus, physician to Augustus, and the Roman poet Attius Labeo who translated Homer, and whose name became synonymous with bad verse.

wrote over five hundred plays) that Pound discusses twenty years earlier in *The Spirit of Romance.* In an earlier draft, Pound introduces yet another speaker and another character:

> And he a [*sic*] was there playing at the palla
> Ugo, Parisina,
>   take two doves for the sacrifice
> But you[r] job is to keep the peace, Lionel,
>   and you Borso,
> Two doves, blood on the altar,
>   and the head on the altar, speaking.
> E[t] il Marchese stava per divinir pazzo,
> Mine next, mortichino ["dead child"]
> and the prince came here, the prince, Troia profugens ["fleeing from Troy"]
> came here, condit Atesten,
>   ere that Rome town was timbered
> or roofs set there over rock hole.[39]

Here, it is clearer that Ugo was the one playing palla. Pound makes reference to Leonella d'Este ("Lionello"), Niccolò's first born son by Stella de' Tolomei. He alludes to Niccolò's request that his own head be cut off as well ("mine next"). "Morticinio" might be a word from Pound's source or a reference to Ugo, although he was twenty. The "head on the altar, speaking" is probably the head of Ugo, so vividly depicted by Byron: "His eyes and lips a moment quiver, / Convulsed and quick."[40] The line, "take two doves for the sacrifice" also makes it clearer that Niccolò regrets his sacrifice. But Pound mercifully cut the talking head, along with the mention of Lionel, probably deciding that four speakers (Niccolò, Roland, Sancho, and Ancures) was sufficiently confusing.

Homer Pound was puzzled by this section of the poem and the whole of Canto 20, prompting Pound to respond with the "outline of main scheme" of *The Cantos* as well as a helpful gloss about how the Niccolò sequence fits into this canto:

> Nicolo d'Este in a sort of delirium after execution of Parisina and Ugo. (For facts vide, I spose, the *Encyclopedia Britan.*)
>   "'*And the Marchese*
>   *was nearly off his head*

[39] Ezra Pound, "Canto XX: Typescript." *EPP*, 3187. I corrected a few of Pound's obvious typing mistakes.

[40] Byron, *Parisina*, lines 459–60.

> *after it all.'"*
>
> Various things keep cropping up in the poem. The original world of gods; the Trojan War, Helen on the wall of Troy with the old men fed up with the whole show and suggesting she be sent back to Greece.
>
> Rome founded by survivors of Troy. Here ref. to legendary founding of Este (condit (founded) At*esten,* Este).
>
> Then in the delirium, Nicolo remembers or thinks he is watching death of Roland. Elvira on wall or Toro (subject-rhyme with Helen on Wall). Epi purgos (on wall); peur de la hasle (afraid of sunburn); Neestho (translated in text: let her go back); ho bios (life); cosi Elena vivi [*sic*] (thus I saw Helen, misquote of Dante).
>
> The whole reminiscence jumbled or "candied" in Nicolo's delirium. Take that as a sort of bounding surface from which one gives the main subject of the Canto, the lotophagoi: lotus eaters, or respectable dope smokers, and general paradiso. You have had a hell in Canti XIV, XV, purgatorio in XVI etc.[41]

Niccolò's jumbled or "candied" delirium is a springboard into the main subject of the poem: the Lotophagoi, and a "doped" vision of general paradiso. Pound repeats the fact that Niccolò is delirious to his father three times. His delirium organizes all the remaining material of Canto 20. History is "charged" in the mind of Niccolò, crazed by betrayal, regret, and guilt. Like the mad Hieronomo of *The Spanish Tragedy,* the final poet persona of *The Waste Land*, who gathers together his incomprehensibly polyglot revenge play, Niccolò fuses his own moment of crisis into a constellation of shifting identities: Roland, the old men on the Skaian gate, and the figure of King Sancho II of Castile and León. Niccolò's luminous "rereading" of these texts allows him to transcend his own grief and recognize the primordial force of Eros. This leads to a "magic moment": a glimpse of "general paradiso" and an even more insightful critique of the *Odyssey*.

Niccolò "remembers or thinks he is watching death of Roland," Pound explains. Niccolò identifies with Roland, betrayed by Ganelon, whom Niccolò initially fuses with Parisina, hence: "Some bitch has sold us / (that was Ganelon)." Niccolò's regret for killing Ugo (and Parisina) mirrors Roland's regret in destroying his "best horn," the oliphant. Pound's summary of *La Chanson de Roland* in *The Spirit of Romance* is helpful here:

> Marseille attacks this rearguard; Oliver sensibly advises Roland to sound his horn to call back the Emperor. Roland bombastically refuses. The warrior Bishop Turpin blesses the French, but neither Roland's hardihood nor the sanctity of the

41 *L*, 285–6.

> Bishop avert the natural result. Roland, dying, sounds the "olifan," and recalls the Emperor, who, by the way, is already thirty leagues off.[42]

Pound argues that Roland is "a victim, not to the treachery of Ganelon, but to that pride which forbade him to sound the horn for aid."[43] The author of *Roland*, however, doesn't exactly suggest that Roland is to blame. Oliver begs Roland to blow his horn. Roland argues that blowing the horn would be an act of cowardice and put France to shame. Their quarrel represents a deadlock summarized in the final lines of the *laisse*: "Rollant est proz e Oliver est sage. / Ambedui unt merveillus vasselage." ("Roland is brave and Oliver is brave. / Both are marvelously courageous."[44]) Later, Roland learns of his mistake. He blows the oliphant so forcefully that his brains burst from his ears. But Roland dies a hero's death. Angels descend and take his soul to paradise. Charlemagne finally arrives and fights off the Saracens. The final section of the poem recounts the trial and execution of the wicked Ganelon.

Pound's summary of Roland's death in his letter to his father is equally revealing of Niccolò and Pound's unusually pacifist interpretation of the epic.

> Tan mare fustes: is Roland's remark to moor who comes up to finish him off, as nearly as I can remember his sword is broken, but he smashes the moor over the head with his horn (olifans: elephant: olifant tusk) and then dies grumbling because he has damaged the ornaments on the horn and broken it. Tan mare fustes, colloquial: you came at a bad moment. Current cabaret song now: J'en ai marre: I'm fed up.[45]

Pound misremembers, perhaps deliberately, in order to cast Roland as the tragic hero who commits hubris or makes a tragic mistake (*hamartia*). Roland does not die "grumbling" about the loss of the oliphant and Durendal is not broken. Roland, with his brains seeping out of his ears, crawls up a steep hill under a pine tree near four great sardonyx blocks. He faints while clutching his sword, Durendal. A Saracen, who was feigning death, sneaks up to steal the sword and take it to Arabia. Just as he pulls it out of its sheath, Roland revives and smashes the oliphant down on the Saracen's helmet, killing him with one blow. Roland exclaims, "Fenduz en es mis olifans el gros, / Caiuz en est li cristals e li ors" ("Now my oliphant is split at its wide end; / The crystal

[42] *SR*, 74.
[43] *SR*, 77.
[44] *La Chanson de Roland*, Oxford text, ed. Joseph Bédier (Paris: Édition d'Art, 1922), lines 1093–4. My translation.
[45] *L*, 285–6.

has come away, and the gold").[46] Realizing that he is about to die, Roland tries in vain to break Durendal against the blocks. He laments to his sword, briefly catalogues its marvels, and prays that no pagan or coward shall ever wield it. Finally, he stretches his right hand to God and dies. Pound quotes most of this passage in *The Spirit of Romance,* calling it the "finest passage in the poem": "one feels that perhaps he and the rest of the characters are not wooden figures, that they are simply French. Heroic he is, and his hands are joined, in death he forgets not etiquette."[47] In his letter to his father, Pound casts Roland in a more pathetic light, conflating the oliphant with Durendal, and assuming that Roland dies "grumbling" about the oliphant rather than cataloguing the marvels of Durendal. To both Pound and Niccolò, Roland's shame is in destroying a work of art, an instrument of music, and a symbol of his fertility, not a symbol of war or his bravery. However, Pound astutely recognizes the irony of Roland's death. Roland should have used the oliphant earlier to call for help; eventually he uses it and it injures him gravely. Roland can't use Durendal to kill the Saracen; he uses his oliphant and renders it useless. Roland tries to render his sword useless; he fails and dies fearing that his sword will get into the hands of the enemy.

Pound is also mistaken about the meaning of the line, "tan mar fustes" in his letter to his father. It does not mean, "you've come at a bad time," but, "so unfortunate are you." Pound probably thought the Old French "tan" was a shortened form of "tans" (*temps*, "time") rather than "tant" ("so"). The word "mar" means "bad" (*mal*), "unfortunate," or marks a negative. The modern French "marre" which forms the expression "j'en ai marre" ("I've had enough") probably derives from "mar," a slang word from the 1880s, meaning "a share of stolen goods." Moreover, Roland does not say "tan mar fustes" to the Saracen. Archbishop Turpin says it to Roland. After surveying all of his dead peers on the battlefield, including Oliver, Roland faints. "Dist l'Arcevesques: 'Tant mare fustes ber!"[48] ("The Archbishop says: 'so unfortunate are you, baron!'").[49] Bédier translates this as, "Baron, c'est pitié de vous." ("Baron, I'm sorry for you.") Turpin takes the oliphant to fill it with water from the stream, but he collapses and dies of blood loss. The line "tant mar fustes" occurs two other times in *La Chanson*

[46] *La Chanson de Roland,* lines 2295–6.
[47] *SR,* 75–6, 77.
[48] *La Chanson de Roland,* line 2221.
[49] *La Chanson de Roland,* line 2221.

de Roland, but this is certainly the instance Pound was thinking of, based on an early notebook draft of Canto 20, which preserves the "ber":[50]

> bigod I have broke my best horn
> + he said "Tan mare fustes ber"
> pulled himself over the gravel."[51]

The Old French "ber" can also mean "good," or "considerable," but that doesn't make sense in this context. It more commonly occurs as the oblique case of "baron."[52] Pound might have dropped the "ber" because he couldn't make sense of the word, or he was confused why Roland would address the Saracen as "baron." Pound was probably working from old notes. Had he consulted the actual text and seen the line in full, he wouldn't have confused it for Roland's.

Regardless of Pound's misreading, Niccolò's delirious recall of Roland's death fixates on the beautiful object destroyed out of pride. "I have broken the horn, bigod, I have / "Broke the best ivory, l'olofans." Niccolò deliriously regrets having killed Parisina (the oliphant) foolishly when he should have properly "used" her in the past; or perhaps Niccolò regrets having killed his own son Ugo (the oliphant) in his own selfish desire to protect his property or good name. Generally, Niccolò destroys a precious possession out of pride and wrath, and now dies grumbling about the beauty he has lost. To Niccolò, the oliphant is more important than Durendal: Roland dies thinking of a beautiful musical object, which recalls the theme of the lost music of the bard(s) from the opening sequence: Bernart's viel, Homer's lyre, the Sirens' song.

Niccolò's thoughts jump to an obscure Lope de Vega play, *Las almenas de Toro,* reflecting on the innocence of sexual passion, even when it is illicit. Ugo and Parisina's incest is punishable by death, but the comic scene in Lope's play reminds Niccolò that passion is innocent and can happen to anyone. Pound summarizes the action of the play in *The Spirit of Romance.* King Sancho (Sancho II of Castile and León [1036/8–1072]), upset that his father (Ferdinand I of León) divided his kingdom among Sancho's siblings (Alfonso, Garcia, Elvira,

[50] "Tant mare fustes ber"; "Dient Franceis: 'Barun, tant mare fus!'"; and "tant mar fustes hardiz" ("how sad that you were so bold") (*La Chanson de Roland,* lines 350, 1604, and 2027).

[51] Ezra Pound, "Canto XX: Autograph ms." *EPP*, 3186.

[52] Pound's consistent writing of "tan" instead of "tant" in all his drafts suggests that he was working with the Venice text, which reads, "tan mare fustes." On the back page of a notebook for Canto 20 Pound writes, "Tan mare fustes. / Roland, / etc. / L. 2 - P. 12. / ? / [illegible: 'maens oc'?]" (Ezra Pound, "Canto XX: Autograph ms." *EPP*, 3186). Presumably, this means "livre 2, page 12," but I've found no two-volume edition of *Roland* that corresponds to this pagination. See *Das Rolandslied: Oxforder und Venediger Text*, ed. Conrad Hofmann (Munich: G. Franz, 1868), 124.

and Urraca) before he died, stands with the Cid (Rodrigo Díaz de Vivar) and Conde Ancures before the battlements of Toro, now occupied by his sister Elvira. ("Alf[53] left that town to Elvira, and Sancho wanted / It from her, Toro.") Sancho sees Elvira on the battlements, does not recognize her, and falls in love. As Pound explains:

> The King sees his sister on the battlements, and, without knowing who she is, falls in love with her.
>
> *King.* On the battlements of Toro
> There passed a damozel, or
> To speak more truly
> 'Twas the sun's self passed us,
> Far the form and light the passing.
> [...]
>
> The Cid tells him that it is his sister.
>
> *King.* An ill flame be kindled in her!
>
> Pastoral action is brought into the play as relief, "contra el arte," as Lope says in his preface.[54]

Niccolò's version is much bawdier. In his mind, King Sancho's love for his sister translates to an erection: "'My God what a woman' said the King telo rigido ['with a rigid javelin']." In earlier drafts, Pound was less oblique: "My God what a woman, said the King with a cockstand."[55] This "pastoral action" cuts into the tragedy, but it provides more than just relief. (Tragedy originates in the satyr dance, as Nietzsche puts it.[56]) It presents an alternative route for Sancho: make love, not war; accept Ferdinand's (fair) division of his empire among his sons and daughters. But Sancho does not listen. He attacks the city, and is eventually killed by his brother Alfonzo. Like Roland, who refuses to blow his oliphant at the opportune time, Sancho does not listen to his own "horn" and persists in his pride and greed. It costs him his life.

Elvira on the battlements also reminds Niccolò of the moment the old men of Troy see Helen walking like a goddess toward them on the Skaian gate. Read in the light of Roland and Sancho, the old men's rejection of Helen ("let'er go back") represents their impotence and inability to witness (and so partake) in the cult of Amor: a rejection of divinity, sexual desire, and the mysterium of femininity.

53 Pound presumably means Ferdinand. Alfonzo is the name of Sancho's brother, who succeeded him.

54 *SR*, 203–204.

55 Ezra Pound, "Canto XX: Typescripts." *EPP*, 3191; Ezra Pound, "Canto XX: Typescript." *EPP*, 3188; Ezra Pound, "Canto XX: Typescripts." *EPP*, 145.

56 See Nietzsche, *The Birth of Tragedy*, 39.

Their rejection of Helen's beauty is comparable to Sancho's rejection of his desire and Roland's misuse of his own horn. In an early notebook version of Canto 20 Pound included a more nuanced critique of war and revenge:

> long boredom of slaughter
> and her mind upon Theseus
> ex neosi neestha (ἐν νηυσὶ νεέσθω) ["let her go back to the ships"] = de peur de la hasle.[57]

In a later typescript, this became:

> cosi Elena vidi
>
> By the gate then,
> and in the portico over the gate—
> and she with her mind on Theseus.[58]

Pound moved the line "cosi Elena vidi" to Niccolò's vision of Helen in the "general paradiso" later. "Her mind on Theseus" is a clever mistranslation of *Iliad* 1.139–40. Iris, disguised as Priam's daughter, finds Helen in the main hall penitently weaving a blood-red mantle depicting the sufferings of the Trojans and Greeks. Iris informs Helen that the Trojans and the Greeks have agreed to settle the whole matter by single combat between Paris and Menelaus. "'And whoso shall conquer, his dear wife shalt thou be called.' So spake the goddess, and put into her heart sweet longing for her former lord [ἀνδρός τε προτέρου, *andros te proterou*] and her city and parents."[59] Helen is overjoyed that the "long boredom of slaughter" will soon be resolved. She longs for her "former lord," Menelaus, in contrast with her current one, Paris. But Pound translates "former lord" as Theseus, her *first* lord—that is, her first abductor when she was a youth. After Helen was returned, her father, Tyndarus, held a competition between all the Greek heroes for her hand. Menelaus emerged victorious, and the rest of the heroes swore that if Helen was ever abducted again, they would provide military assistance (the Oath of Tyndarus). Pound's mistranslation of *andros te proterou* for Theseus (πρότερος [*proteros*] means "before" or "in front") is a joke, possibly about Helen's alleged promiscuity, or about how Homer (or Pisistratus) struggles to plausibly represent Helen's subjectivity in the *Iliad*, but more broadly as a comment about the absurd premise of the *Iliad*: that Helen's abduction by

57 Ezra Pound, "Canto XX: Autograph ms." *EPP*, 3186.
58 Ezra Pound, "Canto XX: Typescripts." *EPP*, 3189.
59 *Iliad* 3.132–40.

Paris led to the war in Troy. Pound's translation would have pleased Herotodus, who begins his histories with a tongue-in-cheek account of how Helen's abduction was in fact a retaliation for an earlier abduction. The Phoenicians first abducted Io from Argos; the Greeks then abducted Europa from Tyre and Medea from Colchis; and Alexander (Paris) then abducted Helen as a retaliation for that.[60]

Pound's position on Helen is also similar to that of J. J. Bachofen:

> Helen is not endowed with all the charms of Pandora in order to become the exclusive possession of one man. When she offends against the marriage bond and follows the fair Alexander (Paris) to Ilium, it is less in response to her own wishes than to the commandment of Aphrodite and to the femininity that made her proverbial as the "eternal woman."[61]

Helen embodies what Bachofen calls "haeterism" or "aphroditism": a stage of sexual promiscuity and social anarchy closer to our original state of nature. Helen's beauty is freely given to all. Exclusivity is an infringement of the rights of mother earth. In Pound's early drafts, Helen's blamelessness is a subject-rhyme for both Elvira and Parisina as objects of (possibly) illicit male desire who incite violence and war.

It's too bad Pound cut this clever mistranslation. However, the mere mention of Helen in Canto 20 reinforces the main idea: rejecting beauty and Eros has disastrous consequences. Moments of comic "relief" in the tragic narrative of war—Roland's destruction of his horn, Sancho's cockstand, Helen's runway walk regarded by the impotent old veterans—offer a "way out" of the "long boredom of slaughter" which is history and chronicle: "Scraped flat by the roller / Of wars, wars, wars," as the narrator of Sylvia Plath's "Daddy" puts it.[62] The final lines, "in the autumn.' / 'Este, go' damn you.' Between the walls, arras, / Painted to look like arras" reinforces Este's regret and presents only a fragment of an erotic memory which is fleshed out in Canto 23: "As we had lain there in the autumn / Under the arras, or wall painted below like arras" (23/108). Niccolò recalls making love with Parisina. In his *Pensées*, Pascal suggests that "the sole cause of man's unhappiness is that he does not know how to stay quietly in his room."[63] Pound's version might read: he does not know how to take sex seriously enough. D. H. Lawrence would agree.

The "pastoral" or Bacchic image of Sancho's erection interrupts Niccolò's (somewhat) more weighty reflection of Roland's death. In a moment of crisis and

[60] Herodotus, *The Histories*, trans. Robin Waterfield, ed. Carolyn Dewald (New York: Oxford University Press, 2008), 1:1–3.

[61] Bachofen, *Myth, Religion, and Mother Right*, 138.

[62] Sylvia Plath, *The Collected Poems*, ed. Ted Hughes (New York: Harper and Row, 1981), 222.

[63] Blaise Pascal, *Pensées*, trans. A.J. Krailsheimer (London: Penguin, 1995), 37.

delirium, Niccolò becomes an ideal reader of literary texts, seeing the arrogance and pride of Roland where generations of readers before him saw only a war-hero and martyr; seeing the folly of Sancho, who did not act on the lesson of his own hard-on and check his pride. Like a Cambridge Ritualist, Niccolò reads between the lines of the primary epic to uncover the "pastoral action" which is not only more primitive, but offers clues to unraveling the telos of the epic narrative. Helen is not the cause of the Trojan war (epic); the cult of female beauty and virility, as epitomized by Helen, is the cause of the lyric, or the *Ur*-epic.

Niccolò might have ended up like Byron's emotionally distant grief-stricken figure, his "sealed-up bosom haunted," who channeled his resentment into ruthless military campaigns, but he did quite the opposite. The real Niccolò was so furious with Parisina that he decreed a law that all women within his domains committed of adultery were to be put to death. However, he rescinded the law after realizing that this action would depopulate Ferrara. Pound omits this from *The Cantos* probably because it might reduce Niccolò's conversion into a joke about fifteenth-century Ferrara. Niccolò's advice to his son, which appears at the end of Canto 20 ("'Peace! / Borso . . ., Borso!") and the beginning of Canto 21 ("Keep the peace, Borso!"), epitomizes his conversion, which led to golden age under Borso d'Este as patron of the arts. His court was the center of the Ferrarese school of painting, whose members included Francesco del Cossa and Cosimo Tura, who were commissioned to create the frescoes in the Palazzo Schifanoia and the Borso d'Este Bible.[64] (Pound ignored Borso's notorious stinginess to the artists he patronized.) In this moment of delirium, Niccolò is able to stand outside of history and reach back to what he describes in "The Flame" as the "clear light" of the primordial past burning near the "eternal embers."[65] The stage is now set for Pound to introduce a glimpse of "general paradiso."

Paradise of Lust: The Shelf of the Lotophagoi

"Canto XVII deals with a sort of paradiso terrestre," Pound writes to his father in 1925. "XX lotophagoi; further sort of paradiso. or something in that direction."[66] The next section of Canto 20 reprises what Pound calls the paradiso terrestre

[64] Pound relied on the plates and commentaries of the frescoes in Antonio Frizzi's *Album Estenze* (1850) while writing Canto 20. See Miyake, *Ezra Pound and the Mysteries of Love*, 108.

[65] *PT*, 169.

[66] Ezra Pound, May 1925, Letter to Homer Pound. *Ezra Pound to His Parents: Letters, 1895–1929*, ed. Mary de Rachewiltz, A. David Moody, and Joanna Moody (Oxford: Oxford University Press, 2010), 565.

of Canto 17: A procession of Dionysus Zagreus through chthonic landscapes. The paradiso of Canto 20 blends elements of Virgil's Mourning Fields (*Lugentes Campi*); Dante's borge of carnal lust in *Inferno*; the terrace of the lustful in *Purgatorio* where Dante Pilgrim meets Arnaut; and the Earthly Paradise of *Paradiso.* Pound inverts or "updates" the traditional topos of punishment and purgation into an ecstatic celebration of Amor. The fire of hell and purgatory becomes Francis of Assisi's holy fire of love: "In foco amor mi mise" ("Love has put me in fire").

Canto 17 describes a procession of Dionysius Zagreus through a lush environment and down Venetian canals along with many of the most important figures of *The Cantos.* This includes "the goddess of the fair knees," probably Diana (17/76); Nerea standing in a shell-boat like Botticelli's Venus, "like a great shell curved, / and the boat drawn without sound"; Hermes and Athene; Borso d'Este and Francesco Bussone de Carmagnola ("the men of craft" (17/78]); Sigismundo Malatesta; "Zothar and her elephants" (Zothar is an invented name) with her dancers shaking the sistrum, the rattle used in Isis worship; Persephone and "the brother of Circe" (17/79) which is probably not a reference to Aeetes, the king of Colchis, but to Odysseus as an initiate to Circe's mysteries: a theme developed in Cantos 39 and 47.[67] Canto 20 continues this procession of figures, "each on invisible raft, / On the high current, invisible fluid" (20/92). They are carried towards a cataract, past the "Shelf of the lotophagoi" (20/93). Some are launched off the cataract and burst into flame, while others travel down a steep path past crystal columns on heavy gilded cars into a plain similar to "the plain of Somnus" (20/94). These include Zothar (again) on her elephant; Dionysus (again) and his panthers "chained to the cars"; Zoe, a Byzantine empress who poisoned her husband; Marozia the mistress of Pope Sergius III, and the mother of Pope John XI (as early as 1904, Pound contemplated writing a trilogy about her);[68] and Helen, who stands in (impossible) sunlight.

Pound's chthonic paradiso inverts the classical topos from a place of punishment (in Virgil and Dante) to a subterranean paradise of sacred disorder and mystery. Aeneas boards the Stygian boat and passes the Mourning Fields, where those whom love consumed are still ravaged by love: Phaedra, Procris, Eriphyle, Evadne, Pasiphae, Laodamia, Caenus, and Dido. In Dante's borge of the carnal, reserved for those who "are damned because they sinned within the flesh, / subjecting reason to the rule of lust," lovers such as Semiramis, Dido,

[67] See Miyake, *Ezra Pound and the Mysteries of Love*, 90; and Liebregts, *Ezra Pound and Neoplatonism*, 177.

[68] Kenner, *The Pound Era*, 354.

Cleopatra, Helen, Achilles, Paris, and Tristan, are tormented by a perpetual hurricane.[69] Pound truncates a line by Dante's Virgil. "Elena vedi, per cui tanto reo / tempo si volse" ("See Helen, for whose sake so many years / of evil had to pass") becomes simply: "cosi Elena vedi," meaning, "Thus I saw Helen," as Pound writes to his father.[70] (In fact, "I saw" would be "vidi"; *vedi* means "you see.") Pound's Helen is marveled at like a goddess, exonerated of all crimes.

Pound's paradiso is wild jungle of vegetation which recalls Virgil's "loca turbida," or "land of disorder."[71]

> Jungle:
> Glaze green and red feathers, jungle,
> Basis of renewal, renewals;
> Rising over the soul, green virid, of the jungle,
> Lozenge of the pavement, clear shapes,
> Broken, disrupted, body eternal,
> Wilderness of renewals, confusion
> Basis of renewals, subsistence,
> Glazed green of the jungle (20/91–92)

Virgil's underworld is crowded with primeval forests, vast chasms, both menacing and placid rivers, whirlpools, and elaborate architecture built into cliffs. Pound's "wilderness of renewals, confusion" specifically recalls Virgil's "antiquam silvam" and "silvam immensam," the primeval and boundless forest in which Aeneas must recover the golden bough which will lead him safely into the underworld.[72] Aeneas descends into Avernus; "spelunca alta fuit vastoque immanis hiatu, / scrupea, tuta lacu nigro nemorumque tenebris" ("a deep cave there was, yawning wide and vast, shingly, and sheltered by dark lake and woodland gloom").[73] "Turbidus hic caeno vastaque vorgine gurges / aestuat, atque omnem Cocyto eructat harenam" ("Here, thick with mire and of fathomless flood, a whirlpool seethes and belches into Cocytus all its sand").[74] Charon conveys the dead on a raft over the banks and down the river; Pound's figures travel on invisible boats until they are flung off a cataract. Aeneas passes a castle under a cliff with

69 Dante, *Inferno* 5.38–39.
70 Dante, *Inferno* 5.64–65.
71 Virgil, *Aeneid* 6.534.
72 Virgil, *Aeneid* 6.179, 186.
73 Virgil, *Aeneid* 6.236–37, trans. H. Rushton Fairclough, in *Eclogues, Georgics, Aeneid I–VI* (Cambridge, MA: Harvard University Press, 1978), 523.
74 Virgil, *Aeneid* 6.296–97.

adamantine pillars and an iron tower; Pound's procession passes crystal columns and a city built into a cliff.

Pound's paradisal cortege of "adulteresses" and other nameless figures are flung off the cataract and "take flame in the air," which alludes to Dante's refining fire which leads to Paradise:

> Each man in his cloth, as on raft, on
>   The high invisible current;
> On toward the fall of water;
> And then over that cataract,
> In air, strong, the bright flames, V shaped;
>   Nel fuoco
> D'amore mi mise, nel fuoco d'amore mi mise…
> Yellow, bright saffron, croceo;
> And as the olibanum bursts into flame,
> The bodies so flamed in the air, took flame,
>   "… Mi mise, il mio sposo novella."
> Shot from stream into spiral. (20/92–93)

Pound explains to his father: "The 'nel fuoco' is from St. Francis' 'cantico': 'My new spouse placeth me in the flame of love.'"[75] But it is in fact a hybrid of Francis of Assisi's "Cantico Secondo" (Second Song), "In foco amor mi mise" ("Love has put me in fire")[76] and Dante's description of the refining fire before the entrance to Earthly Paradise on the terrace of the lustful in *Purgatorio:* "Poi s'ascose nel foco che gli affina." ("Then hid himself in the fire that refines them.")[77] Pound's figures do not hide, they burn like olibanum (frankincense) taking flame, a resin commonly used in Hebraic and Christian religions. Dante, Virgil, and Statius climb "la scala / che per artezza i salitor dispaia" "the stairs / that are too narrow for climbers to go in pairs" to a precarious terrace.[78] Dante Pilgrim walks the narrow path between a cliff and a wall of flame, and encounters a group of men walking in single file (the sodomites), along with Arnaut Daniel, who begs that his suffering be remembered. (This might explain why Pound's procession is first described as consisting of women on invisible rafts, but later: "Each man in his cloth, as on raft.") Pound's figures must also walk in single

[75] *L*, 286.

[76] Francis of Assisi, *Cantico, in Grégoire VII, saint Francois d'Assise, saint Thomas d'Aquin*, ed. E. J. Delécluze (Paris: Jules Labitte, 1844), 385–7.

[77] Dante, *Purgatorio* 26.148.

[78] Dante, *Purgatorio* 25.8–9.

file along a vertiginous mountain path. However, they walk down, "inverting" Dante Pilgrim's journey and Dante's meaning.

Niccolò's revision of the epic material leads directly to his revision of Virgil and Dante's paradiso, which allows Pound to introduce to his most complex *translatio* of the *Odyssey,* in which Odysseus's is critiqued not for his hubris and deceitfulness, but for not sharing with his comrades the mysteries of Amor.

The Lotophagoi

Faulting Odysseus is common to the medieval *translatio*. Odysseus was a cultural hero among the Greeks; but Ulysses is the enemy to Virgil, whose *translatio imperii* shifts the focus to Roman destiny and the heroic struggles of pious (Trojan) Aeneas. Virgil's two most common epithets for Ulysses are "dirus" ("dreadful," "detestable") and "pellax" ("seductive," "deceitful," "misleading").[79] Dante puts Ulysses and Diomedes in the eighth circle of hell among the false counselors. Dante's Virgil faults them specifically for the guile of the wooden horse; luring Achilles into the war effort on Skyros so that he abandoned his wife (Deidamia) and son (Neoptolemus); and stealing the Palladium, the wooden image of Pallas Athena, which protected Troy.[80] But Ulysses's gravest sin is fradulent counsel: he convinces the mariners to give up their journey home in favor of pursuing knowledge and undiscovered lands. They cross the limits of the known world (the Straights of Gibraltar), glimpse Mount Purgatory, and are promptly blasted and drowned like Melville's Ahab and company aboard the Pequod. Ulysses's individualism, inspiring enough to beguile both his fellow sailors and readers of Dante like Tennyson, contrass with Aeneas, the paradigm of filial and civic piety. (Aeneas is unmentioned in the *Commedia,* as he is embodied in Dante Pilgrim himself.)

Pound's critique of Odysseus is in the spirit of Latin and medieval *translatio.* In an early draft of Canto 20, Pound adds two details about Odysseus's blameworthiness unmentioned by Dante right after Niccolò's reflection on the folly of King Sancho.

> And when the boats were sailing out, and out and
> again, they said to Odysseus,
> Odysseus, we have heard, about the theft of the

[79] For example, Virgil, *Aeneid* 2.261, 2.762 ("dirus Ulixes") and 2.90 ("pellacis Ulixi").

[80] Dante, *Inferno* 26.58–63.

horses, that was night, yes, yes, that was
a night for the pair of you, and of the dispute for
the armor, we have heard . . . of Odysseus,

toi panth, Of Troy with stone roofs and stone houses.[81]

The "they" here are the Sirens. "When the boats were sailing out" refers to Odysseus leaving Kimmeria, after which, according to Pound, "he sailed, by Sirens and thence outward and away / And unto Circe" (1/5). "Toi panth" ("all the sufferings") echoes the Siren's song from *Odyssey* 12.189. The line appears in *Hugh Selwyn Mauberly: "Ἴδμεν γάρ τοι πάνθ', ὅσ 'ένι Τροίῃ* / Caught in the unstopped ear"[82] (*Idmen gar toi panth, os eni Troie*: "For we know all the toils that in Troy"). Homer's Sirens seduce Odysseus with their knowledge of his sufferings at Troy; Pound's Sirens shame Odysseus with their knowledge of all the rotten things he did at Troy. "The theft of the horses" refers to Odysseus and Diomedes's marauding of the Thracian camp and killing thirteen sleeping men.[83] (Dante might have included this if he had read the *Iliad*.) This is a marked departure from the fair combat depicted elsewhere in the *Iliad*, and, as Gilbert Murray argues, a vestige of the more primitive poem featuring horse raiding and piracy.[84] (An analogy to Murray's primitive *Iliad* might be the *Táin Bó Cúailnge*.) "And of the dispute for the armor" refers to an episode in the lost *Little Iliad* of the Epic Cycle, which tells of the funeral games held for Achilles. Achilles's armor is awarded to Odysseus, with the help of Athena, causing the madness of Ajax and his suicide.

Pound cut this undeveloped sequence because it clashes with the more original critique of Odysseus voiced by the Lotophagoi later in Canto 20. It also has nothing to do with Eros and so doesn't fit with Niccolò's other readings. (Is this Niccolò imagining what the Sirens might have said to Odysseus?) However, like Niccolò, Pound's Odysseus is haunted by his crimes. He wanders in repentance.

In his essay "Hell" (1934), written nine years after he wrote Canto 20, Pound defends Dante's condemnation of Ulysses and Diomedes, pointing out two key elements usually overlooked:

> Re punishment of Ulysses, no one seems to note the perfectly useless, trifling, unprovoked sack of the Cicones in the *Odyssey*. Troy was one thing, they were inveigled.

81 *EPP*, 3, 143.
82 *PT*, 549.
83 *Iliad* 10.471–515.
84 Murray, *Rise of the Greek Epic*, 87.

> Helen's father was trying to dodge destiny by a clever combination, etc., but for the sack of the Ciconian town there was no excuse handy, it is pure devilment, and Ulysses and Co. deserved all they got thereafter (not that there is any certainty that Dante had this in mind).
>
> It gives a crime and punishment motif to the *Odyssey*, which is frequently overlooked, and is promptly and (?) properly snowed under by the human interest in Odysseus himself, the live man among duds. Dante definitely accents the theft of the Palladium, whereon one could turn out a volume of comment. It binds through from Homer to Virgil to Dante.[85]

Pound's critique of Odysseus here might be an echo of Joyce's, who thought the incident was so significant that he planned to add a Cicones chapter to *Ulysses*.[86] The idea appears in *The Pisan Cantos*: "the folly of attacking that island [of the Cicones] / and of the force ὑπὲρ μόρον ['beyond what is destined']" (74/463). But Pound's reading here is problematic. If Homer wanted to highlight the injustice, he would have mentioned the episode again. Neither Tiresias nor any of the gods care about it. Odysseus himself presents it as a hero's right; the only fault was in staying too long.

> From Ilios the wind bore me and brought me to the Cicones, to Ismarus. There I sacked the city and slew the men; and from the city we took their wives and great store of treasure, and divided them among us, that so far as lay in me no man might go defrauded of an equal share. Then verily I gave command that we should flee with swift foot, but the others in their great folly [μέθυ πίνετο, *methy pineto*: "great childishness"] did not hearken.
>
> (9.39–44)

For Murray, of course, this is evidence of a more primitive form of the *Odyssey* featuring Odysseus-as-pirate, like a Cú Chulainn. Regardless, Pound favors the crime and punishment motif because it fits with his own idea of the *Odyssey* as a ritual purgation through adventure and initiation.

The episode of the Lotophagoi occurs right after the attack on the Cicones. Pound's Odysseus is "young" and full of hubris. He has not learned humility through wandering. Homer's Lotophagoi are not hostile to Odysseus men, but Odysseus regards them as a threat so dangerous that he repeats the danger they represent three times.

> Thence for nine days' space I was borne by direful winds over the teeming deep; but on the tenth we set foot on the land of the Lotus-eaters, who eat

85 *LE*, 212–13.

86 See Lynn Childress, "The Missing 'Cicones' Episode of *Ulysses*," *James Joyce Quarterly* 33.1 (1995): 69–82.

> a flowery food [ἄνθινον εἶδαρ, *anthinon eidar*]. There we went on shore and drew water, and straightway my comrades took their meal by the swift ships. But when we had tasted food and drink, I sent forth some of my comrades to go and learn who the men were, who here ate bread upon the earth; two men I chose, sending with them a third as a herald. So they went straightway and mingled with the Lotus-eaters, and the Lotus-eaters did not plan death for my comrades, but gave them of the lotus to taste. And whosoever of them ate of the honey-sweet fruit of the lotus, had no longer any wish to bring back word or to return [νέεσθαι, *neesthai*], but there they were fain to abide among the Lotus-eaters, feeding on the lotus, and forgetful of their homeward way [νόστου, *nostou*]. These men, therefore, I brought back perforce to the ships, weeping, and dragged them beneath the benches and bound them fast in the hollow ships [νηυσὶ δ' ἐνὶ γλαφυρῇσιν ὑπὸ ζυγὰ δῆσα ἐρύσσας, *nēusi d' eni glaphyrēsin hypo zyga dēsa eryssas*]; and I bade the rest of my trusty comrades to embark with speed on the swift ships, lest perchance anyone should eat of the lotus and forget his homeward way [νόστοιο, *nostoio*]. So they went on board straightway and sat down upon the benches, and sitting well in order smote the grey sea with their oars.
>
> (9.81–104)

Like a good anthropologist, Odysseus first wants "to go and learn who the men were, who here ate bread upon the earth." This is a typical response of Odysseus when he encounters a new land; he also needs to replenish his food supply. After his men fail to return, however, he loses all desire to know who the Lotophagoi are. The threat of forgetting the homeward way (nostos) that the Lotus represents is repeated three times, almost to the point of redundancy: "had no longer any wish to bring back word or to return [*neesthai*]"; "forgetful of their homeward way [*nostou*]"; and "forget his homeward way [*nostoio*]."

Odysseus's extreme reaction is justifiable within the *Odyssey*. He and his men just fought ten years overseas for a Greek cause, and the lotus fruit makes them forget their Greekness. Odysseus needs his crew to get home, and because they are as unruly as children, which both the proem and the earlier episode with Cicones makes clear, they need to be treated like children. However, For Pound, this episode represents the selfish and hubristic Odysseus before he is initiated into Circe's mysteries, and loses all desire to return home. (Odysseus's men need to remind Odysseus after a year that they should be on their way.) It also stages the tension between the vehement teleology of the epic structure and its primordial lyric and ritual origins. Nowhere is Odysseus (and the *Odyssey*) so insistent on nostos.

For Pound, the epic structure destroys the possibility of revelation—or, for that matter, even a good yarn. Pound's version calls attention to what was missed. Pound's Lotophagoi, knowing the fate of Odysseus's men, argue that they would have been better off remaining with them. Surprisingly, Pound's Lotophagoi are not the insular and hedonistic people one might expect them to be. Nor do they, like Tennyson's Lotus-eaters, make the flaccid argument that "slumber is more sweet than toil."[87] The Lotophagoi's critique of Odysseus's single-minded quest is surprisingly cogent. In the spirit of Dante and Cicero, they suggest that Odysseus's quest was never one to get home, but for worldly and spiritual gain.[88] His transgression, however, was in hogging all the fragments of paradiso terrestre for himself.

"What gain with Odysseus,
"They that died in the whirlpool
"And after many vain labors,
"Living by stolen meat, chained to the rowingbench
"That he should have a great fame
"And lie by night with the goddess?
"Their names are not written in bronze
"Nor their rowing sticks set with Elpenor's;
"Nor have they mound by sea-bord.
"That saw never the olives under Spartha
"With the leaves green and then not green,
"The click of light in their branches;
"That saw not the bronze hall nor the ingle
"Nor lay there with the queen's waiting maids,
"Nor had they Circe to couch-mate, Circe Titania,
"Nor had they meats of Kalüpso
"Or her silk shirts brushing their thighs.
"Give! What were they given?

87 Tennyson's poem attempts to rationalize the lure of the Lotophagoi: "Surely, surely, slumber is more sweet than toil, the shore / Than labor in the deep mid-ocean, wind and wave and oar; / O, rest ye, brother mariners, we will not wander more" (Tennyson, *The Major Works*, 51). This might be plausible of the mariners on Thrinacia, three years into the journey, but not at the outset. Odysseus's mariners would be as eager to return as Odysseus; they are the ones who remind Odysseus after a yearlong stay on Circe's island to think about home. "The Lotus Eaters" is a weak counterargument to the worldview presented in "Ulysses" (1833): "to strive, to seek, to find, and not to yield," which is itself a facile version of Dante's Ulysses minus the theology (80). Pound's opinions of Tennyson's Victorian *translatio* of the *Odyssey* were evidently so low he refrained from comment entirely.

88 Cicero remarks that Odysseus seems to be driven by a love of knowledge and wisdom that is dearer than his home. See Cicero, *De Finibus Bonorum et Malorum*, ed. Th. Schiche (Leipzig: Teubner, 1915), 5.18.49.

Ear-wax.

"Poison and ear-wax,

and a salt grave by the bull-field,

"*neson amumona,* their heads like sea crows in the foam,

"Black splotches, sea-weed under lightning;

"Canned beef of Apollo, ten cans for a boat load."

Ligur' aoide. (20/93–94)

Pound's Lotophagoi, ironically, do not forget. They bear witness to Odysseus's crimes. His men were wrested away from their only taste of paradise and "chained to the rowing bench": Pound's translation of Homer's "*nēusi d' eni glaphyrēsin hypo zyga dēsa* eryssas" ("dragged into the hollow ships and tied by a yoke"). "Ear-wax" prevented them from hearing the Siren's song. "Poison" presumably refers to Circe's *pharmaka,* which can mean "drugs" but also "magic philters" or "poisons," and which appears later in Canto 39, "kaka pharmak edoken" ("she gave them evil drugs") (39/193). They never lay in Circe's bed, and nine-tenths of them never even saw Circe's ingle and bronze halls or slept with Circe's waiting maids, since the Laestrygonians ate them. And, obviously, they never lay with Calypso. After eating the Cattle of Helios ("canned beef for Apollo") on his island ("*neson amumona*") the last ones drowned ("heads like sea crows in the foam"). They never received homage or burial mounds like Elpenor—at least not until Canto 20.

This might seem like a bad reading of Homer. It has led to a lot of bad readings of Pound. It is tantalizingly argumentative, but also overburdened with allusions to and re-interpretations of the *Odyssey.* The Lotophagoi's argument is weak when read in the context of Homer, a little less weak in the context of Virgil, Ovid, and Dante, but rich in the context of Pound's own attempt to read Odysseus as a solar hero and mystery initiate.

Odysseus's "renown" in the *Odyssey* is not that he gets to hear the Sirens or sleep with Calypso (he doesn't seem to enjoy that at all), but his reputation as strategist and a warrior who can outsmart Trojans, Greeks, giants, and sometimes gods. Pound's Lotophagoi make no mention of the fact that (in Homer at least) the men who drowned near Thrinacia really had it coming, especially after foolishly opening the bag of winds right when they were nearing the shores of Ithaca, and then deciding to eat the Cattle of Helios, having sworn to Odysseus they would not, and knowing full well that it would incite the god's wrath. Their names are not really worthy of being set in bronze. Pound's Lotophaghoi also never mention that the goal of Odysseus and his men was nostos. Perhaps the Lotophagoi mean to imply that the nostos quest was never anything more than a pretext for

Odysseus to hog all the revelation for himself, but it seems more likely that this is Pound's reinterpretation of the wanderings of Odysseus in which the nostos quest does not exist, or it is so inconsequential that it warrants no attention.

The Lotophaghoi begin by lamenting those who "died in the whirlpool," which is an allusion to Dante, not Homer. In Homer, Odysseus and his men opt to go the way of Scylla rather than the sucking whirlpool Charybdis. Later Odysseus faces it alone and almost drowns. In Dante, a "whirlwind" (*turbo*) spins Ulysses and his men around three times and then the sea swallows them right as they glimpse Mount Purgatory beyond the Pillars of Hercules.[89]

Pound's lament of the Lotophagoi is in part a *translatio* of Odysseus's men themselves when they decide to open the bag of winds from Aeolus:

> Out on it, how beloved and honored this man is by all men, to whose city and land soever he comes! Much goodly treasure is he carrying with him from the land of Troy from out the spoil, while we, who have accomplished the same journey as he, are returning, bearing with us empty hands. And now Aeolus has given him these gifts, granting them freely of his love. Nay, come, let us quickly see what is here, what store of gold and silver is in the wallet.
>
> (10.38–45)

However, Pound's Lotophagoi do not focus on riches or worldly goods but experiences of Pound's paradiso terrestre. Cantos 39 and 47 present Odysseus's union with Circe as is a rite of spring and mystic initiation. Odysseus never saw "the olives under Spartha / 'With the leaves green and then not green, / 'The click of light in their branches." Odysseus probably visited Helen and his brother in Sparta, but the image is not from Homer. It alludes to Allen Upward's 1908 discovery that Athena's epithet, *glaukopis* or "owl-eyed," refers to how the owl's eyes "suddenly leave off glaring like lighthouses whose light is shut off."[90] Pound quoted the passage in full in "Allen Upward Serious" (1914):

> We may see the shutter of the lightning in that mask that overhangs Athene's brow and hear its click in the word glaukos. And the leafage of the olive whose writhen trunk bears, as it were, the lightning's brand, does not glare but glitters, the pale under face of the leaves alternating with the dark upper face, and so the olive is Athene's tree and is called glaukos.[91]

[89] *Inferno* 26.137. Pound might also be echoing Eliot's "Death by Water" in *The Waste Land*: "A current under sea / Picked his bones in whispers. As he rose and fell / He passed the stages of his age and youth / Entering the whirlpool" (lines 315–18).

[90] Allen Upward, *The New Word* (London: A. C. Field, 1908), 234.

[91] Upward, *The New Word*, 239; *SP*, 407.

Pound praises Upward as a genius because, although a non-specialist, "has had much of it at first hand," and "has never forgotten the very real man inside the event or the history."[92] Odysseus is a "real man" like Upward and Pound: one who makes philological discoveries (*glaukopis, noigandres*) by "reading" nature. Like Leo Frobenius, and unlike James Frazer, Upward knows his subject first-hand. For Pound and his Lotophagoi, discovering the meaning of the epithet *glaukopis* by the turning olive trees in Sparta is tantamount to laying with a goddess: accessible to anyone who has a mind willing and free to observe and contemplate nature.

Odysseus's crime is that he does not let his comrades linger with the Lotus-eaters as he might have. He bars them that paradise. The Lotophagoi echo Pound's attacks of war as the tragic waste of individual potential to build and create rather than destroy and be destroyed; "to be men not destroyers" (117/823). "Canned beef" refers to bully beef (corned beef), the popular ration of the trench soldier in the First World War. The word was synonymous to Pound with easily palatable culture. In a 1935 letter to the editor of *New Democracy*, Pound describes himself as one who "did NOT believe that all kulchur shd. be hammered down to the level of Armour's and cos. canned beef."[93] Canto 16 elaborates on the tragedy of the war as a waste of creative men at the whim of stupid uncreative politicians: "And because that son of a bitch, / Franz Josef of Austria… / And because that son of a bitch Napoléon Barbiche…" (16/71); "And Henri Gaudier went to it, / and they killed him, / And killed a good deal of sculpture, / And ole T.E.H. he went to it". Similarly, Canto 27 ventriloquizes the exploited common man or "tovarisch" during the failed Russian revolution. Pound echoes the Lotophagoi's lament of a wasted life, reflecting on the companions of Cadmus:

> I neither build nor reap.
> That he came with the gold ships, Cadmus,
> That he fought with the wisdom,
> Cadmus, of the gilded prows. Nothing I build
> And I reap
> Nothing; with the thirtieth autumn
> I sleep, I sleep not, I rot
> And I build no wall.
> […]

92 *SP*, 403, 404.

93 Ezra Pound, 1935 Letter to *New Democracy*. *EPC*, Box 2, Folder 5.

I sailed never with Cadmus,
lifted never stone above stone. (27/132)

Pound's "democratic" interpretation of myth couldn't be more explicit here. Anyone who is open-minded and free can become a part of myth and build monuments. Cadmus is a much older hero than Odysseus, whose voyage took him from Samothrace to Delphi and eventually Thebes. There, legend has it, he slayed a dragon and sowed a new race of men with its teeth. The men helped him build the Mycenaean Cadmea. His companions were his equals: they sailed with him and built with him. Odysseus, by contrast, does not allow his men to participate in the fruits of his mystic and sensual journey.

The final phrase "Ligur' aoide" alerts the reader to the parallel between Pound's Lotophaghoi and Homer's Sirens. Both sing to passersby on ships, and both are surrounded by bones. Circe describes the bone pile around the Sirens: "The Sirens beguile him with their clear-toned song [λιγυρῇ θέλγουσιν ἀοιδῇ, *ligyrē thelgousin aoidē*], as they sit in a meadow, and about them is a great heap of bones of moldering men, and round the bones the skin is shriveling" (12.44–47). Pound's Lotophagoi rest on a "high shelf" of a cliff; "And beneath: the clear bones, far down, / Thousand on thousand" (20/93). Homer's Sirens speak from a meadow on an island. However, in Virgil, the sirens live on a projecting shelf of rock amidst sea-bleached bones: "Iamque adeo scopulos Sirenum advecta subibat, / difficiles quondam multorumque ossibus albos"; "And now, onward borne, it was nearing the cliffs of the Sirens, perilous of old and white with the bones of many men."[94] Homer's Sirens appeal to Odysseus's desire that his sufferings be remembered: "For we know all that has happened at Troy." Pound's Lotophagoi know all that has happened *since* Troy: but their knowledge would only strike shame into his heart, like Pound's Sirens from the earlier draft of Canto 20.

Pound "translates" the Sirens' song by transposing it onto the Lotophagoi. "Ligur aoide" is Homer's description of the ineffable beauty of the sound of the Sirens which he cannot reproduce. The opening of Canto 20 attempts to recreate the lost folkloric *sound* of the *Ur-Odyssey.* Pound's Lotophagoi, by contrast, represent a step toward understanding the lost forkloric *content* of the *Ur-Odyssey.* The Lotophagoi read Odysseus's adventures not as a series of (interesting) impediments to his victorious and gruesome nostos, but as steps or stages of initiation with primordial goddesses through direct observation

[94] Virgil, *Aeneid* 5.864–65.

of the natural world: hearing the sound of the Sirens, eating the lotus of the Lotophagoi, or sleeping beside Circe.

In Canto 20, the critical work of solving a philological puzzle becomes "real": Arnaut's "flor don lo fruitz sia amors" ("flower that breeds love") blooms into a visionary reading of Homer's "ἄνθινον εἶδαρ" (*anthinon eidar*, "flowery food").[95] While Canto 2 attempts to recreate the "hurley-burley" of a Dionysian transformation, the "wilderness" of Canto 20 more emphatically leads to a "Basis of renewal, renewals" (20/91). It presents a Babelic music difficult to hear, a philological quest with no clear resolution, a narrative of one man's delirious readings of other texts, a visionary poetry difficult to visualize, and a critique of Odysseus that implies his journey was never one to arrive home. (One could go on: a cryptic and inaccurate reading of *La Chanson de Roland;* a paradise rebuilt out of hell and purgatory; Lotophagoi that resemble Sirens.) This "Wilderness of renewals" leads to "confusion / Basis of renewals" (20/92).

Confusion, like forgetting, is the enemy of the Homeric text: the sign of disorder and chaos, the frightening undemocratic and impulse-driven chthonic gods, the irrational and seductive feminine gods, and the monsters like Polyphemus who violate the law of hospitality (*xenia*). Confusion in Homer marks a crisis of democracy and selfhood: an angry god sows confusion among the troops; a bad leader like Agamemnon creates confusion among his men; the underworld is a place of confusion and fear. The hero puts an end to confusion: he pulls out his sword and demands that the ghosts approach him in an orderly fashion; he chains the dope fiends to the rowing benches.

For Pound, however, confusion, delirium, and forgetting undermine the teleology of the epic. Confusion recreates the state of mind of the initiate in the Dionysian mysteries, who experiences the metaphoric *sparagmos* ("abscission") of his individuation and glimpses a deeper truth. In Nietzsche's words: "Whenever this breakdown of the *principium individuationis* occurs, we catch a glimpse of the essence of the *Dionysiac*, which is best conveyed by the analogy of *intoxication*."[96] Dionysus, the god of delirium, of wine and altered states, and Eros, the force of desire and love-sickness that torments so many of the heroes of medieval *translatio*s like Benoît's Achille or Enéas in the *Roman d'Enéas*, presages the return of the old gods. Pound's Lotophagoi represent the essential getting-lost that will wrench epic out of its dangerous teleology and war-mongering; the hashish dreams of Thomas De Quincey

95 Daniel, Arnaut, *Les Poèsies d'Arnaut Daniel*, ed. Réne Lavaud (Toulouse: Édouard Privat, 1910), 80; *Odyssey* 9.84.

96 Nietzsche, *The Birth of Tragedy*, 17.

which are the "keys of Paradise";[97] the guilt-ridden delirium of Pound-Odysseus in *The Pisan Cantos*. When Dionysus Zagreus returns to the epic from which he was banished, as Harrison describes, he restores literature as ritual and a cult of Eros: an *Iliad* that consists of nothing but (haetarchic) Helen-worship; an *Odyssey* of the nameless fertility hero's nomadic wanderings making amends for his crimes against the "democratic" spirit of Eleusis. Pound's poetics calls for the cultivation of confusion, which is the confusion that comes about through interrogating the work by means of the mythic method. This "delirious" or "drugged" reading makes the coherent *Odyssey* deteriorate into visionary fragments and "clear shapes, / Broken, disrupted, body eternal" (20/91): a procession of chthonic gods and goddesses, a mythic repetitive text of a hero endlessly wandering, forever forgetting his way.

[97] Thomas De Quincey, *Confessions of an Opium Eater and Suspira de Profundis* (Boston: Ticknor, Reed, and Fields, 1850), 68. De Quincey argues that opium, delirium, and near-death experiences present a paradise that normally lies dormant in the creative mind by habit.

5

Erotic Circe

The progress of civilization is not favorable to woman. She is at her best in the so-called barbaric periods; later epochs destroy her hegemony, curtail her physical beauty.[1]

Of insects the female is nearly always the superior individual.[2]

In Cantos 39 and 47, Pound connects Odysseus and Circe's lovemaking with a rite of spring tied to the worship of Feronia, Demeter, Adonis, Tamuz, and Mithra. Although Pound claimed to have no "Aquinas-map" for his long poem, the structural parallels between *The Cantos* and the *Odyssey* here are hard to ignore. Homer's two Circe episodes occur roughly in the middle of the *Odyssey* in two distinct sections: books 10 and 12 of 24. They are the sixth and eighth of the thirteen main episodes of Odysseus's wanderings: Cicones, Lotophagoi, Cyclopes, Aeolus, Laestrygonians, Circe, Kimmerians, (back to) Circe, Sirens, Scylla, Thrinacia, Charybdis, and Calypso. Pound's "fertility cantos" are placed in a similar position in *The Cantos:* Cantos 39, which is a *translatio* of *Odyssey* 10, and Canto 47, which is a *translatio* of *Odyssey* 12, in what Pound estimated as "about 100 cantos in all" in 1939 in a letter to Eliot—at least as many as Dante.[3]

Pound's *translatio* of *Odyssey* 10 and 12 is irreverent, pornographic, pedagogic, and celebratory: a kind of satyr play. Like the Lotophagoi episode in Canto 20, Pound denies Odysseus his privileged role of narrator. Canto 39 begins with Elpenor's schoolboyish and hedonistic account of Circe's paradise island of "fucked girls and fat leopards" (39/193). Elpenor trips through Homer's Greek and muddles the story of his transformation into a pig until he arrives at the (imagined) bedroom scene, where he presents a jazzy or ragtime version of Circe's

1 Bachofen, *Myth, Religion, and Mother Right,* 171.

2 Remy de Gourmont, *The Natural Philosophy of Love*, trans. Ezra Pound (New York: Boni and Liveright, 1922), 34.

3 Ezra Pound, September 29, 1939 Letter to T. S. Eliot. *EPP*, 670. As early as 1922, Pound writes to Felix Schelling: "Having the crust to attempt a poem in 100 or 120 cantos long after all mankind has been commanded never again to attempt a poem of any length, I have to stagger as I can" (*L*, 247).

seduction of Odysseus, followed by a Latinate (and Tennysonian) celebration of Circe's erotic mystery: the young bride who has "swallowed the fire-ball" and exclaims, "his rod hath made a fire in my belly" (39/196). Elpenor in part adapts the medieval version of the story, itself derived from the lost *Telegony* (576/7 BCE), that Odysseus and Circe conceived a child. Elpenor's perverted and phallocentric account of the *hieros gamos* is "revised" by Circe's gynocentric and pedagogic account in Canto 47. Pound grafts Circe's directions to Odysseus in *Odyssey* 12 with Hesiod's advice to his brother Perses in *Works and Days* (*c.* 700 BCE): give up adventuring, pick up the plow, observe the seasons, and reflect on the gods' indifference to man. Odysseus finally speaks, ecstatically transformed into the new Pound hero: a dying-and-resurrecting god whose weight is "less than the shadow / Yet hast thou gnawed through the mountain" (47/238).

The fertility cantos represent an evolution of Pound's Homeric *translatio*. The aesthetics of confusion in Canto 20—the delirium of Niccolò III d'Este and the "dope smoking" Lotophagoi—gives way to an ecstatic ritual of "fucking" Circe and Odysseus's transformation into a fertility god. The Lotophagoi's critique of Odysseus as fundamentally selfish in Canto 20 returns as Circe's imperative that Odysseus learn Hesiodic αιδώς (*aidōs*) in Canto 47: shame, decency, and humility. Pound dismantles the mythos of the epic hero, from the "sacker of cities" (Homer) or one who "sails after knowledge" (Dante) to a dying and resurrecting god of spring, who enters Circe's hill "by prong" and is reborn as soil, plant, and tree: "That the grass grow from my body, / That I hear the roots speaking together, / The air is new on my leaf, / The forked boughs shake with the wind" (47/238).

Although there are more allusions and indirect references to Odysseus than any other classical figure in *The Cantos,* Circe is a close second. Her name actually appears more often than Odysseus's: twenty-five times versus seventeen times. This is eclipsed only by sixty-eight mentions of "[John] Adams" (not counting references to John Quincey Adams) and twenty-eight mentions of "Washington"—but many of these are epistolary citations: "Adams to Jefferson 1815" (71/419). "Yeats" and "Dante" both appear sixteen times.[4] Like Odysseus (and unlike Adams and Washington), Circe's name recurs throughout *The Cantos:* Cantos 1, 17, 20, 39, 41, 47, 74, 80, 91, and 106. Some of these appearances are cryptic or obscure, such as the reference to the "brother of Circe" in Pound's Venetian paradise (17/79); and Circe's "swine-sty" compared to the Pisan

4 By my count, there are over sixty five appearances of "[John] Adams" and twenty eight of "Washington." There are sixteen appearances of both "Yeats" and "Dante," and ten of "Eliot/ Possum."

camps and her *kaka pharmaka* ("evil drugs") as a metaphor of "every bank of discount" (74/436, 74/457). Homer's generic epithet, "Κίρκη εὐπλόκαμος" (*Kirkē euplokamos,* "Circe of the goodly locks") even prompts Pound to make her hair a simile for "the law of discourse" which is Horace's dictum, "simplex munditiis" ("elegance in simplicity") (*Odyssey* 11.8, 80/494).

Pound's Circe is a priestess of the mysteries of Adonis and Tamuz. She plays the role of mystagogue to Odysseus's transition from the self-interested hubristic war criminal to the humble farmer, lover, and devotee of the matriarchal goddess. She undermines and transforms Homer's epic into a ritual of spring fecundation. Pound's reading of Circe is mostly consistent with Homer. Homer's Circe is the only pre-Olympian deity who plays a significant role in the *Odyssey*. Circe is of Titan heritage ("Kirke Titania"), and a *Potnia Theron* ("Queen of the Beasts"), or, as Pound puts it, one "that hath the gift of healing, / that hath the power over wild beasts" (47/239). This connects her to the ancient pre-Achean matriarchal goddesses like Inara, who tames the wild animals that live around her temple in a παράδεισος (*paradeisos*), from the Avestan *Pairidaeza*, meaning "enclosure" or "park." Circe's association with the pig and φάρμακον (*pharmakon*, "drug," "poison," "spell") also connects her with the purification rituals of mystery religions like Eleusis. Even Homer specifies that once Circe reverses her spell, the mariners "became men again, younger than they were before, and far comelier and taller to look upon" (10.395–96). Circe is also a more important guide to Odysseus than Tiresias. She teaches him not only how to enter Hades, hear the Sirens, bypass Scylla and Charybdis, and conduct himself on Thrinacia, but also how to change his model of questing from active and aggressive or "σχέτλιε" (*schetlie,* "rash," "merciless," "cruel") to passive and non-violent by learning how to "yield" [ὑπείκω, *hypeikō,* "retire," "withdraw," "depart"] (12.116). Tiresias's advice, by contrast, focuses on what Odysseus must do after he returns home in order to appease Poseidon: the action of the *Telegony*. Finally, Odysseus's year-long stay with Circe is an unusual aberration of Homer's nostos-plot. Unlike his seven-year stay with Calypso, Odysseus takes such pleasure in Circe that his own men remind him after a year that it is time to leave.

In the following, I first examine how Pound's account of Odysseus's return to Aeaea in Canto 23 and a typescript fragment of Canto 20 present Odysseus as a solar deity returning from under-earth to Circe's "temple of the dawn." I then argue that Pound's *translatio* of *Odyssey* 10 and 12 in Cantos 39 and 47 evolves from a patriarchal, hedonistic, teleological story to a matriarchal, gnomic, and cyclical one. Circe debases men in order to liberate them from their swinish nature. Pound does the same to Homer's Circe. Elpenor's retelling of *Odyssey* 10 is not just a bad translation, it is a provocation. Sloppy verse, obscenity, perversion, and parody of the mythical method gives way to satyr-like celebration. Canto 47, by contrast, carefully dismantles Odysseus's quest into a ritual of fecundation, excavating Circe's role as mystagogue and lawgiver in Pound's ideal matriarchal or agricultural-based society. Pound also makes this very shift from epic to lyric part of the "action" of his story. Circe's restoration as primordial goddess and Odysseus's transformation into a fertility daimon is the climax of Canto 47. The confrontation of the traditional epic climax (Hector versus Achilles, Odysseus versus the suitors) is replaced by the confrontation of the (traditional?) lyric climax (orgasm, *hieros gamos*). While Pound's *translatio* in the fertility cantos employs many of the earlier techniques (disorder, confusion, delirium, intoxication), its "technic" might best be best described as "erotic" in its obsession with the *mysterium* of coitus, but also because the word connotes bawdy, ribald, pornographic, and ecstatic.

While there has been a lot of excellent criticism on Pound's Circe and the *hieros gamos* of Odysseus and Circe,[5] little has been written about Pound's unique *translatio* of *Odyssey* 10 and 12, especially the focalization. Canto 39 is loosely told through the perspective of Elpenor. The opening lines make this explicit: "When I lay in the ingle of Circe," directly refers back to Elpenor's line in Canto 1: "I slept in Circe's ingle" (39/193, 1/4). If the hapax legomena "fucked" and "fucking" fail to alert the reader that this is not the poet of paradise speaking, the cartoon version of Circe's pleasure island with talking leopards; nonsense (Eliotic) lyrics like "girls leery with Circe's tisane"; and Latinate Tennysonians like "cunni cultrix, of the velvet marge" ought to (39/193). Canto 47 is loosely constructed as a dialogue between Circe and Odysseus. Circe's nautical and tactical advice begins the canto, which evolves into a series of *gnomai* (maxims) adapted from *Works and Days*. Odysseus's ecstatic response concludes the canto.

Odysseus Helios (Canto 23)

In Canto 1, Pound summarizes Odysseus's departure from Kimmeria: "And he sailed, by Sirens and thence outward and away / And unto Circe" (1/5). Pound originally intended for an account of Odysseus's return to appear at the end

[5] For example, Liebregts, *Ezra Pound and Neoplatonism*, 224–31; Sean Pryor, *W.B. Yeats, Ezra Pound, and the Poetry of Paradise* (Burlington, VT: Ashgate, 2011), 135–44; Peter Nicholls, *Ezra Pound: Politics, Economics, and Writing* (London: Macmillan, 1984), 71–4; and Leon Surette, *A Light from Eleusis: A Study of Ezra Pound's Cantos* (New York: Oxford University Press, 1979), 39–65.

of Canto 20; he expands on this return in Canto 23; Cantos 39 and 47 further elaborate this return. Why does Pound dwell on such a minor episode of Odysseus's wanderings—that of passing by Circe's to bury Elpenor and receive more directions? Because leaving and returning to Circe represents the basic (fugal) narrative model of his primitive solar *Odyssey*: leaving Circe (the dawn sky), traveling west beyond Oceanus and descending underground (nekyia), and returning to Circe (the dawn sky) in the morning.

In an early typescript, Canto 20 ends with an extended translation of *Odyssey* 12.1–11, recounting Odysseus's return to Aeaea. Pound connects Odysseus's return with the dawn, suggesting that Canto 20 is a solar nekyia: a chthonic procession of the sun traveling underground back to the east. Canto 20 ends with the image of "Vanoka, leaning half naked, / waste hall there behind her" (20/95). In the typescript, the procession continues down from Vanoka to an old woman bent like (or over) a loom, to another description of Dionysus's cortege which includes the Renaissance painters Domenico Ghirlandaio and Petrus de Burgo. The action then shifts to Odysseus's men arriving on Circe's beach—although the last page is unpaginated, meaning that Pound might not have known where to place it. My transcription begins at the end of Pound's page "i":

and Vanoka leaning, half naked,
waste hall stretching behind her.
~~and then in the rock, down, two stone stair-flights~~
~~an[] old woman bent in a loom,~~

[page j:]

Ghirlandaio and Petrus de Burgo ~~meeting me~~ in that road,
and the cliff bent like the folds of a curtain,
and the road suave, in the cliffs edge,
and the cars with us, that had fi[r]st shown
coming out of the mist,
the black feet of the panthers
the strong pasterns, suave impact,
and the sleepers wrapped in their cloaks,
indigo, russet, and orange, and gold worked
soft over the cloaks,
each on his side, and the head on the right elbow
~~the beneficent, wise in the senses,~~
~~now columns of brighter colour~~
~~as rose-quartz~~

[unpaginated:]

In this place, the temple of dawn,
Hither Odysseus; from the great coil of ocean,
returned, and from 'Ades; this place of Aiaeos
the place of Kirké Titania,
　　　　in dawn born-of-the-Spring,
here landed in sea-break; beached their keel
　　　　　　　in the sand dunes,
with sacks over their heads, landed their empty casks
brought sea-gear ashore here;
　　　　　　　here bur[]ied Elpenor
here faced again Circe.[6]

The colors in the Ghirlandaio section reflect the imminent glow of the "temple of dawn" that will follow: "indigo, russet, and orange, and gold worked / soft over the cloaks." As the procession descends, the light returns: "now columns of brighter color / as rose quartz." Dante Pilgrim's descent through hell eventually becomes an ascent to the base of Mount Purgatory. Pound's descent is similar. Pound might not have paginated the last page because he couldn't find a place for it.[7] However, the description of the "old woman bent in a loom" anticipates the image of Circe at the beginning of Canto 39, "In hill path 'thkk, thgk' / of the loom" (39/193), itself an allusion to the mariner's first glimpse of Circe singing as she works on her warp-weighted loom in *Odyssey* 10. The "temple of dawn" segment is Pound's translation of the beginning *Odyssey* 12:

> Now after our ship had left the stream of the river Oceanus and had come to the wave of the broad sea, and the Aeaean isle, where is the dwelling [οἰκία, *oikia*] of early Dawn and her dancing-lawns [ὅθι τ' Ἠοῦς ἠριγενείης / οἰκία καὶ χοροί εἰσι, *hothi t' Ēous ērigeneiēs / oikia kai choroi eisi*], and the risings of the sun, there on our coming we beached our ship on the sands [ψαμάθοισιν, *psamathoisin*], and ourselves went forth upon the shore of the sea, and there we fell asleep, and waited for the bright Dawn. As soon as early Dawn appeared, the rosy-fingered, then I sent forth my comrades to the house [δώματα, *dōmata*] of Circe to fetch the body of the dead Elpenor.
>
> (12.1–10)

6 Ezra Pound, "Canto XX: Typescripts." *EPP*, 3189.

7 Akiko Miyake and Peter Liebregts both ignore the middle "Ghirlandaio" section, quoting the final Vanoka lines and then adding an ellipsis before the Circe section, suggesting that Pound intended it to follow directly. See Miyake, *Ezra Pound and the Mysteries of Love*, 133; and Liebregts, *Ezra Pound and Neoplatonism*, 184.

Pound turns Circe's dwelling (*oikia*) of Dawn into a temple. Homer's river of Oceanus encircling the earth becomes Pound's "coil" of Ocean. Pound's invented epithet, "dawn born-of-the-Spring" connects Circe's house with the dawn as well as spring rituals and the return of the warmer months. Pound highlights something only implicit in Homer, that Circe is associated with the rebirth of the sun. Homer describes Aeaea as close to "where the dwellings and dancing floors of early-born Dawn are, and the rising places of the Sun." Pound also reminds his readers of Circe's primordial lineage by referring to her as "Kirke Titania." Circe is also the daughter of Helios, the son of the Titan Hyperion, and the Oceanid nymph Perse. In Canto 106 Pound is more explicit: "Helios, Perse: Circe" (106/774).

Pound also adds two unusual details or "overchange" to his *translatio*: Odysseus and his men wear "sacks over their heads"; and they unload their tackle or "brought sea-gear ashore here." The first alludes to the Persian sun god Mithra, who was often depicted in a Phyrgian cap; while the second is to the Egyptian solar deity Ra, who dumps desert sand from Atet, his sun boat, as he ascends the sky in the morning. Pound develops these connections more fully in his more cryptic and condensed version of Odysseus's return to Aeaea in Canto 23. This canto has received careful exegesis by a number of critics, but few have recognized that it is a *translatio* of *Odyssey* 12.1–15 as well as a continuation and reworking of the "temple of dawn" sequence in the Canto 20 typescript.[8] In Canto 23, "the idiot Odysseus furrowed the sand" (23/107). His men are "in the Phrygian head-sack / Barefooted, dumping sand from their boat" (23/108). This is repeated: "And the men dumping sand by the sea-wall / Olive trees there on the hill / where a man might carry his oar up." Homer's Odysseus specifies that he and his men "beached our ship on the sands." (Pound earlier translates this as "sand dunes," and here, "furrowed the sand.") The other lines echo Homer's description of Elpenor's funeral:

> Straightway then we cut billets of wood and gave him burial where the headland runs furthest out to sea [ὅθ' ἀκροτάτη πρόεχ' ἀκτή, *hoth' akrotatē proech' aktē*], sorrowing and shedding big tears. But when the dead man was burned, and the armor of the dead, we heaped up a mound [τύμβον χεύαντες,

[8] See, for example, Michael Davidson, *Ghostlier Demarcations: Modern Poetry and the Material Word* (Berkeley: University of California Press, 1997), 100–102; Demetres Tryphonopoulos, *The Celestial Tradition: A Study of Ezra Pound's The Cantos* (Waterloo, ON: Wilfrid Laurier University Press, 1992), 127–31; Leon Surettte, *The Birth of Modernism: Ezra Pound, T.S. Eliot, W.B. Yeats and the Occult* (Montreal: McGill-Queen's University Press, 1993), 151–9; and Liebregts, *Ezra Pound and Neoplatonism*, 187–90.

> *tymbon cheuantes*] and dragged on to it a pillar, and on the top of the mound we planted his shapely oar.
>
> (12.11–15)

Pound condenses this to: "The men dumping sand by the sea-wall / Olive trees there on the hill / where a man might carry his oar up." The "sea wall" is Homer's *aktē* or "promontory"; "dumping sand" is Pound's version of the men *tymbon cheuantes*, "heaping" or "throwing up" (the verb χέω [*cheō*] means "pour," but in this context, "throw up" earth so as to form a mound); and the oar is carried up and planted on the mound. These reflect the directions of Elpenor in Canto 1: "Heap up mine arms, be tomb by sea-board [...] And set my oar up" (1/4).

Pound's *translatio* of *Odyssey* 12.1–15 in Canto 23 is stitched together with a translation and philological investigation of a fragment of *Geryoneis* by Stesichorus (*c*. 630–555 BCE) which recounts Heracles's tenth labor to acquire Geryon's cattle. This is arguably the most cryptic and condensed *translatio* of Homer in *The Cantos*—a close second being Canto 91, where Pound interlaces Leucothea's rescue of Odysseus with Philostatus's account of the last days of Apollonius of Tyana (15–100) and details from John Heydon's *The Holy Guide*.[9] Nietzsche contrasts the Dionysian "folk" lyrics of Archilochus (680–645 BCE) with the Apollonian epic of Homer; Pound prefers Stesichorus, who retold epic stories like the story of Helen or the Sack of Troy in lyric meters. Stesichorus embodies Pound's ideal "classicist" poet who translates epic material back into lyric. Stesichorus also associates Heracles's journey across the Libyan desert with the course of the sun. Heracles crosses the Libyan desert en route to Erytheia in the Hesperides (from *Hesperos* or "evening"), the westernmost isle in Oceanus, in order to recover the cattle of the giant Geryon. As Apollodorus recounts: "But being heated by the Sun on his journey, he bent his bow at the god, who in admiration of his hardihood, gave him a golden goblet in which he crossed the ocean."[10] Once Hercules defeats Geryon and rescues the cattle, he takes the golden goblet and the cattle to Tartessus. Stesichorus's fragment recounts the moment when Heracles returns the cup to Helios.[11] Terrell translates the passage with square brackets around the Greek words Pound leaves out of Canto 23:

> The sun, Hyperion's child, stepped down into his golden bowl and then after crossing the stream of ocean [he reached] the depth of black [and holy] night

[9] See chapter 7.

[10] Apollodorus, *The Library*, vol. 1, trans James George Frazer, 2.5.10.

[11] Stesichorus's fragment is preserved by the late-first-century AD writer Athenaeus in his *Deipnosophistae* ("Scholars at Dinner") 11.38. Pound derived his classical text from an 1802 Greek and Latin edition of the book by Johannes Schweighäuser.

> and joined his mother, his faithful wife, and his dear children. [Meanwhile the son of Zeus] entered [on foot] the laurel-shaded [grove].[12]

Pound suppresses the reference to the son of Zeus (Heracles) so as to make Odysseus the subject of the fragment. His use of this fragment is a virtuosic act of creative philology and the mythic method, although he certainly ventures into the obscure wood (*selv' oscura*) of references.

> With the sun in a golden cup
> 		and going towards the low fords of ocean
> Ἅλιος δ' Ὑπεριονίδας δέπας ἐσκατέβαινε χρύσεον
> Ὄφρα δὶ ὠκεανοῖο περάσας
> 		ima vadis noctis obscurae
> Seeking doubtless the sex in bread-moulds
> ἥλιος, ἄλιος, ἄλιος = μάταιος
> ("Derivation uncertain." The idiot
> Odysseus furrowed the sand.)
> alixantos, aliotrephès, eiskatebaine, down into,
> descended, to the end that, beyond ocean,
> pass through, traverse
> 				ποτὶ βένθεα
> νυκτὸς ἐρεμνᾶς,
> ποτὶ ματέρα, κουριδίαν τ' ἄλοχον
> παῖδάς τε φίλους.... ἔβα δάφναισι κατάσκιον
> Precisely, the selv' oscura. (23/107–8)

Taking Stesichoros's cue, Pound links the hero with the course of the sun. Pound first assays a translation of the first two lines of the fragment: "With the sun in a golden cup / and going towards the low fords of ocean." He then reverts to Schweighäuser's Latin translation, "ima vadis noctis obscurae" ("the lowest depths of darkest night").[13] Earlier in the canto, Pound celebrates scientific advancements of the 1920s, including turbine energy, penicillin, and Marie Curie's discovery of radium. Here, the word "noctis" prompts Pound to imagine a "darker" moment for science: a futile experiment to find the "sex" of bread molds (which are made in the dark).[14] Pound interrupts his translation to

[12] Terrell, *A Companion*, 93.

[13] Stesichorus, *Αθηναιου Ναυκρατιτου Δειπνοσοφισται/Athenaei Naucratitae Deipnosophistarum*, ed. and trans. Johannes Schweighäuser, vol. 4 (Argentorati [Strassburg]: ex typographia Societatis Bipontinae, 1804), 237–8.

[14] Pound might have been thinking of Freud's earliest research in 1876 under Carl Claus in Trieste, which involved dissecting hundreds of eels in search for their male reproductive organs. His first published paper was a concession of his failure.

account for why he replaces the god's name in Stesichorus, Ἀέλιος (*Aelios*), by a variant pointed out by Schweighäuser in footnote 3: Ἅλιος (*Halios*), which Schweighäuser explains is a variant of ἥλιος (*helios*). Pound opened up his abridged *Greek-English Lexicon* and found these five entries clustered together relating to ἅλιος, all of which he adds to Canto 23:

ἁλί-ξαντος, ον, (ἅλς, ξαίνω), *worn by the sea*
ἅλιος, ὁ, Dor. for ἥλιος, *the sun* [ᾱ]
ἅλιος, α, ον, also ος, ον, (ἅλς), *of, from*, or *belonging to the sea*, Lat. *marinus.* [ᾰ]
ἅλιος, α, ον = μάταιος, *fruitless, unprofitable, idle, erring*: also in neut. as Adv. *in vain* [ᾰ] (Deriv. uncertain)
ἁλί-τρεφής, ές, (ἅλιος, τρέφω), *sea-nurtured.*[15]

The three different definitions of ἅλιος are presented in Canto 23 as "ἥλιος, ἅλιος, ἅλιος = μάταιος / ('Derivation uncertain.' The idiot / Odysseus furrowed the sand.)" This allows Pound to make a number of connections between Odysseus, Heracles, and Helios. The first definition of ἅλιος (*halios*) is Doric for ἥλιος (*hēlios*), "the sun," which is the only point Schweighäuser was trying to make. The second definition means "from the sea," and derives from ἅλς or ἅλος (*hals* or *halos*) meaning both "the sea" and "salt." (The English word "salt" derives from the Greek *hals*.) Liddell and Scott didn't know the derivation of the third definition of ἅλιος as "μάταιος" (*mataios*) meaning "fruitless." Pound suggests his own: the story of Odysseus, who faked madness by sowing his crops with salt (*hals*) to get out of the Trojan expedition. This hints at another meaning of "furrowed the sand." "Idiot" refers to Odysseus's feigned madness but is also Pound's translation of the third meaning of ἅλιος as μάταιος (*mataios*) or "fruitless." It refers back to the fruitless search for the sex of bread molds, as well as anticipates Circe's admonition of Odysseus and his men as "rash" (*sketlie*) when he returns from Hades (12.21). Circe will confront Odysseus on his own selfish, hubristic, "idiotic" (in the etymological sense of *idios*: "own," "private") and fruitless (*mataios*) sense of questing.[16] The word further recalls Heracles's fruitless journey across the Libyan sands until he was given Helios's golden cup.

[15] Liddell and Scott, *A Lexicon Abridged from Liddell and Scott's Greek-English Lexicon* (Oxford: Clarendon Press, 1871), 33.

[16] Homer twice uses ἅλιος in *The Odyssey* in the third sense of "fruitless," both times with ὁδός ("way," "road"), in reference to a "fruitless journey." Athena, disguised as Mentor, reassures Telemachus: "οὔ τοι ἔπειθ' ἁλίη ὁδὸς ἔσσεται οὐδ' ἀτέλεστος [*ou toi epeith' haliē hodos essetai oud' atelestos*, 'So then shall this journey of thine be neither vain nor unfulfilled']" (2.273). Telemachus echoes Athena's words a few lines later when he tells Antonius: "For go I will, nor shall the journey be in vain [οὐδ' ἁλίη ὁδὸς ἔσσεται (*oud' haliē hodos essetai*)] whereof I speak, though I voyage in another's ship, since I may not be master of ship or oarsmen" (2.318–19).

Just as Heracles lands back on the sandy shores of Tartessus with the cattle and returns the ship to Helios, so Odysseus returns to Circe (daughter of Helios) after reaching Hades by means of her magical directions.

Pound's philological investigation of one ordinary word in Stesichorus allows him to make the connection between the legend of Heracles and that of Odysseus as well as suggest that they both originate as solar myths. "Derivation uncertain," invites readers to search for her own. Both Heracles and Odysseus derive from solar deities: Helios, or the much older Hyperion, invoked in the line that follows ("'Yperionides!" [23/108]). Stesichorus's fragment describes Helios's *katabasis* which is mirrored by Heracles: the sun goes down under the western horizon, just as Heracles goes down into the laurel-shaded ("δάφναισι κατάσκιον" [*daphnaisi kataskion*]) grove.

For good measure, Pound includes the surrounding cognates of ἅλιος: *alixantos* ("worn by the sea"), and *aliotrephès* ("feeding in the sea") from the *Abridged Greek-English Lexicon,* then returns to the Stesichorus fragment, looking up the next word, ἐσκατέβαινε (*heskatébaine*), which he transliterates and then defines: "eiskatebaine, down into, / descended, to the end that, beyond ocean, / pass through, traverse." Pound's transliteration appears to be an error until one looks up the verb in Liddell and Scott, which informs the reader that ἐσκαταβαίνω (*eskatabainō*) is a variant of εἰσκαταβαίνω (*eiskatabainō*): *eis* ("into") + *kata* ("down") + *bainō* ("to go"). The word "katabasis" ("descent") derives from this word, an important motif of *The Cantos:* "live man goes down into the world of the dead."[17] The rest of Stesichorus's fragment is creatively fragmented by Pound: "ποτὶ βένθεα ['to the depths'] / νυκτὸς ἐρεμνᾶς ['of the dark night'], / ποτὶ ματέρα, κουριδίαν τ'ἄλοχον ['to mother, wedded wife'] / παῖδάς τε φίλους.... ἔβα δάφναισι / κατάσκιον ['and dear children .... walked shaded by laurels']." Pound's fragmenting obscures the distinction between Heracles, Odysseus, and Helios, as well as Dante Pilgrim ("Precisely, the selv' oscura"). In an incredibly complex way, Pound suggests that, "precisely," all derive from the same story.

This is immediately followed by the invocation of dawn, which invokes Odysseus's returning to Aeaea in the morning from Hades and the return of the solar deity, golden cup, or "sun boat" which rises over the Phyrigian (eastern) desert and gains buoyancy by dumping sand.

> And in the morning, in the Phrygian head-sack
> Barefooted, dumping sand from their boat
> 'Yperionides! (23/108)

[17] *L*, 285.

Helios is here referred to as Hyperionides (Ὑπεριωνίδης), or "son of Hyperion." Hyperion is an obscure figure in Greek mythology, one of the twelve Titan children of Ouranos and Gaia. Homer conflates Hyperion with Helios, while Hesiod (and Stesichorus) specifies that Hyperion is the father of Helios. Pound is less interested in tracing Helios's lineage than in invoking the oldest Greek solar deity. Although Helios is traditionally represented as driving a chariot, Pound reimagines him here as the ancient Egyptian solar deity (Ra) in his sun-boat (Atet). Solar ships were commonly buried near Egyptian pyramids, possibly as funeral barges, or as vessels meant to carry the resurrected king across the heavens with Ra. Upon resurrection, they would presumably dump their sand and ascend. "Dumping sand" is more generally a metaphor for the solar boat losing its earthly weight so that it can ascend the sky. Stesichorus's Heracles steps out of the golden cup and Helios floats away in it; in his draft for Canto 20, Pound specifies that Odysseus and his men land on Aeaea "with sacks over their heads, landed their empty casks / brought sea-gear ashore here." In Canto 23, Pound echoes the idea in his description of heaping up Elpenor's burial mound, comparing the boat's sail to a weightless cloud: "The boat's sails hung loose at the mooring, / Cloud like a sail inverted, / And the men dumping sand by the sea-wall" (23/108).

Leon Surette points out that the Phyrigian head-sack is an attribute of Mithra, the Persian sun god, detailed in George Mead's pamphlet, *The Mysteries of Mithra* (1907), which Pound probably read.[18] Mead mentions a carving of "a young man, quite naked, except for his Phrygian cape" cutting from a tree branch.[19] Surette argues that this is a reference to the soul's "transmigration from the astral or etheric plan to the material or hylic plane," and that Pound is making a direct reference to this in Canto 23. Pound does compare Odysseus's union with Circe to the Mithraic mysteries in Canto 47, but the Phrygian cap was associated by ancient authors with everyone in Eastern Europe and Anatolia, including Phrygians and Trojans. Greek earthenware depicts Paris and Aeneas with Phrygian caps in order to distinguish them as non-Greek. Titian depicts the mythical Phrygian King Midas in *Flaying of Marsyas* (1570) wearing one. Massimo Bacigalupo also points out that from his terrace in Rapallo, Pound could "the heavy boats with lateen sails (called *leudi*) that brought over sand from Sardinia."[20] The sailors wore burlap sacks or paper bags which appeared to Pound to look like Phrygian caps.

[18] Surette, *The Birth of Modernism: Ezra Pound, T.S. Eliot, W.B. Yeats and the Occult* (Montreal: McGill-Queen's University Press, 1993), 153–4.

[19] George Robert Stow Mead, *The Mysteries of Mithra* (London: Theosophical Publishing Society: 1907), 81.

[20] Massimo Bacigalupo, *The Forméd Trace: The Later Poetry of Ezra Pound* (New York: Columbia University Press, 1980), 380.

A more plausible explanation for the Phyrigian cap is that, in Roman times, the cap came to be associated with the *pileus*, the felt cap of the emancipated slave. In a section that influenced Joyce's "Circe," Victor Bérard argues that the Roman fertility goddess Feronia was Homer's Circe.[21] Her main cult was at Anxur, Terracina, on the promontory of Monte Circeo, so named because it was identified by Virgil as Circe's island. The mountain of calcareous rock contains many caves, long considered by locals to be the "caves of Circe." Feronia's cult was one of the oldest rustic religions in Italy. "Feronia" means goddess of wild, untamed, uncultivated, "feral" places. A chthonic deity, she was syncretized by Greco-romans into Proserpine. Bérard explains that her cortege of nymphs were often depicted as lions and wolves, and that visitors to her land associated the wild pigs and boars of nearby towns with her. Feronia was also known as the goddess of freedom from slavery. Newly freed slaves would go to her shrine and receive the *pileus*, a hat symbolizing their liberty, on their shaved heads.

Just as Feronia changes brutes (slaves) into men (citizens) by means of a symbolic pileus, Circe transforms Odysseus's swinish comrades into better men with a tap of her wand on their heads. Pound's mariners therefore wear the *pileus* because they have been "freed" from their brutish slavery by Circe (as Feronia) in book 10 (Canto 39).[22] In Canto 39, Pound associates Circe with Terracina and imagines her temple on the top of the mountain: "Flank by flank on the headland / with the Goddess' eyes to seaward / By Circeo, by Terracina, with the stone eyes / white toward the sea" (39/195). Pound's Circe also lives in both a temple ("house of smooth stone") as well as a "cave" (47/237). Pound never refers to Feronia, but he associates Circe with the Roman fertility goddesses Flora in Canto 39 and Tellus (Terra) in Canto 47.

Fucking to Fac Deum (Canto 39)

In Canto 39, Elpenor recounts the story of Circe's seduction of Odysseus with the help of Ibycus, Virgil, Catullus, the *Pervigilium Veneris,* and Dante. Elpenor's version of *Odyssey* 10 is a parody of the mythical method, replete with sloppy

[21] Victor Bérard, *Les Phéniciens et l'Odyssée*, vol. 2 (Paris: Colin, 1902–3), 285–7.

[22] Bérard further points out that Servius records a joint cult of "the boy Jupiter" (*puer Iuppiter*) under the name "Anxyrus" and "Juno the Virgin" (*Iuno virgo*) whom he identifies as Feronia. *Atriplex halimus*, also known as sea orache or Mediterranean saltbush, was associated with Jupiter Axour/ Anxur, and therefore was Homer's moly. The herb was used by the Marsicans in the Apennine mountains, who were associated with magicians. See Bérard, *Les Phéniciens et l'Odyssée*, vol. 2, 305.

verse, obscenity, arbitrary obscurity, misuse of words, nonsense repetitions, reflecting his hedonistic and perverted point of view. His satyr song eventually transforms into a celebration of a rite of spring. Circe may transform men into pigs, but she also restores them.

Pound associates Elpenor with a hedonist and an aesthete in *Hugh Selwyn Mauberly* (1920). Out of key with his time, Mauberly "observed the elegance of Circe's hair / Rather than the mottos on sundials."[23] Roman sundials offer gnomic reminders of the transience of life. Mauberly would rather muse on Greek depictions of female beauty. Nearing his end, however, the old aesthete compares himself to Elpenor:

> A consciousness disjunct,
> Being but this overblotted
> Series
> Of intermittences;
>
> Coracle of Pacific voyages,
> The unforecasted beach;
> Then on an oar
> Read this:
>
> "I was
> And I no more exist;
> "Here drifted
> An hedonist."[24]

Mauberly knows only enough to recognize the disorder and insignificance of his own life. Like Prufrock, he recognizes that he is no Prince Hamlet but an attendant lord or a fool. Mauberly is no Odysseus. He is that drunken mariner "not over valiant in war nor sound of understanding" who falls from the roof (*Odyssey* 10.552). Mauberly's death, for Pound, marks the end of a hedonistic (Victorian and Pre-Raphaelite) age: those artists who can muse on the elegance of Circe's hair (like John William Waterhouse) but not penetrate her mysteries, like Odysseus or Pound can.

In *Odyssey* 11 and in Canto 1, Elpenor is crippled in Hades with the realization of his life's insignificance: "an overblotted / Series / Of intermittences." His lament

[23] *PT*, 549.
[24] *SP*, 111.

Figure 5.1 *Circe* (1911) by John William Waterhouse.

is moving because he is the last person the audience expects to pity. Odysseus's describes Elpenor's comically literal downfall in book 10.

> There was one, Elpenor, the youngest of all, not over valiant in war nor sound of understanding [οὔτε τι λίην ἄλκιμος ἐν πολέμῳ οὔτε φρεσὶν ᾗσιν ἀρηρώς, *oute ti liēn alkimos en polemō oute phresin hēsin arērōs*], who had laid him down apart from his comrades [ἄνευθ' ἑτάρω, *aneuth' hetarō*] in the sacred house of Circe, seeking the cool air, for he was heavy with wine [οἰνοβαρείων, *oinobareiōn*]. He heard the noise and the bustle of his comrades as they moved about, and suddenly sprang up, and forgot to go to the long ladder that he might come down again [ἐκλάθετο φρεσὶν ᾗσιν ἄψορρον καταβῆναι ἰὼν ἐς κλίμακα

> μακρήν, *eklatheto phresin hēsin apsorron katabēnai iōn es klimaka makrēn*], but fell headlong from the roof [τέγεος, *tegeos*].
>
> (10.552–559)

Young people in Homer tend to be inexperienced and undeveloped, like Telemachus or Polydamus. Elpenor is not only young, but also he is neither brave (*alkimos*) in battle nor *phresin hēsin arērōs*, which means literally "of heart joined together." (The Greek *phren* refers to the heart but is considered the "mind" or the "seat of thought"; ἀραρίσκω (*arariskō*) means "to be joined," "constructed," or "furnished.") Heavy with wine (*oinobareō*), Elepenor settles apart or distant from (*aneuthe*) his comrades in the house. Odysseus could have been more precise, but that would have ruined the joke. In the morning, Elpenor (and the listener) realize that he is on the roof (*tegeos*). Elpenor forgets entirely (*eklatheto*) to mind ("to heart": *phresin*) to go down the ladder back the way he came.

In Hades, Elpenor explains that "an evil doom of some god was my undoing, and measureless wine. When I had lain down to sleep in the house of Circe I did not think [οὐκ ἐνόησα, *ouk enoēsa*] to go to the long ladder that I might come down again" (11.61–63). According to Odysseus, Elpenor's lack of a fully "joined" or sound mind is why he forgets he's on the roof; here Elpenor presents it as the kind of oversight anyone might make, reinforcing the idea that he was the victim of some unfair god. The gods do not need to punish drunks. They manage it on their own.

The humor is lost if *Odyssey* 11 or Canto 1 is read in isolation. But in Canto 39, Elpenor wistfully remembers his last evening, satiated by wine and fucking, as he fell asleep to the metronomic sound of Circe at the vertical loom in her "ingle"—he can't seem to admit it is a roof and so settles on this nonsensical translation of *tegeos*. Now, in Hades (or in Rapallo), the landscape seems to him desolate and cruel—especially the roof he happens to be looking at. The girls are gone, the panthers are gone, even the cat from that morning is gone.

> Desolate is the roof where the cat sat,
> Desolate is the iron rail that he walked
> And the corner post whence he greeted the sunrise.
> In hill path: "thkk, thgk"
>   of the loom
> "Thgk, thkk" and the sharp sound of a song
>   under olives
> When I lay in the ingle of Circe

> I heard a song of that kind.
>   Fat panther lay by me
> Girls talked there of fucking, beasts talked there of eating,
> All heavy with sleep, fucked girls and fat leopards,
> Lions loggy with Circe's tisane,
> Girls leery with Circe's tisane. (39/193)

Terrell situates the scene as the "sound of the looms on the hill path leading up from Rapallo" and "the guard railing at Lake Garda,"[25] but that level of biographical specificity isn't illuminating because Pound is not that specific. There is a vague invocation of contemporary Greece or Italy—blacksmiths in Homer's time did not make railings—in which the folk continue the artisanal practices of Homer's day (working at the loom and farming olives) and still sing the songs Homer might have sung. Just as Arnaut's music is reborn from the landscape near Perigord in Canto 20, Circe's Aeaea returns to the poet. The sound of a loom becomes the sound of Circe's warp weighted loom; the peasant's song becomes Circe's divine song; the cat becomes one of Circe's tame panthers.

But this is not Ezra Pound speaking. This is the childish, obscene, sloppy, and botched song of a still-intoxicated mind. "Desolate" means deserted, dismal, or bleak. It is the wrong word to describe a roof that a local cat has abandoned to get out of the noonday sun, a worse word to describe an iron rail lacking that cat, and an even worse word to describe a corner post lacking that cat. It is also the kind of Miltonic anastrophe that Pound abhorred.[26] A clunky quest for anaphora overpowers sense. The girls are talking of fucking; the lions are loggy with Circe's tisane; and the beasts are talking of eating. Elpenor sacrifices sense for the sake of drunken melopoeia. "Leery" means wary or suspicious, and is almost always followed by "of," not "with." An archaic form of leery means "alert," and a slang version means "boisterous." But if the girls are "all heavy with sleep" and wine, "leery" is the wrong word. Elpenor wants a word that sounds like "loggy" but has the sense of "bleary" or "weary."

Elpenor's song devolves into a barely coherent half-assed translation of *Odyssey* 10:

> κακά φάρμακ ἔδωκεν ["she gave them evil drugs"]
> kaka pharmak edōken

[25] Terrell, *A Companion*, 160.

[26] Milton is "chock a block with Latin" and does "wrong to his mother tongue" (*ABCR*, 51). Pound's example is: "Him who disobeyes / Mee disobeyes" to mean, "Who disobeys him disobeys me" (Milton, *Paradise Lost*, ed. John Leonard [New York: Penguin, 2003], 5.611–612).

The house of smooth stone that you can see from a distance
λύκοι ὀρέστεροι ἠδὲ λέοντες ["we saw lions and leopards"]
lukoi oresteroi ede leontes
        wolf to curry favor for food
-born to Helios and Perseis
        That had Pasiphae for a twin
Venter venustus, cunni cultrix, of the velvet marge ["beautiful belly, cunny tender"]
        ver novum, canorum, ver novum ["new spring, singing, new spring"]
Spring overborne into summer
        late spring in the leafy autumn
καλὸν ἀοιδιάει ["she sings beautifully"]
KALON AOIDIAEI
        Ἡ θεὸς ἠὲ γυνή.... φθεγγώμεθα θᾶσσον
        ["whether goddess or woman.... let us call out quickly to her"]
        e theos e gune   ptheggometha thasson

First honey and cheese
        honey at first and then acorns
Honey at the start and then acorns
        honey and wine and then acorns. (39/193–94)

Elpenor's *translatio* consists of a handful of Greek phrases and transliterations; some animal and food vocabulary words; and dirty Latin verses. Eurylochus's account of what happened to his search party is narrated out of order: she gave them evil drugs; her house was of smooth stone; we saw lions and leopards. Elpenor connects Circe with her zoophilic sister Pasiphae perhaps to justify a reflection on Circe's "beautiful belly, cunny tender," and the Tennysonian image of "velvet marge," which recalls Golding's "velvet curtain," but seems to be a euphemism for her genitalia. Elpenor returns to a lazy summary of *Odyssey* 10 without translations: "KALON AOIDIAEI" ("she sings beautifully"); "e theos e gune" ("whether goddess or woman"); "ptheggometha thasson" ("let us call quickly to her"). The reader with a bit of Greek might know "kalon," "theos," and "gune," but not "ptheggometha thasson." Elpenor's résumé of what the mariners were fed stumbles forward as if he could not remember the order: the honey, cheese, and wine mixed with *pharmakon kakon.*

Elpenor's slipshod translation compels the reader to return to book 10 in order to make sense of it. The relevant passages are underlined:

Within the forest glades they found the house of Circe, built <u>of polished stone</u> [ξεστοῖσιν λάεσσι, *xestoisin laessi*] in a place of wide outlook [περισκέπτῳ ἐνὶ

> χώρῳ, *periskeptō eni chōrō*], and round about it were mountain wolves and lions [ἀμφὶ δέ μιν λύκοι ἦσαν ὀρέστεροι ἠδὲ λέοντες, *amphi de min lykoi ēsan oresteroi ēde leontes*], whom Circe herself had bewitched; for she gave them evil drugs [κακὰ φάρμακ' ἔδωκεν, *kaka pharmak' edōken*]. Yet these beasts did not rush upon my men, but pranced about them fawningly, wagging their long tails. And as when hounds fawn around their master as he comes from a feast, for he ever brings them bits to soothe their temper, so about them fawned the stout-clawed wolves and lions; but they were seized with fear, as they saw the dread monsters. So they stood in the gateway of the fair-tressed goddess [θεᾶς καλλιπλοκάμοιο, *theas kalliplokamoio*], and within they heard Circe singing with sweet voice, as she went to and fro before a great imperishable web [ἀειδούσης ὀπὶ καλῇ, ἱστὸν ἐποιχομένης μέγαν ἄμβροτον, *aeidousēs opi kalē, histon epoichomenēs megan ambroton*], such as is the handiwork of goddesses, finely-woven and beautiful, and glorious. Then among them spoke Polites, a leader of men, dearest to me of my comrades, and trustiest: "Friends, within someone goes to and fro before a great web, singing sweetly [καλὸν ἀοιδιάει, *kalon aoidiaei*], so that all the floor echoes; some goddess it is, or some woman. Come, let us quickly call to her [ἢ θεὸς ἠὲ γυνή: ἀλλὰ φθεγγώμεθα θᾶσσον, *ē theos ēe gynē: alla phthengōmetha thasson*]." So he spoke, and they cried aloud, and called to her. And she straightway came forth and opened the bright doors, and bade them in; and all went with her in their folly. Only Eurylochus remained behind, for he suspected that there was a snare. She brought them in and made them sit on chairs and seats, and made [ἐκύκα, *ekyka*: "mixed"] for them a potion of cheese and barley meal and yellow honey with Pramnian wine; [τυρόν τε καὶ ἄλφιτα καὶ μέλι χλωρὸν οἴνῳ Πραμνείῳ, *tyron te kai alphita kai meli chlōron oinō Pramneiō*] but in the food she mixed baneful drugs [φάρμακα λύγρ', *pharmaka lygr'*], that they might utterly forget their native land. Now when she had given them the potion, and they had drunk it off, then she presently smote them with her wand, and penned them in the sties. And they had the heads, and voice, and bristles, and shape of swine, but their minds [νοῦς, *nous*] remained unchanged even as before. So they were penned there weeping, and before them Circe flung mast and acorns [ἄκυλον βάλανόν τε, *akylon balanon te*], and the fruit of the cornel tree, to eat, such things as wallowing swine are wont to feed upon.
>
> (10.210–244)

Elpenor's translation is hardly the masterful condensation of Homer of Canto 1. It is a disordered riffing of a few phrases from Homer, possibly mimicking the syncopation or "ragged" rhythm of ragtime. Perhaps Elpenor, unlike Eurylochus, is so broken down by grief that he can't tell the story coherently. More likely, Elpenor is too lazy or incapable of working through Homer's Greek. Elpenor describes Circe's "house of smooth stone that you can see from a distance." Homer, by contrast, describes Circe's palace as a "place of wide outlook," meaning *from* which you can see a great distance. The nonsensical line, "wolf to curry favor for food," which comes right after "lukoi oresteroi ede leontes" ("wolves there were and lions") is a lazy condensation of Homer's epic simile: "as when hounds fawn around their master as he comes from a feast, for he ever brings them bits to soothe their temper." Circe's wolves fawned on the men *like* dogs trying to curry favor from their masters for food. They are not actually looking for food.

The next two lines might baffle even a close reader, unless she were reading it alongside the original:

> Song sharp at the edge, her crotch like a young sapling
> illa dolore obmutuit, partier vocem
> ["she was dumb with grief, in like matter her voice"]. (39/194)

Elpenor already described Circe's transformation of the men into animals, so why does he return to a description of Circe's song? Why qualify it as "sharp at the edge" (recalling Pound's favorite word, *ligur*) when Homer calls it sweet or beautiful (καλῆ, καλὸν)? Why the image of Circe's "crotch like a young sapling"? Unlike Calpyso or Nausicaa, Homer does not specify that Circe is young. A phallic sapling seems like the wrong simile for a yonic crotch. And why juxtapose this with a botched fragment of Ovid's description of Hecuba's speechlessness before the death of her son Polydorous? "The Trojan women shrieked at the sight; but she was dumb with grief; her very grief engulfed her powers of speech, her rising tears. Like a hard rock, immovable she stood, now held her gaze fixed on the ground."[27] Is this Elpenor's subject rhyme for the sudden speechlessness of the mariners once they are transformed? Sean Pryor suggests that Circe herself goes silent here, at least in the reader's mind, because Pound follows this passage with five lines of Circe's directions to Odysseus at the end of book 10 in Greek without transliterations, allowing the "muteness" of Greek text to speak.[28] It's an elegant suggestion. But a more plausible answer is found by reading on in Homer's text:

> But Eurylochus came back straightway to the swift, black ship, to bring tiding of his comrades and their shameful doom. <u>Not a word could he utter, for all his desire, so stricken to the heart was he with great distress, and his eyes were filled with tears</u>, and his spirit was set on lamentation. But when we questioned him in

[27] Ovid, *Metamorphoses*, trans. Frank Justus Miller (Cambridge, MA: Harvard University Press, 1984), 13.538–41.

[28] Pryor, *W.B. Yeats, Ezra Pound, and the Poetry of Paradise*, 137–8.

> amazement, then he told the fate of the others, his comrades. "We went through the thickets [ἀνὰ δρυμά, *ana dryma*], as thou badest, noble Odysseus. We found in the forest glades [ἐν βήσσῃσι, *en bēssēsi*] a fair palace, built of polished stones [δώματα καλὰ ξεστοῖσιν λάεσσι, *dōmata kala xestoisin laessi*] in a place of wide outlook. There someone was going to and fro before a great web, and singing with clear voice [λίγ' ἄειδεν, *lig' aeiden*], some goddess or some woman, and they cried aloud, and called to her."
>
> (10.244–255)

Elpenor's version returns to Circe's voice because the story is repeated by Eurylochus, who describes her singing with Pound's favorite word, *ligur.* Hecuba's silent grief over the death of her sons is Elpenor's idiotic subject rhyme for Eurylochus's temporary speechlessness before Odysseus and his men. And could Homer's mention of the δρυμός (*drymos*) or oak coppice and the βῆσσα (*bēssa*) or wooded comb have inspired Elpenor's image of Circe's crotch? Coppices tend to proliferate in saplings.

Elpenor's abuse of the mythical method would hardly be interesting if it didn't redeem itself. The next section, as Pryor suggests, already marks the limit of this technique. Elpenor drops in fives lines of Homer's Greek with the line number: "490/5," asking the reader to look it up for herself, and (if she hadn't already) discover just how bad Elpenor's translation has been so far.[29] Elpenor actually means lines 490–94. Perhaps he forgot that "0" counts as a line. Logicians call this a fencepost error. But the sixth line is relevant:

> but you must first complete another journey, and come to the house of Hades and dread Persephone, to seek soothsaying of the spirit of Theban Tiresias, the blind seer, whose mind abides steadfast. To him even in death Persephone has granted reason, [that he alone should have understanding; but the others flit about as shadows.]
>
> (10.490–5)

Pound didn't get around to translating this until Canto 47, in *The Fifth Decad of Cantos* (1937), which recounts Circe's directions and advice for Odysseus. The sixth line appears first:

> Who even dead, yet hath his mind entire!
> This song came to me in the dark

[29] See Pound's letter to Sarah Perkins Cope in *Selected Letters, 1907–1941*, ed. D. D. Paige (New York: New Directions, 1971), 335.

First must thou go the road
to hell
And to the bower of Ceres' daughter Proserpine,
Through overhanging dark, to see Tiresias,
Eyeless that was, a shade, that is in hell
So full of knowing that the beefy men know less than he,
Ere thou come to thy road's end. (47/236)

After looking up the Greek, and possibly reading ahead to Canto 47, the reader of Canto 39 can't help but feel as though the main point of all this is that Elpenor and Pound have no intention of "getting on" with the story. Cantos 1 and 23 prepare the reader to return "unto Circe" to bury Elpenor. When Pound finally introduces Circe in Canto 39, she is turning the mariners into swine and giving Odysseus directions (back) to Hades in impenetrable Greek.

After this point, even Circe seems confused by the order of events. Elpenor jumps backs to the previous action and transitions to the bedroom scene which he can only imagine. He stitches quotes from Dante together with Samuel Clarke's Latin translation of the *Odyssey.*

Che mai da me non si parte il dieletto ["So that never will the delight pass from me"]
Fulvida di folgore ["Reddish gold in its splendor"]
Came here with Glaucus unnoticed, nec ivi in harum ["nor went I into the pigsty"]
Nec in harum ingressus sum ["nor into the pigsty did I enter"]
Discuss this in bed said the lady
Euné kai philoteti ephata Kirkh ["Making love in bed, said Circe"]
Εὐνῇ καὶ φιλότητι, ἔφατα Κίρκη
es thalamon ["into the bedroom"]
'Ες θάλαμόν
Eurilochus, Macer, better there with good acorns
Than with a crab for an eye, and 30 fathom of fishes
Green swish in the socket,
Under portico of Kirké: ......
"I think you must be Odysseus ....
feel better when you have eaten ....
Always with your mind on the past ....
Ad Orcum autem quisquam? ["But has anyone to the Underworld?"]
nondum nave nigra pervenit ..... ["not yet reached in a black ship"]
Been to hell in a boat yet? (39/194–95)

Two quotations from Dante's *Paradiso* anticipate the paradise of Circe's bed: a praise of the Queen of Heaven from *Paradiso* 23.29 and a description of the river of light in the tenth empyrean in 30.62. The next lines combine Homer's description of the end of Eurylochus's "escape" with Odysseus's resistance to Circe's magic. Eurylochus explains to Odysseus that he didn't enter into Circe's house: "But I remained behind, for I suspected that there was a snare" (10.258). He didn't "enter" the pigsty. He "came" back to Odysseus unnoticed by Circe.[30] "Nec ivi in harum" is a modification from Samuel Clarke's 1804 Latin translation, "Abi nunc in haram, cum caeteris cuba sociis": Circe's words after she smites Odysseus with her wand: "Begone now to the sty, and lie with the rest of thy comrades" (10.320). Elpenor (or Pound) makes a schoolboyish mistake, transcribing *harum* ("these") instead of *haram* ("pen," "coop," or "pigsty"). He attributes the lines to Odysseus. "Came here with Glaucus unnoticed" alludes to how Odysseus "comes to" Circe with the magical herb *moly*. Glaucus, Circe's first love, was made immortal by eating another magic herb, and became a sea god of prophecy.[31] Dante compares the moment Glaucus tastes the herb to his first glimpse of Beatrice in *Paradiso*. "Nowhere is the nature of mystic ecstasy so well described," Pound declares in *The Spirit of Romance*.[32] In this case, *moly* represents the "mystic ecstasy" of glimpsing Circe for the first time. Even Elpenor resists reading Circe as an evil enchantress, despite the efforts of Apollonius, Virgil, Ovid, Augustine, Servius, Gower, Spenser, Milton, and the Pre-Raphaelites, to name but a few.[33]

The scene between Odysseus and Circe that follows is a jazzy version of Circe's seduction of Odysseus, which also requires that the reader follow along with the Greek. "Making love in bed" is a paraphrase of what Circe says to convince Odysseus, "Nay, come, put up thy sword in its sheath, and let us two then go up into my bed, that couched together in love we may put trust in each other" (10.333–35). Odysseus asks her how she can "with guileful purpose biddest me go to thy chamber, and go up into thy bed [*es thalamon*]" while his comrades remain swine? (10.339–40). Elpenor seems only interested in the Greek word for bedroom. The next line, however, does seem to answer Odysseus's implied question. "Eurilochus, Macer, better there with good acorns / Than with a crab

[30] Although not explicit, Homer implies that Eurylochus was unnoticed by Circe: "And she came forth straightway, and opened the bright doors, and bade them in; and they all went with her in their folly. But I remained behind, for I suspected that there was a snare. Then they all vanished together, nor did one of them appear again, though I sat long and watched" (10.257–60).

[31] Ovid, *Metamorphoses*, 8.917–959.

[32] *SR*, 145. See also "An Idyll for Glaucus" (1909) in *PT*, 86–8.

[33] See Yarnell, *Transformations of Circe*, 54-end.

for an eye, and 30 fathom of fishes / Green swish in the socket." Circe echoes Pound's Lotophagoi here. Homer's Circe could not have said this, for Eurylochus was never transformed, and Macer is Ovid's invention: he stayed behind in Cumae rather than brave more perils after Aeaea. Elpenor then radically abridges the rest of the action. "I think you must be Odysseus / feel better when you have eaten / Always with your mind on the past" condenses the action of Circe recognizing Odysseus when she first meets him in 10.330, ("Surely thou art Odysseus") and Circe convincing him to stop brooding after they share her bed and she restores his men:

> No longer now do ye rouse this plenteous lamenting. Of myself I know both all the woes you have suffered on the teeming deep, and all the wrong that cruel men have done you on the land. Nay, come, <u>eat food and drink wine,</u> until you once more get spirit in your breasts such as when at the first you left your native land of rugged Ithaca; but now ye are withered and spiritless, <u>ever thinking of your weary wanderings</u>, nor are your hearts ever joyful, for verily ye have suffered much.
>
> (10.456–65)

Odysseus agrees and spends a year at Circe's palace. Circe then explains to Odysseus that he must journey to Hades, which Pound quotes above. Odysseus responds, "O Circe, who will guide us on this journey? To Hades no man ever yet went in a black ship" (10.501–2). Elpenor puts this into the mouth of Circe by mangling Clarke's Latin translation, "Ad Orcum autem nondum quisquam pervenit nave nigrâ," into the ungrammatical question: "Ad Orcum autem quisquam? / nondum nave nigra pervenit," and then translating it as, "Been to hell in a boat yet?" (10.502) Circe herself seems confused here about the order of events in Elpenor's jumbled *translatio,* perhaps because she already gave Odysseus directions (in Greek) to Kimmeria half a page earlier.

Elpenor's *translatio* of *Odyssey* 10 suggests that our minds, as readers of Homer (and Pound), are "too much on the past." The outcome of the journey is the least interesting part of the *Odyssey.* It only leads to another woman (Penelope), another war (with the suitors, and then their fathers), and another journey (the temple for Poseidon), according to Homer; to a stingray-tipped arrow, according to the *Telegony*; or to a watery grave, according to Dante. "What gain with Odysseus, / They that died in the whirlpool" (20/93). Macer and Eurylochus are better off as swine "than with a crab for an eye, and 30 fathom of fishes / Green swish in the socket." The reader must reject the narrative telos of epic and renounce the past and future for the immediate present, which is Pound's paradise: the mystic ecstasy of Odysseus's union with Circe; the power of classical poetry once we stop "reading for the plot." Elpenor's piggish and perverted translation is a strategy to change the way this story is told. In place of Homer's epic telos, Elpenor the hedonist proposes the ritual eating and fucking of lyric. Elpenor ruminates, regurgitates, and vomits up bits of *Odyssey* 10 and 12 until the story becomes meaningless. Confusion and schoolboyish perversion lay the ground for renewal.

Elpenor's immature translation blossoms into a celebration of Circe as a goddess of spring: a patchwork of Greek, Latin, Middle English, and Italian invocations of spring, flowers, rebirth, and nighttime:

> Sumus in fide ["we have protection"]
> Puellaeque canamus ["and girls let us sing"]
> sub nocte.... ["beneath the night"]
>   there in the glade
> To Flora's night, with hyacinthus,
> With the crocus (spring
>   sharp in the grass,)
> Fifty and forty together
>   ERI MEN AI TE KUDONIAI ["and in spring the quinces"]
> Betuene April and Merche
>   with sap new in the bough
> With plum flowers above them
>   with almond on the black bough
> With jasmine and olive leaf,
> To the beat of the measure
> From star up to the half-dark
> From half-dark to half-dark
>   Unceasing the measure. (39/195)

The first lines hybridize Catullus and Virgil, pairing the idyllic song with Aeneas's *katabasis*. "Dianae sumus in fide / puellae et pueri integri: / Dianam pueri integri / puellaeque canamus"; "We, upright [*integri*: 'untouched'] maids and youths, are in Diana's care: upright youths and maids, we sing Diana."[34] And Virgil: "Ibant obscuri sola sub nocte per umbram"; "They walked exploring the unpeopled night."[35] Flora, the roman goddess of fertility and flowers, the central figure in Botticelli's *La Primavera,* walks the night among hyacinths and crocuses; spring is "sharp" in the grass as Circe's song is sharp; a fragment

[34] Catullus, Carmen 34.
[35] *Aeneid* 6.268.

from Ibycys invokes the quinces in spring; a line from the Middle English lyric *Alisoun* recalls the spring "sap new in the bow." Pound adds plum and almond flowers, jasmine and olive leaves, while his own prosody mimics the beating of the drum, "unceasing the measure" from "star up to half-dark" and "half-dark to half-dark," invoking a pagan spring ritual and a marriage ceremony.

> Flank by flank on the headland
>   with the Goddess' eyes to seaward
> By Circeo, by Terracina, with the stone eyes
>   white toward the sea
> With one measure, unceasing:
>   "Fac deum!'" "Est factus" ["'Make god!'" "'He is made.'"]
> Ver novum! ["New spring!"]
>   ver novum!
> Thus made the spring,
> Can see but their eyes in the dark
>   not the bough that he walked on.
> Beaten from flesh into light
> Hath swallowed the fire-ball
> A traverso le foglie ["Through the leaves"]
> His rod hath made a god in my belly
>   Sic loquitur nupta ["So the bride speaks"]
>   Cantat sic nupta ["So the bride sings"]
>
> Dark shoulders have stirred the lightning
> A girl's arms have nested the fire,
> Not I but the handmaid kindled
>   Cantat sic nupta
> I have eaten the flame. (39/195–96)

Elpenor's former "fucking" has become "Fac deum!" and "Est factus." A procession of drummers climbs up to the temple of Aphrodite/Flora/Circe. They are celebrating the completion of a mystery: the ritual coitus of Odysseus and Circe which has presumably taken place in her cave.[36] This divine coitus of mortal and goddess (Aphrodite and Adonis, Circe and Odysseus) "makes the spring." Pound then connects the pagan mysteries to medieval cults of the

[36] The line, "Can see but their eyes in the dark / not the bough that he walked on" is a vestige from an earlier version of Canto 39, which included a set of animal stories recounted by the "beasts" in Circe's ingle, involving "Hathorstamm" and "Patha." See Jonathan Ullyot, "Ezra Pound's Jungle Book: Hathor and the Canto 39 Typescripts," *Paideuma* 49 (2023).

Blessed Virgin Mary and the "Worship of Amor" in the Middle Ages with the line "Not I but the handmaid kindled." When Gabriel announces to Mary that she will give birth to the son of God, she announces, "Behold the handmaid of the Lord" (Luke 1:38). The flesh of Catholic communion is paganized and eroticized into "I have eaten the flame."

Elpenor's song in Canto 39 transforms from dirty to sacred, from perverted to spiritual, from pornographic to ecstatic. This reflects the way Elpenor and the rest of Odysseus's men were transformed from swine back into men "younger than they were before, and far comelier and taller to look upon" (10.395–96). The comedic transformation of Elpenor's Circe in Canto 39 lays the groundwork for the more "serious" transformation of Odysseus's Circe in Canto 47.

Power over Wild Beasts (Canto 47)

Canto 39 starts as a dirty song and ends as a sacred one. Canto 47 starts with Circe's teleological advice—how to arrive at Hades, how to pass by the Sirens and Scylla—and ends with her gnomic advice—how to live a good life by embodying Hesiod's *aidōs:* the feeling of reverence or shame which restrains people from wrongdoing. By the end of Canto 47, Pound's Odysseus has transformed from the hubristic, proud, self-interested hero to the selfless, passive devotee of the goddess. Canto 47 enacts a ritual transformation of Odysseus from the Homeric hero to the Pound hero; from Odysseus *ptolipórthion* (sacker of cities) to Odysseus *geōrgon* (farmer); from the teleological, battle-hungry, rash (*sketlie*), and vain Odysseus to the humble consort of the goddess and the devotee of grain rites.

Canto 47 begins with Pound's translation of *Odyssey* 10.490–5 that he didn't provide in Canto 39. Circe likens Odysseus's quest home to Dante's Ulysses's quest for knowledge, which she reduces to a paradox.

> Who even dead, yet hath his mind entire!
>   This sound came in the dark
>   First must thou go the road
>   to hell
> And to the bower of Ceres' daughter Proserpine,
> Through overhanging dark, to see Tiresias,
> Eyeless that was, a shade, that is in hell
> So full of knowing that the beefy men know less than he,
> Ere thou come to thy road's end.

> Knowledge the shade of a shade,
> Yet must thou sail after knowledge
> Knowing less than drugged beasts. (47/236)

Circe's directions "came to [Odysseus] in the dark" because he seeks out Circe late at night after everyone has gone to sleep in the "shadowy halls" (10.323–24). The passage can be read as meta-commentary, establishing Circe as the muse of *The Cantos.* Canto 1 begins by going "the road to hell" and visiting Tiresias, in order to resurrect the oldest part of Homer, the original music of Homer and the precise, sharp (*ligur*) sound of Circe's song. What was represented as a chunk of impenetrable (to most) and untransliterated Greek text in Canto 39 is "given voice" by the inspired Odysseus-poet. Like Dante's Beatrice, who leads Dante Pilgrim through heaven and commands him to write his *Commedia,* Circe commands Odysseus-Pound to write *The Cantos,* beginning with book 11 of Homer's *Odyssey.*

Circe's pep talk is also an anti-enlightenment version of Dante's Ulysses, who longs "a divenir del mondo esparto / e de li vizi umani e del valore"; "for experience of the world / Of human vices and virtue."[37] Right before he meets his own salt grave, Ulysses tells his men, "you were not born to live as a mere brute does, / But for the pursuit of knowledge and the good."[38] Circe's speech, by contrast, asserts the paradox: "You were made to live your life as brutes, and follow knowledge." For Circe, the pursuit of knowledge is the most brutish of all.[39] By continuing to quest, you are no better than a beast. She repeats the verb "to know" five times in five lines until it is emptied of significance. Tiresias, she explains, has "his *mind entire*"; "So full of <u>knowing</u> that the beefy men <u>know</u> less than he"; "<u>Knowledge</u> the shade of a shade, / Yet must though sail after <u>knowledge</u> / <u>Knowing</u> less than drugged beasts." Circe's wisdom would fail to convince any mariner to sail past the limits of the known world. Rather, she suggests that once the quest for knowledge is finally exhausted, human life can begin to recover the fragments of ritual.

37 Dante, *Inferno* 26.98–99.

38 Dante, *Inferno* 26.119–20.

39 Water Baumann singles out the line, "Yet must thou sail after knowledge," as a contradiction of the knowledge Circe elsewhere imparts, which is "inside the sanctum of ritual" (Walter Baumann, "The *Odyssey* Theme in Ezra Pound's *Cantos,*" in *Roses from the Steel Dust* [Orono, ME: National Poetry Foundation, 2000], 88). Baumann argues that the line is also uncharacteristic of Pound. "The only excuse for coining the phrase is that from time to time even Pound had a desire to leave any kind of ambiguity behind and to come out with a piece of self-interpretation, something which even he, the promoter of ideogram-based expression, couldn't do without a dash of the abstract." Deeming the line uncharacteristic of Circe, Baumann assumes that it must be the voice of the poet, only to argue that it is uncharacteristic of Pound. I think Circe (or Pound) is being ironic here. Circe parodies Dante's *Ulysses* to illustrate the paradox of all questing, either for nostos or *gnōsis.*

In the next section, Pound transforms Circe's directions past Scylla and Charybdis into a description of the festival of the Montallegre Madonna which hearkens back to the worship of Adonis and Tamuz.

> *phtheggometha*
> *thasson* ["let us call out quickly to her"]
> φθεγγώμεθα θᾶσσον
> The small lamps drift in the bay
> And the sea's claw gathers them.
> Neptunus drinks after neap-tide.
> Tamuz! Tamuz!!
> The red flame going seaward.
> By this gate art thou measured.
> From the long boats they have set lights in the water,
> The sea's claw gathers them outward.
> Scilla's dogs snarl at the cliff's base,
> The white teeth gnaw in under the crag,
> But in the pale night the small lamps float seaward
> Τυ Διώνα ["You Dione"]
> TU DIONA
> Και Μοῖραι' 'Άδονιν ["And the fates for Adonis"]
> KAI MOIRAI' ADONIN
> The sea is streaked red with Adonis,
> The lights flicker red in small jars.
> Wheat shoots rise new by the altar,
> flower from the swift seed. (47/236–37)

Pound ties the festival of Montallegre Madonna to early vegetation rites celebrating the dying-and-resurrecting gods: the return of the Ancient Mesopotamian god of the shepherds, Dumuzid (Tamuz), to Innana after spending half the year with the gallu demons of the underworld; which was adapted as the Greek celebration of Adonis to Aphrodite (Dione) in the spring after spending the winter months with Persephone. Tamuz is Frazer's archetype of the dying-and-resurrecting god. During the hot, dry, summer months of the month Tamuz in the Babylonian calendar (roughly July), festivals involved public lamentation over Tamuz's death in order to bring the rain again. The Homeric phrase from Canto 39 "let us call out quickly to her," returns in a new context. What was originally Eurylochus's mistake of calling out to Circe and suffering her bewitchment, now signifies the necessity of participating in the ritual of "calling out" in lamentation, "Tamuz!" Pound quotes a fragment of Bion of Smyrna, "Και Μοῖραι' Ἄδωνιν," "And the fates [cried] for Adonis," removing the verb "to cry" because it is already supplied above (*phtheggometha*) (even if it's the wrong tense). The lights going out to sea mimic how mourners in the rite of Adonis "bore the image of the dead Adonis to the sea-shore and committed it to the waves."[40] Adonis was fatally gored by a boar and his blood purportedly stains the sea red every year in the spring.

Pound juxtaposes the cult of Adonis and Tamuz with details of Homeric geography and monsters taken from Circe's second set of directions for Odysseus in book 12, after he returns from Hades: "the sea's claw"; the snarling of "Scylla's dogs" and their "white teeth"; and the "gate" by which Odysseus is measured. Pound's *translatio* inverts Circe's frightful description of Scylla and Charybdis into the beautiful ritual of Montallegre Madonna, turning the telos of Odysseus's quest into a lyric celebration of ritual death and rebirth. Circe explains to Odysseus that, after having sailed by the Sirens and not chosen the way of the Planctae (Wandering Rocks), he will come across a path where "are two cliffs, one of which reaches with its sharp peak to the broad heaven, and a dark cloud surrounds it" (12.73–77).

> Therein dwells Scylla, yelping terribly. Her voice is indeed but as the voice of a new-born whelp, but she herself is an evil monster, nor would anyone be glad at sight of her, no, not though it were a god that met her. Verily she has twelve feet, all misshapen, and six necks, exceeding long, and on each one an awful head, and therein three rows of teeth, thick and close, and full of black death. Up to her middle she is hidden in the hollow cave, but she holds her head out beyond the dread chasm, and fishes there, eagerly searching around the rock for dolphins and sea-dogs [κύνας, *kynas*] and whatever greater beast she may haply catch, such creatures as deep-moaning Amphitrite rears in multitudes past counting. By her no sailors yet may boast that they have fled unscathed in their ship, for with each head she carries off a man, snatching him from the dark-prowed ship. But the other cliff, thou wilt note, Odysseus, is lower—they are close to each other; thou couldst even shoot an arrow across—and on it is a great fig tree with rich foliage, but beneath this divine Charybdis sucks down the black water. Thrice a day she belches it forth, and thrice she sucks it down terribly. Mayest thou not be there when she sucks it down, for no one could save thee from ruin, no, not the Earth-shaker. Nay, draw very close to Scylla's cliff, and drive thy ship past quickly; for it is better far to mourn six comrades in thy ship than all together.
>
> (12.85–110)

[40] Frazer, James, *The Golden Bough*, vol. 5 (London: Macmillan, 1914), 225.

Pound's description of "Scilla's dogs snarl at cliff base" combines the idea of her six dog heads, her voice like a young whelp, and the "dogs" (*kynas*) that she eats from the sea. Pound also incorporates the contrast between Scylla (possibly from *skyllein*, "to tear") and Charybdis ("sucker down"). Pound mentions twice how the sea's claw gathers the red flames outward, invoking the sucking pull of Charybdis's swallowing, while at the same time suggesting Scylla's tearing claw that snatches up men, dolphins, sea-dogs, which would "streak the sea red" as with Adonis's blood. Odysseus will be "measured by this gate," as Circe puts it, insofar as he makes the right choice: to go by way of Scylla and to allow six of his men to be sacrificed, rather than lose everything in the whirlpool. Odysseus will also be "measured by this gate" in the sense that he will be tested and have to endure, rather than battle, this monster: to passively accept Scylla's attack.

In the next section, Pound links Scylla's "dread chasm" with Circe's cave. Circe (and women) represent the "natural" oblivion involved in the *katabasis* of mystery religions.

> Two span, two span to a woman,
> Beyond that she believes not. Nothing is of any importance.
> To that is she bent, her intention
> To that art thou called ever turning intention,
> Whether by night the owl-call, whether by sap in shoot,
> Never idle, by no means by no wiles intermittent
> Moth is called over mountain
> The bull runs blind on the sword, *naturans*
> To the cave art thou called, Odysseus,
> By Molü hast thou respite for a little,
> By Molü art thou freed from the one bed
>   that thou may'st return to another
> The stars are not in her counting,
>   To her they are but wandering holes. (47/237)

Woman is characterized by non-knowledge: a natural animal force which draws the male principal toward it. She is "two span" or approximately eighteen inches wide, but the words recall the "narrow gate" between Scylla and Charybdis, which Circe says "they are close to each other; thou couldst even shoot an arrow across," meaning that one cannot sail between them (12.102). Odysseus is called to Circe's cave as he is to Scylla's cave, as the sacrificial bull is called onto the sword. The self-effacing ritual of *katabasis*, coitus, and death are united. Circe's next lines parody Homer's teleological Odysseus, who relies on herbs (*moly*) and cunning to "escape" and "defeat" the female monster. Such efforts are as futile as the quest for knowledge. All *moly* offers is a brief "respite" from the inevitable. In the light of the ultimate telos, what is the point of Odysseus being freed from one bed (Circe's) just in order to return to another's (Penelope's)? If the *Odyssey* is read as merely a series of adventures and hindrances towards a goal, rather than a spiritual journey, everything blends together: Circe is no different from Scylla who is no different from Penelope.

Some critics have suggested that Pound contrasts here the rational male (who reads the stars) with the female brute (to whom they are but wandering holes), projecting a level of misogyny on Pound's poetry that is neither tenable here nor consistent with the rest of *The Cantos.*[41] *The Cantos* works tirelessly to dismantle patriarchial models and the "virtue" of male rationality. "Female" here stands in for the very *katabasis* into the cave and the loss of identity or selfhood (*sparagmos*) that the hero must experience. *Naturans* is an active participle of the invented verb "to nature," which means "naturing." The Latin tag, *Natura naturans,* coined in the middle ages, means "nature doing what nature does." "Moth is called over mountain" also recalls many of the descriptions in Remy de Gourmont, in which the male insect is "drawn" irrevocably to the female in order to inseminate her, and often perishes in order to do so. A paragraph describing beetles, butterflies, and flies sheds light on Pound's own "natural" philosophy of love.

> Coleoptera are given to cavalage, of duration varying from ten hours to two days. The male cockchafer pursues the female with fervor, he is so ardent that he often mounts other males, deceived by the odour of rut floating in the air. He seizes the female and holds her clamped by his forelegs and genital hooks. The union continues a day and a night, finally the male, exhausted, falls over backward, and still hooked by the penial pincers, is dragged along on his back by the impassive female who moves on feeding, pulling him over the leaves until death detaches him; then she lays and dies in her turn. Butterflies are likewise very fervent, the males make veritable voyages in quest of females, as Fabre has proved. They often fly coupled, the stronger female easily carrying the male: it is a quite frequent sight in the country, these butterflies with four wings who roll, a little bewildered from flower to flower, drunken ships going where the sails bid them. With flies, feminism is brought frankly into the love mechanism. The females have the copulative apparatus; they force their oviduct, then a veritable

[41] See, for example, Mary Gibson, *Epic Reinvented: Ezra Pound and the Victorians* (Ithaca, NY: Cornell University Press, 1995), 145–8; and Robert Casillo, *The Genealogy of Demons: Anti-Semitism, Fascism, and the Myths of Ezra Pound* (Evanston, IL: Northwestern University Press, 1988), 84–94.

> prong, into the male's belly; it is the females who make the mastering gesture, the male merely grips this gimlet with the hooks which surround his genital fent. It is this same augur which the female uses to bore the wood, or earth or flesh where she deposits her eggs. The coupling is end to end, and one of the easiest to observe.[42]

In the insect world, the mysteries of copulation are indeed sexist, but in infinite variations, and rarely favoring the male. Pound's image of "bull runs on the sword" suggests bullfighting, but more specifically the desire of the male victim to be sacrificed. In Greek and Roman religion, water was sprinkled on the head of bulls before the sacrifice so that they would "nod" their consent. Here Odysseus becomes the consenting victim, who is significantly femininized as the one who is pierced by the phallic object (Circe's oviduct?). It also reminds the readers of Odysseus's connection to Adonis, who was gored to death by a wild boar. The young Odysseus was gored by a bull as a child, and Homer puns on one of the possible etymologies of Odysseus's name as a result: ὀδύρομαι (*odýromai*), "to lament, bewail."

Another significant allusion here is to the Mithraic mysteries practiced in the Roman Empire. The religion is inspired by the Iranian worship of Mithra, the Zoroastrian angelic divinity known as the guardian of cattle and the harvest god. In "Terra Italica" (1931) Pound mentions that Nino Burrascano's brochure *I Misteri di Mithra nell'antica Roma* (1929) "will allow the reader to disentangle more confusions [about medieval literature] than any commentary on medieval poetry yet written."[43] Little is known about the mysteries, except that Mithra was worshiped in underground temples and natural caves (*mithraea*). The centerpiece in every temple was a representation of Mithra killing a sacred bull after he has hunted it and exhausted it by riding it (Figure 5.2). Mithra is depicted kneeling or straddling the exhausted white bull, wearing a Phrygian cap, holding the horns or nostrils and stabbing the bull as he looks over his shoulder to Sol, the ancient Roman solar deity, with whom he will share his feast. Animals, usually a dog and a snake, drink his blood while a scorpion eats his genitals; shoots of wheat sprout from his tail, or sometimes his wounds, hence the line, "wheat shoots rise new by the altar." The relief emphasizes the connection between sacrifice and fecundation, even down to the almost sexual nature of Mithra's position with regards to the bull.

[42] Gourmont, *The Natural Philosophy of Love*, 94–5.

[43] *SP*, 56.

Figure 5.2 Roman tauroctony relief from Aquileia (*c.* 175 CE; Kunsthistorisches Museum, Vienna).

Pound turns the Homeric hero into a Hesiodic one. (Bachofen calls Hesiod the "poet of the matriarchy."[44]) Circe repeats the motif of the gates by which Odysseus is measured — the Pillars of Hercules, the strait of Messina (Scylla and Charybdis) — and interprets it as the "gates" of a day (sunrise to sunset), ventriloquizing the gnomic advice in Hesiod's *Works and Days* about how to live a good life: observe the seasons and participate in the fecundation of the earth.

Begin thy plowing
When the Pleiades go down to their rest,
Begin thy plowing
40 days are they under seabord,
Thus do in fields by seabord
And in valleys winding down toward the sea.
When the cranes fly high
        think of plowing.
By this gate art thou measured

[44] Bachofen, *Myth, Religion, and Mother Right*, 84.

> Thy day is between a door and a door
> Two oxen are yoked for plowing
> Or six in the hill field
> White bulk under olives, a score for drawing down stone,
> Here the mules are gabled with slate on the hill road.
> Thus was it in time.
> And the small stars now fall from the olive branch,
> Forked shadow falls dark on the terrace
> More black than the floating martin
>   that has no care for your presence,
> His wing-print is black on the roof tiles
> And the print is gone with his cry.
> So light is thy weight on Tellus
> Thy notch no deeper indented
> Thy weight less than the shadow
> Yet hast thou gnawed through the mountain,
>   Scylla's white teeth less sharp.
> Hast thou found a nest softer than cunnus
> Or hast thou found better rest
> Hast'ou a deeper planting, doth thy death year
> Bring swifter shoot?
> Hast thou entered more deeply the mountain? (47/237–38)

The adventure of Homer's epic transforms into the aphorisms of Hesiod's almanac. All sense of telos is abandoned. Odysseus will be measured by the gate of a day: how well he performs his plowing, worship, and fecundation. The Pillars of Hercules become the pillars of the day (sunrise to sunset), the yoked oxen, and the "gate" of cunnus. This speech is also Pound's *translatio* of Circe's description of Scylla's mountain cave.

> Now on the other path are two cliffs, one of which reaches with its sharp peak to the broad heaven, and a dark cloud surrounds it. This never melts away, nor does clear sky ever surround that peak in summer or in harvest time. No mortal man could scale it or set foot upon the top, not though he had twenty hands and feet; for the rock is smooth, as if it were polished. And in the midst of the cliff is a dim cave, turned to the West, toward Erebus, even where you shall steer your hollow ship, glorious Odysseus.
>
> (12.73–82)

Pound's Odysseus successfully endures Scylla by partaking of her mysteries, for allowing himself to be "eaten" by her. The paradox of Circe's "dreadful" counsel is that once Odysseus learns proper humility—that his weight is less than a shadow—can he gnaw through a mountain faster than Scylla.

Circe quotes almost verbatim from *Works and Days,* including the lines, "When the Pleiades, daughters of Atlas, are rising, begin your harvest, and your ploughing when they are going to set. Forty nights and days they are hidden and appear again as the year moves round, when first you sharpen your sickle."[45] Hesiod champions the virtue of αιδώς (*aidōs*), "decency," "modesty," which carries with it connotations of both respect for one's own conscience or self-respect as well as regard for the person of others: reverence and deference.[46] Hesiod means to contrast this with ὕβρις (*hybris*), the personified spirit (daimon) of violence, insolence, reckless pride, arrogance, and outrageous behavior in general which curses the Age of Iron (the world Hesiod believed he lived in). The word σωφροσύνη (*sophrosyne*) "soundness of mind," "moderation," "discretion," "temperance" can be read as a substitute for Hesiod's concept of *aidōs*.[47]

Pound emphasizes the idea of *aidōs* as a kind of radical humility which is the result of reflecting on one's own cosmic insignificance. Circe's stunning simile of the shadow of an indifferent martin's wing momentarily imprinting itself on the roof tile of a house as being tantamount to the presence of Odysseus on earth is a more coherent version of her "difficult knowledge" earlier stated: that Odysseus is doomed to quest after knowledge while knowing less than a drugged beast. Circe demands of Odysseus the most difficult journey: first beyond the limits of Oceanus, then through the "gates" of Scylla and Charybdis where there is no hope to escape unscathed. But here she is explicit: if Odysseus can conceive of his life as the indifferent martin regards him, if he can grasp his own radical unimportance, then he can become a true (Poundian) hero, if not a god: Odysseus *geōrgon*, Oysseus Adonis, Odysseus Sol. Pound juxtaposes an image of radical selflessness with a feat outside the scope of Homer's imagination: of a modernist beast with teeth that can bore through mountain: Odysseus Rock-Drill.

45 Hesiod, *Works and Days* from *Hesiod, The Homeric Hymns, Homerica*, trans. Hugh Evelyn-White, lines 383–7. Pound's Circe also echoes this line by Hesiod: "Mark, when you hear the voice of the crane who cries year by year from the clouds above, for she gives the signal for ploughing and shows the season of rainy winter" (lines 448–50).

46 See T. A. Sinclair, "On ΑΙΔΩΣ in Hesiod," *Classical Review* 39.7–8 (1925): 147–8.

47 See Richard Hunter, *Hesiodic Voices: Studies in the Ancient Reception of Hesiod's Works and Days* (Cambridge: Cambridge University Press, 2014), 138–9.

Circe's advice here is not a celebration of the male "rational" principal over the female chaos,[48] but, if anything, a sublation of the two principals Pound has presented so far: the male (rational, conquering, adventuring, teleological: Homer and Dante's Odysseus) and the female (irrational, chaotic, mysterious, oblivious) becomes Pound's version of the Hesiodic (cyclical, creative, humble, reverent). The stars are not used as directions (for the male guilding his ship) nor are they unknown (to the woman in the cave) but "fall down from the trees" indicating the seasons and times to plow. Man observes the seasons (again) which tells him when to plow and when to pray, but he is subservient to the feminine principal of the harvest and her "cunnus": not "liberated" in any Neoplatonic sense to a higher astral plane from base matter, the world of the senses, or the "hylic," as Liebregts and Surette argue.[49] As Robert Casillo rightly notes, Pound was probably inspired by Bachofen's concept of matriarchy which emerges from hetaerism.[50] Bachofen describes the male's role in the agrarian matriarchy:

> The principal of agriculture is the principle of ordered sexual union. Mother right pertains to them both. Just as the grain of the field emerges from the furrow opened by the plow, so the child issues from the maternal *sporium* (womb), from the κῆπος [*kēpos*] (garden, vagina); for the Sabines called the feminine field *sporium*, whence *spurii*, "the sowed ones," from σπείρω (I sow.) So Plutarch relates. His, too, was the idea that the principle of love lies in wounding, which is why Amor bears arrows. The earth is wounded by the plowshare, the woman's womb is wounded by the man's *aratrum* (plow). Both these relations justify the connection between the plow and Poseidon, the fecundating water god. What is born from the *sporium* has only a mother, whether it be earth or woman. The father is of no more importance than the plow, than the sower who passes over the tilled field, casting the grain in the opened furrow, and then disappears into oblivion. The Romans formulated this principle in juridical terms. "All produce is gathered not according to the right of the seed, but the right of the soil," says Julian.[51]

[48] The lines from Canto 29, "the female / Is a chaos / An octopus / A biological process" as Guy Davenport points out, originate in a letter to Marianne Moore of 1919: "The female is a chaos, / the male / is a fixed point of stupidity." (29/144, Guy Davenport, "Marianne Moore," in *Geography of the Imagination* [San Francisco: North Point Press, 1981], 118n4.)

[49] See Liebregts, *Ezra Pound and Neoplatonism*, 232–6; and Surette, *Birth of Modernism*, 154–6.

[50] See Robert Casillo, "Bachofen and the Conquest of the Swamp," in *The Genealogy of Demons: Anti-Semitism, Fascism, and the Myths of Ezra Pound* (Evanston, IL: Northwestern University Press, 1988), 84–94.

[51] Bachofen, *Myth, Religion, and Mother Right*, 131–2.

This paragraph might have directly influenced Canto 47, especially Bachofen's emphasis on the insignificance of man ("the planter") compared to woman ("the soil"): an inversion of Apollo's argument in Aeschylus's *Eumenidies*. Hesiod does not make this emphasis.

Unlike Hesiod, Pound introduces a spiritual dimension to the life of farming and radical humility. Circe ends by echoing Ben Jonson's "hast ou" refrain from "A Celebration of Charis: Her Triumph" (*c.* 1623), which invokes the simple beauty of the natural world. Jonson's rhetorical questions become Circe's, who points out the paradox that by ceasing to quest, and focusing on plowing, Odysseus can experience all the fruits of paradise. She even puts it in the language of nostos: "Hast thou found a nest softer than cunnus / Or hast thou found better rest / Hast'ou a deeper planting, doth thy death year / Bring swifter shoot? / Hast thou entered more deeply the mountain?"

The final lines of Canto 47 are given over to Odysseus's response, which is mostly a reiteration of Circe's long monologue. Odysseus bears ecstatic witness to Circe's mysteries.

> The light has entered the cave. Io! Io!
> The light has gone down into the cave,
> Splendor on splendor!
> By prong have I entered these hills:
> That the grass grow from my body,
> That I hear the roots speaking together,
> The air is new on my leaf,
> The forked boughs shake with the wind.
> Is Zephyrus more light on the bough, Apeliota
> more light on the almond branch?
> By this door have I entered the hill.
> Falleth,
> Adonis falleth.
> Fruit cometh after. The small lights drift out with the tide,
> sea's claw has gathered them outward,
> Four banners to every flower
> The sea's claw draws the lamps outward.
> Think thus of thy plowing
> When the seven stars go down to their rest
> Forty days for their rest, by seabord
> And in valleys that wind down toward the sea

Και Μοῖραι' 'Άδονιν
KAI MOIRAI' ADONIN
When the almond bough puts forth its flame,
When the new shoots are brought to the altar,
Τυ Διώνα, Και Μοῖραι
TU DIONA, KAI MOIRAI
Και Μοῖραι' 'Άδονιν
KAI MOIRAI T' ADONIN
that hath the gift of healing,
that hath the power over wild beasts. (47/238–39)

Like Circe, Odysseus combines the ritual of Adonis and the festival of the Montallegre Madonna with Hesiod's description of plowing. He enters the cave of the goddess, partakes of the *hieros gamos*, cries out for Adonis/Tamuz, and is born again with the crops. Pound's rigorous mythical method of condensation and allusion takes a holiday here. Odysseus, the "student" of Circe, repeats her ideas less compellingly. Odysseus becomes earth and soil again ("that the grass grow from my body"); and then plant ("the air is new on my leaf") and tree ("the forked boughs shake with the wind"). Odysseus has multiplied into the spring, and takes on the characteristics of all spring springing. Odysseus recognizes himself as Adonis, citing Bion's *Epitaphios Adonidos* line 94 (without the verb), "χαὶ Μοῖραι τὸν Ἄδωνιν ἀνακλείουσιν Ἄδωνιν'"; "Even the fates [weep] for Adonis [calling, 'Adonis']." Adonis, unlike Orpheus, is not known to have any particular power over animals. The last reference points back to Circe as *Potnia Theron.* Pound has liberated Circe from Homer's patriarchal text. She is a nature goddess who "natures" (*naturans*). She no longer enslaves men with *kaka pharmakon*; she liberates men through her mysteries. Odysseus is orgasmically reborn: restored via Pound's erotic *translatio* to his primordial status as a dying-and-resurrecting god.

It's easy to get so buried in Pound's comparative anthropology, his heteroglossia, and his obscure allusions, that one forgets Pound's almost naive ambition: to turn antiquated mythology back into close observation of nature, to turn organized religion and dogma back into mystery and ritual, and to turn the banality or drudgery of work back into reverence and worship. The pleasure of reading *The Cantos* is that by means of the complex one returns to the simple: stars and leaves and mist, almond trees, lights floating out to sea, an excellent sausage. "The caverns are less enchanting to the unskilled explorer" (74/448). Delirium, disorder, and even (haetarchic) "chaos" clears the way for a vision of the natural world as paradise. After all the work Pound does here in "restoring" Circe as a goddess, she never takes on the role as a definitive goddess or muse of *The Cantos,* the way Athena presides over *Odyssey* 13–24. Pound never allows his divinities to be set in stone. He never tires of exploring new guises, of getting tangled in webs of allusions and even dead ends. A late passage from Canto 106 turns the very disorder of naming, trying to name, and not naming Circe into an act of reverence itself:

This is grain rite
        Luigi in the hill path
                this is grain rite
near Enna, at Nyssa:
                Circe, Persephone
so different is sea from glen that
                the juniper is her holy bush
between the two pine trees, not Circe
        but Circe was like that
                coming down from the house of smoothe stone
"not know which god"
                        nor could enter her eyes by probing
        the light blazed behind her
                        nor was this from sunset.
Athene Pronoia,
                in hypostasis
Helios, Perse: Circe
Zeus: Artemis out of Leto
Under wildwood
                Help me to neede
By Circeo, the stone eyes looking seaward
        Nor could you enter her eyes by probing. (106/774)

One does not know which god, but that does not prevent Pound from trying and trying again. *The Cantos* cannot offer revelation, but its tangled allusive structure attempts to recreate in the reader the sacred confusion before revelation. As Harrison describes Orphism: "In theology as in ritual Orphism reverted to the more primitive forms, lending them deeper and intenser significances. These primitive forms, shifting and inchoate, were material more malleable than the articulate accomplished figures of the Olympians."[52] Pound's own comparative

[52] Harrison, *Prolegomena,* 650.

method approaches an aesthetics of the "unaccomplished," of confusion ("not Circe / but Circe was like that") in order to invoke the Protean, inchoate nature of pre-Olympian worship. Circe is a grain rite. She is Persephone and Enna. She is the sacred juniper bush of the Na-Khi. She is Athena not as the master of stratagem but *Pronoia,* meaning "foresight" or "before the temple," referring to the sacred precinct at Delphi before the great temple of Apollo, first revered by the Mycenians in the fifteenth century BCE, and later attributed to Athena in the eighth century BCE. She is the product of the Titan Helios and the water nymph Perse. She is Artemis, the child of Zeus with Leto. She is the goddess atop Mount Circeo (Aphrodite, Feronia). One does not enter Circe's eyes by probing, but by looking away and seeing her afterimages.

6

Pisan Wreck

"and this grass or whatever here under the tent flaps / is, indubitably, bambooiform." (74/466)

Pound's philological task of excavating Odysseus as a dying-and-resurrecting god was more or less complete by Canto 47, which ends with the apotheosis of Odysseus as a solar hero and fertility daimon. By 1937, Calliope was satisfied, but Clio was not. "An epic is a poem containing history."[1] Pound's next task was a sustained revision of Chinese and eighteenth-century American history in light of the monetary theories of Alexander del Mar, the ethnography of Leo Frobenius, and ethnology of Thaddeus Zielinski (to name but a few), even if it would tax the patience of his most devout readers. There is only one Homeric allusion in all 166 pages of *Cantos LII-LXXI* (1940): Tchan-y (Chang I), a Chinese condottiere during the Zhou dynasty, was so well-traveled that, like Odysseus, "POLLON IDEN" (of many [men] he saw) (53/274, *Odyssey* 1.3).

The Pisan Cantos (1948) marks an abrupt change from that poetic agenda. To many readers, Pound's long poem finds its path again. It returns to the personae, texts, and themes of the first fifty-one cantos. It introduces a confessional voice that vacillates between urgency and resignation, hope and despair. It is more lyrical, fragmented, and self-referential than ever before. *The Pisan Cantos* is grounded in a present time and place: 1945, the American Disciplinary Training Center (DTC) north of Pisa. The poet sings from the six-by-six-foot steel cage in which he was incarcerated for three weeks, where he learned "to know the ground and the dew", and from the pyramidal officer's tent with a smoke hole in the top, where he observed the ascent of butterflies and processions of constellations (76/474).

With access only to the Bible, a text and translation of Confucius, and a copy of the *Pocket Book of Verse* "found on the jo-house seat at that / in a cheap edition!", Pound's poetic technique becomes less philological and learned and

1 *LE*, 86.

more contemplative and ruminative (80/533). The poet-persona reflects on the failure of fascism and (possibly) on his misguided politics. At the same time, he's full of defensive self-assertions and reminders of his own self worth: "I surrender neither the empire nor the temples / plural / nor the constitution nor yet the city of Dioce" (74/454). He resembles Eliot's hero (or Fisher King) who is trying to "set his lands in order."[2] He also resembles Ezra Pound, a poet who is about to be put on trial for treason and had better figure out how to prove to his readers that he's not a monster. Remarkably, Pound weaves just enough humility and seeming regret into its verses that those formerly disgusted with his virulent racism, like T. S. Eliot, Katherine Anne Porter, and W. H. Auden, would marshal in support of his winning the Bollingen Prize in 1949. The "technic" of the Pisan sequence might be called a poetics of shipwreck: radically fragmentary, confessional, and ephemeral, both in the sense of diaristic as well as intangible, fleeting, and "interrupted."

The Pisan sequence relies heavily on cues from the *Odyssey* to achieve a poetics of shipwreck. Many of Pound's Homeric references seem like a hodge-podge of recycled material from Cantos 1 to 51: the nekyia and the catalogue of women; Elpenor; Tiresias; the Lotophagoi; the Sirens; Scylla and Charybdis; Polyphemus; the Cattle of Helios; Circe; Anticlea; and Nausicaa.[3] Pound also introduces the Cicones episode.[4] Seemingly random details are marshaled into the language of the *Odyssey*. Nausicca going down to help her handmaidens with the washing is compared to the delusions of socialism (78/502); students at a university who can't scan the beginning of a Sappho's "To Anactoria" are "lacking the wind sack" of Aeolus (74/465).

The Pisan Cantos seems to reduce the *Odyssey* to a soupy homogeny: flotsam of the wreck of *The Cantos*. However, it is anchored in a specific Homeric episode: Odysseus's shipwreck after he leaves Calypso's island of Ogygia until he is washed up on Scheria, the island of the Phaeacians (5.269–493). Naked, at the mercy of the fierce winds, and engulfed by giant waves, Odysseus is at

[2] Eliot, *The Waste Land*, line 426.

[3] "NEKUIA where are Alcmene and Tyro" (74/451); "Tiro, Alcmene" (74/463); "'with a name to come' / εσσομένοισι" (74/466); "men of no fortune and with a name to come" (80/534); "and have speech with Tiresias, Thebae" (83/553); "Nothing but death, said Turgenev (Tiresias) / is irreparable / ἀγλαος ἀλάου πόρνη Περσεφόνεια / Still hath his mind entire" (80/514); "eating lotus, or if not exactly the lotus, the asphodel" (83/502); "the sharp song with sun under its radiance / λιγύρ'" (74/459); "beware of their charm, / ΣΕΙΡΗΝΕΣ" (74/463); "the Charybdis of action" (74/451); "OY ΤΙΣ, OY ΤΙΣ? Odysseus / the name of my family" (74/445); "ΝΗΣΟΝ 'ΑΜΥΜΟΝΑ" (81/483); "ac ego in harum / so lay men in Circe's swine sty" (74/456); "nec benecomata Kirkê, mah! κακὰ φάρμακ' ἔδωκεν" (74/457); Anticlea, who "appreciated [Odysseus's] conversation" (74/463); "Nausikaa / took down the washing or at least went to see that the / maids didn't slack" (48/502).

[4] "No sooner out of Troas / than the damn fools attacked Ismarus of the Cicones" (79/505).

his most destitute. He fears his imminent and wretched death, and regrets not having died honorably at Troy.[5] *The Pisan Cantos* are shot through with Homer's veering winds (Zephyr, Boreas, Eurus, and Apeliota) and Homer's great waves that shatter ships, dash men against cliffs, and suck them out to sea. Pound's Odysseus clings to his raft, "with the mast held by the left hand" (74/463). He reflects on his great hubris, "the folly of attacking that island [Ismarus] / and of the force ὑπὲρ μόρον [*hyper moron*, 'beyond what is destined']" (80/532). Eventually, "the raft broke and the waters went over me" (80/533). With nothing to cling to, Pound's Odysseus swims in the "fluid ΧΘΟΝΟΣ [*CHTHONOS*], strong as the undertow / of the wave receding" (82/546). Like Eliot's drowning Phoenician, who, "as he rose and fell / He passed the stages of his age and youth / Entering the whirlpool," Pound's Odysseus reflects on his former adventures and wanderings.[6] Eventually, he washes up on Scheria, the island of the Phacaeans, prays to "GEA TERRA," and falls asleep, feeling himself "drawn" deep into the earth with Athena (82/546).

Pound identifies himself with the destitute Odysseus at sea; without friends; having lost his credibility and freedom; reduced to "no one" (*outis*); who has "πολλά παθεῖν" (*polla pathein*, "suffered much") (76/477); is now "au bout de mes forces" (80/532); faces "the loneliness of death" (82/547); and fears that all his work has been in vain: "I will come out of this knowing no one / neither they me" (82/546). He has emerged from the "gates of death"; "out of hell, the pit / out of the dust and glare evil" (74/469) where he "swum in a sea of air strip" (80/532). (The cages at the DTC were reinforced with pieces of heavy steel "mats" normally used to lay down temporary runways.) Pound turns Homer's frequently repeated description of Odysseus as "δακρύων" (*dakryōn*, "weeping," from δάκρυον, *dakryon*, "tear")[7] into a refrain: "δακρύων δακρύων δακρύων" (76/480); "the loneliness of death came upon me / (at 3 P. M., for an instant) δακρύων" (82/547); "DAKRUON, ΔΑΚΡΥΩΝ" (83/552).

At the same time, Pound asserts that his suffering "is of the process" and the necessary condition for building his paradise (74/445). *The Pisan Cantos* continues the philological and comparative anthropological method at work in

5 *Odyssey* 5.306–12.

6 Eliot, *The Waste Land*, lines 317–18.

7 Homer uses δάκρυον three times when he first describes Odysseus on Calypso's island: "Him she found sitting on the shore, and his eyes were never dry of tears [δακρυόφιν], and his sweet life was ebbing away, as he longed mournfully for his return, for the nymph was no longer pleasing in his sight. By night indeed he would sleep by her side perforce in the hollow caves, unwilling beside the willing nymph, but by day he would sit on the rocks and the sands, racking his soul with tears [δάκρυσι] and groans and griefs, and he would look over the unresting sea, shedding tears [δάκρυα]" (5.151–58).

Canto 1: to strip down the epic into its lyric and ritual origins. Pound introduces a sustained lyrical "I," while adopting an even more chaotic and polyphonic style. Similar to his treatment of the Lotophagoi, the Sirens, and Circe, however, Pound also inverts the storm's narrative role from menacing to beneficial. Homer's terrible winds become Pound's suave airs that blow from paradise; Homer's frightful booming waves become a percussive ritual of the Pound hero's chthonic descent; Homer's foreboding chaos of water manifests Pound's sacred disorder which leads to "the mind indestructible" and the mental state of paradise (74/450).

Despite many of these obvious parallels, no critic has examined how *The Pisan Cantos* is a *translatio* of Odysseus's shipwreck in *Odyssey* 5. Many readers have suggested the connection, including Guy Davenport, George Kearns and Leon Surette.[8] Richard Sieburth points out that the line "the raft broke over me," is an allusion to *Odyssey* 5.289, but he only casually describes Pound as a "shipwrecked poet" in Pisa.[9] My intention is not to ignore the historical or political circumstances that led to the composition of *The Pisan Cantos,* but to illuminate how Pound reshaped this experience into the evolving methodology of *The Cantos.* Odysseus's shipwreck was not just a handy metaphor that Pound borrowed to represent his own experience at the DTC. It was, to echo Eliot's definition of Joyce's mythical method, "a way of controlling, of ordering, of giving a shape and a significance to the immense panorama of futility and anarchy which is contemporary history"—as well as Pound's traumatic incarceration.[10] It was also Pound's way of taking ownership of it, of asserting it formally, of making it part "of the process." Ironically, Pound's "epic" downfall—from a crackpot living in Rapallo broadcasting virulent anti-Semitic propaganda on the radio, to a war criminal about to be tried by the US government and possibly hanged—is precisely what made him worthy of becoming one of the visionary heroes of his long poem. Pound found himself, in 1945, at just that moment of crisis, delirium, despair, and regret which made Niccolò III d'Este worthy of the divine vision in Canto 20. In Canto 82, Pound, lying in his cage watching clovers and mint sprout from the ground, compares himself to the hero-king Niccolò, who left a testament that he be buried naked: "Where I lie

[8] Davenport, *Geography of the Imagination*, 158; George Kearns, *The Cantos of Ezra Pound* (Cambridge: Cambridge University Press, 1989), 27; Leon Surette," Having His Own Mind to Stand by Him," *The Hudson Review* 27.4 (1974–5), 503.

[9] Richard Sieburth, "Introduction," *The Pisan Cantos*, ed. Richrd Sieburth (New York: New Directions, 1993), xxii–xxiii.

[10] Eliot, *Selected Prose of T. S. Eliot*, 177.

let the thyme rise / and basilicum / let the herbes rise in April abundant / By Ferrara was buried naked, fu Nicolo" (82/546).

A lot of criticism of *The Pisan Cantos* leans on Pound's biography to account for its abrupt change of tone and style. But it is problematic to assume that when a work of literature is (or becomes) self-referential, it ought to be interpreted more biographically. Critics who task themselves with assessing whether *The Cantos* "succeeds" tend to find in *The Pisan Cantos* Pound's admission of failure and the breakdown of his epic into confessional fragments. These fragments, according to them, comprise some of the most beautiful passages in an otherwise bothced epic. Ronald Bush's recent genetic analysis of *The Pisan Cantos* puts to rest the facile idea "that *The Pisan Cantos* were confessions wrung out of a repentant fascist by a dark night of the soul and the healing force of nature."[11] Bush identifies three distinct stages of composition.

> Writing *The Pisan Cantos* was a protracted, complex, and fractured process. The actual composition took place in three distinct stages, each corresponding with changes in Pound's circumstances, his self-assessment, and his political outlook. First, while residing in Sant'Ambrogio and months before his imprisonment, Pound began a series of lyrical fragments that were overtly symbolist in style and avowedly fascist in viewpoint. Then, after circumstances had wrenched him out of his wartime retreat and into the prison camp in Pisa, his manner and subject changed. The literary model for his writing became a realistic poetic diary in the manner of Villon, and (though he incorporated from memory swatches of material from the earlier drafts) the center of his attention became the lives of the rough crew of soldiers around him. Having thus fashioned an easy mixture of very different perspectives, Pound believed that he had finished the poem, then suddenly changed his mind. Jolted by reports that close friends had died, and increasingly faced with the possibility that he himself might be executed, he began writing once more. In a surge of defensiveness, he imposed a polemical framework on the poem, which gave it a force and coloring that often contradicted what he had recently written.

Bush's genetic analysis helpfully deflates both sentimental and ideological readings:

> Because of the succeeding frames that Pound incorporated into the manuscript and typescript texts of *The Pisan Cantos,* it seems to me that George Kearns is

[11] Ronald Bush, "Modernism, Fascism, and the Composition of Ezra Pound's Pisan Cantos," *Modernism/Modernity* 2.3 (1995), 70.

> as justified arguing that Canto 81 is a "confession of [Pound's own] failure and vanity" as Peter D'Epiro is when he holds it confesses nothing. Pound provided encoded instructions for both, with the result that neither reading by itself suffices.[12]

Bush's analysis, however, assumes that contradictory authorial intentions result in a product that is contradictory. According to Bush, Pound "began" with symbolist fascist fragments; "changed" his model to that of Villon's confessional and a description of the lives of the soldiers at the DTC; and then later "imposed" a new polemical framework on the poem. But a process is not a result. Works of art evolve and change as they are made; organizing frameworks are imposed upon them, then discarded; they are rewritten, revised, and reconceived. Bush ultimately agrees with Jerome McGann's claim that, because Pound left the telos of his writing indeterminate as he composed, it results in a "discourse [that] accumulates a structure that grows increasingly overdetermined."[13] But why attribute the contradictory agendas of *The Pisan Cantos* as a flaw? Why not assume that if *The Cantos* grows increasingly overdetermined, it is because Pound intended it? The (implied) author's admission of failure; his inability to structure his work coherently which is mirrored by the seeming lack of structure of the work itself; an overdetermination of meaning; abrupt changes of poetic style and voice: these are all paradigmatic features of the modernist aesthetic Pound and Eliot pioneered with *The Waste Land*. By 1945, the modernist aesthetics of failure, featuring radically unreliable (if not neurotic) implied authors, had been firmly established by authors like Céline, Kafka, and Beckett.

The Pisan Cantos is consistent with the fugal structure of the first half of *The Cantos*: to create a divine disorder and reveal the primordial polyphonic lyric behind the epic narrative. It employs abrupt changes of voice; self-assertion followed by self-doubt; a mania for system followed by a breakdown of system. *The Cantos* is an insecure epic, whose implied author (and perhaps real author) is subject to all the moods or "states of mind" of hell, purgatory, and heaven. Revision is key to the restless schema of *The Cantos*: not only does it revise itself; it asks the reader to constantly revise her opinion of what the poet is trying to achieve. The consciousness of *The Cantos* ruminates its material; it makes it cohere, then admits it is incoherent; it gives up, then takes it up again. *The Pisan Cantos* moves this "delirium" into the foreground. Pound restlessly returns to the

12 Bush, "Modernism, Fascism, and the Composition of Ezra Pound's *Pisan Cantos,*" 81. References are to George Kearns, *Guide to Ezra Pound's Selected Cantos* (New Brunswick: Rutgers University Press, 1980), 167; and Peter D'Epiro, "Whose Vanity Must be Pulled Down," *Paideuma* 13.2 (1984), 252.

13 Jerome McGann, *Towards a Literature of Knowledge* (Chicago: Chicago University Press, 1989), 119.

previous leitmotifs of his earlier cantos, and makes the struggle to continue *The Cantos* and not surrender his mythical method and his vision part of the "plot." He repeatedly asserts that disorder, periplum, revision, or veering winds are his poem's schema or form.

In the following, I'll first situate Pound's idea of the "new" Odysseus or Pound hero as *outis* or "no one": which includes the solar deity as he travels under the ocean by night, an unrecognizable hero without companions or godly protection, and a man *achronos* or outside of historical and chronological time. Next, I'll look at the three major events of shipwreck in Pound's *translatio:* the storm that destroys Odysseus's raft and his near-drowning off the coast of Scheria; Odysseus's wreck and his prayer to the grain and his first sleep on dry land; and his "rebirth" in the morning. I'll illustrate how these four allusive clusters represent stages in the Pound hero's—and ideally the reader's—transformation: stripping away the self to *outis* and *achronos;* experiencing the catastrophe as revelation; a ritual drowning or death; and rebirth as a vigilance to the ephemeral world. Pound's lyrical *translatio* of *Odyssey* 5 allows him to give way to the veering winds of chaos and embrace the "process" of his rudderless periplum; to visit with goddesses and share in their *hilaritas* and speed in mind; and to gather and retain the "unblastable" images of the permanent world. Ultimately, *The Pisan Cantos* cultivates in the reader a vigilance to the interruptions of ephemera, which are fragments of paradise.

Odysseus *Outis* and *Achronos*

Canto 74 establishes the figure of a shipwrecked Odysseus who is *outis* ("no man"). In Homer, *outis* is a name Odysseus gives himself to trick Polyphemus; in Pound, *outis* becomes an epithet of Odysseus that links him to a fertility daimon and solar deity. Canto 74 begins with a voice mourning the death of Mussolini and failure of fascism; the "twice crucified" Mussolini (killed by partisans and then strung up by his heels at the Piazzale Loreto) is linked to Dionysus and Christ (74/445). The poet staunchly reasserts his aesthetic goals and introduces the image of the shipwrecked Odysseus washed up on Scheria:

> To build the city of Dioce whose terraces are the color of stars
> The suave eyes, quiet, not scornful,
>   rain also is of the process
> What you depart from is not the way

> and olive tree blown white in the wind
> washed in the Kiang and Han
> what whiteness will you add to this whiteness,
>   what candor?
> "the great periplum brings in the stars to our shore."
> You who have passed the pillars and outward from Herakles
> when Lucifer fell in N. Carolina
> if the suave air give way to scirocco
> ΟΥ ΤΙΣ, ΟΥ ΤΙΣ? Odysseus
>   the name of my family
> the wind also is of the process. (74/445)

The question as to what whiteness can be added to the whiteness of something washed in the Han or Kiang (Yangzee) river is from an anecdote in *The Menicus* about how irreplaceable Confucius is: "What has been washed in the waters of the Këang and Han, and bleached in the autumn sun:—how glistening it is! Nothing can be added to it."[14] Pound connects this to Allen Upward's discovery that flashing-eyed Athena holds an olive branch because the leaves of an olive tree flip over and become white in the wind.[15] This is tied to the image of the shipwrecked Odysseus. Dante's Ulysses drowns "in the whirlpool" (20/93) after he passes the Pillars of Hercules and is "reborn" as the white "horn" of flame with Diomedes in hell. Homer's Odysseus strips naked and is washed in salt water for three days and sun-bleached on the shore of Scheria. "All his flesh was swollen, and sea water flowed in streams up through his mouth and nostrils" (5.455–56). Before Nausicaa's maidens, he is frightfully naked and "κεκακωμένος ἅλμῃ" (*kekakōmenos halmē*, "befouled with brine") (6.137). The Greek ἅλμ (*halm*), from ἅλς (*hals*), or "salt," refers to sea-water but also spray that has dried on the skin. Odysseus is stained white. In Canto 23, Pound makes an elaborate connection between Odysseus, Helios (*Aelios/Halios*), and *hals* in his reading of Steisochorus[16] (23/107–8).

Pound also associates Odysseus's wanderings with the "periplum" of the solar deity across the sky passing through various constellations. The term (which should be "periplus") is borrowed from Victor Bérard's scholarship on the *Odyssey*.[17] Read as a solar deity, all of Odysseus's adventures in Homer are

[14] *The Menicus* in *The Four Books*, trans. James Legge (Shanghai: Commercial Press, 1923), 635.
[15] Upward, *The New Word*, 234.
[16] See chapter 5.
[17] "Another French scholar has more or less shown that the geography of the Odyssey is correct geography; not as you would find it if you had a geography book and a map, but as it would be in a 'periplum,' that is, as a coasting sailor would find it" (*ABCR*, 43–4).

necessary stages: every misfortune or delay is "the way"; "What you depart from is not the way." Odysseus/Ulysses is engulfed by waves just as the sun passes the bounds of the navigable world (the Pillars of Hercules) and "crashes" into the ocean, and just as Lucifer seems to crash into North Carolina from Pound's perspective in Pisa. The stars are "brought" to the shore with the departure of the sun each night. The sun lies in wait under the ocean or under the earth, only to reawaken (in the east) and begin its ascent all over again.

After blinding and humiliating Polyphemus, Odysseus cannot help but reveal his true name: No longer "ΟΥ ΤΙΣ" or "No one" but "Odysseus / the name of my family." This allows Polyphemus to call on his father Poseidon to revenge him. Pound turns Homer's joke into an epithet of shipwrecked Odysseus. He is reduced to "no one," without comrades, without the protection of the gods, held captive by the veering winds. He is "ΟΥ ΤΙΣ / a man on whom the sun has gone down" (74/450). This is a literal reading of Homer, for when Poseidon learns that Odysseus has left Calypso's island, he "gathered the clouds, and seizing his trident in his hands troubled the sea, and roused all blasts of all manner of winds, and hid with clouds land and sea alike; and night rushed down from heaven [ὀρώρει δ' οὐρανόθεν νύξ, *orōrei d' ouranothen nyx*]" (5.292–4). Pound also uses the epithet to connect Odysseus to Elijah:

and Rouse found they spoke of Elias
in telling tales of Odysseus   ΟΥ ΤΙΣ
                                                ΟΥ ΤΙΣ
"I am noman, my name is noman". (74/446)

Elijah became so sick of sea-travel that he walked inland with an oar slung on his back until he came to a place where no one knew what an oar was. Tiresias commands Odysseus to do the same.[18] *Outis* therefore connotes the hero who is sick of sea-travel and is no longer recognized as a hero by others.

The *outis* epithet returns in Canto 80 to describe the poet who is *achronos* or outside of time. Pound reflects on the hackneyed Battle Hymn of the Republic:

"mi-hine eyes hev"
                    well yes they *have*
seen a good deal of it
          there is a good deal to be seen
fairly tough and unblastable

[18] See *Odyssey* 11.121–33.

and the hymn . . .
well in contrast to the *god*-damned crooning
put me down for temporis acti
ΟΥ ΤΙΣ
ἄχρονος
now there are no more days
οὔ τις
ἄχρονος
the water seeps in under the bottle's seal
Till finally the moon rose like a blue p.c. (80/518–19)

Horace defines himself as "laudator temporis acti," "one who praises past times."[19] The Greek "ἄχρονος" (a*chronos*), which is not found in Homer, can mean "instantaneous" (that which lasts but a moment of time), "short-lived" (as of infants), or "non-temporal" and "outside of time" (as the immortals). The author of Galatians uses it in reference to the φύσις (*physis*) or "soul"; Plotinus uses it to describe the νόησις (*neēsis*), or "intelligence," "understanding."[20] In a letter to Dallam Simpson, Pound describes his little magazine, *Four Pages*, as "relatively a-chronos, out side time."[21] In Canto 80, Pound connects *outis* with *achronos* and a vision of a post-human world. There are no more days ("He is trampling out the vintage where the grapes of wrath are stored"); there is "no one"; there is "no time"—at least in the chronological, teleological, or historical sense. Only the processes of nature endure, which are immortal, "unblastable": the time of aeons (Aeon) and the Horae. These processes outlast mankind's industry and preservation ("water seeps in under the bottle's seal") as well as man's hackneyed sentimentality and crooning verses: the moon rising like a blue post card.

Outis, therefore, is Pound's epithet for Odysseus washed up on the coast of Scheria after his shipwreck; bleached white by salt and sun; a solar deity that does not shine (when it is "buried" in the earth or plunges into the ocean); and the hero that no one recognizes as such. *Outis* also gestures to a post-human consciousness that exists outside of time and can witness the indestructible processes of nature.

[19] Horace, *De Arte Poetica* in *The Works of Horace*, ed. C. Smart (Philadelphia: Joseph Whetham, 1836), line 173.

[20] Galatians 7.448; Plotinus, *Enneads*, trans. Stephen Mackenna, ed. E. R. Dodds, Paul Henry, and B. S. Page (London: Faber and Faber, 1969), 4.4.1.

[21] Ezra Pound, [?] 1950 Letter to Dallam Simpson. *EPC*, Box 9, Folder 2. Earlier in the letter, Pound suggests that *The Pisan Cantos* don't suffer the "time-lag" of other authors: "FROBENIUS, Gesell, Brooks Adams, you can figure the time-lag for ourselves. In fact that only thing you can read without enormous time-lag is Pound's Pisan Cantos. The Chinese and Adams cantos should have been read long ago."

As the Winds Veer

Descriptions and invocations of winds overwhelm *The Pisan Cantos.* In Canto 74, the olive tree is "blown white in the wind" (74/445); "the wind also is of the process" (445); "the wind came as hamadryas" (451); "Zephyr [is] behind her" (455); there is "Boreas Apeliota libeccio" (458); the Charities flow "in the soft air" (463); "this air as of Kuanon"; "this air brought [Aphrodite] ashore"; and "the wind under Taishan" is soft (469). In Canto 76, the "leaves turn under Scirocco" (47/473); there is "timeless air over the sea-cliffs" (475); "the wind [is] coming down / out of the mountain" (479); and "Came Eurus as comforter" (480). In Canto 77, "Il Scirocco è geloso ['the sirocco is frigid']" (77/485); "Came Boreas and his kylin"; "nor does the martin against the tempest / fly as in the calm air" (488); and "the wind [is] mad as Cassandra" (495). In Canto 80, "This wind is lighter than swansdown" (80/534). In Canto 81, a "hot wind came from the marshes" (81/537); and "the season died a-cold / Borne upon a zephyr's shoulder" (539). In Canto 82, the wind speaks the lines from Theocritus's second idyll: "ἐμὸν τὸν ἄνδρα [*emon ton andra,* 'to me the man']" (82/546).

In contrast to Homer's blasting winds, Pound's winds are "as mad as Cassandra / who was as sane as the lot of 'em" (77/495). They are "part of the process," or the natural beauty of the indestructible world. They guide the *periplum* of Odysseus-Pound on his song's journey:

> between NEKUIA where are Alcmene and Tyro
>   and the Charybdis of action
>   to the solitude of Mt. Taishan
> femina, femina, that wd. not be dragged into paradise by the hair,
> under the gray cliff in periplum
>   the sun dragging her stars
>   a man on whom the sun has gone down
> and the wind came as hamadryas under the sun-beat. (74/451)

Pound contrasts Odysseus's passive reception of the spirits of the dead in the nekyia with his active negotiation past Charybdis, in which Odysseus must grab hold of the fig tree growing on a rock above her to avoid being swallowed (12.430–50). These are both contrasted with the beauty of Mount Tai in Shandong province. Odysseus is invoked in his many guises: as a solar deity dragging the stars after him; as Homer's Odysseus about to be smashed against the menacing cliffs of Scheria, which first appear to Odysseus as "ὄρεα σκιόεντα" (*orea skioenta*) or "shadowy mountains" (5.279) (the Greek name

Φαίακες is also derived from φαιός [*phaios*] or "gray"); and as Pound in Pisa who has lost favor with the world, but still feels the divinity of the wind's visitation like a tree-nymph.

Equally important, this passage identifies the competing poetic agendas of *The Cantos* that Ronald Bush finds inconsolable: the poetic and philological task of resurrecting the *Ur-Odyssey* and the "feminine" gods (who can't just be dragged up to heaven by their hair, and nor should they be: Pound's paradiso is mostly chthonic); "the Charybdis of action," or political task of rewriting and correcting history through the lens of Alexander del Mar, Zielinski, and others; and the task of merely asserting the indestructible "processes" that exists beyond the human world.[22] The *Cantos* are intentionally overdetermined.

Overdetermination of meaning reaches a near breaking point at the end of Canto 74. Pound describes Odysseus clinging to his mast in the storm and then aligns his own poetic technique to the veering winds. The sequence begins with fascist bluster, which flags and changes course to present the image of a dreamy Odysseus visited by goddesses that ride on the wind:

> Said Von Tirpitz to his daughter: beware of their charm
> ΣΕΙΡΗΝΕΣ this cross turns with the sun
> and the goyim are undoubtedly in great numbers cattle
> whereas a jew will receive information
>   he will gather up information
>   faute de … something more solid
>   but not in all cases
> ΣΕΙΡΗΝΕΣ   had appreciated his conversation
> ΧΑΡΙΤΕΣ possibly in the soft air
> with the mast held by the left hand
> in this air as of Kuanon
> enigma forgetting the times and seasons
> but this air brought her ashore a la marina
> with the great shell borne on the seawaves
>   nautilis biancastra. (74/463)

Alfred von Tirpitz, the German admiral who developed submarine and torpedo warfare against the allies in the First World War, warns his daughter to "beware the English charm," which he (or Pound) compares to the charm of the Sirens.

[22] Joyce similarly, and much more explicitly, divides Scylla and Charybdis into two philosophical "positions": roughly Aristotelian, realistic, historical; and Platonic, idealistic, theosophical. Pound never revisits the idea of Charybdis as representing action, but in Canto 47 he associates Scylla with non-aggression and passivity.

Pound then reminds the reader that the grammate cross adopted by the Nazis with arms to the right represents the vernal progress of the sun. A Jewish voice compares non-Jews to cattle that can be easily manipulated. But the lines, "faute de… something more solid / but not in all cases" take the air out of this anti-Semitic caricature as if Pound grew tired of beating that drum—or he realized the danger of beating it. The scene transforms into Odysseus on his raft. He recalls the Sirens' beautiful song and his mother's lament in the underworld: "It was longing for thee, and for thy counsels, glorious Odysseus, and for thy tender-heartedness, that robbed me of honey-sweet life" (11.202–3). The poetic "winds" change abruptly. The Sirens were first associated with malicious flatterers and now with paradise and "the soft air."

Pound uses this poetic conceit of himself as Odysseus in the storm in "*Et Faim Sallir les Loups des Boys*," which first appeared in *Blast* (1915). In this case, clinging to the mast means not allowing the faddism of the press change his opinions about timeless beauty:

I cling to the spar,
Washed with the cold salt ice
I cling to the spar –
Insidious modern waves, civilization, civilized hidden snares.
Cowardly editors threaten: "If I dare."[23]

Clinging to the mast means resisting the opinions of the day and asserting the immortal aesthetic beauties. Similarly, in Canto 74, Pound holds the mast in order to reassert what is immortal amid the chaos of recent events and perhaps his own desire to defend a now-repugnant political position.

Pound's Odysseus hears the voice of the gods "with the mast held by the left hand": a specificity that is partly illuminated by *Odyssey* 5. Odysseus leaves Calypso's island and sails for seventeen days without sleeping, holding "the steering oar" (πηδάλιον, *pēdalion*) in order to keep to the "left side" (ἀριστερός, *aristeros*) of the Wain or Big Dipper, as Calypso advised: a constellation believed in Homer's day never to sink below the horizon (5.270, 5.277). Pound might have misremembered Calypso's directions. More likely, he deduced that if a right-handed Odysseus was steering, he was holding the mast with his left hand.[24]

[23] *PT*, 1178.

[24] In Canto 94, Pound describes Apollonius of Tyana, subject-rhyme of Odysseus, as "keeping the Ganges on his right hand / went down ten days toward the sea" (94/657).

Of course, Pound's Odysseus is not steering at all; he is carried by the kind air "as of Kuanon" or Kuan-yin, of the Chinese goddess of mercy. He is visited by the Charities or Graces, part of the retinue of Aphrodite and associated with the Eleusinian Mysteries. Like Aphrodite who was carried to the shore on her *nautilis biancastra* or "white-colored shell," Odysseus (who is later carried to shore on the white veil of Leucothea) has become an enigma "forgetting all times and seasons." Pound transforms Homer's fierce winds into beneficent and godly ones. Homer's Odysseus clings to the steering oar and mast as he sails in one direction for seventeen days; Pound's Odysseus drifts with the veering winds, visited by graces and drunk as if with the lotus, holding the mast lest he topple over. But this transformation is part of the action of this passage: the proto-fascist bluster gives way to the timeless air of Kuanon; the "Charybdis of action" dissipates into the Scylla of passivity, as Pound presents it in Canto 47; Pound drops his political agenda to assert the "enigma" and living air of the gods.

Pound also connects the image of the wind-blown Odysseus with his poem's "schema" by invoking Homer's four cardinal winds. Poet, poem, and hero all meld and float together. Here, Pound Pilgrim is carried through a paradiso that does not ascend through Dante's heavenly spheres but "as the winds veer in periplum": "not to a schema." This idea resonates with the motif of the "rudderless boat" in the medieval romance, in which the hero abandons his telos and gives way to errancy or "aventure," allowing God to direct his fate.

By no means an orderly Dantescan rising
but as the winds veer
tira libeccio
now Genji at Suma , tira libeccio
as the winds veer and the raft is driven
and the voices , Tiro, Alcmene
with you is Europa nec casta Pasiphaë
Eurus, Apeliota as the winds veer in periplum
Io son la luna". Cunizza
as the winds veer in periplum
and from under the Rupe Tarpeia
drunk with wine of the Castelli
"in the name of its god" "Spiritus veni"
adveni / not to a schema
"is not for the young" said Arry, stagirite
but as grass under Zephyrus
as the green blade under Apeliota

Time is not, Time is the evil, beloved
Beloved the hours βροδοδάκτυλος ["rosy-fingered"]
    as against the half-light of the window
    with the sea beyond making horizon
le contre-jour the line of the cameo
profile "to carve Achaia"
    a dream passing over the face in the half-light
    Venere, Cytherea "aut Rhodon"
    vento ligure, veni. (74/463–64)

Pound's erratic spacing and punctuation here only emphasizes the lyrical "speed in mind" and "forward rush" of his lyric song. As Bush puts it, such "revolutionary poetic techniques [...] subsequently set a standard of poetic immediacy and influenced the most important poetry in the English language for the rest of the century."[25] Pound wrote to James Laughlin, who was preparing the 1946 edition of *The Pisan Cantos:* "God damn & buggar the punctuation—the important thing is for the 1st time to emphasize the articulation of the thought."[26] Pound wants his readers to participate in the radical immediacy: to witness poetry—and poetic consciousness—in its most primordial, godlike state. Pound makes a similar point in a 1939 letter to Hubert Creekmore about his polyphonic technique:

> Narrative not the same as lyric; different techniques for song and story. "would, could", et cetera: Abbreviations save *eye* effort. Also show speed in mind of original character supposed to be uttering or various colorings and degrees of importance or emphasis attributed by the protagonist of the moment.[27]

Pound's account of his abbreviated or "hurried" style implies a polyphonic lyric. Abbreviations "show speed in mind of the original character supposed to be uttering" and reflect the "emphasis attributed by the protagonist of the moment." "Speed of mind" reflects Pound's poetic ideal of *hilaritas,* a term he borrows from John Scotus Eriugena and Gemistos Plethon: "But Gemisto: 'Are Gods by hilaritas'; / and their speed in communication" (98/705). Figures like Hermes, Athena, and Odysseus combine gaiety or good humor with communicative mental swiftness.[28]

25 Ronald Bush, "Art versus the Descent of the Iconoclasts: Cultural Memory in Ezra Pound's Pisan Cantos," *Modernism/Modernity* 14.1 (2007), 87.

26 Ezra Pound, *Ezra Pound and James Laughlin: Selected Letters*, ed. David M. Gordon (New York: New Directions, 1994), 145.

27 *L*, 418.

28 Liebregts, *Ezra Pound and Neoplatonism,* 338–9.

Pound's description of the wind-blown Odysseus is a *translatio* of Homer's storm, which details the riot of the four cardinal winds:

> As when in autumn the North Wind [Βορέης, *Boreēs*] bears the thistle-tufts over the plain, and close they cling to one another, so did the winds [ἄνεμοι, *anemoi*] bear the raft this way and that over the sea. Now the South Wind [Νότος, *Notos*] would fling it to the North Wind [Βορέῃ] to be driven on, and now again the East Wind [Εὖρος, *Euros*] would yield it to the West Wind [Ζεφύρῳ, *Zephyrō*] to drive.
>
> (5.328–333)

Pound localizes Homer's four cardinal winds to Pisa. He include Eurus, the south easterly wind; libeccio, the south westerly wind, from the Greek *Libyian* or Libyan; the Apeliota, the easterly Mediterranean wind that comes from the rising sun, also called the Levant (*levant*, "rising"); and the *vento ligure*, a northern wind from Liguria, which may be Pound's invention, and which recalls the *ligur* ("sharp-toned," "shrill") song of the Sirens. Pound-Odysseus hears goddesses speaking in the wind. Like the exiled Prince Genji at the fishing town of Suma, he sees manifestations of the divine playing in the waves. This includes Tyro and Alcmene from Canto 2; the abducted Europa; Cunizza da Romano, whom Pound believed transmitted the lyrical power of Provence to Italy; and the original *casta* ("chaste") Pasiphae—not the figure of bestiality and lust of the *Interpretatio graeca*, but the goddess abducted by Poseidon in his primitive theriomorphic form as a bull.[29]

Pound's assertion that the goddesses come, like his song, "not to a schema," but are carried on the wind, is juxtaposed with Aristotle's comment that such an idea is "not for the young." In the *Nicomachean Ethics*, Aristotle argues that young are not good at political science because, lacking experience, they are led by their feelings.[30] Pound makes Aristotle condone his own non-schematic approach to his "epic" in which divinity arrives by errant winds and through the observation of the movement of grass. There is some comedy—or at least *hilaritas*—in this, given Aristotle's mania for catalogs and schemata, including of poetic and dramatic forms. One cannot imagine Aristotle appreciating or even understanding Pound's fragmented and frenzied lyric.

[29] On Cunizza's complicated role in *The Cantos*, especially in Cantos 72 and 73, see Bush, "Modernism, Fascism, and the Composition of Ezra Pound's *Pisan Cantos*," 72–6.

[30] Aristotle, *Nicomachean Ethics*, trans. David Ross, ed. Lesley Brown (New York: Oxford University Press, 2009), 1095a.1. See also *GK*, 343.

The passage ends with an assertion of Pound's poetic ideal, which is to achieve this state of Odysseus *outis*: a mind *achronos:* "Time is not, Time is the evil." This involves a devotion to the immediate, observable world: Homer's rosy-fingered dawn seen over the sea through a window. The wind carries salvation to us, if we know how to receive it: the flickering of light, the rustling of grass—and with that skill the poet can "carve Achaia": a permanent ("unblastable") image.[31]

Pound inverts Homer's terrible storm into the suave air that blows from paradise, creating the same type of sacred disorder or "Wilderness of renewals, confusion" of the Lotophagoi section, but now in a distinctly lyrical voice (20/92). Pound's veering, chaotic winds are not just part of the "process" but also, the poet insists, the very *schema* of his poem—a paradox if there ever was one. But this is a poetry that invites paradoxes. The lyric voice sings from unstable ground of the amorphous divinities carried to him on the air. And shipwreck is imminent: a catastrophe which threatens to shatter the delicate schema of the lyric song.

The Waters Went over Me

The lyrical voices of *The Pisan Cantos* circulate around a catastrophe: Oysseus's wreck, or Pound's mental collapse in the gorilla cage. Although the catastrophe has already happened, the diffidence of the lyrical voices suggests that it is also still occurring or always about to occur. Pound refers to it directly only once, buried in a dense cluster of *Odyssey* allusions in Canto 80: Pound hearing the *Odyssey* recited in Greek when he was thirteen; Odysseus's hubris in attacking the Cicones; Odysseus's godlike "speed in mind"; Pound being saved from the gates of death by finding *The Pocket Book of Verse* at the DTC; and the wave that engulfs Odysseus's raft.

> and it was old Spencer (, H.) who first declaimed me the Odyssey
> with a head built like Bill Shepard's
> on the quais of what Siracusa?
>   or what tennis court
> near what pine trees?

[31] Pound's 1920 persona, Mauberly, is compared to an engraver, "Not the full smile, / His art, but an art / In profile; / Colourless / Pier Francesca, / Pisanello lacking the skill / To forge Achaia" (*PT,* 558). Like Piero della Francesca's colorless and "dead" tableaus, or Pisanello's profiles on medals, Mauberly is incapable of capturing the "full" figure, only a pretty simulacra. For the connection between Achaia and Pound's theory of the icon, See Ronald Bush, "Art versus the Descent of the Iconoclasts."

care and craft in forming leagues and alliances
    that avail nothing against the decree
the folly of attacking that island
    and of the force ὑπὲρ μόρον ["beyond what is destined"]

with a mind like that he is one of us
    Favonus, vento benigno
    Je suis au bout de mes forces/
That from the gates of death,
    that from the gates of death: Whitman or Lovelace
        found on the jo-house seat at that
in a cheap edition! [and thanks to Professor Speare][32]
hast'ou swum in a sea of air strip
    through an aeon of nothingness,
when the raft broke and the waters went over me (80/532–33)

Pound significantly misremembers Hubert Spencer's recitation of the *Iliad* after their tennis match at the Cheltenham Military Academy: "A fellow named Spenser [*sic*] recited a long passage of *Iliad* to me, after tennis. That was worth more than grammar when one was 13 years old."[33] Rouse discovered that "the liars on the quai at Siracusa / still vie with Odysseus" (77/487). The tennis court becomes Pound's Syracuse, where he first heard the lies of the *Odyssey* from an instructor who resembled (or was succeeded by) William Pierce Shephard, who taught him Provençal and Dante at Clinton College. The memory therefore condenses most of Pound's objectives of his modernist *translatio* of Homer: to recreate the sound of Homer's Greek; to resurrect the folkloric roots of the *Odyssey*; to include the Provençal (Neoplatonic) theology of love; to emulate the medieval classicism of Dante.

Pound emphasizes what he calls the "crime and punishment motif" of the *Odyssey* by linking Odysseus's shipwreck (and his own) to "the force ὑπὲρ μόρον" or "beyond what is destined."[34] "The folly of attacking that island" returns to a topic introduced in Canto 79: "No sooner out of Troas / than the damn fools attacked Ismarus of the Cicones" (79/505). Homer doesn't use the phrase *hyper moron* in reference to the Cicones, but he uses it in two key episodes in the *Odyssey* which illuminate Pound's insertion of it here. Early in the *Odyssey*,

[32] This is Pound's parenthetical in square brackets.
[33] *GK*, 145.
[34] *LE*, 212.

during the council of the gods, Zeus reflects on how mortals often blame the gods for things they themselves deserve:

> Look you now, how ready mortals are to blame the gods. It is from us, they say, that evils come, but they even of themselves, through their own blind folly [σφῇσιν ἀτασθαλίῃσιν *sphēsin atasthaliēsin*], have sorrows [ἄλγε', *alge'*] beyond that which is ordained [ὑπὲρ μόρον, *hyper moron*]. Even as now Aegisthus, beyond that which was ordained [ὑπὲρ μόρον], took to himself the wedded wife of the son of Atreus, and slew him on his return.
>
> (1.32–36)

Hyper moron is not a theological paradox; it simply means going beyond the normal limit, or taking more than one's share. According to Zeus, the reason man suffers or feels pain (*algeō*) beyond what is "ordained" or normal is due to his own *atasthalia*: "presumptuous sin," "recklessness," or "wickedness" ("the damn fools"). The words "σφῇσιν ἀτασθαλίῃσιν" (*sphēsin atasthaliēsin*) echo the proem, in which Odysseus's men are described as perishing "through their own blind folly" (σφετέρῃσιν ἀτασθαλίῃσιν, *spheterēsin atasthaliēsin*) after devouring the Cattle of Helios (1.7). Odysseus uses a similar expression in his account of his sack of Ismarus:

> From Ilios the wind bore me and brought me to the Cicones, to Ismarus. There I sacked the city and slew the men; and from the city we took their wives and great store of treasure, and divided them among us, that so far as lay in me no man might go defrauded of an equal share. Then verily I gave command that we should flee with swift foot, but the others in their great folly [μέγα νήπιοι, *mega nēpioi*] did not hearken. But there much wine was drunk, and many sheep they slew by the shore, and sleek kine of shambling gait.
>
> (9.37–45)

Odysseus's account of the "great childishness" (*mega nēpioi*) of his men for wanting to linger and devour cattle anticipates their reckless presumptuousness (*atasthalia*) of devouring the Cattle of Helios, but the real presumptuousness to readers like Pound and Joyce was in their sacking Ismarus and slaying the Cicones in the first place: a "force ὑπὲρ μόρον."

The phrase *hyper moron* appears significantly only one other time in the *Odyssey:* during Odysseus's shipwreck, right after a great wave engulfs him off the coast of Scheria. A brief analysis of Odysseus's shipwreck will illuminate Pound's condensed *translatio*. Four huge waves engulf Odysseus at sea. The first "giant wave" (μέγα κῦμα, *mega kyma*) breaks his mast (5.513). Odysseus struggles back onto the raft, weighed down by Calypso's clothes. Then a second "giant wave, dread and grievous" (μέγα κῦμα [...] δεινόν τ' ἀργαλέον τε, *mega kyma [...] deinon t' argaleon te*) breaks the raft into fragments (5.366–67). Odysseus straddles a single plank, strips off his clothes, and plunges into the sea with Leucothea's veil. He rides the waves for two nights and two days. On the morning of the third day, Odysseus is raised up by a "big wave" (μεγάλου [...] κύματος, *megalou* [...] *kymatos*) that carries him to the island of Scheria (5.393). But as Odysseus nears, he realizes that the wave will dash him against the sharp crags and sheer rock. He tries to swim away, but another "great wave" (μέγα κῦμα, *mega kyma*) throws him toward the rugged shore (5.425).

> There would his skin have been stripped off and his bones broken, had not the goddess, flashing-eyed Athena, [γλαυκῶπις Ἀθήνη, *glaukōpis Athēnē*] put a thought in his mind. On he rushed and seized the rock with both hands, and clung to it, groaning, until the great wave went by.
>
> (5.426–29)

Odysseus grabs hold of a protruding rock and escapes his death. However, he is hit by the same wave as it recedes: The "great wave covered him" (μέγα κῦμα κάλυψεν, *mega kyma kalypsen*) and flings him far out from shore (5.435).

> Then verily would hapless Odysseus have perished beyond his fate [ὑπὲρ μόρον, *hyper moron*], had not flashing-eyed [γλαυκῶπις, *glaukōpis*] Athena given him prudence [ἐπιφροσύνην, *epiphrosynēn*, "thoughtfulness," "wisdom"].
>
> (5.436–37)

Odysseus decides to swim away from the coast in search of calmer currents. He eventually discovers "the mouth of a fair-flowing river" and prays to the river god to bring him safely to the shore (5.441).

> The god straightway stayed his stream, and checked the waves, and made a calm [γαλήνην, *galēnēn*] before him, and brought him safely to the mouth of the river. And he let his two knees bend and his strong hands fall, for his spirit [κῆρ, *kēr*, "heart"] was crushed [δέδμητο, *dedmēto*] by the sea. And all his flesh was swollen, and sea water flowed in streams up through his mouth and nostrils. So he lay breathless and speechless, with scarce strength to move; for terrible weariness had come upon him.
>
> (5.451–57)

Homer's Odysseus prays to the river god, who makes a "calm" (*galēnēn*) and brings him safely to the mouth of the river; Pound-Odysseus prays to "Favonus, vento benigno" ("West Wind, with kindly breeze"). Homer's Odysseus is "breathless and speechless with scarce strength to move"; Pound-Odysseus is "au bout de mes forces." Homer's Odysseus is saved from death by his quick-wittedness in grabbing a jutting crag; Pound-Odysseus is saved "from the gates of death" by Speare's *Pocket Book of Verse* found in the latrine. Homer's Odysseus is naked at sea for three days; Pound-Odysseus "swum in a sea of air strip / through an aeon of nothingness" for three weeks exposed to the elements until he could no longer endure it. This might explain Pound's strange inversion of the narrative order: Pound's Odysseus swims in a sea of air strip, then the raft breaks.

During the storm, flashing-eyed (*glaukopis*) Athena "puts a thought" in Odysseus's mind and "gives" him prudence. In Pound's reading: it is Odysseus's quick-wittedness and his ability to channel the "speed of mind" of the goddess that allows him to successfully negotiate all the menacing waves and not perish beyond his fate (*hyper moron*). He shares in godly *hilaritas*, which Pound connects to Odysseus's epithet *polymetis* and his translation of *Odyssey* 1.65, in which Zeus admires Odysseus's intelligence: "How should I, then, forget godlike Odysseus, who is beyond all mortals in wisdom, and beyond all has paid sacrifice to the immortal gods, who hold broad heaven?" (1.65–67). Pound's version is: "with a mind like that he is one of us"; or, in *Guide to Kulchur*: "A chap with a mind like THAT! the fellow is one of us. One of US."[35] Homer's phrase *hyper moron* here refers to the fact that Odysseus's death would be more than he deserved. However, it recalls Zeus's complaint that mortals blame the gods when in fact it is their "blind folly" in doing things that are *hyper moron* which leads to their punishment. Pound links the phrase to Odysseus's sack of Ismarus, inviting the reader to make the association that, like Odysseus, Pound went beyond what is destined (*hyper moron*) and Pisa is his punishment.

However, Pound never makes this explicit, and such a reading is complicated by Pound's portrayal of the DTC and Odysseus's shipwreck as (also) not a punishment at all, but the hero's initiation into a mystery: stripping away his indivualism (*sparagmos*) to become *outis* and *achronos;* giving way to the veering winds and the "process" of his rudderless periplum; visiting with goddeses; and retaining those "unblastable" images of the permanent world. Pound's line, "hast'ou swum in a sea of air strip," aligns his experience in the Pisan cage with Circe's mysteries in Canto 47, and Odysseus's rebirth in nature: "Hast thou found a nest softer than cunnus"; "Hast thou entered more deeply the mountain?" (47/238).

[35] *GK*, 146.

One can read *The Pisan Cantos* as a lyrical representation of the trauma of incarceration. The poet is unable to gain perspective on his situation and narrate the catastrophe or admit his faults. The lyrical voice(s) sing from hell, trying pathetically to build a paradise and make the vision cohere, finding goddesses only in wasps and ladybugs. The poet, likewise, tries to map his own personal experience onto his convoluted reading of Odysseus's shipwreck and ultimately fails. But one can also read *The Pisan Cantos* as a breathless poetics of revelation and an assertion of divinity. The lyrical voice(s) sing from paradise, invoking a catastrophe that never quite arrives, because it is part of a sacred disorder leading to illumination. The poet grounds his experience through his own philological excavation of Odysseus's shipwreck as a ritual of the solar hero and fertility daimon. While my emphasis leans toward the latter reading, it is this very chiasmus, or this vacillation between these two readings which, creates Pound's own complex or "participatory" version of sacred disorder.

When Pound returns to Odysseus's shipwreck at the end of Canto 82, the poetic voice alternates between hope and despair, between wreck as revelation and wreck as catastrophe. This passage alludes specifically to Odysseus's prayer to the earth once he arrives on Scheria and his first sleep on dry land, and to the undertow of the wave which flings Odysseus away from Scheria.

> How drawn, O GEA TERRA,
> what draws as thou drawest
> till one sink into thee by an arm's width
> embracing thee. Drawest,
> truly thou drawest.
> Wisdom lies next thee,
> simply, past metaphor.
> Where I lie let the thyme rise
> and basilicum
> let the herbes rise in April abundant
> By Ferrara was buried naked, fu Nicolo
> et di qua de la del Po,
> wind: ἐμὸν τὸν ἄνδρα ["to me the man"]
> lie into earth to the breast bone, to the left shoulder
> Kipling suspected it
> to the height of ten inches or over
> man, earth: two halves of the tally. (82/546)

After releasing the veil of Leucothea in the river, Odysseus "sank down in the reeds [σχοίνῳ ὑπεκλίνθη, *schoinō hypeklinthē*, 'reclined in the rushes'] and kissed the earth, the giver of grain [ζείδωρον ἄρουραν, *zeidōron arouran*]" (5.462–63). Odysseus does not merely thank ἤπειρος (*ēpeiros*), meaning "terra firma" or "dry land," he prays to *aroura*, meaning "tilled or arable land," because it is *zeidōros*: "*zea*-giving" or "life-giving." Odysseus then notices a natural shelter of "two bushes that grew from the same spot, one of thorn and one of olive" (5.476–77). Homer's complex simile deepens Odysseus's connection to the *zea*-giving earth:

> And the much-enduring goodly Odysseus [πολύτλας δῖος Ὀδυσσεύς, *polytlas dios Odysseus*] saw it, and was glad, and he lay down in the midst, and heaped over him the fallen leaves. And as a man hides a brand beneath the dark embers in an outlying farm [ἀγροῦ ἐπ' ἐσχατιῆς, *agrou ep' eschatiēs*], a man who has no neighbors [ᾧ μὴ πάρα γείτονες ἄλλοι, *hō mē para geitones alloi*], and so saves a seed of fire [σπέρμα πυρὸς, *sperma pyros*], that he may not have to kindle it from some other source, so Odysseus covered himself with leaves. And Athena shed sleep upon his eyes, that it might enfold his lids and speedily free him from toilsome weariness [δυσπονέος καμάτοιο, *dysponeos kamatoio*].
>
> (5.476–93)

This is the only epic simile in Homer that contains a metaphor: the fire's seed (*sperma pyros*). The itinerant man (possibly a herdsman) must bury an ember of fire in an outlying farm (*agros* can mean a tilled land or just a field) where he presumably sleeps because there are no neighbors or borderers (*geitones*) from whom to borrow it. Odysseus, therefore, is both the man who plants the seed and the fire seed itself, both the tucked and the tucker. He covers himself with leaves, preserving the last ember of himself.

Pound reads this moment in Homer as a "connubium terrae," or "marriage of the earth," similar to Odysseus's union with Circe in the fertility cantos. Odysseus-Pound prays to GEA TERRA who draws people into the earth: "Drawest, / truly thou drawest." She is the "universe of fluid force."[36] The fertility hero Odysseus is the seed that fructifies the earth and renews the vegetation by his real or symbolic death: "Where I lie let the thyme rise." Similiar to the solar deity or Jessie Weston's Fisher King, Odysseus has undergone his ritual drowning or descent and is reborn or ascends again on dry land like the *anodos* of Persephone. Pound's wind carries fragments of the "fire-spell" sung by the maiden of Theocritus's Idyll 2 who wants her neglectful lover to come back to

[36] *SR*, 92.

her, reinforcing the *connubium terrae* motif, and recalling Homer's *sperma pyros*. Pound also connects the naked Odysseus sleeping by the river on Scheria to Niccolò buried by the Po: "By Ferrara was buried naked, fu Nicolo / et di qua de la del Po ['was Nicolo / and here beyond the Po']."

"Wisdom lies next thee, / simply, past metaphor" can be read as Pound's literal interpretation of Homer's line, "and Athena shed sleep upon his eyes": the goddess of wisdom would have had to be lying next to Odysseus in order to do so. This also explains why Pound's description of Odysseus being "drawn" into the earth is also so literal and specific: he sinks into her "by an arm's width"; "earth to the breast bone, to the left shoulder"; "to the height of ten inches or over." Rudyard Kipling also "suspected" that Mother Earth was a restorative power in *Kim* (1901). After his arduous journey through the Himalayas, Kim convalesces on a cot in the house of an old lady (the "Sahiba") and has a crisis of identity similar to Pound's Odysseus. Kim feels "that his soul was out of gear with its surroundings—a cog-wheel unconnected with any machinery."[37] He wanders out of the house in search of a better resting place:

> There stood an empty bullock-cart on a little knoll half a mile away, with a young banian tree behind—a look-out, as it were, above some new-ploughed levels; and his eyelids, bathed in soft air, grew heavy as he neared it. The ground was good clean dust—no new herbage that, living, is half-way to death already, but the hopeful dust that holds the seed of all life. Kim felt it between his toes, patted it with his palms, and, joint by joint, sighing luxuriously, laid him down full length along in the shadow of the wooden-pinned cart. And Mother Earth was as faithful as the Sahiba. She breathed through him to restore the poise he had lost lying so long on a cot cut off from her good currents. His head lay powerless upon her breast, and his opened hands surrendered to her strength. The races who shoe their feet with iron and the skins of dead animals, who pack boards and concrete between themselves and the clay of their fashioning, do not understand, except when they go camping, how Earth, that gives all the fevers, can also take them away. The many-rooted tree above him, and even the dead man-handled wood beside him, knew what he sought, as he himself did not know. Hour upon hour he lay deeper than sleep.[38]

Kim's predicament resonates with Pound's own, who slept on a cot in an officer's tent writing about the traumatic and transformative three weeks he slept on the bare earth in the cage. Kim discovers the "seed of all life" just as Odysseus

[37] Rudyard Kipling, *Kim* (New York: Doubleday, 1912), 346.
[38] Kipling, *Kim*, 347–8.

represents the *sperma pyros* in his leafy burrow. Kipling's Mother Earth restores "the poise he had lost lying so long on a cot cut off from her good currents" just as Circe restores the mariners who "became men again, younger than they were before, and far comelier and taller to look upon" (10.395–96). Pound likens the cage to Circe's "swine-sty" and, in the passage above, to a shipwreck, where he is sucked into the fluid *chthonos* like Odysseus the solar deity crashing into the ocean. It is both horrific and rejuvenating: a ritual death (74/456).

Odysseus's burial on Scheria is alluded to in the paradisal procession of Canto 17. There Pound explicitly links Odysseus's self-burial to a fertility rite.

> "In the gloom the gold
> Gathers the light about it." . . .
> Now supine in burrow, half over-arched bramble,
> One eye for the sea, through that peek-hole,
> Gray light, with Athene.
> Zothar and her elephants, the gold loin-cloth,
> The sistrum, shaken, shaken,
> the cohorts of her dancers.
> And Aletha, by bend of the shore,
> with her eyes seaward,
> and in her hands sea-wrack
> Salt-bright with the foam.
> Koré through the bright meadow,
> with green-gray dust in the grass:
> "For this hour, brother of Circe." (17/78–79)

Odysseus in the gloom as *sperma pyros* is the gold that "gathers the light about it." Odysseus is "burrowed in" specifically over the "arched bramble" that Homer describes as a bush of thorn and of olive that grew from the same spot. Odysseus peeks out at the sea from his peephole. The line, "grey light, with Athene" suggests another reading of "Wisdom lies next thee, / simply, past metaphor" in Canto 82. Athena *glaukopis* is associated with the eyes of the owl, the greyish-brown foliage of the *Athene noctua* or "little owl" of Greece, as well as the white undersides of the olive tree which, as Upward points out, "glitters, the pale under face of the leaves alternating with the dark upper face," producing a greyish light.[39] Odysseus is, in other words, "with" Athene "past metaphor" in the sense that the light he sees from his peephole is cast through the olive leaves that arch over his burrow. Odysseus sees Zohar leading the chthonic procession of Persephone's *anodos* or

[39] Upward, *The New Word*, 234.

ascent, as well as Aletha (possibly a reference to Lethe) who gathers up Odysseus's sea-wrack, which is "salt-bright." Canto 17 anticipates Odysseus emerging from the sea as a solar god on the first page of Canto 74: "olive tree blown white in the wind / washed in the Kiang and Han / what whiteness will you add to this whiteness / what candor?" (74/445). It also foreshadows the fertility cantos, in that Persephone (Kore) addresses Odysseus as "brother of Circe," meaning initiate to Circe's mysteries, and leads him out of the underworld.

Odysseus's *anodos* in Canto 17 illuminates the second half of Pound's *translatio* of Odysseus's union with GEA TERRA in Canto 82. Pound interrupts his comparison between himself and Odysseus or Kim, both of whom "came out" much the better: Odysseus wakes up to Nausicaa and is received by the Phaeacians who agree to take him home. Kim is restored and his companion the Tibetan lama achieves enlightenment. Pound, however, doesn't know his ending. His trial still awaits him. "The loneliness of death" still plagues him. But he hears a distant procession in the rhythmic booming of Homer's sea:

> but I will come out of this knowing no one
> neither they me
>   connubium terrae   ἔφατα πόσις ἐμός ["she said my husband"]
>   ΧΘΟΝΙΟΣ, mysterium
> fluid ΧΘΟΝΟΣ o'erflowed me
>   lay in the fluid ΧΘΟΝΟΣ;
>   that lie
> under the air's solidity
>   drunk with ἸΧΩΡ of ΧΘΟΝΙΟΣ
>   fluid ΧΘΟΝΟΣ, strong as the undertow
>   of the wave receding
> but that a man should live in that further terror, and live
>   the loneliness of death came upon me
>   (at 3 P. M., for an instant)   δακρύων. ["weeping"]
>   ἐντεῦθεν ["on each side"]. (82/546–7)

Clytemnestra's words from *Agamemnon* 1404, "ἔφατα πόσις ἐμός" (*ephata posis emos*, "she said my husband"), refer to an anecdote Pound recounts a few pages earlier. After a delirious Swinburne was rescued from a watery death near Étretat in Normandy in 1869, he recited Aeschylus to the fishermen in thanks.

> When the french fisherman hauled him out he
> recited 'em
>   might have been Aeschylus

till they got into Le Portel, or wherever
in the original

"On the Atreides' roof"
"like a dog … and a good job"
ΕΜΟΣ ΠΟΣΙΣ … ΧΕΡΟΣ ["my husband … hand"]
hac dextera mortus
dead by this hand. (82/543)

Pound gets the anecdote intentionally wrong; Swinburne recited Victor Hugo.[40] But Swinburne ranked *The Oresteia* as among the greatest works of literature, and, like Pound, devoted himself to reviving the classics. Pound imagines Swinburne as himself, rescued from drowning in the gorilla cage, now reciting the two passages of *Agamemnon* that Pound had previously tried to translate in 1919, both with the help of Thomas Stanley's Latin "crib" which Pound praises in "Aeschylus" (1919) and cites here. The first is the opening monologue by the watchman ("On the Atreides' roof"); and the second is Clytemnestra's boast: "οὗτός ἐστιν Ἀγαμέμνων, ἐμὸς / πόσις, νεκρὸς δέ, τῆσδε δεξιᾶς χερὸς / ἔργον, δικαίας τέκτονος," which Pound translates as "This is Agamemnon, / My husband, / Dead by this hand, / And a good job."[41] The Greek means, literally, "dead by this right hand: a just workman."

Why recall only a fragment of Clytemnestra's boast? It may allude to Pound himself, who braved the storm of history, holding the mast with his left hand, while asserting the Roman (Fascist) salute with his right. Or this could be Pound's acknowledgment that his adoption of "right" politics was as vile an act as Clytemnestra's, which is why he will "come out of this knowing no one." However, a more plausible answer is that Clytemnestra makes a comparison between her act of murder, Zeus *chthonos,* and the regeneration of the earth:

> Twice I struck him, and with two groans his limbs relaxed. Once he had fallen, I dealt him yet a third stroke to grace my prayer to the infernal Zeus, the savior of the dead [χθονὸς / Διὸς νεκρῶν σωτῆρος εὐκταίαν χάριν, *chthonos / Dios nekrōn sōtēros euktaian charin*]. Fallen thus, he gasped away his life, and as he breathed forth quick spurts of blood, he struck me with dark drops of gory dew; while I rejoiced no less than the sown earth [σπορητὸς, *sporētos*] is gladdened in heaven's refreshing rain at the birthtime of the flower buds.[42]

[40] *LE*, 291.
[41] *LE*, 270.
[42] Aeschylus, *Agamemnon,* trans. Herbert Weir Smyth, lines 1384–92.

A Greek audience would find Clytemnestra's comparison sacrilegious. But any reader of Harrison or Frazer would recognize a vestige of a much older "drama" here: the murder of the fertility hero or king in order to revivify the earth. This is the main reason Pound places it in this cluster: "connubium terrae" and "ἔφατα πόσις ἐμός / ΧΘΟΝΙΟΣ, mysterium."

Odysseus's literal *connubium terrae* evolves into the image of him being swallowed by the watery earth, or the "ΧΘΟΝΙΟΣ, mysterium"; "Fluid ΧΘΟΝΟΣ o'erflowed me"; "fluid ΧΘΟΝΟΣ, strong as the undertow / of the wave receding." The specific reference is to the forth wave that draws Odysseus away from Scheria:

> Thus then did he escape this wave, but in its backward flow [παλιρρόθιον, *palirrothion*] it once more rushed upon him and smote him, and flung him far out in the sea. And just as, when a cuttlefish is dragged from its hole, many pebbles cling to its suckers, even so from his strong hands were bits of skin stripped off against the rocks; and the great wave covered him. Then verily would hapless Odysseus have perished beyond his fate [*hyper moron*], had not flashing-eyed Athena given him prudence.
>
> (5.430–37)

Palirrothion, which means "back-rushing" or "refluent," is used only one other time in the *Odyssey.* After Odysseus mocks the blind Polyphemus, Polyphemus pulls off the top of a mountain and hurls it in front of Odysseus's ship:

> And the sea surged beneath the stone as it fell, and the backward flow [παλιρρόθιον, *palirrothion*], like a flood from the deep, bore the ship swiftly landwards and drove it upon the shore.
>
> (9.484–6)

Odysseus's hubris in mocking the blind Polyphemus continues its refluent retribution in the waves off the Scherian coast, just as Homer's repetition of *hyper moron* suggests that the storm is Odysseus's punishment for an earlier transgression.

The image of the "fluid ΧΘΟΝΟΣ" and the receding wave also recalls Pound's favorite onomatopoetic line of Homer's Greek. He explains to Rouse in 1935: "Para thina poluphloisboio thalasses: the turn of the wave and the scutter of receding pebbles."[43] Pound invokes the sound in Canto 74 as the "diminutive poluphloisboios" (74/447). In Canto 82, Pound repeats the words CHTHONOS and CHOTHIONOS as though trying to recreate the sound of the waves crashing against the shore of Scheria as Odysseus sleeps. Homer's description

[43] *L*, 364.

of Odysseus nearing Scheria contains many of the onomatopoetic words that Pound delights in.

> But when he was as far away as a man's voice carries when he shouts [βοήσας, *boēsas*], and heard the boom of the sea upon the reefs [δοῦπον ἄκουσε ποτὶ σπιλάδεσσι θαλάσσης, *doupon akouse poti spiladessi thalassēs*]—for the great wave thundered against the dry land [ῥόχθει γὰρ μέγα κῦμα ποτὶ ξερὸν ἠπείροιο, *rhochthei gar mega kyma poti xeron ēpeiroio*], belching upon it in terrible fashion [δεινὸν ἐρευγόμενον, *deinon ereugomenon*], and all things were wrapped in the foam of the sea.
>
> (5.400–403)

The word δοῦπος (*doupos*) connotes any dead, heavy sound, such as a thud. The word ῥοχθέω (*rhochtheō*) means "to dash with a roaring sound," and derives from ῥόχθος (*rhochthos*), or "roaring," along with the closely related ῥόθος (*rhothos*, "rushing"), ῥοῖβδος (*rhoibdos*, "rushing"), ῥοῖζος (*rhoizos*, "whistling"), and, of course, *poluphloisboios*, or "many-whistling." The word ἐρεύγομαι (*ereugomai*) means "to belch," "bellow," or "roar." Homer's most "divine" aspects are, according to Pound, his melopoeia, or "ear for the sea-surge" (2/6). It is fitting that Pound attempts a translation of the hero's descent in which the words CHTHONOS and ICHOR boom like Homer's *rhothos* and *rhoibdos* of the sea.

Odysseus-Pound's chthonic prayer is abruptly cut short by "but that a man should live in that further terror, and live." The mythology of death as rejuvenation gives way to the sheer claustrophobic fact of being incarcerated. Real time invades: "the loneliness of death came upon me / (at 3 P. M., for an instant) / δακρύων / ἐντεῦθεν." The final adverb which means, "from this place," or "on each side," reinforces the claustrophobia. The ephemeral aesthetic of *The Pisan Cantos* "swings by a grass blade" and veers as the winds veer (83/553). The poetic drive to mythologize the landscape breaks down, or is under constant threat of breaking down. And yet even this very breakdown is "of the process," and can itself be re-mythologized. The final section will link Pound's ephemeral poetics to Pound's concept of *hiliaritas*, or god-like thinking.

Ephemera, Odysseus *Vespa*

The Pisan Cantos, which Pound began writing on scraps of toilet paper, are characterized by a minute attention to the impermanent and a diaristic attempt to seize what is immediately present. "Ephemeral" derives from *epi* ("on") and *hēmerā* ("day"), meaning "that which lasts only a day." The Greek word εφημερίς (*ephemeris*) means "diary" or "journal" ("diary" from Latin *dies*, or "day"; "journal" from Old French *journal,* or "daily"). Pound's desire for minute and immediate observation is unchecked by a paucity of vocabulary: "and this grass or whatever here under the tent flaps / is, indubitably, bambooiform" (74/466). Minuscule events are granted complex similes: "And now the ants seem to stagger / as the dawn sun has trapped their shadows" (83/551). The lyric voice is repeatedly interrupted by insect and animal life. Pound's prayer to a grasshopper in Canto 74 struggles to unite the present, ephemeral world with the permanent world of myth.

> grass nowhere out of place
> χθόνια γέα, Μήτηρ, ["chthonic goddess, Mother"]
> by thy herbs menthe thyme and basilicum,
> from whom and to whom,
> will never be more now than at present
> being given a new green katydid of a Sunday
> emerald, paler than emerald,
> minus its right propeller
> this tent is to me and ΤΙΘΩΝΩΙ
> eater of grape pulp
> in coitu illuminatio. (74/455)

Pound vacillates between the *achronos*, universal, or mythological world and the specific ephemeral present (Sunday) grounded in close observation. His observance of the perfect grass in his tent ("nowhere out of place") leads to a prayer to the chthonic mother GEA, invoking her sacred herbs: mint, thyme, and basil. Pound then asserts that such a myth "will never be more now than at present," invoking the green katydid (bush cricket) "given" to him on this Sunday, specifically missing its right propeller. Once again, the present is subsumed into the mythical or universal: the cricket relates to Thithonus, lover of Eos who was granted eternal life without eternal youth, like the Cumaen Sibyl, and is (in some versions) turned into a cicada or cricket; Dionysus and his maenads, eaters of grape pulp; and a *connubium terrae* rite of Eleusis. The green katydid, therefore, is not a representation or a metaphor of the myth, but an instance of it, the "presence" of Tithonis.

Pound directly links his poetics of ephemerality with the manifestation of paradise in a well-known but often misunderstood passage:

Le Paradise n'est pas artificial
but spezzato apparently
it exists only in fragments unexpected excellent sausage,
the smell of mint, for example (74/458)

Paradise is not just *spezzato* ("fractured"); it is fractured apparently, which means literally "as far as one can see" but also marks a realization and a concession, as in, "it would appear that paradise is not artificial, but fragmented." The run-on sentence that follows, "it exists only in fragments unexpected excellent sausage," reflects the "speed in mind" by which this revelation occurs. Pound's assertion that paradise "exists only in fragments" is often misread as a reference to his poetics of textual fragmentation. Here, "fragments" signifies ordinary interruptions or elements of (sensory) surprise in ordinary life: a surprisingly good sausage, the smell of mint. Throughout *The Pisan Cantos* Pound associates butterflies, mint, basil, and thyme with paradise and a chthonic reunion with the earth mother Gea or Tellus.[44] Pound's paradise therefore is linked to discoveries made by being observant to fragmentary sensory interruptions. Paradise is not something the poet "builds" like Dante builds his *Paradiso;* it is more like cultivating an openness toward the interruption.

One of the most comic interruptions in the Pisan sequence juxtaposes the "hard work" of the mythical method with the playful presence of the everyday. First the sound of the drill sergeant and then a cat interrupts Pound as he ponders medieval conceptions of the resurrection and Eliot's *Ash Wednesday.* Pound hilariously tries to "hold on" to his complex network of images and update them with as the cat explores his meager belongings.

there is according to some authors a partial resurrection
of corpses
on all souls day in Cairo
or perhaps all over Egypt
in identity but not atom for atom
but the Sadducees hardly give credence
to Mr Eliot's version
Partial resurrection in Cairo.
Beddoes, I think, omits it.
The bone *luz,* I think was his take off
Curious, is it not, that Mr Eliot
has not given more time to Mr Beddoes

[44] For example, 74/455, 79/507, and 82/546.

(T. L.) prince of morticians
where none can speak his language
centuries hoarded
to pull up a mass of algae
(and pearls)
[Ideogram: Ho (M2109), "how"]
[Ideogram: Yüan (M7734), "far"]
or the odour of eucalyptus or sea wrack
cat-faced, cioce di Malta, figura del sol
to each tree its own mouth and savour
"*Hot hole hep cat*"
or words of similar volume
to be recognized by the god-damned
or man-damned trainee
Prowling night-puss leave my hard squares alone
they are in no case cat food
if you had sense
you wd/ come here at meal time
when meat is superabundant
you can neither eat manuscript nor Confucius
nor even the hebrew scriptures
get out of that bacon box
contract W, II oh oh 9 oh
now used as a wardrobe
ex 53 pounds gross weight
the cat-faced eucalyptus nib
is where you cannot get at it. (80/517–18)

The wayward thoughts of the poet are interrupted by a wayward night cat. Pound reflects on Eliot's own fear of the afterlife, which contrasts with the Sadducees, a sect of Jews at the time of Christ, who denied immorality and resurrection. Pound wonders if Eliot ever read Thomas Lovell ("T. L.") Beddoes's *Death's Jest Book*, which describes how the bone *luz* is immune to decay. According to rabbinical teaching, this hazelnut-shaped bone was the *os coccygis* or coccyx; anyone missing this bone was condemned to hell. (And that is why, Pound believed, "they dug [Eriugena] up out of sepulture" [74/449][45].) Beddoes would be able to answer Eliot's question in *Ash Wednesday:* "And God said / shall these bones live? / Shall these bones live?"[46] Pound then reflects on the theme of shipwreck;

[45] Terrell, *A Companion*, vol. 2, 433. In fact, it was Almaric that was disinterred.
[46] Eliot, *The Poems of T. S. Eliot*, vol. 1, 89.

Eliot's drowned Phoenician ("those are pearls that were his eyes"); and the eucalyptus pip that he took as a talisman on the path from Rapallo to Zoagli under guard, which is "cat-faced" but also resembles a "cioce di Malta, figura del sol" ("Cross of Malta, figure like the sun"). Next Pound invokes—or hears—the drill sergeant outside, whose words have meaning to the trainee condemned to endless parade. The cat appears, sniffs Pound's hardtack, or possibly his hopjes (hard squares of candy made with coffee and sugar and vanilla flavoring), then explores the bacon box Pound uses as a wardrobe, upon which is stamped the contract number W-110090: "contract W, II oh oh 9 oh." Pound assures the cat that the eucalyptus pip is out of his reach.

In other words, had Eliot known about the immortal bone *luz,* it would have allayed his fears of the afterlife and answered the questions posed in *Ash Wednesday.* At the same time, Eliot and Beddoes "horded centuries" only to pull up a mass of algae and pearls smelling of eucalyptus. Pound, by contrast, finds salvation in his eucalyptus pip. This magical cat-faced talisman becomes Pound's *luz,* and—lo and behold—a cat comes in looking to consume it, as the church fathers dug up and "destroyed" Eriugena's luz.

The paucity and precariousness of the poet's living and work space, made from packing crates, with a few measly volumes, and some dried biscuits, is reflected in the precariousness of his mythical method and attempt at poetic coherence. The present interrupts and ultimately undermines the mythical method. The cat-faced eucalyptus-pip hastily "foreshadows" the cat's entrance. But a eucalyptus pip does not resemble a coccyx. And although Koala bears may eat eucalyptus trees, they are toxic to cats. The cat is looking for scraps of food; he is not an evil spirit looking to condemn the poet to hell.

This is different than Elpenor's drunken poetics in Canto 39, which is also inspired by watching a cat ("Desolate is the roof where the cat sat, / Desolate is the iron rail that he walked" [39/193]). Here, the "prowling night puss" threatens to topple Pound's menagerie of images. The poet's struggle to bring the cat in line with these ephemeral images is part of the comedy, and marks Pound's own acknowledgment of their ephemerality. A cat cares nothing for poetry or the mythical method—just as the world after fascism (or Hitler) will care nothing for poetry—at least not Pound's poetry. But Pound will not surrender: even if he must find paradise in the mere interruptions of the everyday.

In Canto 83, Pound more successfully incorporates an interruption into his mythical method. Here Pound's observation of the birth of a baby wasp interrupts his serious lament and transforms it into *hilaritas*:

> Will I ever see the Guidecca again?
>   or the lights against it, Ca' Foscari, Ca' Giustinian
> or the Ca', as they say, of Desdemona
> or the two towers where are the cypress no more
>   or the boats moored off le Zattere
> Or the north quai of the Sensaria   DAKRUON   ΔΑΚΡΥΩΝ.
>   and Brother Wasp is building a very neat house
>   of four rooms, one shaped like a squat indian bottle
>   La vespa, *la* vespa, mud, swallow system
> so that dreaming of Bracelonde and of Perugia
> and the great fountain in the Piazza
> or of old Bulagaio's cat that with a well timed leap
>   could turn the lever-shaped door handle
> It comes over me that Mr Walls must be a ten-strike
> with the signorinas (83/552)

The poet laments that he will never see the Guidecca canal in Venice, the Ca' Foscari, Palazzo Giustinian, and the Palazzo Contarini Fasan (also known as the Casa di Desdemona), as well as moored boats by the Zattere quai in Dorsoduro or near the Sensaria. This ends with the Odysseus-cry of "DAKRUON." During this lament, however, "Brother Wasp" is building a neat little house of four rooms through the "mud, swallow system." The common wasp uses wood fibers broken down into pulp with its saliva, but Pound might be referring to mud dauber wasp, which does build its nest with mud, although they build long cylindrical nests, not bottles. The wasp is "brother" to the poet, for his humble abode reflects the poet's own, and the poet likewise ruminates ("re-chews") material to build his poem. But only metaphorically: Pound observes that this a female building a home for her eggs: "La vespa, *la* vespa." The mood of the lyric suddenly changes, marked by the "so that" refrain common to *The Cantos*. The poet now dreams about the enchanted Arthurian forest; the Fontana Maggiore in Perugia carved by Nicola Pisano and his son Giovanni; and a dexterous cat of his old Venetian friend. This culminates in a comic conclusion that "Mr Walls," a trainee who "who has lent me a razor" in Canto 82, must be very attractive to women (82/543).

The inanity of the revelation suggests that what is important here is the change of tone, not content. The poet's monotonous DAKRUON ("Will I ever... or the... or the... or the... or the") is lifted and he channels a godlike *hilaritas* and swiftness of thought. This initial sequence prepares the reader for what follows. While the poet was busy thinking and writing these thoughts, a baby wasp was gestating. By sunrise, it pokes its head out of the bottle. This new interruption, which continues without break from the previous thought about Mr. Walls, transforms the atmosphere into a "living" landscape of fragmentary paradise in which the myths are present and alive again:

> and in the warmth after chill sunrise
> an infant, green as new grass,
> has struck its head or tip
> out of Madame La Vespa's bottle
> mint springs up again
> in spite of Jones' rodents
> as had the clover by the gorilla cage
> with a four-leaf
> When the mind swings by a grass-blade
> an ant's forefoot shall save you
> the clover leaf smells and tastes as its flower
> The infant has descended
> from mud on the tent roof to Tellus,
> like to like colour he goes amid grass-blades
> greeting them that dwell under XTHONOS ΧΘΟΝΟΣ
> ΟΙ ΧΘΟΝΙΟΙ; to carry our news
> εἰς χθονιους to them that dwell under the earth,
> begotten of air, that shall sing in the bower
> of Kore, Περσεφόνεια
> and have speech with Tiresias, Thebae
> Christo Re, Dio Sole
> in about ½ a day she has made her abode
> (la vespa) the tiny mud-flask
> and that day I wrote no further. (83/552–3)

Here Pound's own salvation relies upon the presence of the baby wasp. The mind swings by a grass blade that moves when an ant's forefoot steps on it. The mint springs up that morning again, despite the lieutenant and provost officer Jones who made what he called his "rodents" pull up the grass. (Pound had to explain that reference to Marcella Spann Booth.) The lucky clover springs by the gorilla cages each morning. The green wasp falls to the earth from the tent roof of mud to Tellus, finds the grass, searching for "like color" just as the cat earlier sought out the cat-faced eucalyptus pip. The newborn wasp greets them that dwell under the earth, carrying "our news" and will eventually make his way down to sing in Persephone's bower and talk to Tiresias. The baby wasp becomes Odysseus on his nekyia; he is a solar deity ("Dio Sole") who goes under the earth each night; he is a Christ figure ("Christo Re") bearing the "good news" from heaven to those who live on earth. Pound also makes sure to directly connect Odysseus's nekyia to rite of spring: Persephone's abduction (in winter) by Hades and her rescue (in the spring) by Hermes; the fertility daimon's nekyia to perform a *hieros gamos* and fertilize the crops. The scene also echoes Odysseus's reunion with GEA TERRA in Canto 80, "XTHONOS ΧΘΟΝΟΣ / ΟΙ ΧΘΟΝΙΟΙ." In fact, this passage can also be read as a "continuation" of it: the next morning, Odysseus awakes from his leaf bed, meets Nausicca, and is taken to the court of the Phacaeans, where he will tell them the "news" of his long journey (and they will receive the "good news" that he is still alive, as his is the only nostoi that bards do not sing about) and finally achieve safe passage back to Ithaca. The passage ends with an inversion of Francesca's famous last line from *Inferno* 5: "quel giorno più non vi leggemmo avante" (5.138), "that day we read no further"—that is, in the story of the Lancelot romance, so overtaken with desire. Dante wrongfully condemned this servant of Amor to hell. Here Pound is overwhelmed by evidence of paradiso terrestre that his ephemeral poetry ends for the day.

Pound's link between the baby wasp and Odysseus the fertility demon was not arbitrary. In *The Philosophy of Love,* Gourmont describes the organization of wasp society as a "matriarchate."[47]

> A fecundated female after passing the winter, constructs, by herself, the first foundations of a nest, lays the eggs, from which sexless individuals are born; these workers then assume all material labours, finish the nest, watch the larvae which the female continues to produce. These are now males and females: after coupling the males die, then the workers, the females become languid, those who survive will found as many new tribes.[48]

The matriarchate of wasp society resembles the matriarchal religions of the original dying-and-resurrecting gods: fertility demons and solar deities who work in the service of the earth goddess, as the sexless infants and male wasps work on the nest to continue the "harvest" (Odysseus *geōrgon*), until they partake of the mysteries of coitus by fecundating the earth. Gourmont's elaborate description of the mating rituals of wasps concludes with the complete annihilation of the male.

[47] Gourmont, *The Natural Philosophy of Love*, 157.
[48] Gourmont, *The Natural Philosophy of Love*, 165.

> Copulation takes place in the air; as is the case with ants, it is only possible after a long flight has filled with air the pouches which cause the male's organ to emerge. Between these pockets, or aeriferous bladders shaped like perforated horns, emerges the penis, a small white body, plump and bent back at the point. In the vagina, which is round, wide and shallow, the sperm-pouch opens; it is a reservoir which can contain they say, a score of million of spermatozoides, destined to fecundate the eggs, during several years in proportion as they are to be laid. The form of the penis and the manner in which the sperm is coagulated by a viscous liquid into a veritable spermatophore, cause the death of the male. The copulation ended, he wishes to disengage himself but only manages to do so in leaving in the vagina not only the penis but all the organs attached to it. He falls like an empty bag, while the queen, returned to the hive, stops at the entrance, makes her toilet, aided by the workers who crowd about her: with her mandibles she gently removes the spine which has remained in her belly, and cleans the place with lustral attention. Then she enters the second period of her life: maternity. This penis which remains fast in the vagina makes one think of the darts of fighters which also remain in the wound; be it love or war the over-courageous beastlet expires, worn out and mutilated; there is in this a peculiar facility of dehiscence which seems very rare.[49]

Pound's infant wasp that descends to "Tellus" and "goes amid grass blades / greeting them that dwell under XTHONOS" will not literally burrow under earth to speak to Tiresias and retrieve Persephone. He will soon take flight, return to the hive to make it larger, and copulate in the air. Odysseus *vespa* is the dutiful worker in the matriarchate who will be graced one day to enter the mysterium of coitus and fecundation, and subsequently die via *sparagmos*—his spine hulled from his body, then "lustrally" ripped from his "beastlet" penis which will wither and eventually be "dehisced"—only to be reborn in the womb of the fecundated female.

The redemptive force of ephemera demands of the poet (and reader) that he cultivate this ability to be interrupted and consumed by it. He becomes a "reader" of the book of nature. When the mind swings by a grass blade, it can be saved by an ant's forefoot: the mere presence of this tiny wasp as it struggles through the grass. The Homeric myths, which represent the "permanent world," is manifest before us provided we know how to look, how to wait, and how to bear witness. As Acoetes puts it: "And I worship. / I have seen what I have seen" (2/9).

[49] Gourmont, *The Natural Philosophy of Love*, 158.

The Pisan Cantos present themselves as a *translatio* of Odysseus's final and most perilous journey before his salvation. Odysseus is stripped of his identity into no one (*outis*); he experiences his own ritual death and drowning; he is reborn in the morning and begins the final "ascent" of his wanderings. The Pound hero's ecstatic loss of self through the mystery of this union with the earth is staged in the very dissolution and breakdown of the poetic voice and the "epic" structure. "Old Ez" seems on the verge of a crack-up, but the effect is intentional. The lyric voice that Pound invents in *The Pisan Cantos* is ultimately a participatory one, for paradise is not manifest by merely talking about it but by cultivating a *hilaritas* or godlike "speed in mind" in the reader. The "head over heels rush" of Dionysian lyric is meant to disarm and surprise us. The insistence on a poetic schema and the diffidence of the poetic voice which gives way to periodic despair demand that we detach ourselves and assess even the poet's own mythical method. Even readers who find Pound's mythical method too elitist and his politics too repugnant often find the uncanny and fragmentary beauty of *The Pisan Cantos* hard to dismiss. This particular kind of beauty, which "is difficult" as Pound repeats, is not simply a collection of good lines: it involves the reader's particiaption, recognition, and discovery of those lines. The effect is intentional. Pound's final stage of *translatio* of Leucothea in *Rock-Drill* and *Thrones* is the culmination of this technique: it is at once the most explicit statement of what paradiso terrestre looks like, but also demands the reader's "anagogic" participation in decoding it.

7

How to Read Leucothea

My son, you've seen the temporary fire
and the eternal fire; you have reached
the place past which my powers cannot see.[1]

The use of characters and motifs from the *Odyssey* is markedly different in Pound's late cantos. *Rock-Drill* (1955) and *Thrones* (1959) transform Homer's *Odyssey* into a mystic guide book, full of arcane facts, hidden meanings, and inscrutable details. Circe is glimpsed "coming from the house of smoothe stone"; "the stone eyes looking seaward / Nor could you enter her eyes by probing" (106/774). The Sirens are associated with "the crystal body of air"; Circe's enchantments; and the "mental velocity" of divine thought (93/6562): "deep green over azure / Sirens σῆραγξ [*sēranx*, 'sea cave'] as crystal Σειρῆν [*Seirēn*] / dark hippocampi θελκτήριν [*thelktērin*, 'enchantment,' 'spell'] / god's antennae" (107/782). Zeus makes his first appearance in *The Cantos,* cryptically associated with the six-winged seraphs that fly around the throne of God in *The Book of Enoch* and the *Book of Revelation,* as well as *themis*, meaning "right custom," "proper tradition," or "social order": "Zeus with the six seraphs before him" (90/627); and "Zeus, six bluejays before him / THEMIS against leagues of princes" (104/761). This might be an allusion to the primitive Zeus described by Jane Harrison. Her study, *Themis,* begins with an investigation of the "Hymn of the Kouretes" recovered from Crete, in which Zeus is presented as a young god accompanied by daimons or fertility spirits.[2] He was later associated with Dionysus. Generally, however, the *Odyssey* allusions in the late cantos are cryptic, mysterious, and even trivial. "'A cargo of Iron' / lied Pallas / and as to why Penelope waited / keinas… e Orgei. line 639" (102/748) refers to Athena's claim, disguised as the merchant Mentes, to have a ship full of iron in *Odyssey* 1.184; and Penelope's claim in 4.693 (not 639) that Odysseus "never

1 Dante, *Purgatorio,* 27.127–9
2 Harrison, *Themis,* 1–29. See also Mikaye, *Ezra Pound and the Mysteries of Love*, 186.

wrought iniquity at all to any man." Pound juxtaposes these facts mainly to make the point that most readers of the *Odyssey* don't remember them.

The Leucothea episode from *Odyssey* 5.333–53 is the only sustained *translatio* in the late cantos. Formerly Ino, the first maenad and nurse of Dionysus, Leucothea emerges from the sea and advises Odysseus to strip off his clothes, abandon his raft, and rely solely on her magic veil or κρήδεμνον (*kredēmnon*) to reach dry land. Pound reserves Leucothea for his final Homeric *translatio* because she is the last theophany and mystagogue of Odysseus's wanderings. Having made no appearance in the earlier cantos, including *The Pisan Cantos,* which (also) recounts Odysseus's shipwreck, Leucothea's name appears seventeen times, while Odysseus's name appears only seven times. The episode is narrated in ten fragmentary sequences between Cantos 91 and 100;[3] Leucothea is recalled in Cantos 102 and 109;[4] and there are four separate references to the Phaeacian worship of Leucothea that continued still "after 500 years": a detail which Pound seems to have invented (96/674).[5] The ordering is roughly chronological. *Rock-Drill* recounts Leucothea's intervention while Odysseus is at sea. *Thrones* recounts how Odysseus releases her veil back to the sea on Scheria and how Leucothea was worshiped in Phaeacia after Odysseus left. The Leucothea segments also appear in structurally significant places: in the last lines of *Rock-Drill;* in the first lines of *Thrones*; in the numerically significant Canto 100, which completes the story of Leucothea as Homer presents it; and in the last lines of *Thrones.*[6]

Pound's Leucothea represents the "plunge" into difficult knowledge and arcana that the reader must take in order to follow the late cantos. Pound links Leucothea's demand that Odysseus "get rid of parap[h]ernalia" with Dante's warning to his readers in *Paradiso* 2 (91/635).

> "Oh you," as Dante says,
>   "in the dinghy astern there"
> There must be incognita
>   and in sea-caves
>   un lume pien' di spiriti ["a light filled with spirits"]
>   and of memories
> Shall two know the same in their knowing?

[3] 91/635, 636; 93/643; 95/664, 665, 667; 96/671; 98/704, 705; and 100/736–7.

[4] 102/749; and 109/794.

[5] 96/674; 98/705; 102/728; and 102/748.

[6] 95/667; 96/671; 100/736–7; and 109/794.

> You who dare Persephone's threshold,
> Beloved, do not fall apart in my hands. (93/651)

Dante warns the reader who has never "stretched through time to reach for angel bread" to turn his little boat (*picolleto,* Pound: "dingy") around and not try to follow him.[7] "Do not set out upon these open seas / lest losing me you end confused and lost. / The waves I ride have never yet been crossed."[8] Pound associates Dante's open seas and Leucothea's veil with the plunge into (Homeric) "incognita" which must remain incognita. "The mysteries are *not* revealed, and no guide book to them has been or will be written."[9] Details of the *dromena* ("things done"), *deiknumena* ("things shown"), and *legomena* ("things said") of the Eleusinian Mysteries were known as τὰ ἀπόρρητα (*ta aporrēta*) or "things forbidden." The penalty for divulging them was death. The late cantos attempt to cultivate the mind to receive mystery: to "dare Persephone's threshold."[10] This refers to the *dromena*: a dramatic reenactment of the Demeter/Persephone myth. If scrutinized or over-analyzed, that mystery is cheapened and deteriorates. "Beloved, do not fall apart in my hands."

Pound and Dante are explicit that only a select few can follow them on these open seas where no poet has crossed before. Dante's readers who want to eat heavenly bread must labor to understand Beatrice's account of why Aquinas is better equipped than Averroes to explain the dark spots on the moon: a notoriously difficult section of *Paradiso* which stymies Beckett's Belacqua in "Dante and the Lobster" (1934).[11] Dante's readers must learn complex theological arguments. Pound's readers must learn how to read both anagogically and ideogrammatically: to grasp his poetry as a struggle or thought exercise to grasp the unknowable. Pound's references and allusive clusters aim to manifest the phanopoetic and melopoetic "mental velocity" of the Divine Mind rather than a luminous coherence (93/652). To be "skilled in fire," Pound warns his reader before he introduces Leucothea for the first time, involves "Waiving no jot of the arcanum" (91/635). Leucothea therefore also represents the difficulty of Pound's anagogic poetry itself: the challenge of understanding what Apollonius of Tyana and Richard of Saint Victor and John Heydon and Porphyry of Tyre have to do with her "bikini."

7 Dante, *Paradiso*, trans. Robin Kirkpatrick (New York: Penguin, 2007), 2.10–11.

8 Dante, *Paradiso*, 2.5–7.

9 *L*, 423.

10 See Demetres Tryphonopoulos, *The Celestial Tradition* (Waterloo, ON: Wilfrid Laurier Press, 1992).

11 Dante, *Paradiso*, 2.53–148. See Samuel Beckett, *More Kicks than Pricks* (New York: Grove Press, 1970), 9–22.

The difficulty of understanding Leucothea's role in *Rock-Drill* and *Thrones* is intertwined with the difficulty of understanding Pound's paradise as it is presented, especially in Cantos 90–95. In earlier manifestations, paradise took the form of a "sacred disorder" of Dionysian transformations (Canto 2); a visionary Venetian and chthonic procession of factive personalities (Cantos 17, 20, and 21); an ecstatic but humiliating experience of ritual fucking and farming (Cantos 39 and 47); and a storm-tossed ride through a chaos of winds visited by goddesses while becoming attuned to the sacred interruption of ephemeral or elemental life (Cantos 74 to 83). Paradise in the late cantos is best described as interactive and anagogic. Pound's goal, as he puts it, is to "stimulate anagogico" (99/730). Traditionally, the anagogic, meaning "ascent" or "climb," concerns the afterlife. In Pound's case, however, since his goal is a terrestrial and mental paradise, the anagogic represents the very struggle to achieve a state of divine or philosophical contemplation: to move from what Richard of Saint Victor calls *cogitatio* and *meditatio* to *contemplatio.* Pound summarizes: "In the first the mind flits aimlessly about the object, in the second it circles about it in a methodical manner, in the third it is unified with the object."[12] For Pound, the bridge to *contemplatio* is love. Pound echoes Dante's description of Beatrice that "raised me [*mi levasti*]."[13] In Canto 90, Pound turns this into a refrain: "m'elevasti / from the dulled edge beyond pain, / m'elevasti / out of Erebus, the deep-lying" (90/626). Love draws one "Out of heaviness where no mind moves at all" (90/627). Dante compares the way Beatrice's eyes allow him to pass "beyond the human" to Glaucus who tastes the magical herb, which Pound earlier compares to *moly.*[14] Pound compares Odysseus's nostos or arrival in Phaeacia thanks to Leucothea to the myth of Glaucus in one condensed passage: "mortal once / Who now is a sea-god: / νόστου [*nostou*, 'arrival'] / γαίης Φαιήκων [*gaiēs Phaiēkōn*, 'land of the Phaeacians']" (95/667). Leucothea is the anagogic goddess of Pound's late poetry. She is the bridge to Pound's paradise: "the path wide as a hair" (93/652).

Pound is less concerned in these final books with excavating the oldest part of the *Odyssey*—reading Odysseus as a Helios or Mithra and reading Leucothea as a primitive goddess—as he is about trying to represent the "mental velocity" of the divine mind as well as the very struggle to achieve mental paradise. The "technic" of the Leucothea sections therefore is anagogic and interactive, ideogrammatic, lyric (devotional), mystic, and revelatory.

12 *GK*, 77.
13 *Paradiso*, 1.75.
14 *Paradiso*, 1.70; *C* 39/194; see chapter 5.

Pound's late style exasperated even his most devout followers, and continues to irritate readers today. Ronald Bush remarks how "the truncated and gnomic style of *Thrones* is inappropriate to the point of absurdity."[15] In Canto 91, Richard Parker explains,

> Pound relies on a small selection of unusual texts and seems to insist on their useful veracity, yet he also seems relatively unconcerned with the final "truth" of those texts, exhibiting an almost cavalier disregard from the internal consistency of his sources.[16]

Daniel Pearlman suggests that Pound's technique is deliberate:

> It is obvious that if the poet had wanted to be "clear" and "coherent," he could have been; but if he chose not to be, what irritating ulterior motive could he have had? Perhaps exactly that: *to irritate.* [...] We are given the choice of either sticking with Pound at these exasperating junctures, or throwing up our hands.[17]

Pearlman doesn't really explore what motive Pound might have in irritating his reader. The common critique is that Pound's late ideogrammatic style doesn't offer coherence in the traditional luminous way. Pound seems to have "botched it," but intentionally.

Critical frustration over *Rock-Drill* and *Thrones* often results from the attempt to make the Pound's late poetry luminous through the (old) mythical method. Many critics have read Leucothea as simply another eccentric manifestation of Pound's many ideal ladies and goddesses in his transcultural stew: Princess Ra-Set, Elizabeth 1, Cunizza da Romano, the swan maiden from the Noh play *Hagoromo* (*The Feathered Mantle*), or Diana from Layamon's *Brut.*[18] Peter Liebregts links Leucothea with "arcanum" but doesn't emphasize her connection to a new kind of reading or interpretation. Instead, he reads her as "selfless action," and tries to fit her within a Neoplatonic schema.[19]

More recently, critics have sought to illuminate the oddness of Leucothea through biography. A. David Moody suggests that Leucothea ought to be read as

15 Ronald Bush, "Late Cantos LXXII-CXVII," in *The Cambridge Companion to Ezra Pound*, ed. Ira Nadel (Cambridge: Cambridge University Press, 1999), 123.

16 Richard Parker, "Some Contexts for Canto XCVI," *Glossator* 10 (2018), 13.

17 Daniel Pearlman, "Alexander del Mar in *The Cantos*: A Printout of the Sources," *Paideuma* 1.2 (1972), 161–2.

18 For example, see K. L. Goodwin, "The Structure of Ezra Pound's Later Cantos," *Southern Review* 4 (1971), 300–7; Christine Brooke-Rose, *A ZBC of Ezra Pound* (London: Faber and Faber, 1971), 138–56; Miyake, *Ezra Pound and the Mysteries of Love*, 208–9; and Surette, "Having His Own Mind to Stand by Him," 491–510.

19 Liebregts, *Ezra Pound and Neoplatonism*, 310–11.

little more than a *nom à clef* of Sherri Martinelli.[20] He argues that Leucothea isn't an important Homeric figure in *The Cantos*. "One should not make too much of this use of the *Odyssey*," he warns his readers about Leucothea's sixth and seventh appearances at the end of *Rock-Drill* and the beginning of *Thrones*.[21] "Pound's *nostos* is not his Penelope's bed but a just society." That is true, but it does not follow that Leucothea's intervention in the *Odyssey* is unimportant. Moody cites as evidence Pound's letter to Mary de Rachewiltz, "Div Comedy the main structure. Not Odyssey."[22] This is also true, given that Pound is explicit that *Rock-Drill* adapts Dante's third sphere of heaven (Venus), where the souls of blessed lovers dwell, and that *Thrones* is an inquiry into models of good government inspired by Dante's sixth sphere of heaven (Jupiter), inhabited by the just rulers.[23] But to suggest that the sixteen distinct appearances of Leucothea is unimportant begs the question.

Michael Kindellan and Alec Marsh argue that knowing about Martinelli is essential to interpreting both Leucothea and the Paradise Cantos (90–95). "The importance of Martinelli can hardly be overstated when it comes to an understanding of Pound's paradise," argues Kindellan.[24] Martinelli "figures as these cantos' first and only intended audience." "If so," Marsh concludes, "we have to change our approach to these poems."[25] "We must now understand that these cantos were inspired by her, written *with* her, *specifically for her to read*." But Pound never claimed this to be true. Neither Martinelli's name nor any explicit reference to her appears in the late cantos. Unlike *The Pisan Cantos*, which constantly invites the reader to draw comparisons between the mythic and the actual, Pound avoids personal references almost entirely in *Rock-Drill* and *Thrones*. There are almost no details of Pound's living situation or any reference to the inhabitants of St. Elizabeths or the countless visitors and acolytes he received. The fact that Sherri Martinelli may have partly inspired Leucothea, or that Martinelli recognized "hidden" references to her, does not mean that Leucothea must (or ought to) be read biographically. One could easily make the biographical counterargument (although no one has) that Pound projected

[20] A. David Moody, *Ezra Pound: Poet*, vol. 3 (New York: Oxford University Press, 2015), 311–18.

[21] Moody, *Ezra Pound: Poet*, vol. 3, 364.

[22] Ezra Pound to Mary de Rachewiltz, May 18, 1956. *EPP*. Quoted by Moody, *Ezra Pound: Poet*, vol. 3, 364. (Moody does not provide the folder number.)

[23] Ezra Pound to James Lauglin, November 14, 1955. Quoted in Ezra Pound, *New Selected Poems and Translations*, 2nd edition, ed. Richard Sieburth (New York: New Directions, 2010), 338.

[24] Michael Kindellan, *The Late Cantos of Ezra Pound: Composition, Revision, Publication* (London: Bloomsbury Academic, 2017), 103.

[25] Alec Marsh, *Ezra Pound's Washington Cantos and the Struggle for Light* (London: Bloomsbury Academic, 2021), 113.

onto Martinelli aspects of Leucothea and even "played out" his unique vision of paradise in Cantos 90–95 with her simply in order to seduce her—as he did to just about every young attractive woman who showed any interest in him at St. Elizabeths. In other words, Martinelli inspired Pound to be inspired by her.

Leah Flack argues that even the metapoetic aspects of Leucothea should be read biographically. "While in St. Elizabeths, Pound used Homer in complex ways as he grappled with his epic's failure to cohere."[26]

> Rather than turning to the *Odyssey* as a narrative scaffold to stabilize his poem in its final movements, Pound uses it to remake his poem, to begin again on new terms. After his poem is shipwrecked, Pound writes a new beginning by imagining he is rescued by Leucothea. [...] Pound uses Leucothea to write a self-conscious drama of his own remaking of a literary tradition he continued to believe would rescue him and his poem from collapse.[27]

Flack details how James Laughlin launched a campaign to depoliticize *The Cantos* by indirectly insisting that the *Odyssey*-theme kept his long poem "legitimate," high-modernist, and Joycean.[28] For Flack, Leucothea represents both Pound's failure to make the *Odyssey* meaningful to *The Cantos* as well as the "selling out" of his long poem by trying to convince the reader that Homer (still) matters. Flack assumes that Pound intended Leucothea to be as "coherent" as any other of his (Homeric) goddesses. But Pound is explicit in many ways that Leucothea is a limit case of Homeric allusion. As the anagogic goddess, Leucothea is a mystery that must remain a mystery.

In the following, I analyze Leucothea's role as a spiritual guide to both Odysseus and the reader in *Rock-Drill* and *Thrones*. I argue that Leucothea's main role is to challenge the reader to read differently. She represents what Pound calls "reading by fire," which involves contemplation of arcana, reading with love, and thinking with the birdlike swiftness and *hilaritas* of a god. I also argue that *Thrones* acts as an envoi or "letting go" of the *Odyssey* as the guiding hypertext. The *Odyssey* is reduced to irrelevancies in order to reinforce the struggle to make paradise now. Pound goes so far as phanopoetically grafting Leucothea to a non-Homeric character, Leucothoe, simply to frustrate those readers still in search of philological and mythical luminosity. The worship of Leucothea remains long

[26] Flack, *Modernism and Homer*, 154.

[27] Flack, *Modernism and Homer*, 155.

[28] Flack, *Modernism and Homer*, 157–61. See also Greg Barnhisel, *James Laughlin, New Directions Press, and the Remaking of Ezra Pound* (Amherst, MA: University of Massachusetts Press, 2005), 127–96.

after the action of the *Odyssey* as a set of paradigmatic rituals that society must practice in order to cultivate good governments, peaceful societies, and artistic flourishing on earth.

Rock-Drill: Leucothea as Arcanum

In *Rock-Drill,* Pound weaves the story of Leucothea's rescue of Odysseus with Philostratus's account of Apollonius of Tyana in Rome under Domitian, John Heydon's encounter with the goddess Euterpe in *The Holy Guide* (1662), and the troubadour adoration of the Lady. Leucothea represents a new way of reading, or being "skilled in fire" which involves allowing arcana to remain arcana (91/635). Pound equates this way of reading as emulating adoration and love to the (absent) object of desire.

After Calypso reluctantly agrees to release Odysseus, she bathes and clothes him "in fragrant raiment. On the raft the goddess put a skin of dark wine, and another, a great one, of water, and provisions, too, in a wallet. Therein she put abundance of dainties to satisfy his heart" (5.264–67). Ten days later, Odysseus is thrown off his raft near the coast of Scheria and nearly drowns because "the garments which beautiful Calypso had given him weighed him down" (5.321). Leucothea intervenes to offer Odysseus a new type of garment. This encounter is crucial to understanding the methodology of both *Rock-Drill* and *Thrones.*

> But the daughter of Cadmus [Κάδμου θυγάτηρ, *Kadmou thygatēr*], Ino of the fair ankles [καλλίσφυρος, *kallisphyros*], saw him, even Leucothea, who of old was a mortal of human speech, but now in the deeps of the sea has won a share of honor from the gods. She was touched with pity for Odysseus, as he wandered and was in sore travail, and she rose up from the deep like a sea-mew [αἰθυίῃ, *aithuiē*] on the wing, and sat [ἷζε, *hize*] on the stoutly-bound raft, and spoke, saying: "Unhappy man, how is it that Poseidon, the earth-shaker, has conceived such furious wrath against thee, that he is sowing for thee the seeds of many evils? Yet verily he shall not utterly destroy thee for all his rage. Nay, do thou thus; and methinks thou dost not lack understanding [δοκέεις δέ μοι οὐκ ἀπινύσσειν, *dokeeis de moi ouk apinyssein*]. Strip off these garments [εἵματα ταῦτ᾽ ἀποδὺς, *heimata taut' apodys*], and leave thy raft to be driven by the winds, but do thou swim with thy hands and so strive to reach the land of the Phaeacians [ἀτὰρ χείρεσσι νέων ἐπιμαίεο νόστου / γαίης Φαιήκων, *atar cheiressi neōn epimaieo nostou / gaiēs Phaiēkōn*], where it is thy fate to escape. Come, take this veil [κρήδεμνον, *krēdemnon*], and stretch it beneath thy breast. It is immortal; there

> is no fear that thou shalt suffer aught or perish. But when with thy hands thou hast laid hold of the land, loose it from thee, and cast it into the wine-dark sea far from the land, and thyself turn away." So saying, the goddess gave him the veil, and herself plunged again into the surging deep, like a sea-mew [αἰθυίῃ ἐικυῖα, *aithuiē eikuia*]; and the dark wave hid her [μέλαν δέ ἑ κῦμα κάλυψεν, *melan de he kyma kalypsen*]. Then the much-enduring [πολύτλας, *polytlas*], goodly Odysseus pondered.
>
> (5.333–354)

Homer contrasts the earthly *heimata* of Calypso (εἷμα [*heima*] can mean a "garment" or "clothes," but also a "cover," "rug," or "carpet") with the unearthly *kredēmnon* of Leucothea. Leucothea is the opposite of the clingy and possessive Calypso, who refuses to let Odysseus leave her island for seven years. Calypso's gifts burden the receiver; Leucothea's gift unburdens the receiver. Leucothea reappears throughout *Rock-Drill* in order to remind the reader to abandon his traditional sense of poetic coherence.

Pound introduces the story in Canto 91, interlacing it with details of the final days of the Neopythagorean philosopher Apollonius of Tyana (15–100) as told by Philostratus (*c.* 170–*c.* 247), and the Rosicrucian Neoplatonic John Heydon (1629–*c.* 1667). The complex ideogram acts as an introduction on "how to read" Pound's anagogic late poetry.

> They who are skilled in fire
> shall read 旦 tan the dawn.
> Waiving no jot of the arcanum
> (having his own mind to stand by him)
> As the sea-gull Κάδμου θυγάτηρ ["daughter of Cadmus"] said to Odysseus
> KADMOU THUGATER
> "get rid of parap[h]ernalia"
> TLEMOUSUNE ["endurance"]
> And that even in the time of Domitian
> one young man declined to be buggar'd.
> "Is this a bath-house?"
> ἄλλοτε δ'αὖτ' Εὖρος Ζεφύρῳ εἴζασκε διώκειν
> ["now again the East Wind would yield it to the West Wind to drive"]
> "Or a Court House?"
> Asked Apollonius
> who spoke to the lion
> charitas insuperabilis ["love invincible"]

to ascend those high places
wrote Heydon
stirring and changeable
"light fighting for speed"
and if honor and pleasure will not be ruled
yet the mind come to that High City...
who with Pythagoras at Taormina
Souls be the water-nymphs of Porphyrius
Νυχρὸς δ'αὔτ'αἴθηρ τε χαὶ ἡμέρα Ζηνὸς πυρὸς
["But of the night both sky and day were born Zeus's wheat"]
Formality. Heydon polluted. Apollonius unpolluted
and the whole creation concerned with "FOUR"
"my bikini is worth your raft"
And there be who say there is no road to felicity
tho' swallows eat celandine
"before my eyes into the aether of Nature." (91/635–66)

At the outset, Pound suggests that the arcana here presented leads not to a deeper meaning but a new poetic faculty. The reader must be "skilled in fire" and able to see the phanopoeia of 旦 as the sun rising over the wheat fields, as Gaudier-Brzeska was able to do having "spent only a fortnight in the museum studying the Chinese characters."[29] "He was used to consider all life and nature in the terms of planes and of bounding lines." Pound links the reader's plunge into his arcana with Odysseus's plunge after divesting himself of paraphernalia. "Having his own mind to stand by him" is Pound's *translatio* of Leucothea's line, "methinks thou dost not lack understanding" (*dokeeis de moi ouk apinyssein*). The verb ἀπινύσσω (*apinyssō*) derives from πινυτός (*pinytos*), meaning "prudent," "discreet," or "sensible." Pound's version emphasizes Odysseus's unique and original mind (like Gaudier-Brzeska's), echoing Pound's earlier version of Zeus's admiration of Odysseus from *Odyssey* 1.65, "with a mind like that he is one of us" (80/532). Just as it is sensible for Odysseus to throw off Calypso's heavy garments, the reader must "get rid of parap[h]ernalia" in order to navigate Pound's difficult seas. The Greek word παράφερνα (*parapherna*) originally denoted those goods which a wife brings over and above (*para*) her dowry (*phernē*). Unlike the *phernē*, which became the husband's property, the *parapherna* remained the wife's property. Pound's

[29] Ezra Pound and Ernest Fenollosa, *The Chinese Written Character as a Medium for Poetry*, ed. Haun Saussy, Jonathan Stalling, and Lucas Klein (New York: Fordham University Press, 2008), n59.

Leucothea reminds us that these garments were originally Calypso's property, and they cling to and impede him like she did.

Pound compares Odysseus's treatment by Poseidon to Apollonius's treatment by Domitian. Apollonius, a pagan miracle worker with similarities to Christ, first taught in Taormina in Easy Sicily and claimed to be a spiritual descendant of Pythagoras: hence he was "with Pythagoras at Taormina." He rid himself of worldly possessions (paraphernalia) and traveled the earth. He entered Rome in defiance of Domitian's banishment of philosophers and was thrown in prison, where he lectured to the hopeless prisoners that they must "bear in mind the words of Archilochus of Paros who says that the patience under adversity which he called endurance [τλημοσύνην, *tlēmosynēn*] was a veritable discovery of the gods."[30] (Conybeare's translation renders *tlēmosynēn* as "endurance," but it can also mean "misery" or just "suffering.") This is Pound's *translatio* of Odysseus's epithet, *polytlas*, or "much-enduring," used by Homer after Leucothea disappears into the waves (5.354). The word invokes a vortex of references and condensations: Pound citing Apollonius citing Archilochus to put Homer's epithet of Odysseus into the mouth of Leucothea. It is also an example of what Pound calls "overchange": when a translator improves upon the original.[31] Archilochus's words are: "Yet to woes incurable, my friend, the Gods have ordained the remedy of staunch endurance."[32] In other words, the gods merely ordain the remedy of endurance for men. Apollonius improves on this: the gods themselves discovered the virtue of endurance through their own sufferings, meaning that to endure is to emulate them.

Pound's other allusions to Philostratus are cryptic ideogrammatic fusions. Apollonius "declined to be buggered" by Domitian only metaphorically. But the literal reference is to a handsome young Arcadian that Apollonius meets in prison, who refused the lecherous intentions of Domitian and his court: "I am master of my person and shall guard it inviolate."[33] The reference to the courts as a "bath house" fuses two separate anecdotes. When Apollonius is first summoned to Domitian's court,

> he halted at the Palace and beheld the throng of those who were either being courted or were courting their superiors, and heard the din of those who were

[30] Philostratus, *Life of Apollonius of Tyana*, vol. 2, trans. F. C. Conybeare (Cambridge, MA: Harvard University Press, 1912), 7.29.

[31] See chapter 3.

[32] Archilochus *Elegy and Iambus*, vol. 2, trans. J. M. Edmonds (Cambridge, MA: Harvard University Press, 1931), 103.

[33] Philostratus, *Life of Apollonius of Tyana*, vol. 2, 7.42.

> passing in and out, he remarked: "It seems to me, O Damis, that this place resembles a bath; for I see people outside hastening in, and those within, hastening out; and some of them resemble people who have been thoroughly well washed, and others those who have not been washed at all."[34]

Months later, on the day of his trial, Apollonius revisits the simile:

> As he waited before the court another secretary came up and said: "Man of Tyana, you must enter the court with nothing on you." "Are we then to take a bath," said Apollonius, "or to plead?" "The rule," said the other, "does not apply to dress, but the Emperor only forbids you to bring in here, either amulet, or book, or any papers of any kind."[35]

Pound quotes only the latter passage, but knowing the former explains why he splices in Homer's description of the winds tossing Odysseus from *Odyssey* 5.332: "'Is this a bath-house?' / ἄλλοτε δ'αὖτ' Εὖρος Ζεφύρῳ εἴζασκε διώκειν / 'Or a Court House?'" Apollonius likens the palace court to a bath house because some hasten in, some hasten out, some appear washed, some appear unwashed. Pound therefore equates the storm with the "insidious modern waves, civilization, civilized hidden snares," as he puts it in "*Et Faim Sallir les Loups des Boys.*"[36]

Pound's impetus for pairing Apollonius with Leucothea is suggested by an earlier passage in Philostratus. When Apollonius arrives in Rome, he is accused of wizardry and treason. His accuser wants to bring him before the emperor immediately, but Aelian, one of Domitian's sentinels, warns Apollonius in advance and advises him how to delay his trial in order to learn more about the court system. When Apollonius recounts his conversation with Aelian to his disciple Damis, Damis introduces a Homeric analogy, which is common to their discourse:

> Now I am ready to believe that Leucothea did really give her veil to Odysseus, after he had fallen out of his ship and was paddling himself over the sea with his hands. For we are reduced to just as awful and impossible a plight, when some god, as it seems to me, stretches out his hand over us, and we fall not away from all hope of salvation.
>
> But Apollonius disapproved of the way he spoke, and said: "How long will you continue to cherish these fears, as if you could never understand that wisdom amazes all that is sensible of her, but is herself not amazed by anything."

[34] Philostratus, *Life of Apollonius of Tyana*, vol. 2, 7.31.
[35] Philostratus, *Life of Apollonius of Tyana*, vol. 2, 8.3.
[36] *PT*, 1178.

> "But we," said Damis, "are brought here before one who is quite insensible, and who not only cannot be amazed by us, but would not allow anything in the world to amaze him."
>
> "Seest thou not," said Apollonius, "O Damis, that he is maddened with pride and vanity?"
>
> "I see it, how can I not?" said the other.
>
> "Well," said Apollonius, "you have just got to despise the despot just in proportion as you get to know him."[37]

Damis's comparison between Aelian and Leucothea is rejected by Apollonius, who suggests instead that Wisdom (himself, Odysseus) causes amazement in others (Aelian, Leucothea) but is not amazed by them. In other words, Leucothea's rescue of Odysseus is the wrong comparison: Apollonius is "saved" by his virtue and philosophical mind. (And he is right; after speaking to Apollonius, Philostratus explains that Aelian "himself formed the conviction that here was a man whom nothing could terrify or startle, and who would not flinch, even if the head of the Gorgon were brandished over him."[38]) Apollonius also revises Damis's analogy between Poseidon and Domitian: if the despot Domitian (Poseidon) cannot be amazed like Aelian (Leucothea), then they (Odysseus) must despise him back, in the same way that the philosopher despises pride and vanity.

This failed analogy is cleverly (albeit confusingly) explored by Philostratus in order to make a comparison between myth and reality. Apollonius, unlike Odysseus, does not need to rely on magical objects or empathetic goddesses to receive safe passage; reason and virtue are his salvation. Pound's comparison between Apollonius and Odysseus at sea is therefore partly ironic, in that Apollonius rejects the analogy. Like Apollonius himself, who has "his own mind to stand by him," Pound's readers are invited to reject Pound's Homeric analogy, like they will later have to reject Pound's mythical Frankenstein: a grafting of Leucothoe onto Leucothea. A few lines down, Pound juxtaposes Odysseus's initial hesitation to remove his clothes with Apollonius's hesitation before the "buggering" court of Domitian. This may be Pound's *translatio* of the brief moment when Odysseus considers whether Leucothea is tricking him, but the comparison is absurd. Leucothea is not in league with Poseidon and she is not a Calypso who wants to seduce and entrap Odysseus. In both texts, getting rid of paraphernalia is a good thing. Odysseus sheds his clothing and raft and

[37] Philostratus, *Life of Apollonius of Tyana*, vol. 2, 7.22.
[38] Philostratus, *Life of Apollonius of Tyana*, vol. 2, 7.21.

saves himself by his wits. Apollonius sheds his clothing, meaning his papers and books, possibly including a copy of the *Odyssey*, in order to defend himself with naked reason alone and exonerates himself.

Pound next suggests that Apollonius emulates Richard of Saint Victor's "charitas insuperabilis" or "love invincible" and compares Apollonius to the Rosicrucian Neoplatonic John Heydon who describes his ascent to the City of Heaven through the pursuit of wisdom and virtue in *The Holy Guide* (1662). Only those readers who might have recently have read Heydon's obscure text—or, better yet, have Pound's copy, to review the passages he underlined—could make sense of the fragments that follow, which refer to Heydon's belief that the number four was mystically important; that swallows eat medicinal plants like celandine to deal with their digestive problems; a few lines by Hesiod about the birth of the sky and day from the night that Heydon misattributes to Plato (and Pound adds "Ζηνὸς πυρὸς" or "wheat of Zeus" at the end for a grain-rite resonance);[39] and Heydon's muse, Euterpe, who, after advising him in the use of her arcana, "past before my eyes into the ether of Nature," like Leucothea into the sea wave after offering her divine counsel.[40]

In this case, the source text barely illuminates anything. Rather, it helps Pound conjure the process of the divine mind and Cavalcanti's "ardor of thought" at work: flashing and fading away, "fighting for speed," arcane, playful, Protean, and polyglot.[41] The fact that Heydon believed that swallows were intelligent eaters is less important than the simple appearance of swallows which invoke the bird-like swiftness of divine thought, as Richard of Saint Victor emphasizes. "Out of heaviness where no mind moves at all / 'birds for the mind' said Richardus" (90/627). Likewise, nothing is gained by knowing why Heydon believed that "the whole universe [is] concerned with FOUR." It is just arcana. Nor is the line, "Souls be the water-nymphs of Porphyrius" Pound's suggestion that his readers study Porphyry's allegorical interpretation of the Cave of the Nymphs to understand Leucothea, whom the Neoplatonists were mostly silent about. The point is to invoke the arcane, not explain it.

The irony of Pound's late style is that it demands an intuitive, instinctive, and even superficial reading along with a great deal of work. The late cantos cultivate mystery. Pound wants his reader to feel that there is always something more to be interpreted. "The mysteries are *not* revealed, and no guide book to them has

39 See Terrell, *A Companion*, 554.

40 John Heydon, *The Holy Guide* (London: Printed by T.M. and are to be sold by Thomas Whittlesey, 1662), book 6, page 34. Each book is paginated separately.

41 *LE*, 156.

been or will be written." Except for *The Holy Guide,* of course. But even in it, Euterpe warns Heydon to be silent about her gifts.

> My love I freely give you, and with it these tokens—mystery and signet; the one opens, the other shuts; be sure to use both with discretion. As for the mysteries of the Rosie Cross, you have my Library to peruse them all. There is not anything here but I will gladly reveal it unto you; I will teach you the virtues of numbers, of names, of angels, and genii of men. I have one precept to commend to you—you must be silent. You shall not in your writings exceed my allowance; remember that I am your love, and you will not make me a prostitute. But because I wish you serviceable to those of your own disposition, I give you an emblematical type of my sanctuary, namely, the Axiomata of the R. C., the secrets of numbers, with a full privilege to publish it. And now I am going to the invisible region, amongst the ethereal goddesses.[42]

The veil of Nature might be lifted to the select few; but to describe a naked undine or a naked Sherri Martinelli would be to make her a prostitute. The reader must be "skilled in fire" and read in "terms of planes and of bounding lines," discovering enough of the source material in order to discern (momentarily) the ideogram being presented.

Pound's translation of "κρήδεμνον" (*krēdemnon,* "a woman's headdress" or "veil") as "bikini" is an example of the godlike *hilaritas* required to read his *translatio.* Like throwing a Frigidaire into Sextus Propertius, it calls attention to itself: in this case, Pound's struggle to translate a difficult word in Homer, which later appears in *The Cantos* as "veil" and "scarf."[43] Liddell and Scott explain that "it seems to have been a sort of *veil* or *mantilla with lappets,* passing over the head and hanging down on each side, so that at pleasure it might be drawn over the face."[44] "Bikini" cheapens the translation, especially in the context Pound renders it: as a commodity of equal value to a raft: "My bikini is worth your raft." The word shifts our attention away from the magic properties of the veil to a comedic transaction: "I'll get naked if you do"; or even: "I'll take my top off if you accept death by drowning."

But how can a seagull wear a bikini? Homer explains that Leucothea emerges from the waves like an *aithuia* ("shearwater," "seagull"), and settles (ἵζω or *hizō:* "sit down," "settle") on the raft. But she is still a sea-nymph that can take off a *kredēmnon.* Leucothea was never transformed into a seagull, although Homer

[42] Heydon, *The Holy Guide,* book 6, page 32.

[43] *C,* 98/704, 100/736.

[44] Liddell and Scott, *A Lexicon Abridged from Liddell and Scott's Greek-English Lexicon,* 393.

suggests that she might have actually assumed that form. By calling her "the sea-gull," Pound hints that Odysseus can hear the green language and follow the bird-like swiftness of divine thought. The vegetarian Apollonius could also could talk to animals. The ideogram reappears in Canto 93: "having his own mind to stand by him / Κάδμου θυγάτηρ / Apollonius made his peace with the animals" (93/643).

Pound also invites a comparison between himself and Apollonius of Tyana. Although Pound makes almost no references to his confinement in *Rock-Drill,* his infamy guaranteed that his readers would be on the hunt. Apollonius is thrown into prison by a tyrant for refusing to leave Rome and exercising his freedom of philosophical inquiry. There, he receives visitors and acolytes and is eventually given a room where he can prepare his defense. He openly defies the emperor in blunt terms. He is acquitted and undergoes heavenly assumption. Pound was thrown in a cage for refusing to leave Fascist Italy and continuing to exercise his freedom to broadcast. He was eventually put in a mental institution, where he continued to write poetry and lecture to his rag-bag of acolytes. The immortality of *The Cantos* (he hoped) would exonerate him. Odysseus, Apollonius, and Pound "decline to be buggered" through "endurance" and making a virtue of necessity: set on building paradise here on earth, of realizing their "nostos": "the palpable / Elysium, though it were in the halls of hell" (81/541).

Later in *Rock-Drill,* Pound associates Leucothea with the divine Lady of Bernart and Cavalcanti, introducing the idea that Leucothea is also the "love" that lifts one up to mental paradise. In Canto 95, Pound reflects on the etymology of Leucothea as "white goddess" and links her to Beatrice's light-emanating eyes.

> Κάδμου θυγάτηρ
> bringing light *per diafana*
> λευκός Λευκόθοε [*leukhos Leukothoe*, "white Leucothoe"]
> white foam, a sea-gull. (95/664)

Pound's (mis)spelling possibly anticipates his fusion of Leucothea with Leucothoe in *Thrones.* Leucothoe was a princess loved by Helios and changed into an incense plant. Ovid recounts both stories and (confusingly) spells them both "Leucothoe."[45] More relevant, Ovid suggests that Ino received the name Leucothea because she threw herself into the foam of the sea. Pound associates her name here with "white foam."[46] Milton connects Leucothea

[45] See below.
[46] Ovid, *Metamorphoses,* 4.542.

with the light-bringing dawn.[47] Pound's Leucothea brings light "per diafana": a reference to Cavalcanti's metaphor of how love originates by the imprint of the beloved on the *tabula rasa* of memory. "In quelle part dove sta memora / Prendre suo stato si formato chome / Diafan dal lume d'una schuritade."[48] Pound translates this in 1934 as: "Where memory liveth, / it [love] takes its state / Formed there in matter as a mist of light / Upon dusk."[49] Then, in Canto 36: "Formed like a diafan from light / on shade" (36/177). Pound's Leucothea is that very diaphanous light of the beloved cast onto the darkness of the mind. This is reinforced later:

> "My bikini is worth yr/ raft". Said Leucothae [*sic*]
> And if I see her not
> No sight is worth the beauty of my thought. (95/665)

The lines of Bernart de Ventadorn first appear in Canto 20: "Si no'us vei, Domna don plus mi cal, / Negus vezer mon bel pensar no val" (20/89). Pound offers no other goddess in Homer this honor. Leucothea (misspelled again) is here equivalent the divine Lady of Bernart or Cavalcanti. She is a bridge toward understanding the *Odyssey* in a mystic sense, one who can raise the poem up to a new form like Beatrice raises the mind to comprehend *Paradiso.* Leucothea is the love that lifts the poet and reader up to divine *hilaritas, contemplatio,* or the mental state of paradise.

Rock-Drill ends with a condensed translation of *Odyssey* 5.315–46. Pound reiterates Leucothea's role as a bridge to mental paradise, comparing her to Dante's Glaucus, while also suggesting that his *translatio* is coming to its final "arrival" (*nostos*) or end.

> That the wave crashed, whirling the raft, then
> Tearing the oar from his hand,
>   broke mast and yard-arm
> And he was drawn down under wave,
>   The wind tossing,
> Notus, Boreas,
>   as it were thistle-down.
> Then Leucothea had pity,

[47] "Meanwhile, / To re-salute the world with sacred light, / Leucothea wak'd, and with fresh dews imbalmd / The Earth." (Milton, *Paradise Lost,* 11.133–5.)

[48] Quoted in *LE*, 164.

[49] Quoted in *LE*, 155.

"mortal once
Who now is a sea-god:
νόστου
γαίης Φαιήκων." (95/667)

Homer's lines are: "Far from the raft he fell, and let fall the steering-oar from his hand; but his mast was broken in the midst by the fierce blast of tumultuous winds that came upon it, and far in the sea sail and yardarm fell" (5.315–18). "Thistle down" is interpolated from a later image of Odysseus being tossed about in the waves: "As when in autumn the North Wind bears the thistle-tufts [ἀκάνθας, *akanthas*] over the plain, and close they cling to one another, so did the winds bear the raft this way and that over the sea" (5.328–31). "Notus, Boreas" is lifted from the next line in Greek: "ἄλλοτε μέν τε Νότος Βορέῃ προβάλεσκε φέρεσθαι" (*allote men te Notos Boreē probaleske pheresthai*) "Now the South Wind would fling it to the North Wind to be driven on" (5.332). When Leucothea witnesses this "she was touched with pity [ἐλέησεν, *eleēsen*] for Odysseus" (5.336). The Greek verb ἐλεέω comes from ἔλεος (*éleos*, "mercy"). The open quotation marks suggests that Leucothea is about to speak, but Pound first cites Homer's earlier description of Leucothea "who of old was a mortal of human speech, but now in the deeps of the sea has won a share of honor from the gods" (5.334–36) and then jumps to Leucothea's direction to Odysseus: "do thou swim with thy hands and so strive to reach the land of the Phaeacians [νόστου / γαίης Φαιήκων]" (5.344–46). Pound also makes a clever substitution: Leucothea is not really the "mortal once / Who now is a sea-god." She is a goddess, after all. The line refers to Glaucus in Dante's simile for "passing beyond the human" when he gazes at Beatrice.

In watching her, within me I was changed
as Glaucus changed, tasting the herb that made
him a companion of the other sea gods.
Passing beyond the human cannot be
worded; let Glaucus serve as simile—
until grace grant you the experience.
Whether I only was the part of me
that You created last, You—governing
the heavens—know: it was Your light that raised me [*mi levasti*].[50]

[50] Dante, *Paradiso*, trans. Robin Kirkpatrick, 1.67–75.

Just as Glaucus will have to serve as Dante's simile so will Leucothea have to serve as Pound's. Her light raised Odysseus beyond the human. Now it is up to the reader to take the plunge.[51]

In the final lines of *Rock-Drill,* the word "νόστου" appears in *The Cantos* for the only time. It is not translated or transliterated, meaning that it must be understood only in its context. The Greek *nostos* can mean a return home, but also more generically, a travel or journey. In this case, *nóstou* merely means "arriving," and refers to Phacaia, not Ithaca. Pound's final line reasserts the importance of the *Odyssey* as a guiding structural element of *The Cantos* and signals that the Pound's *Odyssey* is not a homecoming (*nostos*) story but a story of Odysseus's (repetitive) spiritual "arrival" (*nostos*) or transformation. Leucothea represents the last demand of self-sacrifice and complete abandonment in order to achieve paradise. Odysseus "arrives" when he plunges out into the void holding nothing but Leucothea's veil, and passes beyond the human: beyond the desire for home (Homer) or even the love of knowledge (Dante). *Thrones* outlines what this brave new world might look like, sans even the *Odyssey* as guide.

Thrones: Leucothea's Lack

In *Rock-Drill,* Leucothea represents the difficult plunge into arcana and "ardor of thought" that the reader must attempt in order to glimpse paradise. In *Thrones,* Pound's emphasis shifts to how love and devotion to the absent goddess or Lady leads to good government. As Pound explains to Donald Hall in 1962:

> The thrones in Dante's *Paradiso* are for the spirits of people who had been responsible for good government. The thrones in *The Cantos* are an attempt to move out from egoism and to establish some definition of an order possible or at any rate conceivable on earth.[52]

Once Pound recounts how Odysseus returns Leucothea's veil to the sea, his story is complete. Pound lingers on Homer's Phaeacians as a representation of "an order possible or at any rate conceivable on earth." Homer describes how the Phaeacians became devout to Poseidon after he punished them for bringing Odysseus home. In his final *translatio,* Pound substitutes Poseidon with Leucothea. Pound also "releases" the *Odyssey* as his guiding hypotext through four subtle techniques: he bookends *Thrones* with the image of Leucothea's

[51] For more on Glaucus, see chapter 5.
[52] Hall, "Ezra Pound, an Interview," 49.

departure and translates Odysseus's "envoi" to Leucothea's veil in Canto 100, where Dante's *Commedia* ends; he (cryptically) alludes to Odysseus's return to Ithaca and makes the only allusion to Penelope in *The Cantos*; he reduces the *Odyssey* to trivial facts and insignificant details; and he fuses Leucothea with Leucothoe, undermining her specific Homeric context, and creating a deliberately meaningless philological puzzle.

Thrones begins with Leucothea's disappearance and then an image of a ritual that marks her absence. Pound picks up the translation right where he left off at the end of *Rock-Drill:* "So saying, the goddess gave him the veil [κρήδεμνον], and herself plunged again into the surging deep, like a sea-mew; and the dark wave hid her" (5.351–53).

> Κρήδεμνον…
> κρήδεμνον…
> and the wave concealed her,
>   dark mass of great water.
> Aestheticisme comme politique d'église, hardly religion.
> & on the hearth burned cedar and juniper…
>   that should bear him thru these diafana (96/671)

The aestheticism of Mauberly and Henry James fails, like church politics, to create religion the way that modernism does: "Words like the locust-shells, moved by no inner being; / A dryness calling for death" (7/26). Pound here introduces the main concern of *Thrones*: how to identify successful models not of individual but civic and religious life. Beauty and mystery (represented by Leucothea) lead to meaningful devotion and ritual. Cedar was often used to purify homes and temples, and sacred to Artemis Kedreatis or "Lady of the Cedar"; while juniper was associated with potency. The line specifically alludes to Homer's description of Calypso's cave: "A great fire was burning in the hearth, and from afar over the isle there was a fragrance of cleft cedar and juniper as they burned" (5.59–60). Just as Odysseus must take the plunge with only Leucothea's veil, this simple ritual will bear Odysseus (and future civilizations) "through these diafana," meaning the white foaming sea, but the image also recalls Leucothea's diaphanous veil and the "imprint" of Cavalcanti's Lady upon memory. The light of Leucothea bears mankind through the diafana of earthly life.

This image is developed two cantos later when Pound compares Circe's drugs to Leucothea's veil: "Make it new / Τὰ ἐξ Αἰγύπτου φάρμακα [*Ta ex Aigyptou pharmaka,* 'drugs from Egypt'] / Leucothea gave her veil to Odysseus" (98/704). The veil of Leucothea, Calypso's burning cedar and juniper, and the drugs of

Circe, are all gifts from the gods that purify and raise men up to live better lives. They represent the vestiges of divine life that become the basis for meaningful ritual: the sacred intoxication of Dionysus, the mysteries of Circe's *kykleon* (Greek mystery religions were imported from Egypt, the purification ceremonies of Eleusis involved bathing with pigs); incense offerings to goddesses; the sacred herbs of Glaucus or Hermes's *moly;* and the veil (*kredēmnon*?) symbolizing death worn by the initiate of Eleusis, which is lifted by the priestess to symbolize his or her rebirth.

Pound singles out the Phaeacians as the example of "good government" from the *Odyssey*. This develops into a philological mystery that the reader struggles to solve. Rather than alluding to their great hospitality and generosity toward Odysseus, Pound focuses on the legacy Leucothea had on the Phaeacians. The idea, which is not found in Homer, first appears buried between a passage about *The Eparch's Book* and the history of seventh-century Briton in Canto 96:

> After 500 years, still sacrificed to that sea gull
> a colony off Phaeacians θῖνα θαλάσσης ["shore of the sea"]. (96/674)

In the *Odyssey*, Poseidon punishes the Phaeacians for bringing Odysseus home by turning their ship into stone. The Phaeacians sacrifice twelve bulls to Poseidon, and thereafter, Homer tells us, cease to give convoy to men who arrive in their country: hence "after 500 years": roughly the time from the action of the *Odyssey* (*c.* 1250 BCE) and Homer's day (*c.* 850 BCE).[53] Pound's *translatio* replaces the major god Poseidon with the minor goddess Leucothea. Although Ino, the daughter of Cadmus, lived in Boeotia, which is nowhere near Scheria (generally associated with Corfu), the cult of Leucothea was widespread among seafaring city states. Pausanias describes cults of Leucothea in Megara, Corinth, and Laconia, all of which are in Southern Greece; and Strabo mentions a temple to Leucothea in Colchis near the Black Sea.[54]

More important, Leucothea is a goddess of seafaring, for which the Phaeacians are famous. The Greek "thina thalasses," refers to one of Pound's favorite onomatopoetic phrases, "para thina polyphloisboio thalassēs" from *Iliad* 1.34, and means literally, "along the shore of the loud-resounding sea." Homer describes the Phaeacians as "Φαίηκες δολιχήρετμοι, ναυσίκλυτοι ἄνδρες" (*Phaiēkes dolichēretmoi, nausiklytoi andres*) "the Phaeacians of the long oars,

[53] *Odyssey*, 13.180–3.

[54] Pausanias, *Description of Greece*, trans. W. H. S. Jones and H. A. Ormerod (Cambridge, MA: Harvard University Press, 1918), 1.42.7 and 1.44.7 (Megara); 2.2.1 and 2.3.4 (Corinth); 3.23.8 and 3.26.1 (Laconia).

men famed for their ships"; and "φιληρέτμοισι" (*philēretmoisi*, from φιλήρετμος, *philēretmos*) or "lovers of the oar" (8.369, 13.36). King Alcinous outlines their supernatural seafaring abilities:

> For the Phaeacians have no pilots, nor steering-oars such as other ships have, but their ships of themselves understand the thoughts and minds of men, and they know the cities and rich fields of all peoples, and most swiftly do they cross over the gulf of the sea, hidden in mist and cloud, nor ever have they fear of harm or ruin.
>
> (8.557–563)

In Canto 97, Pound echoes Homer's own epithet for the Phaceacians, "δολιχήρετμοι" or "long-oared" in connection with six Chinese ideograms from the *Ta Hio* about the Ch'u state which does not collect wealth "but counts fair-dealing its treasure" (8.191, 97/696).[55] In Canto 98, these connections are gathered together in the context of Pound's poetic principles, and especially the idea of reading and seeing "by fire":

> "Ut facias pulchram" ["so that you make beauty"]
> there is no sight without fire.
> thinning their oar-blades
> θῖνα θαλάσσης ["shore of the sea"]
> nothing there but an awareness. (98/704)

In "Remy de Gourmont" (1920) Pound connects Goddeshalk's phrase, "amas ut favias pulcham" (love so that you make beauty) with De Gourmont's notion of love as an "intellectual instigation."[56] He contrasts this to the bloodless aestheticism of the Victorians like Henry James. To "make beauty" involves being "skilled in fire" ("there is no sight without fire"). This includes those who can read the phanopoeia of 旦 as the dawn; and those who can grasp the melopoetic connection between *thina thalasses* and "thinning their oar-blades."

The Phaeacians of the long oars (*Phaiēkes dolichēretmoi*) are lovers of the oar (*philēretmoisi*) and also "thinners" of their oars. Pound's invented epithet is illuminated by Homer's description of the Phaeacians as they set off to take Odysseus home.

55 *Confucius: The Great Digest, the Unwobbling Pivot, the Analects*, trans. Ezra Pound (New York: New Directions, 1969), 75. Pound writes "δολιχηρέτμοι."

56 *LE*, 341.

> As soon as they leaned back, and tossed the brine with their oarblades [ἀνερρίπτουν ἅλα πηδῷ, *anerriptoun hala pēdō*], sweet sleep fell upon [Odysseus's] eyelids, an unawakening sleep, most sweet, and most like to death. And as on a plain four yoked stallions spring forward all together beneath the strokes of the lash, and leaping on high swiftly accomplish their way, even so the stern of that ship leapt on high, and in her wake the dark wave of the loud-sounding sea foamed mightily [κῦμα δ᾽ ὄπισθε / πορφύρεον μέγα θῦε πολυφλοίσβοιο θαλάσσης, *kyma d' opisthe / porphyreon mega thye polyphloisboio thalassēs*], and she sped safely and surely on her way; not even the circling hawk, the swiftest of winged things, could have kept pace with her. Thus she sped on swiftly and clove the waves of the sea [ὣς ἡ ῥίμφα θέουσα θαλάσσης κύματ᾽ ἔταμνεν, *hōs hē rhimpha theousa thalassēs kymat' etamnen*].
>
> (13.78–88)

"Thinning their oar blades" invokes Homer's strong verbs including "throwing up" (*anerriptoun*, from ἀναρρίπτω, *anarriptō*) saltwater and cleaving (ἔταμνεν, *etamnen*) the waves of the sea, which Homer compares to the stroke (πληγή, *plēgē*) of the lash. Pound therefore imagines the Phaeacians "thinning" their oar-blades with such vigorous rowing, echoing the alliteration of πολυφλοίσβοιο θαλάσσης (*polyphloisboio thalassēs*) or loud-roaring sea. In this passage, the vigorous oar-work of the Phaeacians is responsible for the *polyphloisboio thalassēs.*

Although Pound connects the Phaeacians and Leucothea mythically, his goal is to connect them "by fire": ideogrammatically, melopoetically, and phanopoetically. The next time Pound pairs them, he intensifies the confusion by a melopoetic joke, pedantically distinguishing Leucothea from Leucothoe. The reader suspects that Pound's previous "errors" of spelling (Leucothea, Leucothoe, Leucothae) were intentional.

> And that Leucothoe rose as an incense bush
> – Orchamus, Babylon —
>   resisting Apollo.
> Patience, I will come to the Commissioner of the Salt Works
>   in due course.
> Est deus in nobis.   and ["There is a god in us."]
>   They still offer sacrifice to that sea-gull
> est deus in nobis
>   Χρήδεμνον
> She being of Cadmus line,
>   the snow's lace is spread there like sea-foam. (98/705)

Leocothoe appears as a point of clarification: she is not the Leucothea to whom the Phaeacians still offer a sacrifice. Only the alternate spelling signals the change, as well as, "Orchamus, Babylon." Ovid recounts the story of Leucothoe in *Metamorphoses* 4. Sol (Helios) falls in love with the maid Leucothoe, the daughter of Orchamus, the king of Babylon. Sol enters her room disguised as her mother, then reveals himself:

> "Who measures the long year, I am he. I see all things, earth sees all things by me, I, the world's eye. Trust me, you please me." She is afraid, and, in her fear, distaff and spindle fall from her lifeless fingers. Her fear enhances her, and he, waiting no longer, resumes his true form, and his accustomed brightness. And, though the girl is alarmed by this sudden vision, overwhelmed by his brightness, suppressing all complaint, she submits to the assault of the god.[57]

Orchamus finds out, and "in his pride and savagery, buried her deep in the earth, she praying, stretching her hands out towards Sol's light, crying 'He forced me, against my will', and he piled a heavy mound of sand over her."[58] Sol, arriving at the scene a little too late,

> tried to see if he could recall life to those frozen limbs, with his powerful rays. But since fate opposed such efforts, he sprinkled the earth, and the body itself, with fragrant nectar, and, after much lamenting, said "You will still touch the air." Immediately the body, soaked through with heavenly nectar, dissolved, steeping the earth in its perfume. Tentatively, putting out roots, the shoot of a tree, resinous with incense, grew through the soil, and pierced the summit of the mound.[59]

In other words, "Leucothoe rose as an incense bush." But Pound's condensation, "resisting Apollo," is odd. Ovid specifies that she in fact submitted at the moment because of Sol's overpowering light. Daphne, by contrast, does actively resist Apollo, and is transformed into a laurel before Apollo can get to her.

This seems like a good example of Peter Nicholls's argument that "a return to sources often fails to satisfy" when it comes to *Thrones*.[60] However, those who return to *Metamorphoses* book 4 in fact discover that the story of Leucothoe and the story of Leucothea are placed within a few hundred lines of one another, and that Ovid spells them both Leucothoe. To make matters worse, it is Leuconoe, one of the daughters of Minyas who rejects the worship of Bacchus and is later changed into a bat, who recounts the story of Leucothoe, daughter

57 Ovid, *Metamorphoses,* trans. Frank Justus Miller, 4.226–33.
58 Ovid, *Metamorphoses*, 4.237–41.
59 Ovid, *Metamorphoses*, 4.247–55.
60 Peter Nicholls, "'Two doits to a boodle': Reckoning with *Thrones*," *Textual Practice* 18.2 (2004): 233.

of Orchamus.[61] Nor should Ovid's Leuconoe be confused with her namesake, Leuconoe, the young woman addressed in Horace's ode 1.11, which Pound alludes to earlier in Canto 98 with the line, "Tu ne quaesieris" (98/632): "Tu ne quaesieris, scire nefas, quem mihi, quem tibi / finem di dederint, Leuconoe, nec Babylonios / temptaris numeros" ("Do not ask, as we may not know, Leuconoe, / What the gods plan for us. Don't attempt Babylonian / calculations"). Five years after *Thrones*, Pound translated this poem, and seemed intent on continuing the confusion (or the joke): "Ask not ungainly askings of the end / God send us, me and thee, Leucothoë: / Nor juggle with the risks of Babylon."[62] Distinguishing Leucothea (and Leucothae) from Leucothoe from Leuconoe from Leucothoë can be a daunting task.

Pound's attempt to discern Leucothea from "that Leucothoe" parodies the philologist's monocular mania for orthographic precision. In the words of old Levy: "'Noigandres, eh *noi*gandres, / 'Now what the DEFFIL can that mean!" (20/90). The line about the Salt Commissioner can be read in the same spirit of *hilaritas*. Pound has not mentioned a salt commissioner before this, and those who have read *The Cantos* thus far have abandoned all hope of the author getting to a "point." The joke reappears on the next page, now via the voice of a doddering German philologist: "But the salt works…"; "Patience, ich bin am Zuge ['I'm getting to it']"; "Until in Shensi, Ouang, the Commissioner Iu-p'uh / volgar' eloquio" (98/706). Finally the Salt Commissioner appears, and we learn that this is a reference to the editorial history of *The Sacred Edict*. Originally published in 1670 in the high literary style by K'ang Hsi, the text was simplified by K'ang Hsi's son Iong Cheng (whom the reader might recall as "YONG TCHING" from Canto 61, although Pound makes no mention of *The Sacred Edict* there); a high official Uang-iu-p'uh who was Salt Commissioner in Shensi translated it into colloquial Chinese (as Dante wrote *De Vulgari Eloquentia* in the Tuscan vernacular) and so allowed others to receive its message. The idea is repeated a few pages later as, "*Ouang -iu- p'uh* / on the edit of K'ang -hsi / in volgar' eloquio taking the sense down to the people" (98/708). Finally, in Canto 99, Pound offers a *translatio* of the Salt-commissioner's version.

Pound's repeated deferral of his "point" here is like his endless deferral of Odysseus's homecoming. *The Pisan Cantos* recounts Odysseus's shipwreck and arrival on Phaeacia; *Rock-Drill* recounts the shipwreck again; *Thrones* recounts the arrival on Phaeacia and then jumps ahead five hundred years, seemingly

[61] Ovid, *Metamorphoses*, 4.214–55.
[62] *PT*, 1145.

lost in a pedantic digression about the worship of Leucothea in Scheria. In both cases, the joke is on us. Pound finally "arrives" at the Salt Commissioner's version in Canto 99, but Canto 100 (where Dante ended) has Odysseus releasing the veil of Leucothea back to sea. *The Cantos* never gets to Ithaca: "am Zuge."

Canto 100 presents the last sustained *translatio* of the *Odyssey* in *The Cantos.* Pound resolves the Leucothea story as Homer presents it but implies that the poet is letting go of the Homeric structure.

> So that the mist was quite white on that part of the sea-coast
> Le Portel, Phaecia
> and he dropped the scarf in the tide-rips
> KREDEMNON
> that it should float back to the sea,
> and that quickly
> DEXATO XERSI ["she gathered it in her hand"]
> with a fond hand
> AGERTHE ["gathered back"]. (100/736–7)

Leucothea asks Odysseus to return the veil to the sea when he reaches dry land: "But when with thy hands thou hast laid hold of the land, loose it from thee, and cast it into the wine-dark sea far from the land, and thyself turn away" (5.348–50). Pound translates the moment that Odysseus gives the veil back:

> But when he revived, and his spirit returned again into his breast [ἐς φρένα θυμὸς ἀγέρθη, *es phrena thymos agerthē*], then he loosed from him the veil of the goddess and let it fall into the river that murmured seaward; and the great wave bore it back down the stream, and straightway Ino received it in her hands [αἶψα δ' ἄρ' Ἰνὼ / δέξατο χερσὶ φίλῃσιν, *aipsa d' ar' Inō / dexato chersi philēsin*].
> (5.458–61)

Pound borrows Homer's word that describes Odysseus's gathering his strength and applies it to Leucothea's gathering of the veil. Homer explains that Leucothea "swiftly" (*aipsa*) "takes into the hand" (*dexato chersi*) her veil. Her hand is not "fond" in Homer. This may have been inspired by Rouse's translation: "until Ino quickly received it into her kind hands."[63] "Le Portel, Phaecia" recalls the story from Canto 82 when Swinburne, saved from drowning, recites Aeschylus to the French fishermen.[64] Swinburne returns the favor with the only gift he

[63] Homer, *The Story of Odysseus*, 5.458–61.
[64] See Pound, *LE*, 218; and *C*, 82/523, as well as the chapter above.

possesses: his knowledge of classical poetry. Likewise, Odysseus's release of the veil is his own offering of thanks to the goddess that spared him, but it also acts as Pound's own return of the Homeric model to his higher muse. Although Michael Kindellan points out that "Canto 100 is famously a let down," it does adequately conclude the solar *Odyssey* theme.[65] Odysseus's periplum is essentially over; he has achieved his arrival (*nostou*); the "story" of *The Cantos* is complete; the sun has run its course (for roughly the hundredth time); it now is up to the reader to preserve the arcana of mystery religions and create "good government" on her own.

Pound knew that his readers would not be satisfied with such an end to his *Odyssey.* But rather than end with a bang (and satisfy James Laughlin), he reprises the pedantic Leucothea/Leucothoe distinction in Canto 102 in order to frustrate the reader's desire for coherence, consistency, and closure. Pound parades a detritus of Homeric trivia and mis-citations only to end by fusing the Leucothea myth with the Leucothoe myth. Many of Pound's most devoted readers and supporters asked him to clarify and "correct" his method here, but Pound insisted on this conflation, despite his earlier emphasis on their difference.[66]

> This I had from Kalupso
>   who had it from Hermes
> "eleven literates and, I suppose,
>   Dwight L. Morrow"
> the body elected,
>   residence required, not as in England
> "A cargo of Iron"
>   lied Pallas
>   and as to why Penelope waited
> keinas ... e Orgei. line 639. Leucothoe
> rose as an incense bush,
>   resisting Apollo,
>   Orchamus, Babylon
> And after 500 years
>   still offered that shrub to the sea-gull,
> Phaecians, [*sic*]
>   she being of Cadmus line
> The snow's lace washed here as sea-foam (102/748)

[65] Kindellan, *The Late Cantos of Ezra Pound*, 181.

[66] See Kindellan, *The Late Cantos of Ezra Pound*, 131–5.

Homeric trivia is randomly compiled. First: Odysseus "had it [i.e., permission to leave] from Kalupso who had it from Hermes" refers to Calypso's words: "Unhappy man, sorrow no longer here, I pray thee, nor let thy life pine away; for even now with a ready heart will I send thee on thy way" (5.160–61). Pound stops to admire the American businessman, ambassador to Mexico, and later senator, Dwight Morrow, because he was well-read in the classics.[67] Second: Athena disguises herself as a trader, Mentes, and explains to Telemachus that she is "on my way to Temese for copper; and I bear with me shining iron [αἴθωνα σίδηρον, *aithōna sidēron*]" (1.183–84). Third: those who don't know "why Penelope waited" for Odysseus for twenty years rather than marry one of the suitors might refer to "line 639." The diligent reader proceeds to check line 639 of all twenty-four books of the *Odyssey* until she discovers that Pound means book 4, line 693: "κεῖνος δ' οὔ ποτε πάμπαν ἀτάσθαλον ἄνδρα ἐώργει (*keinos d' ou pote pampan atasthalon andra eōrgei,* 'he never wrought iniquity at all to any man')" (4.693). (Pound's spelling, "e Orgei," seems to be a typo.) Forth: Pound suggests that Leucothoe's rising "as an incense bush" comprises her "resistance" to Apollo; then claims that the Phaeacians still offer up (that is, burn) Leucothoe (the frankincense shrub) to Leucothea (the sea-gull); only to remind us that Leucothea is *not* Leucothea, the latter "being of Cadmus line."

But there is some mythical method to this ideogrammatic madness. "This I had from Kalupso" can be read as Odysseus explaining to Leucothea where he got his raft, clothes, and treasures. Athena's reference to a "cargo of iron" which she needs to unload is a subject-rhyme of Odysseus's heavy burden. And the sole mention of Penelope in *The Cantos* is hard to ignore. Readers waiting for Odysseus to get home must be satisfied with this meager offering, for it does at least suggest that Odysseus returned to Ithaca. Penelope "waited." She waits no longer. Five hundred years later, Odysseus and Penelope were dead.

To all those *Odyssey* enthusiasts hoping that Pound will end with a bang like the monologue of Molly Bloom, Pound offers them a half-page of *Odyssey* trivia idiogramatically and idiotically arranged into a kind of nostos, however obscure, haphazard, and flaccid. And what better way to indicate the sheer impotence or irrelevance of the *Odyssey* than this last "botched" reading of frankincense offered up to a seagull? Pound suggests that a luminous connection will appear between Leucothea and the Phaeacians, pedagogically reminding them that Leucothea must not be confused with Leucothoe, only to arrive at the absurd image of the Phaeacians offering Leucothoe up to Leucothea: a lily wrung from

[67] See *GK,* 260 and Canto 86.

an acorn. A reader might recall Heydon's swallows eating celandine, and the necessity of bird-like "reading by fire." But compared to pairing of Helen of Troy with Eleanor of Aquitaine as melopoetic subject rhymes in Canto 2, this displays as much mythical method as the pupil Armstrong in Joyce's "Nestor." "You, Armstrong, Stephen said. What was the end of Pyrrhus?" (2.21) "Pyrrhus, sir? Pyrrhus, a pier" (2.26). The joke is on those still clinging to the spar of the mythical method.

Pound's original notebook draft of this section suggests that he intended to contrast poetic precision with poetic vagueness and a pedantic drilling of *Odyssey* facts.

what did Athene says
she was up to?
toting iron
they read the Odyssey + do not
nor see why Penelope waited
κεῖνος.. εώργει
693
Religion not being a racket
That Leucothoe rose as
an incense bush.
Orchamus, in Babylon
resisting twice Apollo
+ after twice 500 years years
her shrub was burnt for
that sea-gull.
~~we presume~~
est deus in nobis.
somebody's colony -
κρήδεμον
she being of Cadmus' line.
A colony of Phaeacians
+ snow's lace
washed there
as sea-foam.[68]

Pound pedantically critiques those who don't read the *Odyssey* with enough attention to detail. Penelope's line about Odysseus's character does reveal an

[68] Ezra Pound, "Notebook 91," *EPP*, 4959.

often-overlooked detail; but it is unclear why Athena's disguise is important, unless Pound is offering evidence that Ithaca was primarily a mercantile community, or highlighting one of Homer's many anachronistic references to iron in a Bronze Age. (Gilbert Murray lists many similar anachronisms in *The Rise of the Greek Epic.*[69]) Surprisingly, Pound was originally correct about the line number (693) and the Greek word ἑώργει. Did he botch them intentionally? The propagation of textual mistakes seems to mimic the larger "mistake" of confusing Leucothoe with Leucothea. Pound is emphatic about the difference between Leucothea and "That Leucothoe," but this draft is full of other strange doublings: she resisted "twice" Apollo and after "twice 500 years years" (in late Classical Athens?) her shrub was burnt to the sea-gull Leucothea. The line "somebody's colony" which becomes "a colony of Phaeacians" suggests that Pound wanted to cast doubt on whether he really means the Phaeacians at all.[70]

Although Pound's late style sometimes reads like merely "notes" for cantos that he couldn't bother to make luminous or even properly research ("somebody's colony"), in this case, Pound went out of his way to make the finished canto more obscure and erroneous than his original draft. Leucothea is a "broken" allusion that the poet keeps returning to and trying to repair, pedantically, philologically, only to arrive at this exquisite corpse of the two Leucotheas. The luminous fusion of hypotext (the *Odyssey*) and hypertext (*The Cantos*) is here definitively broken.

Thrones contains only two more references to Leucothea/Leucothoe, but she has departed from her Homeric context and become part of Pound's pantheon of nameless goddesses that interchange and switch identities, including Circe: "not know which god / but Circe was like that" (106/774). The image of Leucothoe's resistance to Apollo is invoked in Canto 102 amid another cluster of random Homeric trivia. Pound reprises his investigation into Homeric color-words that he began in Canto 2:

> "The libraries" (Ingrid) "have no Domvile." Jan 1955
> as was natural
> "pseudos d'ouk… ei gar pepneumenos ["not a lie… wise indeed"]
> seed barley with the sacrifice (Lacedaemon)
> But with Leucothoe's mind in that incense
> all Babylon could not hold it down.
> "for my bitch eyes" in Ilion

[69] Murray, *The Rise of the Greek Epic*, 180–3.
[70] See Kindellan, *The Late Cantos of Ezra Pound*, 183–4.

copper and wine like a bear cub's
                        in sunlight, thus Atalant
the colour as *aithiops* ["glittering"]
                                the gloss probably
                                                oinops ["wine-dark"]
as lacquer in sunlight
                                haliporphuros, ["sea purple"]
                                                russet-gold
in the air, extant, not carmine, not flame, oriXalko, ["watery copper"]
                                                le xaladines[71]
lit by the torch-flare,
                                and from the nature, the sign. (102/749–50)

Pound's friend Ingrid Davies informed him in a letter that she could not find the work of the anti-Semitic Barry Domvile at local libraries in London. Pound believed this was a case of deliberate suppression, and goes on to compare Domvile to Nestor, about whom Athena, in the guise of Mentes, tells Telemachus, "φεῦδος δ'οὐχ ἐρέει / … γάρ πεπνύμενος" (*pheudos d'ouch ereei / … gar pepnymenos*, "he will not tell a lie / … [he is] wise indeed") (3.20). "Seed barley" may refer to Eurycleia who, after lulling a worried Penelope to sleep in book 4, places barley in a basket and prays to Athena (4.758–61). The parenthesis "(Lacedaemon)" refers back to the earlier "fact" that "Spartans in Mount Taygeto / sacrifice a horse to the winds" (87/702). "But with Leucothoe's mind in that incense / all Babylon could not hold it down" finally illuminates what Pound earlier meant by "resisted." Just as Leucothoe resisted her father (the Babylonian king) as he buried her alive ("hold it down"), so too no one in Babylon can ever forget her father's crimes. The blooming of frankincense speaks out against the cruelty of Sol, and hence "resists" Apollo. The line also connects to Saint Hilary of Poitiers who saw in an oak leaf an example of the divine intelligence: "St. Hilary looked at at an oak-leaf" (95/667). This relates to the final line: "and from the nature, the sign," recalling Homer reading what Joyce calls "the signatures of all things" in the sea-surge, including the voice of the old men seeing Helen on the Skaian gate in Canto 2. Pound links this to Helen's own self-negation of her "bitch eyes" that launched a thousand ships, a translation of Helen's line, "ἐμεῖο κυνώπιδος εἵνεκ' Ἀχαιοὶ / ἤλθεθ'" (*emeio kynōpidos heinek' Achaioi / ēltheth:* "when for the sake of shameless me ye Achaeans came") (4.144–45). The Greek word, κυνώπης

[71] An invented word, probably a combination of the Greek prefix *kali* ("good") with χαλκός (*chalkos*, "copper").

(*kynōpēs*), means "dog-eyed." It usually has a negative connotation. Homer uses it in connection with Aphrodite (8.314) and Hera (*Iliad* 18.396). Pound compares it to the theriomorphic beauty of Atalanta's wild eyes (who was suckled by a she-bear[72]), who also appeared in Canto 2 ("the voice of Schoeney's daughters" [2/6]), and connects it back to Richard of Saint Victor's "UBI AMOR IBI OCULUS" ("where there is love, there is the eye") and the "green deep" of Elizabeth I of England's eye which inspired Drake: "Drake saw the splendour and wreckage in that clarity / Gods moving in crystal / ichor, amor" (91/631).

This passage reinforces the fact that the *Odyssey* has fully dissipated into Pound's other thematic obsessions. The focus, now, is on the "signs" of divinity in the world, the beauty and intricacy of the natural world, the perennial forces of nature, human intelligence, and the importance of worship and keeping "love" alive through memory. The eyes of Helen anticipate the paradisal visions of Canto 106: Circe's stone eyes and the light that blazes from behind her; the beauty of the mind of Artemis; the "great acorn of light bulging outward"; and the "God's eye" (106/775). All of Pound's gods are disordered into that sacred confusion of Dionysian ritual: "He has a god in him, / though I do not know which god" (2/9).

Thrones ends by invoking the muse of Pound's paradise one more time, Leucothea, and reminding the reader of the difficulty of "thinking" paradise. Twice her name is repeated: "INO Ινώ Kadmeia" and "Καλλĭαστρᾰ́γαλος ['beautiful-ankled'] Ino Kadmeia" (109/794). The epithet, *Kallĭastrhagalos*, means the same thing as Homer's word to describe Ino: "Ino of the fair ankles [καλλίσφυρος, *kallisphyros*]" (6.333). Pound ends with "You in the dinghy (piccioletta) astern there!" This merely serves to recall the lines that follow, as presented in Canto 93: " 'Oh you,' as Dante says / 'in the dinghy astern there' / There must be incognita" (93/651). Only a select few can follow Pound on these "open seas" where no poet has crossed before.

In *The Pisan Cantos*, the text of the *Odyssey* is shipwrecked into fragments for the reader to gather up into new luminous combinations. In *Rock-Drill* and *Thrones*, the *Odyssey* is raised to the level of the arcana of mystery religions and its fragments are arranged idiogrammatically, melopoetically, and phanopoetically. Leucothea is the spiritual guide to both Odysseus and the reader. Her goal is to lead the reader toward a new form of anagogic or spiritual interpretation. The reader must abandon (if he hasn't already) not only the desire for narrative

72 Cf. Apollorodorus, *Library*, 3.9.2.

closure (nostos) but the notion that *The Cantos* will present a coherent vision of the paradise it seeks. Ultimately, the reader must abandon the paraphernalia of the *Odyssey* itself, and along with it the desire for that "aha" moment of coherence when the old and the new synthesize with delight. Readers of Joyce's *Ulysses*, by contrast, are increasingly rewarded with such orgasmic moments of trivial coherence. The later books cultivate hypertextual puzzle-solving—How can *moly* be a potato? How are catechisms a *translatio* of Odysseus's revenge on the suitors? In what sense is Stephen Dedalus Leopold Bloom's son?—which lead to a set of (usually) satisfying meta-fictional answers. Pound's vapid *Odyssey* trivia near the end of *Thrones* mocks our desire for coherence. Leucothea resists luminosity. She is a let-down with beautiful ankles. She fails to mean anything other than our struggle to comprehend her and retain her image in the mind. She emerges and re-emerges throughout these cantos for only moments in the void of the churning sea, reminding us to rise up and play.

> the Divine Mind is abundant
> unceasing
> *improvisatore*
> Omniformis
> Unstill. (92/640)

Pound's divinity is, like the sea-swell from which the legendary Homer crafted his poetry, forever roiling and "creating" mythology and poetry. In "The Coming of War: Acteon," Pound describes the sea as "harsher than granite, / unstill, never ceasing; / High forms / with the movement of gods."[73] In the late Canto 113, Pound writes: "The long flank, the firm breast / and to know beauty and death and despair / and to think that what has been shall be, / flowing, ever unstill" (113/807). What is unstill can never be subsumed into Joyce's "Penleope," or a *Paradiso* of fixed spheres. Those who are skilled in fire must learn, gaily, to let Homer go. And eventually, Pound.

[73] *PT*, 285.

Conclusion: Eternal Disorder

In 1944, while Ezra Pound was composing Fascist radio broadcasts and the Italian Cantos 72 and 73, Theodore Adorno and Max Horkheimer completed a critique of the epic elements of the *Odyssey* which would eventually become part of *Dialectic of Enlightenment* (1947). Despite their radically different politics, Adorno and Horkheimer's critique reads as a remarkably cogent gloss of Pound's poetic and philological project of Odyssey-*translatio* in *The Cantos.*

Adorno and Horkheimer argue that "the equation of epic and myth has been undermined by recent classical philology."[1] Citing the work of J. J. Bachofen, Victor Bérand, Johann Kirchhoff, Gilbert Murray, and J. A. K. Thomson, they suggest that Odysseus's goal of nostos runs contrary to the older nomadic narrative structure that contains him. (Unsurprisingly, they ignore the work of Jane Harrison.) "Precipitated in the epic is the memory of an historical age in which nomadism gave way to settlement, the precondition of any homeland."[2] In the *Odyssey,* epic conquers myth; "male" rationality triumphs over "female" (Dionysian, vegetation) ritual; teleological time (Odysseus's quest home) replaces cyclical time (Odysseus's solar journey). Homer is an "antimythological, enlightened character" with a strong "opposition to chthonic mythology."[3]

> The primeval world is secularized as the space he measures out; the old demons populate only the distant margins and islands of the civilized Mediterranean, retreating into the forms of rock and cave from which they had originally sprung in the face of the primal dread.[4]

Homer's Hades is beyond Oceanus, the limits of the known world, and epitomizes the "primal dread" of the old religion. "The farthest point reached on the odyssey

1 Adorno and Horkheimer, *Dialectic of Enlightenment*, 34.
2 Adorno and Horkheimber, *Dialectic of Enlightenment*, 60.
3 Adorno and Horkheimber, *Dialectic of Enlightenment*, 37.
4 Adorno and Horkheimber, *Dialectic of Enlightenment*, 38. They credit Kirchhoff with the insight that "Odysseus's visit to the Underworld forms part of the oldest stratum of the epic." (59)

proper is no such homely refuge. It is Hades."[5] There dwell "matriarchal shades who have been banished by the religion of light."

By championing the individual, Homer suppresses pre-Olympian religion. "Humanity had to inflict terrible injuries on itself before the self—the identical, purpose-directed, masculine character of human beings—was created."[6] Women, intoxication, regression, and forgetting represent the threat of non-identity in the *Odyssey.* They are the enemies of enlightenment and epic, and must be conquered or overcome, even if they are not particularly hostile. Calypso, Circe, and the Lotophagoi represent earlier forms of life, what Bachofen calls the hetaeric worldview.[7]

> The hetaera both bestows joy and destroys the autonomy of its recipient – that is her ambiguity. But she does not necessarily destroy the recipient himself: she holds fast to an older form of life. Like the Lotus-eaters, Circe does not cause lethal harm to her guests, and even those she had turned into wild beasts are peaceable.[8]

Nevertheless, Odysseus must resist these intoxicating and monstrous women. He must resist the Sirens, navigate past Scylla's dread teeth, and pull himself out of Charybdis's sucking hole. This resistance is tantamount to the destruction of myth. "Every mythical figure is compelled to do the same thing over and over again. Each of them is constituted by repetition: its failure would mean their end."[9] "Against this Odysseus fights. The self represents the rational universality against the inevitability of fate."[10] The Sirens boast that no man can resist their charms. What song might they sing after Odysseus sails past them? Do they go silent?

For Adorno and Horkheimer, this tension between the old and the new religion makes the *Odyssey* unique. "In Homer, epic and myth, form and subject matter do not simply diverge; they conduct an argument."[11] The *Odyssey* puts these worlds in deliberate tension. But in the end, epic triumphs. Death loses its dominion. The rational war hero becomes immortal, even if his punishment of Melanthius

[5] Adorno and Horkheimber, *Dialectic of Enlightenment,* 59.

[6] Adorno and Horkheimber, *Dialectic of Enlightenment,* 26.

[7] See Bachofen, *Myth, Religion, and Mother Right,* 132–4.

[8] Adorno and Horkheimber, *Dialectic of Enlightenment,* 55. To this, they add a footnote directing the reader to Thomson's *Studies in the Odyssey,* 153. (263n36) There, Thomson argues that Circe and the other female goddesses of the Odyssey "belong to a primitive nature-religion older than Homer's Olympianism and plainly irreconcilable with it." (153)

[9] Adorno and Horkheimber, *Dialectic of Enlightenment,* 45.

[10] Adorno and Horkheimber, *Dialectic of Enlightenment,* 46.

[11] Adorno and Horkheimber, *Dialectic of Enlightenment,* 37.

and the unfaithful maids borders on the barbaric. Powerful, independent female figures (Circe, Calypso, Leucothea) are overshadowed by female monsters (the Sirens, Scylla, Charybdis, Clytemnestra), and the patriarchal image of feminine virtue is established by the misogynist Agamemnon as Penelope, the faithful wife: "Therefore the fame of her virtue shall never perish, but the immortals shall make among men on earth a pleasant song in honor of constant Penelope" (24.196–98).

Adorno and Horkheimer probably did not read *The Cantos*, but they succinctly outline the very *Odyssey* that Pound tirelessly resists. Pound's *translatio* rejects the enlightened, rational hero of epic for the regressive and passive nomadic solar hero and fertility hero of myth who learns humility (*aidōs*) through adversity and delights in the ephemeral gifts of the gods: the *ligur' aiode* of the Sirens, the meats of Calypso, the ecstasy of Circe's cave. Pound takes on the Sisyphisian philological and mythical task of rewriting the *Odyssey* such that myth triumphs over epic again. Sisyphus, as Harrison points out, is not a paragon of (existential) futility, but a primitive solar hero whose natural repetitive and cyclical action was reframed by Homer as a punishment.[12] Like the rising and setting of and the sun, Pound achieves his goal with every effort.

The Cantos tells Homer's story backwards, unraveling epic into repetition and excavating its mythical roots. Odysseus journeys to the underworld to recover the oldest part of Homer. He lingers on the tales of heroines. He is told to return to Circe. The Lotophagoi shame Odysseus for his selfish and "purpose-directed" individualism. Odysseus returns to Circe's island, only to replay his yearlong stay with Circe before he visits Tiresias. Circe reorients Odysseus's wanderings as a fertility ritual and Odysseus undergoes his own ecstatic Dionysian *sparagmos*. *The Cantos* "ends" by circling endlessly around Odysseus's shipwreck and arrival on Phaeacia: the last of Odysseus's wanderings, but the first adventure recounted in the *Odyssey*. Pound refuses any mention of homeland, opting instead to repeat the story of shipwreck and Leucothea until the *Odyssey* itself is dismembered like the limbs of Osiris into nothing but luminous fragments.

Consider the wealth of material in the last fourteen books of the *Odyssey* that Pound might have employed the late cantos. Odysseus's devotion to his absent Penelope suggests a comparison to the troubadour's deification of the Lady-Love. *Thrones* might have compared Odysseus's restoration of a "good government" to an ideal marriage of the ethics of Confucius with the mysteries of Eleusis. The parasitical suitors could have personified Usura, American Democracy, or

12 Harrison, *Prolegomena to the Study of Greek Religion*, 609.

just plain "kikery" (91/634). Most obvious: Like Odysseus, Pound returns to his native land and is treated like a beggar, mocked, and thrown into a mental institution.

Homer's nonlinear narrative serves a thematic purpose. The *Odyssey* begins with Odysseus at his most destitute and ends with Odysseus fully restored as husband and king. Pound's nonlinear narrative also serves a thematic purpose. *The Cantos* begins with Odysseus as a man on a mission ("till I should hear from Tiresias") and ends with Odysseus *outis,* having shorn his individualism, naked, free of paraphernalia of the enlightened rational man, free of the constraints of the epic machinery, the wind his only schema through the mad folkloric rush of Dionysian lyric, and his mind like Neptunus, "leaping / like dolphins" (116/815). Pound's *Odyssey* resists narrative coherence:

> I have brought the great ball of crystal;
>   who can lift it?
> Can you enter the great acorn of light?
>   But the beauty is not the madness
> Tho' my errors and wrecks lie about me.
> And I am not a demigod,
> I cannot make it cohere. (116/815–16)

This is neither a biographical nor a methodological admission of failure. The errors and wrecks of *The Cantos* are not only deliberate but also necessary to Pound's aesthetics. The coherence of *The Cantos,* at its most developed, is anagogic and mystic. The author does not make it cohere. It is a work of love, not reason. The paradox of *The Cantos* is that it wants to be an epic of self-undoing, one that intentionally goes astray, delaying, critiquing, and ultimately unraveling its master narrative to emanate sparks of paradiso terrestre. *The Cantos* cultivate a special kind of confusion in the reader: not the confusion we encounter facing something difficult or obscure, but the confusion we arrive at after mastering it.

Bibliography

Archives

Ezra Pound Collection. Harry Ransom Humanities Research Center, University of Texas at Austin.

Ezra Pound Papers. YCAL MSS 43. Yale Collection of American Literature, Beinecke Rare Book and Manuscript Library, Yale University.

Works and Translations by Pound

ABC of Reading. New York: New Directions, 1960.

The Cantos. New York: New Directions, 1995.

Cavalcanti, Guido. *Sonnets and Ballate of Guido Cavalcanti*. Translated by Ezra Pound. London: S. Swift and Co., 1912.

Confucius: The Great Digest, the Unwobbling Pivot, the Analects. Translated by Ezra Pound. New York: New Directions, 1969.

"On Criticism in General." *The Criterion* 1.2 (1923): 143–56.

Ezra Pound to His Parents: Letters, 1895–1929. Edited by Mary de Rachewiltz, A. David Moody, and Joanna Moody. Oxford: Oxford University Press, 2010.

Ezra Pound and James Laughlin: Selected Letters. Edited by David M. Gordon. New York: New Directions, 1994.

Gaudier-Brzeska: A Memoir. New York: New Directions, 1970.

Gourmont, Remy de. *The Natural Philosophy of Love*. Translated by Ezra Pound. New York: Boni and Liveright, 1922.

Guide to Kulchur. New York: New Directions, 1970.

"I Gather the Limbs of Osiris." *The New Age*, 10.9 (December 28, 1911): 201–2.

The Letters of Ezra Pound, 1907–1941. Edited by D. D. Paige. New York: New Directions, 1951.

Literary Essays. Edited by T. S. Eliot. New York: New Directions, 1968.

"The New Sculpture." In *Ezra Pound and Visual Arts*. Edited by Harriet Zinnes, 179–82. New York: New Directions, 1980.

Poems and Translations. Edited by Richard Sieburth. New York: Library of America, 2003.

Pound/Ford: Story of Literary Friendship. New York: New Directions, 1981.

"Prolegomena." *Poetry Review* 1.2 (February 1912): 72–6.

"Prolegomena." *The Exile* 2 (1927): 35.

Prolegomena 1: How to Read. Toulon: To Publishers, 1932.

"Raphaelite Latin." In *Ezra Pound's Poetry and Prose: Contributions to Periodicals*. Volume 1. Edited by Lea Baechler, A. Walton Litz, and James Longenbach, 5–8. New York: Garland, 1991.

Selected Letters, 1907–1941. Edited by D. D. Paige. New York: New Directions, 1971.

Selected Prose, 1909–1965. Edited by William Cookson. New York: New Directions, 1973.

The Spirit of Romance. London: Dent, 1910.

The Spirit of Romance. Edited by Richard Sieburth. New York: New Directions, 2005.

A Walking Tour in Southern France. Edited by Richard Sieburth. New York: New Directions, 1992.

Co-authored Works

Pound, Ezra and Ernest Fenollosa. *The Chinese Written Character as a Medium for Poetry*. Edited by Haun Saussy, Jonathan Stalling, and Lucas Klein. New York: Fordham University Press, 2008.

Secondary Sources

Adorno, Theodor and Max Horkheimer. *Dialectic of Enlightenment*. Stanford: Stanford University Press, 2002.

Aeschylus. *Agamemnon*. In *Aeschylus*. Volume 2. Translated by Herbert Weir Smyth. Cambridge, MA: Harvard University Press, 1926.

Aldington, Richard. "The Influence of Mr. James Joyce." *English Review* 32 (1921): 333–41.

Ames, Keri Elizabeth. "The Rebirth of Heroism from Homer's Odyssey to Joyce's Ulysses." In *Twenty-First Joyce*. Edited by Ellen Carol Jones and Morris Beja, 157–78. Gainesville: University of Florida Press, 2004.

Anderson, David. *Pound's Cavalcanti*. Princeton, NJ: Princeton University Press, 1983.

Apollodorus. *The Library*. Volume 1. Translated by Sir James George Frazer. Cambridge, MA: Harvard University Press, 1921.

Aristotle. *The Nicomacean Ethics*. Translated by David Ross. Edited by Lesley Brown. New York: Oxford University Press, 2009.

Bachofen, Johann Jacob. *Myth, Religion, and Mother Right*. Translated by Ralph Manheim. Princeton, NJ: Princeton University Press, 1967.

Bacigalupo, Massimo. *The Formèd Trace: The Later Poetry of Ezra Pound*. New York: Columbia University Press, 1980.

Barnhisel, Greg. *James Laughlin, New Directions Press, and the Remaking of Ezra Pound.* Amherst, MA: University of Massachusetts Press, 2005.

Baumann, Walter. "The *Odyssey* Theme in Ezra Pound's *Cantos*." In *Roses from the Steel Dust: Collected Essays on Ezra Pound*, 83–97. Orono, ME: National Poetry Foundation, 2000.

Beckett, Samuel. "Dante and the Lobster." In *More Pricks Than Kicks*, 9–22. New York: Grove Press, 1970.

Bédier, Joseph. "La tradition manuscrite du *Lai de l'Ombre*." *Romania* 54 (1928): 161–96.

Bédier, Joseph. "The Legend of Tristan and Isolt." In *The Romance of Tristan and Iseut*, Translated by Susan Taber, 121–40. Indianapolis: Hackett, 2013.

Bédier, Joseph. *Le Roman de Tristan par Thomas*. Paris: Didot, 1902.

Bédier, Joseph. *The Romance of Tristan and Iseut*. Translated by Edward J. Gallagher. Indianapolis: Hackett, 2013.

Benoît de Saint-Maure. *Le Roman de Troie*. Edited by Léopold Constans. Paris: Firmin Didot, 1904–12.

Bérard, Victor. *Les Phéniciens et l'Odyssée*. Paris: Colin, 1902–3.

Bernart von Ventadorn. Bernart von Ventadorn: seine Lieder, mit Einleitung und Glossar. Edited by Carl Appel. Halle: Niemeyer, 1915.

Blavatsky, Helena. *Collected Writings*. Volume 12. Edited by Boris De Zirkoff. Wheaton, IL: The Theosophical Publishing House, 1980.

Bollack, Joan. "Odysseus among the Philologists." In *The Art of Reading: From Homer to Paul Celan*. Translated by Catherine Porter, Susan Tarrow, and Bruce King, 16–45. Washington, DC: Center for Hellenic Studies, 2016.

Brooke-Rose, Christine. *A ZBC of Ezra Pound*. London: Faber and Faber, 1971.

Bush, Ronald. "Art versus the Descent of the Iconoclasts: Cultural Memory in Ezra Pound's Pisan Cantos." *Modernism/Modernity* 14.1 (2007): 71–95.

Bush, Ronald. *The Genesis of Ezra Pound's Cantos*. Princeton, NJ: Princeton University Press, 1976.

Bush, Ronald. "Late Cantos LXXII-CXVII." In *The Cambridge Companion to Ezra Pound*. Edited by Ira Nadel, 109–38. Cambridge: Cambridge University Press, 1999.

Bush, Ronald. "Modernism, Fascism, and the Composition of Ezra Pound's Pisan Cantos." *Modernism/Modernity* 2.3 (1995): 69–87.

Byron, George Gordon. *The Siege of Corinth, Parisina*. London: John Murray, 1816.

Byron, Mark. *Ezra Pound's Eriugena*. London: Bloomsbury Academic, 2014.

Camille, Michael. "Philological Iconoclasm: Edition and Image in the *Vie de Saint Alexis*." In *Medievalism and the Modernist Temper*. Edited by R. Howard Bloch and Stephen G. Nichols, 371–401. Baltimore: Johns Hopkins University Press, 1996.

Carpentier, Martha. "Jane Ellen Harrison and the Ritual Theory." *Journal of Ritual Studies* 8.1 (1994): 11–26.

Carpentier, Martha. *Ritual, Myth, and the Modernist Text: The Influence of Jane Ellen Harrison on Joyce, Eliot, and Woolf*. Amsterdam, The Netherlands: Gordon and Breach, 1998.

Casillo, Robert. *The Genealogy of Demons: Anti-Semitism, Fascism, and the Myths of Ezra Pound.* Evanston, IL: Northwestern University Press, 1988.

Catullus. *The Carmina of Gaius Valerius Catullus.* Edited by Leonard C. Smithers. London: Smithers, 1894.

Cerquiglini, Bernard. *In Praise of the Variant.* Translated Betsy Wing. Baltimore, MD: Johns Hopkins University Press, 1999.

La Chanson de Roland. Oxford text. Edited by Joseph Bédier. Paris: Édition d'Art, 1922.

Childress, Lynn. "The Missing 'Cicones' Episode of *Ulysses.*" *James Joyce Quarterly* 33.1 (1995): 69–82.

Cicero, Marcus Tullius. *Cicero on Oratory and Orators.* Translated by J. S. Watson. New York: Harper and Brothers, 1860.

Cicero, Marcus Tullius. *De Finibus Bonorum et Malorum.* Edited by Th. Schiche. Leipzig: Teubner, 1915.

Cicero, Marcus Tullius. *De Oratore.* From *On the Orator: Book 3. On Fate. Stoic Paradoxes. Divisions of Oratory.* Translated by H. Rackham. Cambridge, MA: Harvard University Press, 1942.

Coleridge, Samuel Taylor. "Essays on the Principles of Genial Criticism." In *The Collected Works of Samuel Taylor Coleridge: Shorter Works and Fragments.* Volume 2. Edited by H. J. Jackson and J. R. de J. Jackson, 375–86. Princeton, NJ: Princeton University Press, 1995.

Collins, Derek. "Homer and Rhapsodic Competition in Performance." *Oral Tradition* 16.1 (2001): 129–67.

Connolly, Thomas. *The Personal Library of James Joyce: A Descriptive Bibliography.* Buffalo: University at Buffalo, 1955.

Conrad, Joseph. *Heart of Darkness.* New York: Penguin, 2017.

Corbellari, Alain. "Joseph Bédier, Philologist and Writer." In *Medievalism and the Modernist Temper.* Edited by R. Howard Bloch and Stephen G. Nichols, 269–85. Baltimore: Johns Hopkins University Press, 1996.

Crawford, Robert. *The Savage and the City in the Work of T. S. Eliot.* Oxford: Clarendon Press, 1987.

Crawley, Alfred Earnest. *The Idea of the Soul.* London: Adam and Charles Black, 1909.

Dakyns, Janine. *The Middle Ages in French Literature: 1851–1900.* London: Oxford University Press, 1973.

Daniel, Arnaut. *La vita e le opere del trovatore Arnaldo Daniello.* Edited by U. A. Canello. Halle: Max Niemeyer, 1883.

Daniel, Arnaut. *Les Poèsies d'Arnaut Daniel.* Edited by Réne Lavaud. Toulouse: Édouard Privat, 1910.

Dante Alighieri. *The Divine Comedy.* Translated by Allen Mandelbaum. New York: Bantam, 1982.

Dante Alighieri. *Paradiso.* Translated by Robin Kirkpatrick. New York: Penguin, 2007.

Davenport, Guy. *Geography of the Imagination.* San Francisco: North Point Press, 1981.

Davidson, Michael. *Ghostlier Demarcations: Modern Poetry and the Material Word.* Berkeley, CA: University of California Press, 1997.

D'Epiro, Peter. "Whose Vanity Must be Pulled Down." *Paideuma* 13.2 (1984): 247–52.

De Quincey, Thomas. *Confessions of an Opium Eater and Suspira de Profundis.* Boston: Ticknor, Reed, and Fields, 1850.

Dieterich, Albert. *Nekyia.* Leipzig: B. G. Teubner, 1893.

Diggory, Terrence. *Yeats and American Poetry.* Princeton, NJ: Princeton University Press, 1983.

DiVanna, Isabel. *Reconstructing the Middle Ages.* Newcastle upon Tyne: Cambridge Scholars Publishing, 2008.

Doughty, Charles. *Travels in Arabia Deserta.* Volume 2. London: Jonathan Cape, 1921.

Elegy and Iambus. Volume 2. Translated by J. M. Edmonds. Cambridge, MA: Harvard University Press, 1931.

Eliot, Thomas Sterns. "Review of *Group Theories of Religion and the Religion of the Individual.*" Edited by Clement C. J. Webb" *International Journal of Ethics* 27 (1916): 115–17.

Eliot, Thomas Sterns. *Selected Prose of T. S. Eliot.* Edited by Frank Kermode. London: Faber and Faber, 1975.

Eliot, Thomas Sterns. *The Waste Land.* In *The Poems of T. S. Eliot.* Volume 1. Edited by Christopher Ricks and Jim McCue. New York: Farrar, Straus and Giroux, 2018.

Flack, Leah Culligan. *Modernism and Homer: The Odysseys of H.D., James Joyce, Osip Mandelstam, and Ezra Pound.* Cambridge: Cambridge University Press, 2015.

Francis of Assisi. *Cantico.* In *Grégoire VII, saint Francois d'Assise, saint Thomas d'Aquin.* Edited by E. J. Delécluze. Paris: Jules Labitte, 1844.

Frazer, James. *The Golden Bough.* Volume 1. London: Macmillan, 1906.

Frazer, James. *The Golden Bough.* Volume 6. London: Macmillan, 1914.

Frazer, James. *The Golden Bough.* Volume 7. London: Macmillan, 1912.

Frizzi, Antonio. *Memorie per la Storia di Ferrara.* Volume 3. Ferrara: A. Servadio, 1850.

Ford, Ford Madox and Ezra Pound. *Pound/Ford: Story of Literary Friendship.* New York: New Directions, 1981.

The Four Books. Translated by James Legge. Shanghai: Commercial Press, 1923.

Froula, Marjorie. *To Write Paradise: Style and Error in Pound's Cantos.* New Haven, CT: Yale University Press, 1984.

Gallagher, Edward J. "Introduction." In *The Romance of Tristan and Iseut.* Edited by Joseph Bédier, xi–xlii. Indianapolis: Hackett, 2013.

Gibbon, Edward. *Miscellaneous Works.* Volume 3. London: John Murray, 1814.

Gibson, Mary. *Epic Reinvented: Ezra Pound and the Victorians.* Ithaca, NY: Cornell University Press, 1995.

Gillam, Doreen. "Stephen Kouros." *James Joyce Quarterly* 8 (1971): 221–32.

Gladstone, William. "The Color-Sense." *The Nineteenth Century* 2.8 (1877): 366–88.

Gladstone, William. *Studies on Homer and the Homeric Age*. Volume 3. London: Oxford University Press, 1858.

Goodwin, K. L. "The Structure of Ezra Pound's Later Cantos." *Southern Review* 4 (1971): 300–307.

Guyau, Jean-Marie. *l'Art au point de vue sociologique*. Second Edition. Paris: Félix Alcan Éditeur, 1889.

Hall, Donald. "Ezra Pound: An Interview." *The Paris Review* 7.28 (1962): 22–8, 43–51.

Harmon, William. "T. S. Eliot, Anthropologist and Primitive." *American Anthropologist* 78.4 (1976): 797–811.

Harrison, Jane. *Ancient Art and Ritual*. London: Williams and Norgate, 1914.

Harrison, Jane. *Myths of the Odyssey*. London: Rivingtons, 1882.

Harrison, Jane. *Prolegomena to the Study of Greek Religion*. Second Edition. Cambridge: Cambridge University Press, 1908.

Harrison, Jane. *Themis*. Cambridge: Cambridge University Press, 1912.

Hesiod. *The Homeric Hymns, Epic Cycle, and Homerica*. Translated by H. G. Evelyn-White. Harvard: Harvard University Press, 1914.

Heydon, John. *The Holy Guide*. London: Printed by T.M. and to be sold by Thomas Whittlesey, 1662.

Homer. *Iliad*. Translated by A.T. Murray. Cambridge, MA: Harvard University Press, 1924.

Homer. *Odyssey*. Translated by A.T. Murray. Cambridge, MA: Harvard University Press, 1919.

Homer. *The Story of Odysseus*. Translated by W. H. D. Rouse. London: Thomas Nelson and Sons, 1937.

Honoratus, Maurus Servius. *Commentary on the Eclogues of Virgil*. Edited by Georgius Thilo. Leipzig. B. G. Teubner, 1881.

Horace. *The Works of Horace*. Edited by C. Smart. Philadelphia: Joseph Whetham, 1836.

Herodotus. *The Histories*. Translated by Robin Waterfield. Edited by Carolyn Dewald. New York: Oxford University Press, 2008.

Hesiod, the Homeric Hymns, and Homerica. Translated Hugh G. Evelyn-White. Cambridge, MA: Harvard University Press, 1914.

Houlihan, James. "Incorporating the Other: The Catalogue of Women in Odyssey 11." *Electronic Antiquity* 2.1 (1994). https://scholar.lib.vt.edu/ejournals/ElAnt/V2N1/houlihan.html [Accessed March 19, 2022]

Hulme, Thomas Ernest. "Romanticism and Classicism." In *The Collected Writings of T. E. Hulme*. Edited by Karen Csengeri, 59–73. Oxford: Clarendon Press, 1984.

Hult, David. "Gaston Paris and Courtly Love." In *Medievalism and the Modernist Temper*. Edited by R. Howard Bloch and Stephen G. Nichols, 192–224. Baltimore: Johns Hopkins University Press, 1996.

Hunter, Richard. *Hesiodic Voices: Studies in the Ancient Reception of Hesiod's Works and Days*. Cambridge: Cambridge University Press, 2014.

Isocrates. *Helen*. In *Isocrates*. Volume 2. Translated by George Norlin. Cambridge, MA: Harvard University Press, 1980.

Jones, Chris. *Strange Likeness*. Oxford: Oxford University Press, 2006.

Joyce, James. *Ulysses*. Edited by Walter Gabler. New York: Vintage, 1986.

Kearns, George. *The Cantos of Ezra Pound*. Cambridge, UK: Cambridge University Press, 1989.

Kearns, George. *Guide to Ezra Pound's Selected Cantos*. New Brunswick: Rutgers University Press, 1980.

Keats, John. *The Complete Poems*. New York: Penguin, 1988.

Kenner, Hugh. *The Pound Era*. Berkeley: University of California Press, 1971.

Kenner, Hugh. "Pound and Homer." In *Ezra Pound among the Poets*. Edited by George Bornstein, 1–12. Chicago: University of Chicago Press, 1985.

Ker, Walter. *Epic and Romance*. New York: Macmillan, 1897.

Kindellan, Michael. *The Late Cantos of Ezra Pound: Composition, Revision, Publication*. London: Bloomsbury Academic, 2017.

Kipling, Rudyard. *Kim*. New York: Doubleday, 1912.

Kirchhoff, Johann Wilhelm Adolph. *Die homerische Odyssee*. Berlin: W. Hertz, 1859.

Lang, Andrew. *Homer and the Epic*. London: Longmans, Green, and Company, 1893.

Lavaud, Réne. *Les Poèsies d'Arnaut Daniel*. Toulouse: Édouard Privat, 1910.

Lawrence, David Herbert. *Letters of D. H. Lawrence*. Volume 2. Edited by James Boulton. Cambridge: Cambridge University Press, 1981.

Leaf, Walter. "Appendix L: Homeric Burial Rites." In *The Iliad*. Edited by Walter Leaf. Second Edition. Volume 2, 618–22. New York: Macmillan, 1900.

Levy, Emil. *Provenzalisches Supplement-Wöterbuch*. Volume 4. Leipzig: O. R. Reisland, 1904.

Lévy-Bruhl, Lucien. *Les fonctions mentales dans les sociétées inférieures*. Paris: Félix Alcan, 1910.

Liddell, Henry George and Robert Scott. *A Lexicon Abridged from Liddell and Scott's Greek-English Lexicon*. Oxford: Clarendon Press, 1871.

Liddell, Henry George, Robert Scott, Henry Stuart Jones, and Roderick McKenzie. *A Greek-English Lexicon*. Oxford: Clarendon Press, 1940.

Liebregts, Peter. *Ezra Pound and Neoplatonism*. Madison: Fairleigh Dickinson University Press, 2004.

Liebregts, Peter. *Translations of Greek Tragedy in the Work of Ezra Pound*. London: Bloomsbury Academic, 2019.

Longenbach, James. *Stone Cottage: Pound, Yeats, and Modernism*. Cary, NC: Oxford University Press, 1991.

Makin, Peter. *Provence and Pound*. Berkeley: University of California Press, 1978.

Marsh, Alec. *Ezra Pound's Washington Cantos and the Struggle for Light*. London: Bloomsbury Academic, 2021.

Martin, Timothy. *Joyce and Wagner*. Cambridge: Cambridge University Press, 1991.

McDougal, Stuart. *Ezra Pound and the Troubadour Tradition*. Princeton, NJ: Princeton University Press, 1979.

McGann, Jerome. *Towards a Literature of Knowledge*. Chicago: Chicago University Press, 1989.

Mead, George and Robert Stow. *The Mysteries of Mithra*. London: Theosophical Publishing Society, 1907.

Mills, Jean. *Virginia Woolf, Jane Ellen Harrison, and the Spirit of Modernist Classicism*. Columbus, OH: Ohio State University Press, 2014.

Milton, John. *Paradise Lost*. Edited by John Leonard. New York: Penguin, 2003.

Mirrlees, Hope. *Paris: A Poem*. London: Hogarth, 1919.

Mirrlees, Hope. *Paris: A Poem*. In *Gender and Modernism*. Edited by Julia Briggs, 270–87. Chicago: University of Illinois Press, 2007.

Miyake, Akiko. *Ezra Pound and the Mysteries of Love*. Durham, NC: Duke University Press, 1991.

Moody, A. David. *Ezra Pound: Poet*. Volume 3. New York: Oxford University Press, 2015.

Murray, Gilbert. *Jane Ellen Harrison: An Address Delivered at Newnham College*. Cambridge: W. Heffer, 1928.

Murray, Gilbert. *The Rise of the Greek Epic*. Second Edition. Oxford: Clarendon Press, 1911.

Nicholls, Peter. *Ezra Pound, Politics, Economics and Writing: A Study of the Cantos*. London: Macmillan, 1984.

Nicholls, Peter. "'Two Doits to a Boodle': Reckoning with *Thrones*." *Textual Practice* 18.2 (2004): 233–49.

Nietzsche, Friedrich. *The Birth of Tragedy*. Translated by Ronald Speirs. New York: Cambridge University Press, 1999.

Nykrog, Peter. "A Warrior Scholar at the Collège de France: Joseph Bédier." In *Medievalism and the Modernist Temper*. Edited by R. Howard Bloch and Stephen G. Nichols, 286–307. Baltimore: Johns Hopkins University Press, 1996.

Oderman, Kevin. *Ezra Pound and the Erotic Medium*. Durham, NC: Duke University Press, 1986.

Ovid. *Metamorphoses*. Edited by Hugo Magnus. Gotha, Germany: Friedr. Andr. Perthes, 1892.

Ovid. *Metamorphoses*. Translated by Arthur Golding. London: De La More Press, 1904.

Ovid. *Metamorphoses*. Translated by Brookes More. Boston: Cornhill Publishing Co., 1922.

Ovid. *Metamorphoses*. Translated by Frank Justus Miller. Cambridge, MA: Harvard University Press, 1984.

Ovid. *The Epistles of Ovid*. London: J. Nunn, 1813.

Paris, Gaston. "Études sur les romans de la Table Ronde: Lancelot du Lac, II: Le conte de la charrette." *Romania* 12 (1883): 459–534.

Paris, Gaston. *Mélanges de littérature française du Moyen Age*. Paris: H. Champion, 1912.

Paris, Gaston. "À nos lecteurs." *Revue critique d'histoire et de littérature* 4.1 (1869): 1–4.

Paris, Gaston. "Original Preface by Gaston Paris." In *The Romance of Tristan and Iseut*. Translated by Edward J. Gallagher, 115–20. Indianapolis: Hackett, 2013.

Paris, Gaston. "Paulin Paris et la littérature française du Moyen Age." In *La poésie du Moyen Age*, 211–54. Paris: Librairie Hachette, 1895.

Paris, Gaston and Léopold Pannier. *La Vie de Saint Alexis*. Paris: Franck, 1872.

Parker, Richard. "Some Contexts for Canto XCVI." *Glossator* 10 (2018): 1–26.

Pausanias. *Description of Greece*. Translated by W.H.S. Jones and H.A. Ormerod. Cambridge, MA: Harvard University Press, 1918.

Payne, Edward John. *History of the New World Called America*. Volume 2. Oxford: Clarendon Press, 1899.

Pearlman, Daniel. "Alexander del Mar in *The Cantos:* A Printout of the Sources." *Paideuma* 1.2 (1972): 161–80.

Philostratus. *Life of Apollonius of Tyana*. Volume 2. Translated by F. C. Conybeare. Cambridge, MA: Harvard University Press, 1912.

Pigna, Giambattista. *Historia de Principi di Este*. Vinegia: V. Valgrisi, 1572.

Plath, Sylvia. *The Collected Poems*. Edited by Ted Hughes. New York: Harper and Row, 1981.

Plotinus. *The Enneads*. Translated by Stephen Mackenna. Edited by E. R. Dodds, Paul Henry, and B. S. Page. London: Faber and Faber, 1969.

Pondrom, Cyrena. "Mirrlees, Modernism, and the Holophrase." *Time Present: The Newsletter of the T. S. Eliot Society* 74/75 (2011): 4–6.

Propertius, Sextus. *The Elegies of Sextus Propertius*. Translated by James Cranstoun. London: William Blackwood and Sons, 1875.

Pryor, Sean. *W.B. Yeats, Ezra Pound, and the Poetry of Paradise*. Burlington, VT: Ashgate, 2011.

Rainey, Lawrence. *Ezra Pound and the Monument of Culture: Text, History, and the Malatesta Cantos*. Chicago: University of Chicago Press, 1991.

Rilke, Rainer Maria. *Selected Poetry*. Translated by Stephen Mitchell. New York: Vintage, 1989.

Robinson, Fred. "Pound's Anglo Saxon Studies." In *Ezra Pound*. Edited by Harold Bloom, 105–26. New York: Chelsea House, 1987.

Das Rolandslied: Oxforder und Venediger Text. Edited by Conrad Hofmann. Munich: G. Franz, 1868.

Rosetti, Gabrielle. *Il mistero dell' amor platonico del medio evo*. Volume 1. London: R. e G.E. Taylor, 1840.

Shea, Daniel M. *James Joyce and the Mythology of Modernism*. Stuttgart: Ibidem-Verlag, 2006.

Sieburth, Richard. "Channelling Guido: Ezra Pound's Cavalcanti Translations." In *Guido Cavalcanti tra i suoi lettori*. Edited by Maria Luisa Ardizzone, 249–78. Firenze: Cadmo, 2003.

Sieburth, Richard. "Introduction." In *The Pisan Cantos*. Edited by Richrd Sieburth, ix–xliii. New York: New Directions, 1993.

Sinclair, T. A. "On ΑΙΔΩΣ in Hesiod." *Classical Review* 39.7–8 (1925): 147–8.

Spillman, Deborah. "Miming Made Modern: D. H. Lawrence, Jane Harrison, and the Novel." *The D.H. Lawrence Review* 42.1–2 (2017): 123–45.

Stesichorus. *Αθηναιου Ναυκρατιτου Δειπνοσοφισται/Athenaei Naucratitae Deipnosophistarum*. Edited and translated into Latin by Johannes Schweighäuser. Volume 4. Argentorati, Strassburg: ex typographia Societatis Bipontinae, 1804.

Stock, Noel. *The Life of Ezra Pound*. London: Routledge, 1970.

Surette, Leon. *The Birth of Modernism: Ezra Pound, T.S. Eliot, W.B. Yeats and the Occult*. Montreal: McGill-Queen's University Press, 1993.

Surette, Leon. "Having His Own Mind To Stand by Him." *The Hudson Review* 27.4 (1975): 491–510.

Surette, Leon. *A Light from Eleusis: A Study of Ezra Pound's Cantos*. New York: Oxford University Press, 1979.

Swanwick, Michael. *Hope-In-The-Mist: The Extraordinary Career and Mysterious Life of Hope Mirrlees*. Upper Montclair, NJ: Henry Wessells, 2009.

Tennyson, Alfred Lord. *The Major Works*. New York: Oxford World's Classics, 2000.

Terrell, Carroll F. *A Companion to the Cantos of Ezra Pound*. Berkeley: University of California Press, 1993.

Thomson, J. A. K. *Studies in the Odyssey*. Oxford: Clarendon Press, 1914.

Timpanaro, Sebastiano. *The Genesis of Lachmann's Method*. Edited and translated by Glen Most. Chicago: University of Chicago Press, 2005.

Tindall, William York. "D. H. Lawrence and the Primitive." *The Sewanee Review* 45.2 (1937): 198–211.

Tryphonopoulos, Demetres. *The Celestial Tradition: A Study of Ezra Pound's the Cantos*. Waterloo, ON: Wilfrid Laurier University Press, 1992.

Ullyot, Jonathan. "Ezra Pound's Jungle Book: Hathor and the Canto 39 Typescripts." *Paideuma* 49 (2023).

Ullyot, Jonathan. *The Medieval Presence in Modernism*. Cambridge: Cambridge University Press, 2016.

Upward, Allen. *The New Word*. London: A. C. Field, 1908.

Virgil. *Aeneid*. Translated by Theodore C. Williams. Boston: Houghton Mifflin Company, 1910.

Virgil. *Aeneid*. Translated by H. Rushton Fairclough. In *Eclogues, Georgics, Aeneid I–VI*. Cambridge, MA: Harvard University Press, 1978, 240–571.

The Wanderer. In *Anglo-Saxon and Norse Poems*. Edited and translated by Nora Kershaw. Cambridge: Cambridge University Press, 1922.

Warren, Michelle. *The Collected Works of W. B. Yeats*. Volume 1. Edited by Richard J. Finneran. New York: Scribner, 1996.

Warren, Michelle. *Creole Medievalism*. Minneapolis: University of Minnesota Press, 2011.

Wilhelm, James J. *Dante and Pound: The Epic of Judgment*. Maine: University of Maine Press, 1974.

Wilhelm, James J. *Ezra Pound in London and Paris, 1908–1925*. University Park, PA: Penn State University Press, 1990.

Yeats, William Butler. "Certain Noble Plays of Japan." In *Essays and Introductions*, 220–37. New York: Macmillan, 1961.

Yeats, William Butler. *The Collected Works of W. B. Yeats*. Volume 1. Edited by Richard J. Finneran. New York: Scribner, 1996.

Yeats, William Butler. "Introduction." In *The Oxford Book of Modern Verse*, edited by W. B. Yeats, v–xli. Oxford: Oxford University Press, 1936.

Yeats, William Butler. "Ireland and the Arts." In *Essays and Introductions*, 203–10. New York: Macmillan, 1961.

Yeats, William Butler. "Magic." In *Essays and Introductions*, 28–52. New York: Macmillan, 1961.

Yeats, William Butler. *Per Amica Silentia Lunae*. New York: Macmillan, 1918.

Yeats, William Butler. "The Theater." In *Essays and Introductions*, 165–72. New York: Macmillan, 1961.

Index of Names

Index of Works Published by Pound

Ingram Content Group UK Ltd.
Milton Keynes UK
UKHW022301290323
419396UK00004B/97